The Dow Jones-Irwin Guide To
Bond and Money Market Investments

The Dow Jones-Irwin Guide To
Bond and
Money
Market
Investments

Marcia Stigum
Frank J. Fabozzi

DOW JONES-IRWIN
Homewood, Illinois   60430

This publication is designed to provide accurate and
authoritative information in regard to the subject matter
covered. It is sold with the understanding that the
publisher is not engaged in rendering legal, accounting, or
other professional service. If legal advice or other expert
assistance is required, the services of a competent
professional person should be sought.

*From a Declaration of Principles jointly adopted by a Committee
of the American Bar Association and a Committee of Publishers.*

ISBN 0-87094-892-X

Library of Congress Catalog Card No. 86–71921

Printed in the United States of America

1234567890K43210987

To Fran and Ed Garlicki

Preface

The purpose of this book is to explain how to lend your money to creditworthy banks, corporations, and governments at the highest available rates.

There are many good books written about how to invest in common stocks and real estate. This book describes the other opportunities to invest your money—opportunities with typically lower risk and with commission costs that are usually much less than those on stock or real estate transactions.

This book is about fixed-income instruments: certificates of deposit, Treasury bills, commercial paper, bankers' acceptances, Treasury notes and bonds, federal government agency securities, municipal securities, corporate bonds and mortgage-pass through securities. We also explain special features of some of these instruments that may make them particularly attractive to investors. These include zero-coupon bonds, variable rate bonds, putable bonds, and convertible bonds. Money market funds and bond funds which allow you to invest in a pool of fixed income securities are also explained.

Along the way the book discusses fundamental issues that apply to all forms of fixed income instruments: credit risk, bond price volatility, risk-return tradeoff, taxation, and rate of return determination. Practical aspects of investing in these instruments such as basic strategies, trading mechanics and liquidity considerations are given careful attention.

Ten years ago it was much easier to write on bond and money market investments. There were fewer varieties of fixed-income securities. But creative minds on Wall Street have introduced a blizzard of choices, the most important of which you will learn about in the chapters that follow.

After reading this book, you will know how to increase your hard-earned money at a risk you select and at the highest rate of return available for the level of risk you selected.

ACKNOWLEDGMENTS

There are many professionals on Wall Street who have shared their knowledge and insights with us so that this book would be both theoretically correct and in line with current practices. These include: David Askin (Drexel Burnham Lambert), Peter L. Bernstein (Peter L. Bernstein Inc.), Catherine V. Blake (Merrill Lynch), John Charlesworth (Merrill Lynch), Andrew Davidson (Merrill Lynch), Daniel Delahanty (Bear Stearns), Albert D. Diposti (Merrill Lynch), Emanuel Falzon (Merrill Lynch), Sylvan Feldstein (Merrill Lynch), Michael Ferri (John Carroll University), Gifford Fong (Gifford Fong Associates), Dessa Garlicki (Bentley College), Gary Gastineau (Kidder Peabody), Charles Geiger (First Fidelity Bank of New Jersey), Jim Hight (Bear Stearns), Steven Hueglin (Gabriel, Hueglin & Cashman, Inc.), Frank Jones (Kidder Peabody), Robert Kopprasch (Salomon Brothers Inc), Howard Marks (Trust Company of the West), Eva Laskas (Bear Stearns), Mark Pitts (Shearson Lehman Brothers), Fred Price (Bear Stearns), Sharmin Mossavar-Rahmani (Lehman Management Co.), Jack Ritchie (Temple University), Ronald J. Ryan (Ryan Financial Strategy Group), Harry Sauvain (Indiana University), Rob Smith (Bear Stearns), John B. Stokes (Manufacturers Hanover), Michael Smirlock (University of Pennsylvania), Kenneth Sullivan (Drexel Burnham Lambert), Michael Waldman (Salomon Brothers Inc), Leslie Webster (Chase Manhattan Bank), Richard Wilson (Merrill Lynch), Benjamin Wolkowitz (Morgan Stanley), and Alling Woodruff (Lipper Analytical Services, Inc.). Robin Cohen, Joseph Gaziano, Thomas Radwanski and David Warren provided research assistance at various stages of this project. Our thanks to them and to Mary Driscoll, for her editing contribution.

Marcia Stigum
Frank J. Fabozzi

Contents

Moral Obligation Bonds. Municipal Utility District Revenue Bonds. Tax Allocation Bonds. "Troubled City" Bailout Bonds. Federal Savings and Loan Insurance Corporation-backed Bonds. "Territorial" Bonds. Municipal Notes: *Tax, Revenue, Grant, and Bond Anticipation Notes: TANs, RANs, GANs, and BANs. Construction Loan Notes: CLNs. Tax-exempt Commercial Paper.* Newer Market-Sensitive Debt Instruments: *Zero-coupon Bonds. Put or Option Tender Bonds. Super Sinkers. Variable-rate Notes.* Default Risk. Issuing Procedures: *Underwriting.* The Secondary Market: *Price Quotes.* Buying and Selling Municipals. Risk, Liquidity, and Return: *Return. Liquidity. Risk. Municipal Bond Insurance.*

Services Provided. Closed-End Funds. Unit Trusts.
Types of Bond Funds. Selecting a Fund. Risk, Liquidity,
and Return.

Risk, Liquidity, and Return

$$1$$

The small investor who has some surplus funds is faced with a wealth of different investment opportunities. He can buy a home; put money into other real estate; acquire savings accounts; purchase oil-drilling participations; buy stocks, bonds, or art—the list is endless. Each of these different investment media offers the investor its own unique advantages; these advantages, depending on the instrument, may include high income, low risk, tax avoidance, tax shelter, protection from inflation, or high liquidity.

Unfortunately, despite the array of investment instruments available, many people behave as if they lived in a world in which there were just four assets in which to invest. They buy a house, are sold some whole life insurance, and divide the rest of their savings—depending on their appetite for risk—between stocks and regular savings accounts. This approach to asset selection has the virtue of significantly reducing the amount of effort the investor has to make in choosing his portfolio, *but* such investors ignore, to their cost, many attractive investment opportunities. They end up foregoing high current yields or capital gains, and they may end up paying more taxes than necessary.

This book is about one prominent group of widely ignored investment instruments—interest-bearing IOUs other than regular savings accounts. These debt instruments offer a potential return that is higher than that available on regular savings accounts; however, this is not the only attraction offered by debt instruments such as Treasury bills, certificates of deposit, bonds, and other debt securities. Municipal bonds offer the opportunity of interest free from federal income taxes and possibly state and local taxes; the interest on U.S. governments issues is exempt from state and local taxes. Also, for those who choose to speculate on security price rises, opportunities for leveraging through margin purchases are greater in U.S. government bonds than in common stocks because margin requirements are very low on government issues.[1] Finally, for the individual who wants to speculate on the recovery of a company that has fallen on ill times, the opportunity for capital gains offered by an investment in the company's outstanding bonds is often vastly greater than that offered by an investment in the company's stock.

INVESTMENT CHARACTERISTICS OF DEBT SECURITIES

Since the average small investor does not know much about debt securities, especially negotiable ones, our starting place in this discussion is a quick overview of what debt securities are all about.

A *debt security or instrument,* as we use the term, is simply an IOU. Most of the IOUs we will discuss are interest bearing. Some, however, do not bear interest; such securities yield the investor a return because they are sold at a discount from face value (that is, the amount the issuer of the debt agrees to pay at maturity) but redeemed at maturity for full face value.

For most consumers the most familiar debt security is a savings deposit. When you put money into a regular savings account, you are (whether you think of it that way or not) lending money to your bank, and the return the bank pays you is interest on your loan to it. A key characteristic of a savings deposit is that it is not negotiable; you can not sell your deposit at the local First National Bank to another investor. You can, however, withdraw your deposit (demand repayment of

---

[1]When securities are purchased "on the margin," the investor borrows part of the purchase price from his broker. Leveraging, i.e., using borrowed funds, amplifies the return earned by an investor on his funds. Examples of this are given in Chapter 8.

your loan to the bank) at any time. If you do, you will get back the full amount you deposited plus any interest due.

Most of the debt securities we will discuss in this book are *negotiable*. Unlike regular savings deposits, they have some specific date on which they mature; that is, there is some fixed date on which the borrower promises to pay back to the holders of its IOUs all principal borrowed plus any interest due. An investor who buys a negotiable debt instrument with a fixed maturity might, of course, want to get his money back before the instrument matures. In that case, the only alternative is to sell the instrument for cash to some other investor.

A negotiable debt instrument (for example, a bond and some certificates of deposit), like any other negotiable asset (stocks, a home, or a race horse), sells at a market-determined price that reflects its value at the moment of sale. Just what this value is depends on several factors.

To illustrate, let's look at corporate bonds. A corporate bond is an IOU that generally has a face value of $1,000. Corporate bonds are normally issued (i.e., initially sold to investors) at full face value.[2] Thus, a corporation issuing new bonds borrows $1,000 of principal from the buyer of each bond it sells.

Every corporate bond carries some *coupon rate;* it is the interest rate that the borrower promises to pay to the holder on the bond's face value. If the coupon rate is 8%, this means that the issuer promises to pay the bondholder 8% of $1,000, or $80 of interest each year. One half of the interest is typically paid every 6 months. So, a bond that promises to pay $80 per year will usually pay $40 every 6 months. The coupon rate on a bond is normally set so that it equals the current yield on equivalent bonds. Doing so permits the new bond to be issued at a price equal to full face value. All corporate bonds mature on some fixed date.

Economic conditions naturally change over time and, as they do, interest rates fluctuate up and down. In particular, a boom drives interest rates up, while a recession depresses them. During the period between issue and maturity, the price that a bond commands (its *market value*) will depend in part on *the relationship between the coupon rate it carries and the currently prevailing rate of return on similar securities.*

---

[2]The exception is an original-issue discount bond, which we discuss in Chapter 7.

To illustrate, suppose that you had bought a new corporate bond when prevailing interest rates were 10%, and your bond carries a 10% coupon. A year and a half later you want to sell this bond. Suppose that during the interval, interest rates have fallen as the economy slipped from boom to recession, and yields on new securities of comparable quality and maturity are now down to 8.5%. What price will your bond command? Obviously, all investors wanting to put money into bonds would prefer your old 10% bond to a new 8.5% bond, so they will bid more for your old bond than for new bonds; that is, the price of your old bond will be driven to a *premium* above $1,000. How much of a premium? The investor who buys your bond is going to receive a two-part overall yield: (1) coupon interest, *minus* (2) the capital loss implied by the fact that he is paying more than $1,000 for a bond that will be redeemed for only $1,000 at maturity. Since investors think in terms of overall yield (called *yield to maturity* in financial jargon), they will keep bidding up the price of your old bond until its yield to maturity falls to roughly 8.5%.

Interest rates, instead of falling, might have risen after you bought your bond. In that case, the situation is reversed; your old bond is less attractive than new bonds, and as a result its price will be forced to a *discount* from face value—to a price below $1,000. Because of this discount, the overall return earned by an investor who buys your bond and holds it to maturity will consist of coupon interest *plus* a capital gain. The latter comes into the picture because the investor who buys your bond will get $1,000 when it matures, which is more than he paid you for it.

Falling interest rates drive bond prices up, rising interest rates depress them. By how much? The amount varies depending on a bond's *time to maturity.* For example, if you own a bond that will not mature for 20 years and interest rates fall below the coupon rate on your bond, the investor who buys it may be able to lock in 20 years of extra high yield. Therefore the investor will be willing to pay quite a high premium for your bond. If, on the other hand, you have a high-coupon instrument that is due to mature in one year, the situation is quite different. The investor who buys your bond will be able to enjoy an extra high yield for only one year, so the premium placed on your bond will be relatively small. Generally, the shorter the time to maturity, the lower the premium at which high-coupon bonds will sell and the lower the discount at which low-coupon bonds will trade. Thus, the longer a bond's time to maturity, the more volatile the fashion in which its price will react to changes in interest rates.

A third factor influencing the value of a bond is the *risk of default* attached to the bond by investors. Most corporate bonds are rated by Moody's Investors Service, Inc. and by Standard & Poor's Corp. with respect to risk of default. Top-grade, triple A-rated bonds expose the investor to only a minimal risk of default and therefore command relatively high prices. In contrast, low-rated bonds issued by companies that have fallen upon bad times expose the investor to a real risk of default and consequently command much lower prices. Naturally, the health and credit rating of a company that has issued bonds may change over time, and as they do, so too will the price commanded by the firm's outstanding bonds.

To sum up, the value of a bond depends on three crucial factors: the relationship between its coupon rate and currently prevailing yields, its time to maturity, and the risk of default to which it exposes the investor. Since all these factors vary over time, bond prices fluctuate from day to day, rising with falling interest rates and good news about the issuer, declining in the opposite case.

The fact that the prices of bonds and other debt securities vary means that the investor who buys such securities cannot be sure of the price at which he will be able to sell them. In other words, an investment in bonds subjects the investor to a *price risk*. The existence of this risk is, of course, not all bad news for the investor. It creates possibilities for capital gains and for profitable speculation as well. Naturally, in bonds as in stocks, price risk varies greatly from issue to issue. The conservative investor may be able to lock up a near certain rate of return by investing in high-grade securities and holding them to maturity. To the less risk-averse investor, other securities and other strategies will be more appealing. There will be more about that in later chapters.

THE MONEY MARKET AND THE BOND MARKET

Generally bonds are long-term instruments, maturing anywhere from 5 to 25 years after issue. Straight bonds and other long-term IOUs are traded in what is called the *bond market*.

In addition to such long-term securities, there are a host of negotiable, short-term IOUs that are actively traded: Treasury bills, bankers' acceptances, and some certificates of deposit, to name a few. These short-term instruments, whose maturity is measured in days or months, are traded in what is called the *money market*. The money market is an odd name to give a financial market because it sounds like a place where people trade money for money, an obviously pointless operation. *Actually the money market is a market in which large borrowers raise short-term money by selling various debt instruments; that is, it is a "new-issues" market for short-term securities. The money market is also a secondary market in which such securities, once issued, are actively traded.*

While a few bond issues are listed on the New York Stock Exchange and the American Stock Exchange, the bond market and the money market are both primarily *over-the-counter* markets. As such, they are not located in any one place but instead are made by dealers located in New York and other financial centers. These dealers act as principals in all the trades they enter, buying for their own account and selling from inventory.

ASSETS—REAL AND FINANCIAL

The three key characteristics in terms of which any rational investor should evaluate alternative investment opportunities are *risk, liquidity,* and *return.* Unfortunately, the small investor does not often do a very good job at this. He may fail to consider liquidity, and he typically measures return in the wrong way. Consequently, before we start looking at individual debt securities, a few words about assets and how to evaluate them are in order.

A person's assets are simply things of value that he owns. All assets can be divided into two broad categories, real and financial. *Real* assets are physical goods of value: a car, a house, a motorboat, a diamond, even a race horse. *Financial assets,* in contrast, are *claims* against others, where the "others" may be consumers, the government, financial institutions such as banks, or nonfinancial business firms.[3]

Financial assets can themselves be subdivided into two broad categories, equity and debt claims. *Equity claims* are ownership rights: common stock, interest in a partnership, and ownership of a sole proprietorship are all examples. *Debt claims,* in contrast, are assets that arise from loan-type transactions. They include certificates

---

[3]Banks, S&Ls, credit unions, life insurance companies, finance companies, and other financial institutions are all *financial* business firms. In contrast, firms engaged in such things as manufacturing, retailing, and construction are *nonfinancial* business firms.

of deposit, bonds, and many other instruments described in later chapters.

LIQUIDITY

An asset is said to be *liquid* if it can be converted into cash easily and rapidly without substantial loss in value. Liquidity is not an absolute property; it varies from asset to asset. A savings account is highly liquid because in practice it can be converted on demand into money, with transaction costs equaling at most the expense of a trip to the bank. In contrast, a house is relatively illiquid; selling a house takes time (generally longer the more expensive it is) and transaction costs are substantial. The liquidity of corporate bonds lies somewhere between; bond prices rise and fall as interest rates and other factors determining their value change. Also, markets for some bond issues are *thin;* that is, little trading occurs in them. Consequently, a decision to sell a bond immediately might result in a substantial loss of value to the investor; also transaction costs on such sales, while low, are not zero. In measuring the liquidity of an asset, it is important to remember that often an inverse relationship exists between rapidity of sale and value realized. If you are trying to sell a Picasso drawing on consignment through an art dealer, you will get a higher price the longer you are willing to wait.

RETURN

Money Rate of Return

Most investors tend to think of return in terms of money rates of return. An asset's *money rate of return* equals the annual income yielded by the asset as a percentage of the asset's total value. For example, a $100 debt security that pays $5 of interest once a year yields a 5% money rate of return.

Calculating the money rate of return for some debt instruments is simple. For others, it is a bit more complicated. Suppose, for example, that you buy a corporate bond with a $1,000 face value for exactly $1,000. The bond pays 6% interest on face value, so over the following year you get $60 in interest. If you sell your bond at the end of the year for $1,000—the same amount you paid for it—your money rate of return is 6%. You might, however, get lucky; interest rates fall, and at the end of the year you are able to sell your bond for $1,100. Now your total return is $60 of interest plus $100 of capital gain—a money rate of return of 16%. Of course, you might also be unlucky; rising interest drives down the price of your bond to $900; in that case, your total return becomes $60 of interest minus a $100 capital loss—a money rate of return of −4%.

When an investor looks at a money rate of return, what he is really interested in is how the investment will alter over time the *purchasing power* of the funds invested. For making this sort of judgment, money rates of return are misleading for two reasons. First, the prices of goods change over time. Second, taxes have to be paid on most income.

Real Rate of Return

To deal with the problem posed by changes in the price level, it is necessary to introduce a new concept, the real rate of return.

An asset's *real rate of return* equals the percentage change that occurs in the purchasing power of the money invested in the asset when account is taken of both the money rate of return and changes in the price level.

This sounds complicated but the idea is simple. Suppose you put $1,000 in a savings account paying 5% and hold it there for one year. Suppose also that the price level rises 5%. At the end of the year, you will have more money than you started with—$1,050 as opposed to $1,000—but because of the rise in prices, your $1,050 at year's end will buy exactly the same quantity of goods that you could have bought with $1,000 at the beginning of the year. Consequently, the *real rate of return* on your investment is zero. *On any investment the real rate of return equals the money rate of return minus the inflation rate.* Thus a 10% money rate of return combined with a 5% rise in prices yields a real rate of return of 5%. *Obviously for the investor who wants to conserve purchasing power, as opposed to just dollars, thinking in terms of real rates of return is vital during inflationary periods.*

To end on a more cheerful note, we might add that in the unlikely event that prices fall, the arithmetic works the other way. A 5% money rate of return combined with a 10% fall in prices yields a +15% real rate of return!

After-Tax Real Rate of Return

Since most income is taxable, if you really want to know how a particular investment will change the purchasing power of the funds you invest, you must consider the after-tax real rate of return that this investment will yield.

An asset's *after-tax real rate of return* equals the percentage change that occurs in the purchasing power of the money you invest when account is taken of:

1. The money rate of return yielded by the asset.
2. Taxes you pay on this money return.
3. Changes in the price level.

To illustrate, recall our example of $1,000 invested in a savings account yielding 5%. If you have to pay out 20% of the interest you earn in income taxes, your after-tax money rate of return will equal only 4%. Add now to the picture a 5% inflation rate and your after-tax real rate of return becomes −1%.

In case you still doubt the importance of evaluating return in real after-tax terms, let's work through a slightly more elaborate example. Investment books, the "how to have a secure old age" type, are always proclaiming the advantages of compound interest, setting up tables and graphs to show the monumental dollar sums to which a small dollar amount invested and left to compound at a fixed interest rate will grow over time. We too can play that game. The top line of Exhibit 1–1 shows the dollar sum to which $1,000 invested at 8% would grow over 20 years if all interest were reinvested at the 8% rate. The total is an impressive $4,875. This, however, is an irrelevant number unless you pay no taxes on income and prices do not rise, i.e., unless you earn a real after-tax return of 8%. Unfortunately, that is not likely. Typically, you will have to pay taxes on interest income. So you are not going to accumulate $4,875—a point that the how-to-be-a-millionaire-by-saving-a-penny-an-hour-and-investing-it tracts consistently ignore. Worse still, the dollars you accumulate over 20 years (assume they total $3,300 after taxes), might have much less purchasing power than did the dollars you originally invested. If prices rise by 50% over the period, the real after-tax purchasing power of those $3,300 will be only $2,200, approximately what you could have obtained by investing $1,000 for 20 years at a real after-tax return of +4%.

EXHIBIT 1-1 Real Purchasing Power over 20 Years for $1,000
Invested and Left to Compound at Various Real After-
Tax Rates of Return (*r*)

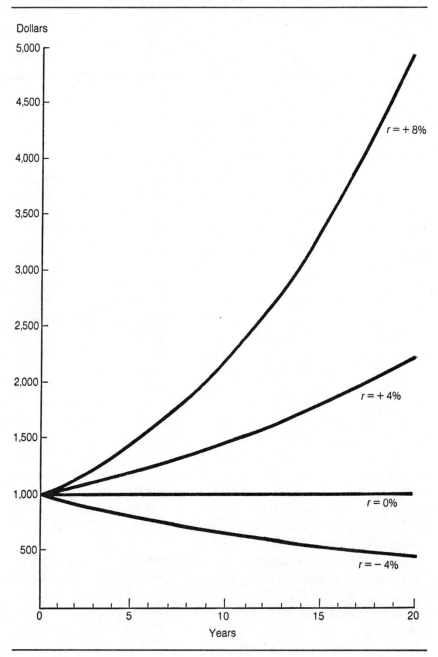

If you are investing to have *purchasing power* as opposed to dollar bills, you *must* think in real after-tax terms. To emphasize this point, we have plotted three other curves in Exhibit 1–1. These show what would happen to the purchasing power of $1,000 invested at 8% and left to compound if taxes and inflation reduced the real after-tax return to (1) +4%, (2) 0%, and (3) −4%. The results vary dramatically.

Marginal Tax Rates.   In calculating the after-tax real rate of return that any investment offers, bear in mind that the federal tax and some state taxes on income are *progressive;* that is, you pay a higher tax rate as your taxable income increases.

The tax rate that an individual must pay on the last dollars of income he earns is called his *marginal tax rate,* or in everyday parlance, his *tax bracket.* For example, suppose your combined marginal tax rate is 30%; if your income rises by $100, you will have to pay $30 additional taxes. At this writing, there are 14 federal marginal rates that rise with income from 11% to 50%. New tax legislation would simplify the code so that there would only be two marginal tax rates, 15% and 28%.[4]

The reason for this digression on marginal tax rates is that marginal rates—federal and state—are what the investor *must* use in calculating the after-tax real rate of return on any asset. Also, because different investors pay different marginal tax rates, the *same* asset will offer *different* after-tax real rates of return to different investors. To illustrate, a bond yielding a 10% money rate of return will, assuming stable prices, offer an after-tax real rate of return of 8.5% to an investor whose marginal tax rate is 15% but only a 6.7% after-tax real rate of return to an investor whose marginal tax rate is 33%.

RISK

Another important factor to consider in evaluating any asset is risk. Holding an asset exposes you to *risk* whenever the asset offers an *uncertain* return. Risk, like liquidity, is not an absolute property; some assets are riskier than others.

The most obvious source of risk is uncertainty with respect to *money rate of return.* To illustrate, consider an investor who has

---

[4]Under the proposal expected to be law, in 1987 investors would face "blended" marginal tax rates—a mixture of current rates and proposed rates. The top rate for married couples with taxable income of $90,000 or more would be 38.5%. In 1988, a surcharge would make the effective top marginal tax rate 33% rather than 28%.

$10,000 he wants to invest for two years. If he puts his money in a certificate of deposit that has a two-year maturity and pays 7%, he is certain to get a 7% money rate of return. Even if the bank president absconds with half of the bank's deposits, federal deposit insurance guarantees the investor his return. In contrast, if the investor puts his $10,000 into, say, IBM stock, his money return over the two-year period is uncertain. IBM might raise or lower its dividend, and the price that its stock will command two years hence is unknown to all but an accurate reader of a crystal ball.

For the investor who is willing to follow a hold-until-maturity strategy, many debt securities are low in risk, but for the investor who might want to liquidate his position on short notice, they are a riskier proposition. This view implies that the investor whose principal aim is to conserve capital and therefore to minimize risk should maintain a portfolio comprised largely of debt securities that he plans to hold to maturity.

During periods of stable prices, such a policy is indeed likely to eliminate risk, but not so when the price level is subject to fluctuations. The reason is that it completely overlooks a *second* important source of risk—unpredictable *changes in the price level* and consequently in an asset's real rate of return. As we have stressed, what the rational investor should focus on is the after-tax *real* rate of return that an asset offers him. Whenever prices are subject to unpredictable changes, up or down, *all* assets, even those offering a certain money rate of return, expose the investor to uncertainty with respect to the real rate of return. Thus, in inflationary periods, *all assets are to some degree risky.*

The risks posed by unpredictable changes in the price level can be illustrated with a simple example. Suppose you put money into a savings account that offers a money rate of return of 5%. Suppose also that the odds are 1 in 3 that prices will not change, 1 in 3 that they will rise 5%, and 1 in 3 that they will rise 10%. Then the real rate of return you will earn is uncertain. Chances are 1 in 3 that your real rate of return will be 5%, 1 in 3 that it will be 0%, and 1 in 3 that it will be −5%.

PLAN OF THE BOOK

Every investor would like to enjoy maximum liquidity, minimum risk, and maximum return on his investments. Unfortunately, it can't be done. Higher yields often mean more risk and less liquidity, and vice versa. Thus, you face a trade-off. If you insist on more return, you have to sacrifice some liquidity or accept some additional risk. This trade-off does not mean that you should not try to increase return but, rather, that you should learn enough about the different options available so that you can increase return without accepting any large or unnecessary loss of liquidity or increase in risk. The trick of the investing game is to understand your options; select carefully; and get the combination of risk, liquidity, and return that best serves your investment goals.

When constructing your financial portfolio, you should think of your assets as a financial pyramid, as shown in Exhibit 1–2. The base or foundation of the pyramid includes funds invested in liquid and safe assets. Examples of such assets are insured savings accounts, insured certificates of deposit, short-term U.S. Treasury securities, money market funds, and money market deposit accounts.

As you move up the pyramid, you are trading off liquidity and/or safety for higher potential return. The layer above the base represents funds invested in assets that have a higher degree of risk and lesser degrees of liquidity but offer higher income and long-term growth potential than those in the base. These assets include high-grade corporate bonds, high-grade municipal bonds, and high-quality stocks. Also included in this second layer of assets are intermediate- and long-term U.S. Treasury securities. As we shall see in Chapter 6, despite the absence of default risk, all intermediate- and long-term bonds expose the investor to substantial price risk that results in less liquidity.

Investment vehicles that offer the potential for extremely high returns but expose the investor to higher degrees of risk are found in the top two layers. The layer labeled "speculative" in Exhibit 1–2 includes lower-quality corporate bonds, lower-quality municipal bonds, and lower-quality stocks. Investment vehicles in the top layer, labeled "high risk," would include tax shelters based on tax benefits rather than economic viability and options and futures not used to hedge an investment position.[5]

---

[5]It is not our position that options and futures per se are high-risk investments. In fact, options and futures can be and are used by many professional money managers to control the risk of a portfolio. Unfortunately, most individual investors buy or sell options and futures solely with the objective of realizing substantial profits and many incur substantial losses.

EXHIBIT 1–2   Financial Pyramid

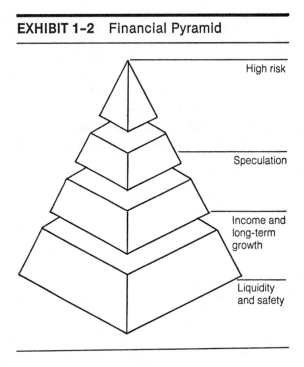

Notice the shape of the pyramid. The base is the widest part and the top is the smallest. This means that an investor with $100,000 should invest, say, $50,000 to $55,000 in safe and liquid assets and only about $5,000 in high-risk assets. Unfortunately, there are investors who take the inverted pyramid approach; that is, they invest the bulk of funds in high-risk assets and, once the expected, big payoff comes in, invest it in safe and liquid assets. If you follow that approach, remember that your financial stability depends on your ability to balance a pyramid on its point!

The purpose of this book is to give you all the information you need to make intelligent choices among different debt obligations. Specifically, the book provides an easy-to-read, nontechnical introduction to the many different debt obligations available to you—answering such questions as: What are these obligations? How do they measure up in terms of risk, liquidity, and return? How does one buy and sell them?

The next four chapters explain the assets housed in the base of the financial pyramid: insured certificates of deposit (Chapter 2), Treasury bills (Chapter 3), other money market instruments (Chapter 4), and money market funds and money market deposit accounts (Chapter 5). Our explorations of the bond market—and the nuances of bond investing—span Chapters 6 through 14. We explain bond funds in Chapter 15, then wind up our discussion with an overview of bond swapping strategies in Chapter 16.

One cannot discuss debt instruments without introducing a lot of jargon. To help you keep it straight, we have included at the end of the book a glossary that defines all of the key terms used.

Certificates of Deposit

2

A certificate of deposit (CD) is a receipt for funds deposited at a depository institution for a specified time period at a specified interest rate. Maturities available typically range from 3 months to 10 years, with a minimum deposit at some institutions of as little as $500. Until recently, small denomination CDs were nonnegotiable. That is, a depositor who wanted to withdraw funds prior to the maturity date could only do so at the discretion of the institution and, if allowed, would typically be subject to severe interest penalties. Negotiable CDs have been available since the early 1960s but require an investment of about $1 million, and are not a practical investment for the small investor.

Today, however, several retail-oriented brokerage firms offer CDs issued by institutions that are insured by federal deposit insurance programs and salable in a secondary market. We begin our exploration of the debt obligations available to you with CDs because we feel that they are ideally suited for building the base of your financial pyramid.

THE ISSUERS: DEPOSITORY INSTITUTIONS

CDs are offered by depository institutions. These institutions include commercial banks and thrifts (savings and loan associations and savings banks). Commercial banks (simply referred to as banks) obtain deposits from consumers, nonfinancial business firms, other financial institutions, and various branches of government. They use these funds to make loans to consumers and business firms and to invest in various debt instruments, such as U.S. government securities and municipal obligations.

Although savings and loan associations (S&Ls) became highly visible and important financial institutions only after World War II, they have a long history in the U.S. They began as local cooperative savings societies, whose purpose was to permit members to finance the construction of homes. Each member of the association deposited what savings he could in the association and, as funds accumulated, the association made home loans to members. Naturally, this procedure, under which actual savers equaled would-be borrowers, meant that some members had to wait a considerable time to obtain a home loan. As a result, outside savers were eventually invited to deposit their funds in S&Ls. Early S&Ls were all *mutual* institutions; that is, they were owned and managed by their depositors. Today, the majority of S&Ls are still mutual institutions, but many of the larger firms in the industry are corporations owned by stockholders who provide equity capital and have the ultimate say in management of the institution. The asset portfolios of S&Ls consist largely of long-term mortgages.

Savings banks also have a long history—over 160 years—in the U.S. They were first established in the early 19th century to promote thrift among industrial workers by providing these people with an institution into which they could make small interest-bearing deposits of savings. Until recently, savings banks did not have stockholders. They were controlled by a governing board of trustees, and all earnings, after provision was made for a reserve against loan losses, were paid to depositors. Consequently, savings banks were known as *mutual* savings banks. The humble origins of these thrift banks are suggested by the names of some of the more prominent ones: Seaman's Bank for Savings, The Dime Savings Bank, Emigrant Industrial Savings Bank, and Boston Five Cents Savings Bank. Although there are fewer savings banks than S&Ls, savings banks are generally larger.

Only 16 states charter savings banks. The bulk of these savings banks are located in the Northeast (New England, New York, and New Jersey). In 1978, Congress granted a federal chartering authority for savings banks, which resulted in the creation of savings banks in

46 states and the Virgin Islands. Most savings banks are state-chartered. Many of the federally chartered savings banks are those that converted from S&Ls to savings bank status.

DEPOSIT INSURANCE

The accounts of depository institutions offering CDs are insured by either a federal agency, a state insurance fund, or a private insurance company. *We strongly recommend that you avoid any depository institution that is not insured by a federal agency.* Consequently, we shall focus our attention on federal deposit insurance programs.

Accounts at banks are insured by the Federal Deposit Insurance Corporation, a $17.9 billion fund that insures about $1.8 trillion of deposits in 14,750 institutions. S&L accounts are insured by the Federal Savings and Loan Insurance Corporation, a $6.6 billion fund that insures $862 billion of deposits in 3,250 institutions. Savings banks may be insured by either of these federal deposit insurance programs.

Federal Deposit Insurance Corporation

Federal deposit insurance for bank depositors was introduced by the federal government in the 1930s in response to the numerous bank failures that occurred. The Federal Deposit Insurance Corporation (FDIC), which administers this program, charges each member bank a small premium calculated as a percentage of its total deposits. In exchange, it guarantees that the bank's depositors will receive cash in full for their deposits (up to a specified limit) in the event that the bank fails.

The beauty of the FDIC system, ironically unforeseen by its founders, is that it significantly reduces the contingency insured against, namely, bank failures. Today, if a bank is weakened by some miscalculation, depositors do not immediately form long lines to pull out their deposits and thereby force the bank to close. Depositors know their funds are safe—if the troubled bank ultimately fails, the FDIC will protect them. Typically, the FDIC does so by injecting funds into the insolvent bank and effecting a rapid merger between it and a strong solvent bank. Today a "failed" bank's doors rarely close, and the unobservant depositor at a failed bank may not even realize that anything unusual has happened at the bank. The existence of the FDIC reduces bank failures in another more subtle way—because depositors know their deposits are safe, they no longer respond nervously to the failure of one bank by creating "runs" on other banks.

The protection that deposit insurance gives to banks and bank depositors is reinforced by another equally important factor. Today, the Federal Reserve System (Fed) recognizes, as it did not during the 1930s, that it has both the power and the responsibility to protect the banking system against any outside shock that threatens either the liquidity or the solvency of the system.

Events in mid-1974 provided a classic example of how the existence of deposit insurance combined with the Fed's commitment to protect the banking system can prevent difficulties at a prominent bank from touching off a major financial crisis. In the spring of 1974 the Franklin National Bank, then the 20th largest bank in the United States, disclosed that it had sustained a $46 million loss through unauthorized speculation by traders in its foreign exchange department. In other times, this announcement could have been counted on to set off a run on the Franklin that would have forced it to close its doors, which in turn might well have cast suspicion on other banks, caused runs on them, and resulted in a wave of bank suspensions or failures. Instead events took quite a different turn. The Franklin's depositors, knowing that they were protected by deposit insurance, left the bulk of their funds on deposit at the Franklin. Meanwhile the Fed, realizing the serious consequences that failure of the Franklin might have on both the national and the international financial systems, promised immediately and publicly to support the Franklin by lending to it at the discount window whatever sums were necessary.[1] Fed loans to the Franklin eventually reached an unprecedented $1.75 billion.

Had the Franklin's troubles been simply a temporary loss of confidence due to a single misstep, the Fed's actions combined with some minimal assistance from the FDIC might have sufficed to permit the Franklin to recover. Unfortunately as a result of chronically weak

---

[1]To meet temporary reserve deficiencies, banks that are members of the Federal Reserve System are permitted to borrow from the Fed. The Fed lends to a bank by discounting, i.e., by buying at a discount, short-term commercial debt instruments from the bank, or by lending directly to the bank against collateral in the form of U.S. government securities. Loans at the discount window are made at the Fed's discretion with the understanding that an individual bank's borrowings are normally to be modest in size and short in duration.

management, the Franklin also suffered from excessive leverage at unfavorable rates, an overloaded and badly depressed bond portfolio, and low-quality business loans. Thus, it was insolvent not only in the technical sense of having liabilities greater than assets but also in a second and more serious sense—it was no longer able to operate profitably. As a result, by fall the FDIC felt compelled to force the Franklin to merge with another large and profitable bank, the European American Bank and Trust Co. In that merger the Franklin's depositors were fully protected.

Federal Savings and Loan Insurance Corporation

In 1934 the federal government, at the same time that it set up the FDIC to insure bank deposits, also set up the Federal Savings and Loan Insurance Corporation (FSLIC) to insure S&L deposits. The FSLIC operates in much the same way as the FDIC does.

Insured Deposits at Banks and S&Ls Are Equally Safe

Essentially what FDIC and FSLIC insurance protects against are losses due to mismanagement or misfortune at an individual bank or S&L. Because of the financial problems facing thrift institutions, some investors have expressed concern that the reserves of FSLIC would be inadequate to meet its obligations in the event of widespread S&L failures, even when recognition is taken of FSLIC's right to borrow from the U.S. Treasury. This is of course true, *just as it is true of the FDIC*. However, it is not particularly relevant, since the federal government today recognizes that it has the responsibility to protect the nation's S&Ls against any widespread failure. Protection against any shock that might threaten the whole system is provided implicitly by the government's commitments to maintain a smoothly functioning financial system and to promote the construction of adequate housing for the nation's population, an area in which S&Ls play a vital role. Therefore, FSLIC offers the S&L depositor the same degree of protection that FDIC offers bank depositors.

Insurance Payoffs

It is also noteworthy that insurance payoffs have been rare. For example, in 1985 there were 177 failures, 120 involving FDIC and 57 involving FSLIC. Only 2 of the 57 involving FSLIC required a payout to depositors; 8 required deposit transfers; 25 were handled through the management consignment program; 22 involved FSLIC-assisted mergers. For the 120 FDIC-insured failures, 87 were handled through purchase and assumption; 4 involved FDIC-assisted mergers; 7 required deposit transfers; 22 required a payout to depositors.

Coverage

Federal deposit insurance programs make a deposit a riskless investment for an amount specified by law. All forms of deposits are covered including: regular savings accounts, checking accounts, NOW accounts, money market deposit accounts, and CDs. The limit on the amount insured for a depositor has been raised periodically. Currently, the insurance fully protects a depositor's principal and interest combined at an institution up to $100,000. Any excess is not covered by the program.

For example, if a depositor obtains a 5-year, 7% CD with a principal deposit of $90,000, interest after the second year, assuming annual compounding, would be about $13,041. Assuming no other deposits at the institution, and assuming interest is left on deposit, principal plus interest would then be $103,041, which exceeds the coverage provided by federal insurance programs by $3,041. Furthermore, if interest is accrued in the CD for the next 3 years until the CD matures, the accrued interest of about $23,189 will be uninsured. So, when you obtain a CD, be sure that the principal plus the projected interest for the account does not exceed $100,000.

Also, keep in mind that coverage for a depositor includes all deposits in the name of the depositor at the insured institution. For example, suppose Mr. X has a $40,000, 1-year CD, a $50,000 2-year CD, a $10,000 3-year CD, a $2,000 checking account balance, and a regular savings account of $4,000, all under Mr. X's name. Should the institution fail, all of Mr. X's deposits would be added to determine his coverage. Since the sum of the deposits is $106,000, there would be no federal insurance coverage for the $6,000 in excess of the $100,000 limit. Nor would the interest on the four interest-bearing deposits be covered.

An individual who wants to deposit more than $100,000 at a particular institution can obtain full insurance protection in several ways. First, deposits maintained in different rights or capacities are each separately insured for $100,000 at an institution. Therefore, a person may have an interest in more than one separately insured account at the same institution. A married couple, for example, could have three accounts at the same institution insured for $100,000 each by having an individual account for the husband, an individual account for the wife, and a joint account. A couple with one child can raise this total to $700,000 by opening accounts in the names of wife; husband; child; husband and wife; husband and child; wife and child; and husband, wife, and child. In addition, other accounts such as IRAs, Keoghs, irrevocable trusts, and testamentary accounts are each insured up to $100,000. In our earlier illustration, for example, if Mr. X's 1-year CD had been in a Keogh plan account at the institution, he would not have exceeded the $100,000 limit for coverage since the $40,000 plus interest would not be included in determining the amount of his deposits for individual coverage.

A second way to increase insurance protection above the $100,000 limit is by simply opening accounts at different institutions since coverage limits are on a per institution basis. Deposits are not added from other institutions in determining coverage limits. Of course, branches of an institution do not constitute different institutions. Deposits from all branches of a failed institution are added together to determine whether the $100,000 limit is exceeded.

INSURED CDs AVAILABLE THROUGH BROKERS

In 1982, Merrill Lynch entered the retail CD business by opening up a primary and secondary market in small denomination (less than $100,000) CDs. In addition to making available to retail customers the CDs of numerous of its banking and savings institutions clients, Merrill Lynch began to provide retail investors the negotiability enjoyed by institutional investors by standing ready to buy back the CDs prior to the maturity date. In its first four years Merrill Lynch has raised more than $30 billion in deposits for more than 130 depository institutions. Over $5 billion worth of these CDs have been traded in its active secondary market.

The CDs available through Merrill Lynch are issued only by institutions that are FDIC or FSLIC insured.[2] The insurance protection flows through to the investor since the CDs are direct obligations of the issuing institutions and are protected by federal deposit insurance just as if they were placed directly: that is, $100,000 per depositor per institution. Any excess is not insured by the FDIC/FSLIC or Merrill Lynch.

---

[2]They are sometimes referred to as brokered CDs; however, the term brokered CD applies to any CD, retail and institutional, in which an intermediary serves as a broker.

Purchasing a CD through Merrill Lynch has several advantages over making a direct deposit at a bank or thrift. First is the wide choice of issuers and maturities. Of the 130 banks and savings institutions which issue CDs through Merrill Lynch, a dozen or more may be active in a given week offering popular maturities from 3 months to 10 years. When its secondary market inventory is considered, the choices of issuer and term are even extensive.

Second, you may be able to avoid the early withdrawal penalty should you need your funds prior to the maturity date. Merrill Lynch's secondary market works like most other markets. If they offer to repurchase a CD, the proceeds you will receive will depend on interest rates prevailing in the market. If interest rates have declined since you acquired your CD, the proceeds you will receive may be greater than the principal plus accrued interest. The opposite is true if interest rates rise: you may get back less than the principal plus the accrued interest. There is also a customary dealer spread which compensates the market maker. As we explained in the previous chapter, these are investment characteristics shared by all debt obligations. Merrill Lynch also offers its CD customers the opportunity to borrow against CDs with its Flexible Credit Account at the same rates available on margined securities.

The third advantage will be important for those who "rate hunt." The rates depository institutions offer on CDs through Merrill Lynch are set in relation to other money market instruments. Although the rates may not be the highest available at the time, the rates are usually higher than U.S. Treasury securities and competitive with national averages of deposit rates. Often higher current yields are available in the secondary market than in the primary market. That is, when you purchase a "secondhand" CD in the secondary market you usually receive a slightly higher yield than is currently being offered by banks and thrifts for new deposits in Merrill's primary market.

In addition, there is the convenience. You can buy and sell insured CDs with a telephone call rather than making a trip to your local bank or thrift, just the same way you buy or sell a stock or bond. When you first open an account, you'll probably present a check for the amount to be invested. After that, you can buy CDs with a telephone call and send in a check or have an account executive transfer funds from another investment. For those who have held on to funds because they did not have the time to run to their local bank or thrift to deposit funds in a CD, this is a big plus in terms of leisure time sacrificed and interest lost by holding on to the funds. In a declining interest rate environment, you don't have to worry about getting to your bank or thrift to lock in a higher rate. Just call, then send a check! And, with a money market account at Merrill Lynch you can eliminate the float associated with sending money through the mail to distant banks. Moreover, you do not pay any commission when you buy or sell a CD. The institution issuing the CD pays the fee to Merrill Lynch.

Furthermore, for those of you who are still concerned with the risk of failure of an institution despite what we said earlier about the safety provided by federal deposit insurance programs, these CDs offer another advantage. There are at least a dozen professional analysts in Merrill Lynch's Corporate Credit Department who analyze banks and thrifts before they can issue insured CDs through Merrill Lynch. The credit analysts look at a wide range of financial performance measures and assess the current strength and long term viability of each potential issuer. Once an issuer is accepted into the program (and many are rejected), the analysts continuously monitor and reevaluate the issuer. Not a single Merrill Lynch insured CD customer has ever lost a penny or had to wait for an insurance payment.

Merrill Lynch's idea caught on quickly. Today several of the major Wall Street firms with large retail customer bases have followed Merrill's lead while most of the regional and local brokerage firms are part of Merrill's selling group and therefore make available the same CDs as Merrill nationwide.

UNDERSTANDING RATES AND YIELDS

Interest-bearing debt obligations have been created with the liberality of design that auto makers apply to producing cars. Some pay interest at maturity, others pay periodic interest; all accrue interest, but they do so in different ways on the basis of different methods for measuring time periods. Consequently, for CDs and the other debt obligations discussed in this book, we must examine the particular calculations that apply to each.

Quotes on CD Basis versus Bond Equivalent Basis

The rate quoted on a CD, commonly referred to as the coupon rate, is typically quoted on an actual 360-day basis. That is, the interest rate for each day in the interest period (up to 365 or 366 days in a year) is equal to:

$$\text{Daily interest rate on CD} = \frac{\text{Coupon rate}}{360} \times \text{Principal}$$

For example, if the coupon rate for a CD is 7% and the principal is $10,000, then the daily interest is:

$$\frac{.07}{360} \times \$10,000 = \$1.94444$$

If the CD is deposited for 365 days, the total annual dollar interest would be $709.72. The depositor earned more than $700 (7% on the $10,000 principal); he earned a simple annual interest rate of approximately 7.10% ($709.72 ÷ $10,000).

When a CD is quoted on the basis of an actual 360-day basis, the rate is said be quoted on a "CD basis." As we just demonstrated, the simple annual interest rate will be higher. How much higher? The following formula shows you how to compute the simple annual interest rate once you know the quoted rate on a CD basis:

$$\text{Simple annual interest rate} = \text{Quoted rate on a CD basis} \times \frac{365}{360}$$

For example, we showed that the simple annual interest rate for the $10,000 CD with a quoted rate on a CD basis of 7% is 7.10%. Using the above formula, we obtain the same result:

$$\text{Simple annual interest rate} = .07 \times \frac{365}{360}$$
$$= .071 = 7.10\%$$

Life would be so simple if all CDs were quoted on a CD basis. Unfortunately, there are some CDs quoted on a "bond equivalent basis." Any debt obligation (such as CD or bond) quoted on a bond equivalent basis pays interest based on 360 days in a 360-day year (or 12 30-day months, or 365 days in a 365-day year). When CDs are quoted on a bond equivalent basis, a depositor who keeps the funds in a CD for 365 days will receive the coupon rate for 365 days. Consequently, if our 7%, was on a bond equivalent basis and the same $10,000 was deposited for one year, the annual dollar interest would be exactly $700. The difference of $9.72 between the annual dollar interest quoted on a CD basis and the annual dollar interest quoted on a bond equivalent basis is equal to the 5 days of interest of $1.94444 per day. The simple annual interest rate for a CD quoted on a bond equivalent basis is the same as the coupon rate.

The moral is clear. When comparing CDs of different issuers, make sure you know how the issuer is quoting the rate.

Effects of Compounding

The more frequently interest payments are made in a year, the greater the dollar interest realized in a year will be. The reason is that the investor can make the dollar interest work for him by reinvesting it to generate additional interest.

The issuer of a CD may pay interest once a year, semiannually, quarterly, monthly, or daily. A bank generally quotes two rates. One is the coupon rate (remember to find out which basis!). The other is the effective annual yield which takes into account the reinvestment of the interest payments as well as the adjustment necessary for a CD basis. For example, for a CD with a coupon rate of 7% quoted on a CD basis that pays interest semiannually, the effective annual yield would be quoted as 7.22%. Had this CD been quoted on a bond equivalent basis, the effective annual yield would be 7.12%.

Keep in mind that the effective annual yield assumes that the depositor reinvests the interest payments in the same CD or one with the same coupon rate. If a depositor withdraws the interest payments, then the actual yield that he will realize depends on the interest rate earned on the withdrawn interest payments. An interest rate earned on the withdrawn interest payments that is lower (higher) than the coupon rate on the CD will result in an actual yield that is less (greater) than the quoted effective annual yield.

The same is true for CDs that do not automatically reinvest interest payments in the same CD. For example, CDs available through Merrill Lynch normally pay interest semiannually for maturities over one year with interest payments being paid out rather than being reinvested in the same CD. Therefore, if an effective annual yield is quoted, it assumes that the semiannual interest payments can be invested in an investment vehicle that offers the same coupon rate.

Zero-coupon CDs

With a coupon bearing CD that pays out its interest, the investor cannot be assured of locking in an effective annual yield because of the uncertainty over the rate at which interest payments will be reinvested. We'll take a closer look at the impact of reinvestment on an investor's return in Chapter 7. However, at this point it is sufficient to say that an investor can lock in an effective annual yield: by investing in a debt instrument that does not pay explicit interest but is instead purchased at a substantial discount from its maturity value and held to its maturity date. The interest earned by the investor is the difference between the maturity value and the price paid.

An instrument with maturity greater than one year that does not make periodic interest payments, but is instead sold at a discount, is called a zero-coupon instrument. Later in this book we will discuss zero-coupon notes and bonds. Zero-coupon insured CDs have become popular with investors who seek to lock in a yield and thereby accumulate enough funds to meet a particular goal such as financing a college education or retirement. There is a tax disadvantage to a zero-coupon CD. The daily interest that accrues on a zero-coupon CD is taxed by the federal government as if it had been actually received by an investor.[3] Consequently, zero-coupon CDs should only be included in tax-deferred retirement accounts or given as gifts to minors who are in a lower tax bracket.

Comparison with Bonds Yields

Thus far we have shown how to compare CD yields offered by institutions. But an investor will want to compare yields on CDs with yields offered on bonds. This can be done by computing the bond equivalent yield. For a CD quoted on a CD basis, the bond equivalent yield is found as follows:

$$\text{Bond equivalent yield} = \text{Quoted rate on a CD basis} \times \frac{365}{360}$$

Notice that this is the same formula as the one for the conversion of the quoted rate on a CD basis to a simple annual interest rate. The bond equivalent yield is equal to the quoted CD rate when the rate is quoted on a bond equivalent basis.

RETURN, RISK, AND LIQUIDITY

As with any investment, it is the combination of return, risk and liquidity which must be considered. The yield offered on new CDs is determined by the management or board of the institution. Such yields have been higher than yields available on U.S. government securities of comparable maturity. For example, when the yield on 1-year Treasury bills was 11.4%, the yield on 1-year CDs was 11.5%.[4] When the

---

[3]The tax treatment of zero-coupon instruments is discussed in Chapter 8.
[4]Treasury bills are the subject of the next chapter.

yield on 1-year Treasury bills declined to 7.7%, the yield on 1-year CDs was 7.9%. How much higher a depository institution will pay above a U.S. government security with the same maturity depends on how aggressive the institution wants to be in attracting funds.

The best way to select a depository institution is to shop around for one with the best terms. Consider the rate for the maturity desired, the minimum balance, and early withdrawal penalties. Some institutions even allow you to add more money to a time deposit within a certain period of time after the account is opened—that gives you the opportunity to invest at a higher rate should interest rates decline. Each of these factors is important in searching for the most appropriate institution. If the ability to sell a CD prior to maturity is important, you should buy your CD through a brokerage firm.

Call several local institutions to check on terms offered. However, if you have $10,000 or more, don't restrict your search to local banks and thrifts. A good way to compare rates offered by banks and thrifts throughout the U.S. is to check the *Banxquote Deposit Index* published in *The Wall Street Journal* every Friday. An example of this information is reproduced as Exhibit 2–1. Notice that there is a wide range of yields offered. Some geographical areas are not as competitive as others in seeking funds, and the yields offered reflect this. Remember that the quoted rates are not always comparable for the reasons discussed earlier in the chapter.

There are certain times during the year (December through April 15th) when banks are particularly aggressive in seeking qualified, tax-exempt retirement fund money such as Keogh Plans. During this period, every piece of literature you receive in the mail from a bank or thrift will have information about the advantages of these plans. Some banks and thrifts will offer a bonus rate such as 1/2% more for Keogh Plan deposits.

At other times, promotional campaigns by banks and thrifts to attract funds will offer bonus rates. Promotional campaigns tying the rate on a new CD to the performance of a sports team have been popular in recent years. Skokie Federal Savings and Loan in Illinois offered a bonus on its 1-year CD if the Chicago Bears beat the New England Patriots in the 1986 Super Bowl. The amount of the bonus was based on the margin of victory, each point being equal to .01%. Since the victory of margin was 36 points, Skokie Federal Savings and Loan had to pay an additional .36%. The bank was able to lure $13.8 million, including $10,000 from a Boston depositor who sent in his deposit explaining that he hated

EXHIBIT 2-1

BANXQUOTE® DEPOSIT INDEX

Wednesday, March 26, 1986

Annual effective savings yields of major banks in key states

	MMA*	30 days	60 days	90 days	Six Months	One Year	2½ Years	5 Years
NEW YORK								
Avg.	6.82%	6.82%	6.82%	7.02%	7.18%	7.39%	7.74%	8.00%
CALIFORNIA								
Avg.	6.27%	6.12%	6.12%	6.55%	6.85%	7.18%	7.40%	7.78%
PENNSYLVANIA								
Avg.	6.50%	6.40%	6.40%	6.79%	6.99%	7.10%	7.28%	7.83%
ILLINOIS								
Avg.	6.98%	6.55%	6.55%	6.92%	7.34%	7.43%	7.69%	8.05%
TEXAS								
Avg.	6.63%	7.15%	7.12%	7.12%	7.18%	7.33%	7.58%	7.92%
FLORIDA								
Avg.	6.53%	6.45%	6.60%	6.91%	7.42%	7.60%	8.08%	8.20%
National								
Avg.	6.62%	6.64%	6.66%	6.89%	7.16%	7.34%	7.62%	7.95%
Wkly Chng	−0.05	−0.02	−0.03	−0.03	−0.02	−0.02	−0.04	−0.03

*Money Market Accounts.

Each depositor is insured by the Federal Deposit Insurance Corp. (FDIC) or Federal Savings and Loan Insurance Corp. (FSLIC) up to $100,000 per institution.

Methods of compounding (continuously, daily, weekly, monthly, quarterly, semiannually, annually or simple interest), minimum balance requirements, number of days in one year (360 or 365), interest payment schedule and other conditions vary among institutions. Effective annual yield can be influenced by these factors, which should be carefully evaluated to obtain a valid rate comparison.

The information included in this table has been obtained directly from the participating institutions, but the accuracy and validity cannot be guaranteed. Rates are subject to change. Yields, terms and creditworthiness should be verified before investing.

HIGH YIELD SAVINGS

Small minimum balance, generally $500 to $2,500

Savings Money Market Accounts	Rate	Yield		Six Months Savings CDs	Rate	Yield
Citisavings, San Antonio Texas	8.38%	8.74%		Community Svgs, Baton Rouge La	8.25%	8.69%
Meridian Svgs, Arlington Texas	8.00%	8.45%		Sharon Svgs, Baltimore Md	8.09%	8.55%
OBA Federal, Washington DC	8.00%	8.33%		Mereidian Svgs, Arlington Texas	8.25%	8.51%
Amer Investment, Salt Lake City	8.00%	8.32%		Guaranty Federal, Dallas	8.25%	8.50%
Vista Federal, Reston Va	8.00%	8.30%		Benjamin Franklin, Houston	4.30%	8.46%

30-Day Savings CDs	Rate	Yield		One Year Savings CDs	Rate	Yield
Community Svgs, Baton Rouge La	7.50%	7.87%		Community Svgs, Baton Rouge La	8.63%	9.09%
Benjamin Franklin, Houston	7.50%	7.76%		Guaranty Federal, Dallas	8.75%	9.04%
Progressive Svgs, Alhambra Ca	7.40%	7.65%		Sun Savings San Diego Ca	8.50%	9.00%
South Bay Svgs, Costa Mesa Ca	7.25%	7.62%		Sharon Svgs, Baltimore Md	8.65%	9.00%
Dixie Federal, New Orleans	7.30%	7.58%		Southern Calif, Beverly Hills Ca	8.50%	9.00%

60-Day Savings CDs	Rate	Yield		2½ Years Savings CDs	Rate	Yield
Sharon Svgs, Baltimore Md	8.25%	8.55%		Sharon Svgs, Baltimore Md	8.96%	9.51%
Commonwealth Svgs, Houston	8.20%	8.49%		Community Svgs, Baton Rouge La	8.88%	9.37%
Community Svgs, Baton Rouge La	7.63%	8.01%		Southern Calif, Beverly Hills Ca	8.73%	9.25%
South Bay Svgs, Costa Mesa Ca	7.50%	7.89%		Baltimore County, Perry Hall Md	8.75%	9.14%
Benjamin Franklin, Houston	7.50%	7.76%		Guardian Fed, Bridgeport Ct	8.75%	9.14%

90-Day Savings CDs	Rate	Yield		5 Years Savings CDs	Rate	Yield
Sharon Svgs, Baltimore Md	8.29%	8.55%		Guardian Fed, Bridgeport Ct	9.75%	10.24%
Commonwealth Svgs, Houston	8.20%	8.46%		Guaranty Federal, Dallas	9.75%	10.11%
Colonial Nat'l Bank, Wilmington Del	8.00%	8.45%		Financial Svgs, Dallas	9.25%	9.71%
Community Svgs, Baton Rouge La	8.00%	8.40%		Baltimore County, Perry Hall Md	9.25%	9.69%
Bell Svgs, Sacramento Ca	7.84%	8.27%		Southern Calif, Beverly Hills Ca	9.09%	9.65%

HIGH YIELD JUMBOS

Large minimum balance, generally $100,000.

Jumbo Money Market Accounts	Rate	Yield		Six Months Jumbo CDs	Rate	Yield
Citisavings, San Antonio Texas	8.38%	8.74%		Spindletop Svgs, Beaumont Texas	8.50%	8.50%
Commonwealth Svgs, Houston	8.25%	8.57%		Guaranty Federal, Dallas	8.50%	8.50%
Vista Federal, Reston Va	8.25%	8.57%		Ben Milam Svgs, Cameron Texas	8.50%	8.50%
Guaranty Federal, Dallas	8.50%	8.50%		Bell Svgs, Sacramento Ca	8.40%	8.40%
Meridian Svgs, Arlington Texas	8.00%	8.45%		Sun Svgs, San Diego Ca	8.38%	8.38%

30-Day Jumbo CDs	Rate	Yield		One Year Jumbo CDs	Rate	Yield
Commonwealth Svgs, Houston	8.00%	8.30%		Bell Svgs, Sacramento Ca	8.75%	8.75%
Ben Milam Svgs, Cameron Texas	8.25%	8.25%		Spindletop Svgs, Beaumont Texas	8.75%	8.75%
Benjamin Franklin, Houston	7.80%	8.08%		Guaranty Federal, Dallas	8.75%	8.75%
American Svgs, Salt Lake City	8.05%	8.05%		Ben Milam Svgs, Cameron Texas	8.75%	8.75%
Creditbanc Svgs, Austin Texas	8.00%	8.00%		Benjamin Franklin, Houston	8.45%	8.72%

60-Day Jumbo CDs	Rate	Yield		2½ Years Jumbo CDs	Rate	Yield
Commonwealth Svgs, Houston	8.30%	8.60%		Bell Svgs, Sacramento Ca	9.00%	9.00%
Ben Milam Svgs, Cameron Texas	8.25%	8.25%		Benjamin Franklin, Houston	8.60%	8.88%
Creditbanc Svgs, Austin Texas	8.13%	8.13%		Community Svgs, Baton Rouge La	8.88%	8.88%
Benjamin Franklin, Houston	7.80%	8.08%		Commonwealth Svgs, Houston	8.63%	8.63%
American Svgs, Salt Lake City	8.05%	8.05%		Unity Svgs, Beverly Hills Ca	8.50%	8.50%

90-Day Jumbo CDs	Rate	Yield		5 Years Jumbo CDs	Rate	Yield
Commonwealth Svgs, Houston	8.25%	8.51%		Guaranty Federal, Dallas	9.75%	9.75%
Ben Milam Svgs, Cameron Texas	8.50%	8.50%		Amer Investment, Salt Lake City	9.50%	9.50%
Benjamin Franklin, Houston	8.10%	8.38%		Guaranty First Trust, Waltham Ma	8.95%	9.36%
Creditbanc Svgs, Austin Texas	8.25%	8.25%		Guaranty First Trust, Waltham Ma	9.00%	9.31%
Guaranty Federal, Dallas	8.25%	8.25%		Bell Svgs, Sacramento Ca	9.30%	9.30%

Source: MASTERFUND INC., New York.
Banxquote is a registered trademark
and service mark of MASTERFUND INC.

SOURCE: Reprinted from *The Wall Street Journal*. Banxquote Online, Published by Masterfund, Inc. 575 Madison Avenue, New York, N.Y. 10022, Tel. (212) 605-0337.

his hometown team.[5] Management must have been pleased with the re-sults—after all, for the 1986 baseball season, Skokie Federal Savings and Loan offered CDs with progressively better rates depending on the success of the Chicago Cubs and Chicago White Sox baseball teams. In 1986, a Louisville bank offered a bonus on its 6-month CD based on the NCAA playoff performance of the basketball teams of the University of Louisville and the University of Kentucky. The bank had to payoff—Louisville won the NCAA Division I basketball title. Another bonus payoff came that year when the Dallas Texas Group offered a higher rate on a 1-year CD if the Dallas Mavericks or the Houston Rockets won five playoff games—a feat accomplished by the Rockets who made it to the NBA finals, losing to the Boston Celtics. Do you think any bank or thrift in Boston offered a bonus tied to the point spread between the Celtics and the Rockets? No way.[6]

As for safety, as we stated earlier in this chapter, as long as a CD is insured by a federal deposit insurance program, and a depositor does not exceed the maximum coverage, the chances of a depositor losing funds are slim to none. Higher rates are available on CDs with a mini-mum balance of $100,000, called "jumbo CDs." However, with the additional yield comes additional risk—the excess over $100,000 in principal deposited and the interest accrued is not covered by federal deposit insurance.

Turning to liquidity, an investor can withdraw funds with no un-certainty about the amount that will be received. However, CDs are subject to an early withdrawal penalty which may result in proceeds from withdrawal that are less than the amount deposited. Brokered CDs offer investors greater liquidity than CDs acquired directly from depository institutions; however, there is uncertainty as to the amount of the proceeds that will be received if the CD is sold prior to maturity. The proceeds depend on whether interest rates have increased or de-clined since the CD was purchased. For short-term CDs, changes in rates may have only a small impact on price, but then there is the deal-er's spread. Long-term, zero-coupon CDs have the greatest price volatility, a point that we shall return to in Chapter 7. Consequently, while they may be sold in a secondary market, long-term, zero-coupon CDs are not considered to be very liquid. This should not be of con-cern to an investor who plans to hold the CD to maturity.

---

[5]"The Price of Being Bearish," *Institutional Investor,* February 1986, p. 17.

[6]Lisa Grace Lednicer, "How to Make Basketball Boring? Leave It to Bankers to Find a Way," *The Wall Street Journal,* June 13, 1986.

Treasury Bills

3

To finance its debt, the U.S. government sells various securities (commonly referred to in the financial community as *governments*) to the investing public. The government issues three types of *negotiable* or *marketable* debt securities to the public—*bills, notes,* and *bonds.*

In this chapter we shall discuss Treasury bills, which are investment vehicles that can be used for building the base of your financial pyramid and for parking funds for a short time period. Treasury bills offer investors several attractive features. Because they are guaranteed by the full faith and credit of the U.S. government, they expose the investor to no risk of default. Although they yield less than comparable maturity CDs and other money market instruments, which we shall discuss in the next chapter, they are the most liquid instruments traded in the money market. Another advantage of Treasury bills is that interest income earned on them is *not* subject to state and local taxation. A final attraction is the wide range of maturities available as a result of the active secondary market. With the exception of liquidity (liquidity have being the certainty of price if sold prior to maturity), Treasury bonds and notes share these attractive investment features. Treasury notes and bonds are discussed in Chapter 9.

The most important reason to be familiar with Treasury bills is that their yields are the most frequently quoted and often the benchmark on which many consumer yields are based.

WHAT ARE TREASURY BILLS?

Treasury bills (often called T bills or bills), which represent about 40% of the total marketable securities issued by the Treasury, are negotiable, non-interest-bearing securities with an original maturity of 1 year or less. Bills are currently offered by the Treasury in minimum denominations of $10,000 and increments of $5,000 thereafter. Bills are issued only in book-entry form.

Bills are always issued at a discount from face value, with the amount of the discount being determined in bill auctions held by the Fed each time the Treasury issues new bills. At maturity, bills are redeemed by the Treasury for full face value. Thus, the investor in bills earns a return by receiving more for his bills at maturity than he paid for them at issue. This return is treated for federal income tax purposes as ordinary interest income and, as such, is subject to full federal taxation at ordinary rates; it is as we noted earlier, however, specifically exempt from state and local taxation.

DETERMINING THE YIELD ON BILLS

The first mystery to unravel concerning bills is how to calculate yield on them. As noted, bills pay no interest. Instead, they are issued at a discount and redeemed at maturity for full face value. Thus the investor who holds bills from issue until maturity realizes a gain; he gets back more for his bills than he paid for them. The amount of this gain can easily be expressed as a percentage yield on the funds invested. For example, suppose that an investor buys a bill maturing in 1 year at a price of $93 *for each $100 of face value*. Then, by holding his bill until maturity, he will realize a gain of $7 on each $93 invested. Dividing $7 by $93, we find that this equals a simple annual interest rate of 7.53% on his investment. The general formula for calculating the simple annual interest rate on a bill maturing in *1* year is as follows:

$$\text{Simple annual interest rate} = \frac{\text{Face value} - \text{Price}}{\text{Price}}$$

For bills maturing in *less than* 1 year, the situation is more complicated. In that case the above formula understates the simple annual interest rate since the investor earns his return in less than a year. To correct for this, we have to divide the above formula by the fraction of the year that the bill must be held before it matures. Thus, if a bill selling at $93 per $100 of face value had a maturity of 300 days, the simple annual interest rate to the investor buying this bill would be

$$\left(\frac{\$7}{\$93}\right) \div \left(\frac{300}{365}\right)$$

or 9.16%. All this can be expressed easily in a general formula. Let

$$t = \text{days to maturity}$$

Then the simple annual interest rate on a bill maturing in one year or less is given by the expression:

$$\text{Simple annual interest rate} = \left(\frac{\text{Face Value} - \text{Price}}{\text{Price}}\right) \div \left(\frac{t}{365}\right)$$

From this formula it is obvious that the yield on a bill depends on both the discounted price paid for the bill and its *current* maturity, which will be something less than its *original* maturity if the bill is purchased some time after issue. For a given current maturity, the lower the discounted price, the higher the yield; and for a given discounted price, the shorter the current maturity, the higher the yield.

Yield on a Bank Discount Basis

Bill dealers quote bill yields in a unique way that makes little sense to an investor. They measure yield on a *bank discount basis;* they quote yield as *the percentage amount of the discount on an annualized basis.* To illustrate, consider again our investor who buys a bill maturing in 1 year at a price of $93 for each $100 of face value. The discount on this bill is $7, so yield on a bank discount basis works out to be 7% ($7/$100). For a bill maturing in 1 year, the expression for the yield on a bank discount basis per $100 of face value is

$$\text{Yield on a bank discount basis} = \frac{\text{Face value} - \text{Price}}{100}.$$

On a bill maturing in less than 1 year, the discount is earned more quickly, so to get the correct annualized bank discount rate, we have to divide the above formula by the fraction of the year over which the bill must be held to reach maturity. Thus, if our bill selling at $93 per $100 of face value had a current maturity of only 300 days, the annual yield on a bank discount basis would be, using a 360-day year (which bankers do): ($7/$100) ÷ (300/360) or 8.40%. For a bill maturing in *t* days, the general formula for annual yield on a bank discount basis per $100 of face value is as follows:

$$\left(\frac{\text{Face value} - \text{Price}}{100} \right) \div \left(\frac{t}{360} \right)$$

When we calculated yield on a simple annual interest rate basis for a bill selling at $93 per $100 of face value and maturing in 1 year, we got a figure of 9.16%. When we redid the same calculation on a bank discount basis, we got a smaller figure, 8.40%. As a comparison of these figures correctly suggests, *yield on a bank discount basis significantly understates yield on a simple annual interest rate basis.*

The absolute divergence between simple annual interest rate and yield on a bank discount basis is not constant but varies depending on both absolute yield and maturity. As Exhibit 3–1 shows, the greater the yield and the longer the maturity, the greater the divergence.

Bond Equivalent Yield

In later chapters of this book, we will describe securities that make periodic interest payments. These are called coupon securities. In the secondary market, bids for and offerings of coupon securities are quoted not in terms of yields (as in the case of discount securities) but in terms of dollar prices.[1] On a dealer coupon quote sheet, however, there is always a number for each security stating what its yield to maturity would be if it were purchased at the quoted asked or offered price. However, the yield to maturity figure on a quote sheet for coupon securities *understates* the effective yield to maturity because it ignores the fact that interest is paid *semiannually;* that is, whatever investors do with coupon interest, it is worth something to them to get semiannual interest payments rather than a single year-end interest payment.

In converting the yield on a T bill to an add-on interest rate, various approaches are possible. One approach is to convert to an equivalent simple annual interest rate as explained above. However, in putting together quote sheets, "the Street" takes a slightly different tack.

---

[1]An exception is municipal bonds. See Chapter 12.

EXHIBIT 3-1 Comparison of Different Yield Measures on Bills

Rate of Discount (Percent)	Simple Annual Interest Rate and Bond Equivalent Yield (Percent)		Simple Annual Interest Rate	Bond Equivalent Yield
	30-Day Maturity	182-Day Maturity	364-Day Maturity	364-Day Maturity
6	6.11	6.27	6.48	6.38
8	8.17	8.45	8.82	8.64
10	10.22	10.68	11.27	10.98
12	12.29	12.95	13.84	13.40
14	14.36	15.28	16.53	15.90

It restates yields on discount securities such as T bills on a basis that makes them comparable to the yield to maturity quoted on coupon securities. A rate so computed is called a *bond equivalent yield.*[2]

The formula for converting yield on a bank discount basis to bond equivalent yield is complicated for discount securities that have a current maturity of longer than 6 months, but that is no problem for investors because bill yields are always restated on dealers' quote sheets in terms of bond equivalent yield at the *asked* rate.[3]

On bills with a current maturity of 6 months (182 days) or less, bond equivalent yield is the simple annual interest rate yielded by a bill. Let

$$d_b = \text{Bond equivalent yield}$$

Then, on a bill quoted at the discount rate *d*, bond equivalent yield is given by

$$d_b = \frac{365 \times d}{360 - (d \times t)}$$

For example, on a 91-day bill purchased at 8%, bond equivalent yield is

$$d_b = \frac{365 \times 0.08}{360 - (0.08 \times 91)} = 8.28\%$$

---

[2]The Treasury uses the term coupon equivalent yield rather than bond equivalent yield.

[3]The asked price is the price the dealer is willing to sell the security for.

Exhibit 3-1 compares the bond equivalent yield with the yield on a bank discount basis and simple annual interest rate. The greater the yield and the longer the maturity of the bill, the greater the divergence between the yield on a bank discount basis and bond equivalent yield. The bond equivalent yield and the simple annual interest rate are identical for the 30-day and 182-day bills. The bond equivalent yield is less than the simple annual interest rate for bills with more than 182 days to maturity.

Money Market Yield

Bond equivalent yield on a bill is calculated on the basis of a 365-day year. Bill rates are—to make them directly comparable to rates on 1-year CDs and other interest-bearing, money market instruments that we shall discuss in the next chapter—often converted to a simple interest rate on a 360-day-year basis. That number, dubbed *money market yield,* is obtained by substituting 360 for 365 in the above equation for bond equivalent yield; specifically,

$$\left(\begin{matrix}\text{Money market yield} \\ \text{on a bill}\end{matrix}\right) = \frac{360 \times d}{360 - (d \times t)}$$

NEW-ISSUE MARKET

Currently all bills are sold through auctions conducted by the 12 regional Federal Reserve banks. These auctions are held on a regular schedule. Bills with 13-week and 26-week maturities are offered each week. Except when holidays interfere, such issues are announced on Tuesdays, auctioned the following Monday, and paid for and issued on the next Thursday. The Treasury also offers bills having a 52-week maturity every 4 weeks. These offerings are announced on a Friday, auctioned the following Thursday, and paid for and issued on the Thursday after the auction.

Money market banks, bond dealers, and other institutional investors who buy large quantities of bills usually submit what is called a *competitive bid* at the auction. The bid must be expressed on a bank discount basis with not more than 2 decimals. For example, an investor who wanted to buy $1 million of 6-month bills might bid 6.45%. It is easy to determine that if this investor gets his bills at that bid, he will pay a price of 98.770. What yields investors bid for bills depend naturally both on what rates are being paid by outstanding money market instruments that compete with new bills for their investment dollars and on what (if any) movement they think is occurring in short-term interest rates.

Once it receives investors' bids, the Fed, which is responsible for selling some specific, previously announced total of bills, allocates the available supply of bills among those bidders who have offered to accept the lowest rates of discount (pay the highest prices). Note that each such bidder gets the quantity of bills he bid for at the specific yield he bid. Thus the system is such that successful bidders will pay different prices for their bills. The range of prices paid runs from the lowest yield received to the *stop-out* yield—the highest yield the Fed has to accept in order to sell all the bills to be auctioned. Obviously the investor who manages to be at or near the stop-out yield is going to get the most favorable return on his investment. Thus, large bidders spend much time studying the market before they submit their bids. Also, because of constantly changing money market conditions, they generally make their bids at the last moment possible; in fact, on an auction day just before the Fed window closes, one can count on seeing a stream of panting runners delivering tenders on which the inked-in bids are still wet.

The less expert investor who is not prepared to work out a bid to 2 decimal points can put in a noncompetitive bid, as noted later in this chapter. This permits him to buy bills at the average accepted bid.

As noted above, there is normally a time lag of several days after the day on which bills are auctioned and the day on which they are actually issued. During this period, the new bill issue, which has been sold but not yet delivered, is traded among investors and dealers on a *when-issued* basis. Securities traded on this basis are denoted *wi* on dealers' quote sheets.

THE SECONDARY MARKET

Once a bill issue has been auctioned, trading in it moves to the *secondary market*. The secondary market for bills and other governments is an over-the-counter market made by about 37 primary dealers in government securities. These dealers all act as principals in the transactions they enter, buying and selling for their own account. Before we discuss how the dealer-made market in governments operates, we need to say a few words about how and why bill prices fluctuate over time.

Fluctuations in a Bill's Price in the Secondary Market

Normally, the price at which a bill sells will rise as the bill approaches maturity. For example, to yield 9% on a discount basis, a 6-month bill must be priced at $95.45 per $100 of face value. For the same bill 3 months later (3 months closer to maturity) to yield 9%, it must have risen in price to $97.72. The moral is clear: If a bill always sold at the same yield throughout its life, its price would rise steadily toward face value as it approached maturity.

A bill's yield, however, is unlikely to be constant over time; instead, it will fluctuate for two reasons: (1) changes may occur in the general level of short-term interest rates, and (2) the bill will move along *the yield curve*. Let's look at each of these factors.

Short-term Interest Rates. T bills are issued through auctions in which discounted prices (yields) are bid. The rate of discount determined at auction on a new bill issue depends on the level of short-term interest rates prevailing at the moment of the auction. The reason is straightforward. Investors who want to buy bills at the time of a Treasury auction have two alternatives—to buy new bills or to buy existing bills from dealers. This being the case, investors will not bid for new bills a rate of discount lower than that available on existing bills. If they did, they would be offering to buy new bills at a price higher than that at which they could buy existing bills. Also, investors will not bid substantially higher rates of discount (lower prices) than those prevailing on existing bills. If they did, they would not obtain bills, since they would surely be underbid by others trying to get just a slightly better return than that available on existing securities. Thus, the prevailing level of short-term rates determines, within a narrow range, the discount established on new bills at issue.

However, the going level of short-term rates is not constant over time. It rises and falls in response to changes in economic activity, the demand for credit, investors' expectations, and monetary policy as set by the Federal Reserve System. If the going level of short-term rates (which establishes the rate at which a bill is initially sold) falls after a bill is issued, then this bill—as long as its price doesn't change—will yield more than new bills. Therefore, buyers will compete for this bill, and in doing so, they will drive up its price and thereby force down its yield until the bill sells at a rate of discount equal to the new, lower going interest rate. Conversely, if short-term rates rise after a bill is issued, the unwillingness of buyers to purchase any bill at a discount less than that available on new issues will drive down its price and thereby force up its yield.

The Yield Curve. Even if the going level of short-term interest rates does not change while an investor holds bills, it would be normal for the rate at which he could sell his bills to change. The reason lies in the *yield curve,* which we will discuss in detail in Chapter 7. Here it suffices to observe that when an investor chooses among alternative securities, he is interested in three things: risk, liquidity, and return. Many investors desire high liquidity and are therefore willing to pay a higher price for (that is, accept a lower rate of return on) a security when its liquidity is greater.

Bills and other debt instruments are more liquid, the shorter their current maturity. To see why, suppose that short-term interest rates rise a full percentage point across the board; then the prices of all bill issues will drop *but the price drop will be greater, the longer an issue's current maturity.* For example, a rise from 7 to 8% in market rates would cause a 3-month bill to fall only $0.25 in price per $100 of face value, whereas the corresponding price drop on a 9-month bill would be $0.80 per $100 of face value. In financial jargon, the longer-maturity bill is less liquid because it exposes the investor to a greater *price risk.*

Because a 3-month bill is more liquid than a 9-month bill, it would be normal for a 3-month bill to yield less than a 9-month bill. In other words, the *bill-market yield curve,* which shows the relationship between yield and maturity, normally *slopes upward,* indicating that *the longer the time to maturity, the higher the yield.* We say "normally" because other factors, such as the expectation that interest rates are going to fall, may alter this generally prevailing relationship.

To give you a concrete feel for a yield curve, we reproduced in Exhibit 3–2 the yield curve based on quotes of Treasury securities for June 28, 1985. While the yield curve for very short maturities is almost always upward sloping, its precise shape and slope vary over time. Thus, it is difficult to pinpoint a "normal" spread between, say, 1-month and 6-month bills. Yield spreads between different securities are always measured in terms of basis points. A *basis point is 1/100 of 1 percentage point.* Thus, if 5-month bills are quoted at 5.25 and 6-

---

EXHIBIT 3-2 Yield Curve for U.S. Treasury
Securities—Bills, Notes, and
Bonds—June 28, 1985

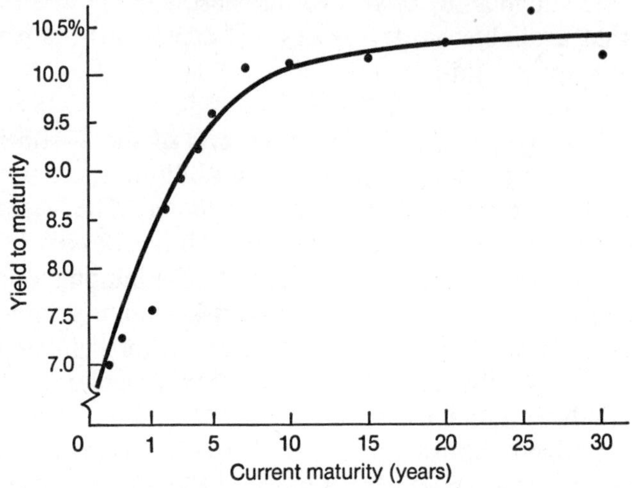

*Dots represent observed yields, yield curve is fitted to them.

SOURCE: J. L. Kochan, "Corporate-to-Treasury Yield Spreads:
A Critical Analysis," in *The Handbook of Fixed Income Securi-
ties,* 2nd ed., ed. F. J. Fabozzi and I. M. Pollack (Homewood, Ill.:
Dow Jones-Irwin, 1987).

---

month bills at 5.35, the spread between the two is said to be 10 basis
points. A yield spread between two securities of 100 basis points
would indicate a full 1% difference in their yields.

Dealers—the Market Makers

As we said, the secondary market for bills and other governments is
made largely by a limited number of primary dealers in government
securities. The market these dealers make is an extremely efficient one
which trades billions of dollars of securities every day under extremely
competitive conditions.

The easiest way to explain what a dealer does would be to say that
he buys securities at one price, his *bid price,* and then turns around
and resells them at a slightly higher price, his *asked price.* If the margin between the two prices, typically very small in governments, is sufficiently large to cover his operating expenses, then he makes a profit,
if not he loses money. Such a description, while it has some validity, is

misleading because it misses a fundamental and inescapable part of the dealer's role, namely that he acts as a speculator in a highly volatile market.

The major dealers in government securities are spread around the country in New York City, Chicago, and other financial centers. Despite this geographic dispersion, they form a single tightly knit market, since they are all linked by direct phones over which they are in constant contact throughout the trading day. A key rule of the dealer game is that each dealer must stand ready to quote at any time to other dealers bid and asked prices on active issues, *and* he must be willing to buy or sell substantial quantities at those prices. In the jargon of "the Street," a series of price quotes is a *run,* a request to sell at a bid price is a *hit,* and a request to buy at an asked price a *take.*

Throughout every trading day, each dealer is constantly trading with other dealers and with his customers, the public. In these transactions the dealer almost always acts as a *principal,* buying and selling for his own account. Thus a fundamental part of a dealer's role is to take a position i.e., to *speculate,* in different government issues. Doing so naturally exposes the dealer to a considerable *price risk.* If interest rates should rise, the value of the securities he holds in inventory will be driven down, resulting in losses. On the other hand, if interest rates should fall, the securities he holds will rise in value, creating profits for him when he sells.

Because they are fundamentally speculators in government securities, dealers constantly seek to adjust their positions in the securities they trade in the light of changing economic conditions. If, for example, dealers expect interest rates to fall, perhaps due to an economic downswing, they will try to build up inventories, or extend their long positions. Since bill dealers never have the funds necessary to finance the huge positions they take in governments, they are constantly borrowing short-term to get required financing. If the rates at which they can borrow are less than the yield on the securities they are carrying, which might occur when rates are falling, they have a *positive carry,* which further encourages them to build up inventories. A *negative carry* has the opposite effect.

If a dealer expects rates to rise rather than fall, he will attempt to cut back his position, even sell some issues short.[4] Among dealers, as-

---

[4] On a *short* sale, the seller sells securities he does not own. Naturally, his short position must eventually be covered by an offsetting purchase.

suming a short position is much less common than going long since shorting requires that the dealer find securities to borrow so that he can make delivery on the short sale, a proposition that is not always easy and can be costly.

From what we have said, it is obvious that what profits a dealer earns over the year depends on how successful he has been in guessing trends in the market and making appropriate changes in his portfolio. It is also clear that all dealers are in strong competition with each other; consequently, they have a strong incentive to hide their buying and selling intentions from each other. The moment word gets around that a certain dealer is trying to build up or cut back his holdings of a given issue, other dealers will alter their quotes on that issue. Keeping the competition in the dark sometimes calls for gamesmanship. For example, a dealer who wants to buy an issue might start out by selling a little of it to force the price down and then reverse his position, hoping to buy back at low prices more than he had sold. Another common practice is to buy and sell through a broker who guards the anonymity of both buyer and seller. In recent years brokered trades have become increasingly common in the dealer market.

In a very real sense the prices of bills and other governments are made in the dealer market through the constant sparring—runs, hits, and takes—that occurs among the dealers. However, since the behavior of the dealers—their bullishness or bearishness—is immediately and highly sensitive to every change in both customer demand and economic conditions, the prices established in the market reflect rapidly and accurately the constantly changing conditions in the credit market.

One major participant in the bill market not mentioned so far is the Fed. In effecting monetary policy, one of the Fed's key tools is *open market operations,* purchases and sales of government securities. When the Fed wants to ease interest rates and increase the money supply, it buys bills, which has the effect of increasing bank reserves and permitting an expansion of bank loans and deposits. When the Fed wants to tighten money, it buys bills.

All Fed open market operations are carried out from the trading desk of the Federal Reserve Bank of New York and are made through the network of primary dealers. Because of the large volume and crucial nature of its operations, the Fed will deal directly only with dealers who have established a performance record. Thus, who becomes a primary dealer is a question determined by the Fed. When a dealer's record is good enough so that the Fed can rely on him, it signs a trading agreement with the dealer, installs a private wire to him from its trading desk, and the dealer becomes a primary dealer. Not all participants in the dealer market are primary dealers, but most of the major market-makers are.

In carrying out open market purchases and sales, the Fed cloaks its intentions for the same reason the dealers do, to get the best prices possible. Consequently when the Fed does a *go-around,* asking all the primary dealers for price runs, these dealers never know whether the Fed is in the market as a buyer or seller, whether the Fed will *hit* their bid price or *take* their asked price. Because of the large size of Fed purchases and sales and because of their direct impact on the money supply and interest rates, dealers are very sensitive to any change in Fed policy. Any hint that the Fed is out to ease credit will cause dealers to buy, and vice versa.

Besides making a secondary market in governments, dealers also act to some extent as underwriters of new issues. For example, when the Treasury auctions a new bill issue through the Fed, dealers typically buy up substantial quantities of the new bills at auction and then turn around and sell these bills to their retail customers.

In this chapter we have talked about bills. In later chapters we will discuss negotiable government notes and bonds. All dealers handle both types of securities and government agency issues as well (Chapters 9 and 10). Since the number of such issues outstanding is large, a dealer operation involves many individuals. At the top of the pile is the account manager who determines from day to day what the organization's overall trading stance in different maturities should be: to stay even, to short the market, or to run a long position. Under the account manager are a number of traders, each responsible for trading a specific group of securities: bills, short-term governments, immediate-term governments, long-term governments, and various agency issues. Finally, surrounding the trading desk are a bevy of salesmen who deal directly with the organization's retail customers, primarily institutional buyers who invest substantial amounts.

Buying Bills

There is no way for an individual to invest in bills unless he has a minimum of $10,000 available or is willing and able to pool funds with other investors. For an individual with more than $10,000 to invest, it is possible to acquire bills in amounts equal to any multiple of 5 by buying an appropriate mix of bills in $10,000 and $15,000 denominations. Bills can be purchased from a bank or at auction.

Buying Bills at a Bank. The easiest way for a small investor to acquire bills is to buy them from a bank. If your bank is a major bank in a large financial center, such as Chicago or New York City, it may well act as a dealer in government securities; in that case it will sell bills to you directly out of its inventory. If your bank is not a dealer bank, it will purchase the required amount of bills from a larger bank with which it has a correspondent relationship.

While buying bills from a bank is convenient, it has one disadvantage: most banks impose a service charge on bill purchases for amounts less than $100,000, the only exceptions being a few small country banks whose relationship with their correspondent bank is such that they can buy bills from them at no fee. The size of purchase charges varies considerably from bank to bank. Typically it is in the range of $20 to $35, with higher rates being charged by smaller banks, which, in order to acquire bills for their customers, have to go through another bank that charges them a fee. Moral: If you are going to buy bills through a bank, shop around and find out where you can get the lowest service charge.

Obviously the imposition of a service charge on bill purchases reduces the yield you get, since the charge in effect raises the price you have to pay for your bills. The net yield (bond equivalent basis) that you receive when you pay a service charge to buy bills can easily be calculated as follows:

$$\frac{\text{Face value} - \text{Price} - \text{Service charge}}{\text{Price} + \text{Service charge}} \div \frac{t}{365}$$

For example, if a $10,000 bill with a 200-day maturity is selling at a discounted price of $9,500, its annual yield would be

$$\frac{\$10,000 - \$9,500}{\$9,500} \div \frac{200}{365} = 9.60\%$$

if there were no service charge. With a service charge of $25, annual yield falls to

$$\frac{\$10,000 - \$9,525}{\$9,525} \div \frac{200}{365} = 9.10\%$$

that is, it drops 50 basis points. Since bank service charges on bill purchases generally are on a per-transaction basis, that is, the same whether you buy $10,000 or $60,000 of bills, the effect of such a charge on the yield will be smaller, the larger the amount you invest. Also the effect will be smaller, the longer the maturity of the securities you buy.

When buying bills from a bank, rate-quote shopping may also be beneficial. Because of the highly competitive conditions that prevail in the bill market, dealer banks normally quote very close if not identical rates on bills of a given maturity. However, this is not always the case. Occasionally money market banks in the same financial center quote rates to the public that differ by as much as 20 or even 40 basis points on very short issues. Thus if you live in a financial center and you are investing a substantial amount (say, $100,000 or more), it might be worthwhile to call around and find out what rates different dealer banks are quoting. The investor who shops around can either buy his bills directly from the bank quoting the best rate or he can direct his own bank to buy bills for him from that source. Generally, suburban and country banks place all customer orders for bills with their correspondent bank but, if requested, they can and will buy from another source.

Bills can also be purchased from any brokerage house. How that compares with buying from a bank depends on which brokerage house you pick. Some large houses, such as Merrill Lynch, are active dealers in government securities and will fill small orders for a $25 service charge. Other brokerage houses that don't have a dealer operation have to go through a bank to purchase bills, with the result that you can end up paying a $50 purchase commission—$25 to the broker and another $25 to cover the bank's service charge to the broker.

Buying Bills at Auction. If you are willing to put yourself out a little, you can escape the service charge that banks impose on bill purchases by buying bills directly from the Fed during one of the periodic auctions at which the Fed sells new issues of T bills.

Naturally, a small investor can't be expected to arrive panting at the Fed just before the bid window closes with a tender tuned to the morning's developments in the money market. That is no problem, however, since the Fed has made provision for the small investor who is unsophisticated and, worse still, has no runner at his disposal. To service such investors, the Fed accepts what are called *noncompetitive* bids for amounts up to $1 million per investor per auction. A person submitting a noncompetitive bid gets bills at a price equal to the average of the competitive bids accepted by the Treasury. Generally, the spread in competitive bids is not very wide, so the noncompetitive bidder does not fare badly.

To submit a noncompetitive bid, the first thing you must do is write to the Federal Reserve bank in your district and ask for information on bill offerings and forms for tendering bids. In response, the Fed will send a circular describing the next bill issue to be auctioned and *tender forms* for bidding on these specific securities. Also the Fed will send a tender form that can be used at any time. The latter, which is reproduced in Exhibit 3-3, is useful for the small investor who plans to tender noncompetitive bids. Such an investor does not really need a detailed circular on a planned T bill offering to submit a bid. All he needs to know is when to submit his bid (something he can determine from the issuing schedule) and roughly the rate of discount at which he can expect to get his bills (something he can estimate by looking in his newspaper at yield quotes on existing bills of comparable maturity).

All this may sound a bid complicated, but once you go through the process of buying bills at auction and learn the ropes, the trouble involved in making subsequent purchases is minimal. However, one caveat is in order. If you are thinking of buying bills at auction, bear in mind that money market rates are at times subject to sharp and unanticipated fluctuations. Thus, an investor who puts in a bid 2 days before an auction expecting to get a 9% return might find that rates had fallen substantially by the day of the auction. How great the danger of a sharp and unanticipated break in interest rates is depends on economic conditions. During the midst of a boom, when employment is high and inflationary pressures are the main worry, the Fed is unlikely to make a sudden switch to an easy monetary policy, which would cause short-term rates to drop. On the other hand, when the Fed has been fighting inflation with tight money for a lengthy period and employment is finally beginning to fall, the danger of a sudden and precipitous drop in rates is real.

For the investor who wants to avoid uncertainty and lock in a rate, the best alternative is to buy existing bills from a bank. Note in this respect that a bank buying bills through its correspondent may offer you a choice—a telephone order that locks in the rate you get versus a cheaper mail order in which you get the rate prevailing when the order is processed. Generally, the secured rate is worth a few extra dollars.

EXHIBIT 3-3   Tender Form for Bidding on Treasury Bills

TB-12 (Rev. 9/85)

IMPORTANT — This is a standard form. Its terms are subject to change at any time by the Treasury. This tender will be construed as a bid to purchase the securities for which the Treasury has outstanding an invitation for tenders. *(See reverse side for further instructions.)*

TENDER FOR 12-MONTH BOOK-ENTRY TREASURY BILLS
(For Use in Subscribing Through a Financial Institution)
Do Not Use This Form for Direct Subscriptions to the Treasury

To Federal Reserve Bank of New York   Dated at ....
   Fiscal Agent of the United States
   New York, N.Y. 10045   .... , 19......

Pursuant and subject to the provisions of Treasury Department Circulars No. 26-76 and No. 27-76, Public Debt Series, and to the provisions of the public notice issued by the Treasury Department inviting tenders for the current offering of 12-month Treasury bills, the undersigned hereby offers to purchase such currently offered Treasury bills in the amount indicated below, and agrees to make payment therefor at your Bank on or before the issue date in accordance with the provisions of the official offering circular.

COMPETITIVE TENDER	*Do not fill in both Competitive and Noncompetitive tenders on one form*	NONCOMPETITIVE TENDER

$................................ (maturity value)
or any lesser amount that may be awarded.

Rate: .... (Bank Discount Basis)

(Rate must be expressed in two decimal places, for example, 7.15 percent. See reverse side of form for additional explanation.)

$................................. (maturity value)
(Not to exceed $1,000,000 for one bidder through all sources)
at the average of accepted competitive bids.

A noncompetitive bidder may not have entered into an agreement, or may not make an agreement with respect to the purchase or sale or other disposition of any noncompetitive awards of this issue in this auction prior to the designated closing time for receipt of tenders.

Certification by Competitive Bidders: The Bidder's☐ Customer's☐ net long position in these bills (including bills acquired through "when issued" trading, and futures and forward transactions, as well as holdings of outstanding bills with the same maturity date as the new offering) as of 12:30 p.m. Eastern time on the day of this auction, was —

   ☐ Not in excess of $200 million.
   ☐ In excess of $200 million, amounting to $ .... million.

Subject to allotment, please issue and accept payment for the bills as indicated below:

Safekeeping or Delivery Instructions	Payment Instructions
(No changes will be accepted)	

Safekeeping or Delivery Instructions
(No changes will be accepted)

Book-Entry—
☐ 1. Hold in safekeeping at FRBNY in-
   ☐ Investment Account (4)
   ☐ General Account (5)
   ☐ Trust Account (6)
☐ 2. Hold as collateral for Treasury Tax and Loan Note Account*(7)
☐ 3. Wire to ....(8)
        (Exact Receiving Bank Wire Address/Account)

Payment Instructions

Payment will be made as follows:
☐ By charge to our reserve account
☐ By credit to the Treasury Tax and Loan Note Account
☐ By check in *immediately available funds*
☐ By surrender of eligible maturing securities
☐ By charge to my correspondent bank

....
        (Name of Correspondent)

*The undersigned certifies that the alloted securities will be owned solely by the undersigned.

Insert this tender in envelope marked "Tender for Treasury Securities"	Name of Subscriber (Please Print or Type)

Address		
City	State	Zip Code
Phone (Include Area Code)	Signature of Subscriber or Authorized Signature	
Title of Authorized Signer		

(Banking institutions submitting tenders for customer account must list customers' names on lines below or on an attached rider)

_____   _____
(Name of customer)   (Name of customer)

PRIVACY ACT STATEMENT: The individually identifiable information required on this form is necessary to permit the tender to be processed and the bills to be issued in accordance with the General Regulations governing United States book-entry Treasury Bills (Department Circular No. 26-76, Public Debt Series). The transaction will not be completed unless all required data is furnished.

One final note: You can always ask your bank to submit in your name a noncompetitive bid for bills. This procedure is simpler than sending in your own tender form, *but* the bank will impose its normal bill-purchase fee on such transactions.

Selling Bills

If you are investing small amounts, because of transactions costs, you will get the best yield on your bills if you hold them to maturity. However, a person investing in bills can never be sure that he will not experience some unexpected need for cash before the bills mature. So the natural next question is: How does one sell bills and what sort of price can one expect to get?

The answer to how to sell is simple. Go to a bank or broker. They handle bill sales as well as purchases, and their service charge on a sale is normally the same as their charge for a purchase.

Determining the price you get on your bills requires a simple calculation, since bills are quoted in terms of yield rather than price. First find the yield on a bank discount basis at which the bills you hold are currently quoted. Then use the following formula to determine roughly the discount from face value at which your bills are currently trading per $100 of face value:

$$\text{Discount from face value} = \text{(Yield on a bond discount basis)} \times 100 \times \left(\frac{t}{360}\right)$$

The price you get is face value minus total discount.

Normally, if you have held your bills for any length of time, the price at which you can sell them will be higher than the price at which you bought them. The reason is that the price a bill commands will gradually rise over time (assuming the rate of discount at which it sells doesn't change); the dollar amount of the discount at which it sells will fall as the bill approaches maturity. For example, for a 6-month bill to yield 9% on a bank discount rate basis, it must be priced at $95.45 per $100 of face value. For the same bill 3 months later to yield 9%, its price must have been bid up to $97.72 per $100 of face value.

Of course the rate at which a bill sells typically does not stand still over time. With an upward sloping yield curve, this rate will tend to fall over the holding period, which means that the bill's price will be bid up even more during the holding period, enough more so that its current yield equals the rate of discount quoted on bills of shorter maturity.

To illustrate, let's look again at our 6-month bill selling initially at a 9% rate of discount. If after 3 months, this bill were still quoted at 9%, its price would have risen by $2.26. If, however, over these 3 months, the rate at which the bill was quoted had fallen to 7%, then the bill's price would have risen from $95.45 to $98.23, or by an extra $0.51 per $100 of face value.

As we explained earlier in this chapter, movement along the yield curve is not the only factor that will alter the rate at which a bill is quoted. So, too, will changes in the general level of short-term interest rates. Moreover, the possible effects of such changes on a bill's price form a two-way street. Although a *fall* in interest rates will cause a bill's price to *rise,* a *rise* in rates will cause a bill's price to *fall.* The latter possibility adds an element of *risk* for the individual who invests money in bills he might not hold to maturity. If rates rise sharply while one holds the bills, the yield on the investment will be substantially below anticipated earning, maybe even negative. Notice, however, that the effect of changes in the level of interest rates on a bill's price will be smaller as the bill gets closer to maturity, and so the price risk inherent in selling a bill before maturity declines as the bill approaches maturity.

The preceding paragraphs can be summed up quite neatly. How high a price you get for bills you sell before maturity depends on how close they are to maturity, on the shape of the yield curve, and on the general level of interest rates prevailing at the time of the sale. Specifically, the price you get will be higher the closer your bills are to maturity, the steeper the yield curve, and the lower the level of short-term interest rates.

If you sell bills before maturity, you may want to know what annual rate of return you have earned on your investment. This return on a bond equivalent basis is easily determined. Essentially, it equals your net dollar gain as a percentage of the full purchase cost divided by the fraction of the year over which the bills were held. That is,

$$\frac{(\text{Sales price} - \text{Sales fee}) - (\text{Purchase price} + \text{Purchase fee})}{(\text{Purchase price} + \text{Purchase fee})} \div \frac{t}{365}$$

RISK, LIQUIDITY, AND RETURN

When evaluated in terms of risk, liquidity, and return, T bills measure up quite favorably much of the time. The risk of default to which bills expose the investor is always zero. The price risk on bills is small, and it diminishes rapidly as they approach maturity.

Since T bills are traded in huge volume at very small spreads in a highly efficient secondary market, their liquidity is extremely high. On small trades, however, sales charges significantly reduce yield, thereby diminishing somewhat the liquidity of these instruments for the small investor.

Commercial Paper and
Bankers' Acceptances

4

In the two previous chapters, we discussed two vehicles that you should use in building the base of your financial pyramid—CDs and Treasury bills. In this chapter, we shall describe two money market instruments that can also be used in building your base, commercial paper and bankers' acceptances. For most investors, however, direct investment in these two money market instruments is not practical because of the large dollar investment involved. Yet, because these instruments are commonly owned by money market mutual funds (the subject of the next chapter), fund investors may indirectly own them. Therefore, you may need to understand their investment characteristics. Thanks to our indepth examination of bills in the previous chapter, we can cover quickly these two money market instruments; their pros, their cons, and how they are traded.

COMMERCIAL PAPER

Commercial paper, whoever the issuer and whatever the precise form it takes, is an unsecured promissory note with a fixed maturity. In plain English, the issuer of commercial paper (the borrower) promises to pay the buyer (the lender) some fixed amount on some future date.

But issuers pledge no assets—only liquidity and established earning power—to guarantee that they will make good on their promises to pay. Traditionally, commercial paper resembled in form a T bill; it was a negotiable, non-interest-bearing note issued at a discount from face value and redeemed at maturity for full face value. Today, however, some paper is interest-bearing. For the investor the major difference between bills and paper is that paper carries some small risk of default because the issuer is a private firm, whereas the risk of default on bills is zero for all intents and purposes.

Firms selling commercial paper frequently expect to roll over their paper as it matures; that is, they plan to get money to pay off maturing paper by issuing new paper. Since there is always the danger that an adverse turn in the paper market might make doing so difficult or inordinately expensive, most paper issuers back their outstanding paper with *bank lines of credit;* they get a promise from a bank or banks to lend them at any time an amount equal to their outstanding paper. Issuers normally pay for this service in one of several ways: by holding at their line banks compensating deposit balances equal to some percentage of their total credit lines; by paying an annual fee equal to some small percentage of their outstanding lines; or through some mix of balances and fees.

Issuers of Paper

Financial and nonfinancial firms (e.g., public utilities, manufacturers, retailers) issue paper. Paper issued by nonfinancial firms, referred to as *industrial paper,* accounts for about 32% of all paper outstanding. Such paper is issued to meet seasonal needs for funds and also as a means of interim financing (i.e., to obtain funds to start investment projects that are later permanently funded through the sale of long-term bonds). In contrast to industrial borrowers, finance companies have a continuing need for short-term funds throughout the year; they are now the principal borrowers in the commercial paper market, accounting for roughly 48% of all paper.

In the recent years of tight money, bank holding companies have also joined finance companies as borrowers in the commercial paper market. Many banks are owned by a holding company, an arrangement offering the advantage that the holding company can engage in activities in which the bank itself is not permitted. Commercial paper is sold by bank holding companies primarily to finance their nonbank activities in leasing, real estate, and other lines. However, funds raised through the sale of such paper can also be funneled into the holding company's bank, if the latter is pinched for funds, through various devices, such as the sale of bank assets to the holding company.

Issuing Techniques

All industrial paper is issued through paper dealers. Typically, dealers buy up new paper issues directly from the borrower, mark them up, and then resell them to investors. The current going rate of markup is very small, 1/8 of 1% per annum. Generally, paper issues are for very large amounts, and the minimum round lot in which most dealers sell is $250,000. Thus the dealer market for commercial paper is a meeting ground for big corporate borrowers and for large investors (the latter including financial corporations, nonfinancial corporations, and pension funds).

Finance companies and banks occasionally place their paper through dealers, but most such paper (over 80%) is placed directly by the issuer with investors. A big finance company, for example, might place $1 million or more of paper with an insurance company or with a big industrial firm that had a temporary surplus of funds. In addition to these large-volume transactions, some finance companies and banks also sell paper in relatively small denominations directly to small business firms and individual investors, as will be discussed later in this section.

Paper Maturities

Maturities on commercial paper are generally very short—between 30- and 90 days being the most common on dealer-placed paper. Generally, dealers prefer not to handle paper with a maturity of less than 30 to 45 days because, on paper of such short maturity, their markup (which is figured on a percent *per annum* basis) barely covers costs. However, to accommodate established borrowers, they will do so. Paper with a maturity of more than 270 days is rare because issues of such long maturity generally have to be registered with the SEC.

Finance companies that place their paper directly with large investors generally offer a wide range of maturities—3 to 270 days. Also they are willing to tailor maturities to the needs of investors and will often accept funds for very short periods, for example for a weekend. Finance companies that sell low-denomination paper to individual investors generally offer maturities ranging from 30 to 270 days on such paper. These companies also issue longer-maturity short-term notes that have been registered with the SEC.

Paper Yields

Some paper bears interest, but much does not. The investor who buys non-interest-bearing paper gets a return on his money because he buys his paper at a discount from face value, whereas the issuer redeems the paper at maturity for full face value. Yields on paper are generally quoted in ⅛ of 1%, for example, at 7⅛% per annum. Paper rates, whether the paper is interest-bearing or not, are quoted on a *bank discount basis,* as in the case of bills.

Bill rates vary over time, rising if business demand for credit increases or if the Fed tightens credit, falling in the opposite cases. The yields offered by paper issuers follow much the same pattern of bill yields except that paper yields are, if anything, even more volatile than bill yields.

The reason paper rates fluctuate up and down in step with the yields on bills and other money market securities is simple. Paper competes with these other instruments for investors' dollars. Therefore, as yields on bills and other money market securities rise, paper issuers must offer higher rates in order to sell their paper. In contrast, if bill yields and other short-term rates decline, paper issuers can and do ease the rates they offer.

The volatility of paper rates has important consequences for the investor. First, it means that the attractiveness of paper as an investment medium for short-term funds varies over the interest rate cycle. It also means that the rate you get on paper bought today tells you relatively little about what rate you would get if you were to roll over that paper at maturity. Paper yields offered in the future may be substantially higher or lower than today's rates, depending on whether money is tightening or easing.

Risk and Ratings

If you are thinking of buying paper, you should consider not only the *return* it yields, but also whether there is any *risk* that you will not get timely payment on your paper when it matures. Basically there are two situations in which an issuing company might fail to pay off its maturing paper: (1) it is solvent, but lacks cash and (2) it is insolvent. How great are the chances that either situation will occur?

Since the early 1930s, the default record on commercial paper has been excellent. In the case of dealer paper, one reason is that, after the 1920s, the many little borrowers who had populated the paper market were replaced by a much smaller number of large, well-established firms. This gave dealers, who were naturally extremely careful about whose paper they handled, the opportunity to examine much more thoroughly the financial condition of each issuer with whom they dealt.

Since 1965 the number of firms issuing at any time a significant quantity of paper to a wide market has increased from 450 to 1,200; of these about 130 are currently non-U.S. borrowers. Only 5 issuers of commercial paper have failed over the past 15 years. Three of these 5 were small domestic finance companies that got caught by tight money; in each case the losses to paper buyers were small, $2–$4 million. The fourth firm that failed was a Canadian finance company that had sold paper in the U.S. market; losses on its paper totaled $35 million. The fifth failure, one that shook the market, was that of the Penn Central Railroad, which at the time it went under had $82 million of paper outstanding.

Although the payments record on paper is good, the losses that have occurred make it clear that an individual putting money into paper has the right—more strongly, the responsibility—to ask: How good is the company whose paper I am buying? Because of the investor's very real need for an answer, and because of the considerable time and money involved in obtaining one, rating services have naturally developed. Today a large proportion of dealer and direct paper is rated by one or more of three companies: Standard & Poor's, Moody's, and Fitch Investors Service.

Paper issuers willingly pay the rating services to examine them and rate their paper, since a good rating makes it easier and cheaper for them to borrow in the paper market. The rating companies, despite the fact that they receive their income from issuers, basically have the interests of the investor at heart for one simple reason: the value of their ratings to investors and thereby their ability to sell rating services to issuers depend on their accuracy. The worth to an issuer of a top rating is the track record of borrowers who have held that rating.

Each rating company sets its own rating standards, but their approaches are similar. Every rating is based on an evaluation of the borrowing company's management and on a detailed study of its earnings record and balance sheet. Just what a rating company looks for depends in part on the borrower's line of business; the optimal balance sheet for a publishing company would look quite different from that of a finance company. Nonetheless, one can say in general that the criteria for a top rating are strong management, a good position in a well-established industry, an upward trend in earnings, adequate liquidity, and the ability to borrow to meet both anticipated and unexpected cash needs.

Since companies seeking a paper rating are rarely in imminent danger of insolvency, the principal focus in rating paper is on *liquidity*—can the borrower come up with cash to pay off his maturing paper? Here what the rating company looks for is ability to borrow elsewhere than in the paper market and especially the ability to borrow short-term from banks. Today, for a company to get a paper rating, its paper must be backed by bank lines of credit.

Different rating firms grade borrowers according to different classifications. Standard & Poor's, for example, rates companies from A for highest quality to D for lowest. It also subdivides A-rated companies into groups according to relative strength, A-1 + down to A-3. Fitch rates firms F-1 (highest grade) to F-4 (lowest grade). Moody's uses P-1, P-2, and P-3, with P-1 being their highest rating.

Rates and Tiering

In the early 1960s, when the commercial paper market was small, all issuers paid similar rates to borrow there. Then, after the Penn Central's failure and periods of extremely tight money, investors became very credit conscious; they wanted top names, and rate tiering developed in the market. That tiering today is a function not only of issuers' commercial paper ratings but of their long-term bond ratings. The market distinguishes between A-1 + issuers with a triple-A bond rating and those with only a double-A bond rating. Many investors want to buy only unimpeachable credits; looking up an issuer's bond rating is a quick way for an investor to check the credit of an issuer with whom he is unfamiliar.

The spread at which A-1, P-1 paper trades to A-2, P-2 paper varies depending on economic conditions. When money is tight and people are more concerned than normal about risk in general and credit risk in particular, they may drive the yield on A-2 paper 200 basis points above that on A-1 paper; this occurred in the summer of 1982. When—after a period of tight money—rates begin to fall, investors, seeking to maintain past portfolios yields, tend to become yield buyers; they switch out of lower-yielding, top-rated paper into higher-yielding, second-tier paper. As they do, they drive down the spread between A-1 and A-2 paper so that, by the time money eases, it may be only ⅜ or even ¼. Whether money is easy or tight, very few institutional investors will buy P-3 paper from dealers.

Commercial paper yields slightly more than T bills of comparable maturity, the spread being widest when money is tight. There are two reasons. First, paper exposes the investor to a small credit risk. Second, commercial paper is much less liquid than bills because there is no active secondary market in it.

Buying Commercial Paper

So far, we looked at what commercial paper is and how it is rated. There is still more to know, so let's start with the mechanics of buying paper.

Buying Dealer Paper. All industrial and some finance company paper is sold through dealers. The dealer is essentially a wholesaler operating on a very small margin. Consequently, he is willing to sell only in large amounts; the minimum round lot which most dealers sell is $250,000 to $350,000. Generally to buy paper in smaller amounts, the buyer has to be lucky enough to pick up the tag end of an issue. For example, a buyer might get $150,000 of paper from a dealer who had bought up a $5 million issue and was left with $150,000 on the shelf after he cut off for large buyers 4 $1 million pieces, a $600,000 piece, and a $250,000 piece.

Unfortunately few individuals are going to have $150,000 to put into a tag end; *and* even if they do, they would not be able to buy it from a dealer. The reason is that the SEC has ruled that paper should not be sold to "unsophisticated" buyers. Just which buyers are "unsophisticated" is left up to the seller to determine. Dealers generally take the position that individuals, no matter how rich or financially savvy they may be, are unsophisticated and consequently they will not sell paper to individuals.

To get dealer paper, an individual has to go to a broker. A number of brokerage houses operate on the assumption that an individual who trades stocks, has a respectable net worth, and owns a reasonably diversified holding of assets is sufficiently sophisticated to buy paper. The reason for the divergence between dealers' and brokers' interpretation of "sophisticated" lies in their contrasting positions. To dealers, who are accustomed to making large transactions with knowledgeable investors on the basis of a brief phone call, sales to individuals would be a time-consuming, money-losing proposition. So dealers are happy to accept a rule that keeps out a few well-heeled, sophisticated investors and a horde of others who would want all sorts of information and would buy in small lots. Brokers are in a different position. They are accustomed to dealing at a retail level and they set a pricing structure that allows them to profit by doing so. A big part of a broker's role in the financial structure is to assist customers in making stock investments. But at times when the stock market looks unpromising or has badly burned investors, some of his customers may choose to pull their money out of the market. To keep that cash in-house, so to speak, until stocks regain their allure, the broker needs an alternative instrument to offer—one that is safe, yields a good return, and is liquid. Paper meets these requirements, so some brokers sell paper to individuals who are established customers.

Retail brokerage houses that sell paper get it in several ways. One is to buy large lots from dealers and have them cut up into small pieces—say, a mix of $25,000, $50,000, and $100,000 denominations. Another way is for the brokerage house to set up facilities to act itself as a dealer in paper.

Buying dealer paper from a broker has several disadvantages from the investor's point of view: not all brokerage houses are prepared to sell paper to individuals; on small purchases transaction costs are significant; and maturities of less than 30 to 45 days generally are unavailable. Fortunately, there is an alternative, direct paper.

Buying Direct Paper.   A number of large, well-known finance companies sell commercial paper in relatively small denominations directly to individual investors and/or through commercial banks. Their ranks include the General Motors Acceptance Corporation (GMAC), Chrysler Financial Corporation, C.I.T. Financial Corporation, Associates Corporation of North America, and other perhaps less familiar names.

Some of these companies are *independent* finance companies which specialize in providing various types of short-term financing to consumers and/or business firms—making installment loans to consumers, buying up accounts receivable from business firms, and so forth. Obviously, these independent finance companies need a lot of funds to carry out their operations. One way they get them is by selling paper, mostly direct but sometimes through dealers.

Other direct paper issuers are *captive* finance companies; that is, they specialize in financing installment and credit sales by their parent company. For example, GMAC uses the money it raises through the sale of paper to buy from GM dealers the installment loan contracts generated when consumers finance car purchases directly through a GM dealer. Similarly, the captive finance companies set up by Sears and Montgomery Ward sell paper to finance the credit sales made at their parent company's retail stores.

To get an idea of what is available in direct paper, let's look at GMAC's menu. GMAC offers investors *paper* ranging in maturity from 30 to 270 days and *notes* registered with the SEC ranging in maturity from 9 months to 5 years. The minimum denomination in which they issue paper or notes is $25,000; above that amount they will accept funds in $100 increments. Also, on investments of $100,000 or more, GMAC will write paper with a maturity as short as 3 days. GMAC issues its notes and paper in either bearer or registered form, as the buyer desires. Also it will issue either non-interest-bearing securities sold at a discount or interest-bearing securities sold at full face value. As you can discover by making a few phone calls to direct issuers, rates, maturities, and terms of issue vary considerably from issuer to issuer. Sears, for example, sets a minimum denomination of $150,000 and issues only paper (not notes). Because of the differences in practice between issuers, shop around. Also, in comparing yields on finance company paper with yields on other instruments, remember that paper yields are quoted on a bank discount basis. Finally, check paper ratings before you buy.

The cheapest way to buy direct paper is from the company issuing it. In the case of GMAC, this can be done in person, by phone, or by mail. To buy GMAC paper, first contact their nearest office and find out what rates, maturities, and minimum denominations they are offering. Then when you have decided what paper to buy, visit the company's office, write a check, and pick up your paper; *or* mail the company a check and have them send your paper or note. Whether you deal by mail or in person, have the security you buy registered in your name. This will protect against loss if you misplace the security or it is stolen. Even with this precaution, keep paper and notes in a safe-deposit box.

When your paper matures, there are several ways to redeem it. If you want to stay in paper, it is easy to roll over maturing paper. Any direct paper you bought was probably accompanied by a renewal form when you got it; if not, you can get one by mail. Simply fill out this form and send it with your maturing paper to the issuing company *before* the maturity date. On the maturity date, they will issue you new paper *and* send you a check for interest due if your paper was interest-bearing. If your paper was not interest-bearing, the check will be for the difference between the face value of your maturing paper and the discounted price of your new paper.

To redeem maturing paper for cash, a few days before maturity send it to the bank that handles collections on the paper you purchased. On the day of maturity, this bank will send you a check for the amount owed you (or issue you a check if you present the security personally).

As you have probably noted, a do-it-yourself purchase of direct paper requires little time and effort on the part of the investor and involves minimal transaction costs—a few phone calls and some postage stamps. An alternative procedure is to have your local bank buy direct paper for you, a route some direct issuers require that you take. The minimum purchase is established by the bank and may depend on the maturity of the paper. For example, a bank may set a minimum purchase of $100,000 for paper with 30 days or less to maturity but only $25,000 for paper maturing after 30 days.

Buying paper through a bank calls for slightly (very slightly) less effort, but you incur a service charge which can easily run to $35 for a purchase. If your local banker buys commercial paper for you, he will probably buy it not directly from the issuing company but through his correspondent bank, which in turn purchases the paper from the issuer. By doing so, your banker incurs a service charge at that bank, which is passed on to you as part of his fee. In return for the correspondent bank's service charge (which you in effect pay), your banker obtains convenience for himself. The correspondent bank holds your paper in safekeeping and automatically redeems it for cash at maturity, relieving your banker from the trouble of taking delivery on the paper, keeping track of it, and then returning it for collection at maturity.

Even if you buy finance company paper directly from the issuer, your bank can cash it in for you. If you use your bank, give them the paper several days before maturity so that they have time to present it for collection on the maturity date. If you are a good customer, the bank may not charge for this service. Paper bought through a bank is automatically redeemed by the bank at maturity and there is no charge. Either way you should ask for and get payment from your bank on the day your paper matures.

Since buying paper from a bank saves little (if any) effort, you should calculate the reduction in return that the bank's service charge is going to entail. For example, paying your banker $35 to buy $25,000 worth of 30-day paper yielding 6% will reduce your yield to 4.32%.[1] Obviously the yield reduction will be smaller the larger the amount invested and the longer the maturity of the paper purchased.

Buying Bank Paper. As noted earlier, many banks obtain funds by having their *holding company* issue commercial paper. Most bank paper sold is direct paper, purchased at the bank whose holding company issues it.

Most large city banks that issue paper set minimum denominations at $100,000. They are interested in catering to large investors and firms rather than to small investors. However, there are suburban and country banks that offer paper in maturities ranging from less than a month to 270 days and in minimum denominations as low as $5,000 or $10,000. You might wonder why small banks would do so since their paper will obviously compete with bank demand and time deposits for their customers' savings dollars. The answer is that a bank following this practice realizes that when money market rates are high, some of its sophisticated depositors are going to put their liquid funds into money market instruments. If the bank itself offers them such an instrument, then chances are greater that when open market rates fall, these depositors will again place their funds on deposit at the bank.

One big advantage of bank paper is that if your bank happens to offer paper in small denominations, the transaction costs—both monetary and in terms of effort expended by you—are reduced to near zero. To buy such paper, you simply write your banker a check

---

[1]For a way to make such calculations, see the section "Buying Bills" in Chapter 3.

for the amount of the purchase. Naturally there is no bank fee on either purchase or redemption.

If you consider buying bank paper, bear in mind that bank paper is *paper,* i.e., unsecured promissory notes. It is not bank deposits and it is not covered by deposit insurance. If your bank fails, you are likely to lose money. Therefore before buying bank paper, check the condition of the company issuing it. As we said, banks don't fail often these days, but when they do, it is only depositors, not paper holders, who are protected.

If you buy bank paper in small denominations, don't count on always being able to roll it over. When money is tight and interest rates are high, a bank holding company may bid aggressively for money through the sale of paper in small denominations both because it wants money and because it knows that its bank's depositors have attractive alternatives to bank deposits. When money eases the situation is quite different. For the small investor, alternatives to bank deposits are less attractive, and the bank is likely to be less strained for funds. Therefore it will bid less aggressively for paper sales and may, besides cutting rates, also increase minimum denominations and lengthen minimum maturities.

Picking a Maturity. An individual who is thinking of buying direct paper or notes will be confronted with a wide choice of maturities—anywhere from a few days to 5 years. This naturally raises the question of what maturity to select. If the investor knows he will need his funds 3 months hence for buying a home or paying for a vacation, a 3-month maturity is the obvious choice. On the other hand, if he intends to keep the funds invested for a long time, say 5 years, this does not mean that he should automatically buy a 5-year note. The choice is more complicated.

Generally paper and notes of different maturities will be quoted at different rates. As we said in the previous chapter, the fact that investors value liquidity means that the yield curve normally slopes upward—the longer the maturity, the higher the yield.[2] Moreover, if people expect interest rates to *rise,* this normal tendency is reinforced because the expectation of rising rates causes investors to hold back on long-term commitments until rates have risen, while simultaneously causing borrowers to scramble for long-term money while rates are

---

[2]See the explanation of the yield curve in Chapter 3.

still low. Naturally both these responses tend to raise long-term rates relative to short-term rates. Alternatively, if rates are expected to *fall,* investors and borrowers behave in the opposite way, thereby tending to reverse the normal slope of the yield curve.

Whatever the slope of the yield curve, the *long-term* investor faces a maturity choice that has to be based on what he *expects* to happen to interest rates over time. Upswings in economic activity and in the pace of inflation both tend to push interest rates up, while downturns and abatements in inflation tend to depress them. Short-term rates respond with much more volatility to changes in economic conditions than long-term rates do. What all this means for the investor is that, at any point in time, the maturity offering the highest yield is not necessarily the best investment. At the top of the cycle, short-term interest rates may be above longer-term rates, but as the economy peaks out and slides into recession, short-term rates will fall more precipitously than longer-term rates. Thus the optimal strategy for the investor with a reliable crystal ball is to lock in a high return over the downswing by switching at the economic peak from short-term longer-term securities. Conversely, during a recession, when long-term rates exceed short-term rates, investing in short-term securities and waiting for rates to rise may be the optimal strategy, provided that the wait is not too long.

Risk, Liquidity, and Return

In comparing paper to alternative investments such as T bills, the investor should think in terms of risk, liquidity, and return. As we noted, the risk of default is extremely small on top-rated paper. It is not, however, zero. Consequently tying up your life savings in paper would not be a good idea. Also if you invest a substantial amount of money in paper, some diversification among issuers would be wise. It might seem that all this should go without saying, but unfortunately that is not so. In the fall of 1975, when New York City declared a moratorium on its notes, newspapers were full of stories about small investors who had tied up all their funds in these notes and found suddenly that they could not finance retirement, needed hospital care, or college education for their children.

So far as the liquidity of paper is concerned, note that there is *no* secondary market for either dealer or direct paper. An investor's need for liquidity is usually satisfied by the very short maturities of commercial paper and, as a result, there has been no need for a secondary market. Should you need funds tied up in paper before it matures, alternatives are limited. You can use paper as collateral for a bank loan or you can request that the company from which you purchased the paper buy it back before maturity in the case of direct paper. How willing the seller will be to do this is likely to depend on why you want the money. If you have a pressing personal need (decide unexpectedly to buy a house), chances are the borrower will return your money early. But if your objective is to increase yield—say, to buy bills because bill rates have risen since you bought paper, the answer will be no. If the paper was purchased from a dealer, the original dealer will usually repurchase the paper in order to accommodate the needs of an investor. However, dealer repurchases of paper will reflect market and interest rate conditions prevailing at the time of the repurchase.

Because there is no secondary market in paper, bills appear to be more liquid than paper. However, because of the high transaction costs involved in selling bills before maturity, you should, if you make only a modest investment in bills, plan to hold them until maturity. Also, given the transaction costs involved in purchasing bills on the open market, you will, if you want to place money for a short period (say, 30 days), do better by buying 30-day direct paper than buying bills with a current maturity of 30 days.

Paper rates, like bill yields, are quoted on a bank discount rate basis. Since a yield quoted on this basis understates actual yield, before comparing yields on paper with those on other securities, you should convert the paper rate quoted from a bank discount basis to a bond equivalent yield basis. This conversion is simple.[3]

Let

r = Annual effective rate of return,
d = Yield on a bank discount basis, and
t = Days to maturity.

Then according to the formula on page 35:

$$r = \frac{365 \times d}{360 - (d \times t)}$$

Example: Commercial paper having a 45-day maturity and quoted at a rate of $8\frac{1}{8}\%$ would give you a bond equivalent yield of

---

[3]See Chapter 3, p. 35.

$$\frac{365 \times 0.08125}{360 - (0.08125 \times 45)}$$

or 8.32%. This yield figure is the one you should compare with the rate you could get on, say, a Treasury bill or CD.

Since the cost of obtaining funds by selling direct paper in relatively low denominations to small investors is greater than that of obtaining funds by selling large denominations to big investors, you might expect rates offered on small-denomination paper (direct or offered by a broker) to be slightly lower than those on regular dealer paper. To some extent this *is* true; however, it is possible to find days on which GMAC (minimum denomination $25,000), Sears (minimum denomination $150,000), and dealer paper (minimum denomination still larger) are being offered at the same rates for a given maturity. Another factor to bear in mind is that the relationship between the rates on direct and dealer paper is likely to vary with business conditions. During periods of monetary ease, rates offered by GMAC are likely to be almost in line with those offered on top-rated paper, ⅛ of 1 point or below; but when money is tight, rates posted by direct issuers may be as much as ¼ to ⅜ below those offered on dealer paper.

Sometimes you may find that the yield on paper you can buy at a brokerage house exceeds the yield on paper offered by, say, GMAC. When this occurs, you should (at least if you are investing less than $100,000) calculate carefully the effect of a $25 commission on the return you are going to get before you jump for the broker's paper. As noted earlier, such charges significantly reduce return when a modest sum is invested in short-maturity paper.

Paper yields consistently exceed the yield on bills by a small margin. The reason is that paper exposes the investor to a small risk of capital loss since there is always the possibility (remote though it may be) that the issuer will fail. The small size of the differential between paper and bill rates indicates the degree of confidence with which the investment community today views paper.

However, it is important to recognize that the yield on paper is subject to state and local income taxes, whereas bills are exempt from such taxes. (Both are taxable at the federal level.) Consequently, an investor facing a high marginal state and local tax rate should compare yields after adjusting for these taxes.

BANKERS' ACCEPTANCES

To the average investor, *bankers' acceptances* are an even more strange and unknown instrument than commercial paper. Explaining them isn't easy because they arise via a variety of involved paths. The best approach is to start with an example.

Suppose a U.S. importer wants to buy shoes in Brazil and pay for them 4 months later, after he has had time to sell them in the U.S. One approach would be for the importer to simply borrow from his bank; however, short-term rates may be lower in the open market. If they are and if the importer is too small to go into the open market on his own, then he can go the bankers' acceptance route.

In that case he has his own bank write a letter of credit for the amount of the sale and then he sends this letter to the Brazilian exporter. Upon export of the shoes, the Brazilian firm, using this letter of credit, draws a time draft on the importer's U.S. bank and discounts this draft at its local bank, thereby obtaining immediate payment for its goods. The Brazilian bank in turn sends the time draft to the importer's U.S. bank, which then stamps "accepted" on the draft (that is, the bank guarantees payment on the draft and thereby creates an "acceptance"). Once this is done, the draft becomes an irrevocable primary obligation of the accepting bank. At this point, if the Brazilian bank did not want cash immediately, the U.S. bank would return the draft to that bank, which would hold it as an investment and then present it to the U.S. bank for payment at maturity. If, on the other hand, the Brazilian bank wanted cash immediately, the U.S. bank would make payment to it and then either hold the acceptance itself or sell it to an investor. Whoever ended up holding the acceptance, it would be the importer's responsibility to provide its U.S. bank with sufficient funds to pay off the acceptance at maturity. If the importer should fail for any reason, his bank would still be responsible for making payment at maturity.

Our example illustrates how an acceptance can arise out of import trade. Acceptances also arise in connection with export sales, domestic shipment of goods, domestic or foreign storage of readily marketable stables, and dollar exchange credit to foreign banks. Currently most bankers' acceptances arise out of foreign trade; the latter may be in manufactured goods but more typically it is in bulk commodities, such as cocoa, cotton, coffee, or crude oil, to name a few. Because of the complex nature of acceptance operations, only large banks possessing well-staffed foreign departments act as accepting banks.

Bankers' acceptances closely resemble commercial paper in form. They are short-term (270 days or less), non-interest-bearing notes sold at a discount and redeemed by the accepting bank at maturity for full face value. The major difference between bankers' acceptances and paper is that payment on paper is guaranteed by only the issuing company, while payment on bankers' acceptances is also guaranteed by the accepting bank. Thus bankers' acceptances carry slightly less risk than commercial paper. The very low risk on acceptances is indicated by the fact that to date no investor in acceptances has ever suffered a loss.

Yields on bankers' acceptances are quoted on a bank discount basis, as in the case of commercial paper, and closely parallel yields on paper. Also, both rates are highly volatile, rising sharply when money is tight and falling in an equally dramatic fashion when conditions ease. This means that when money is tight yields on bankers' acceptances are very attractive.

The big banks through which bankers' acceptances originate generally keep some portion of the acceptances they create as investments. The rest are sold to investors through dealers or directly by the bank itself. Major investors in bankers' acceptances are other banks, foreign central banks, and Federal Reserve banks.

Many bankers' acceptances are written for very large amounts and are obviously out of the range of the small investor; certainly this includes all acceptances that pass through the hands of dealers. However, acceptances in amounts as low as $5,000 or even $500 are not uncommon. Some accepting banks offer these low-denomination acceptances to their customers as investments. An individual investing in a $25,000 acceptance may in fact be buying a single small acceptance arising out of one transaction, or he may be buying a bundle of even smaller acceptances that have been packaged together to form a round-dollar amount. Frequently, bankers' acceptances are available in still smaller odd-dollar amounts. The investor who puts his money into an odd-dollar acceptance should be prepared to experience some difficulty in rolling over his funds. Also the availability of bankers' acceptances varies both seasonally and over the cycle. Generally, availability is greatest when money is tight and banks prefer not to tie up funds in acceptances.

The easiest and cheapest way to buy a bankers' acceptance is from an accepting bank. In that case, service charges will be zero. The rate you get will, of course, be less than the rate that a $1 million investor gets, but when money is tight, it may nevertheless be quite good. If you don't live in the vicinity of an accepting bank, you can have your bank purchase acceptances for you through its correspondent bank. Here you are likely to run into a service charge, and its effect on yield should be carefully calculated.

The rates offered on bankers' acceptances, like those on paper, vary from day to day. Also they may vary slightly on a given day from one accepting bank to another. Thus a few calls to shop for rates are in order if you decide to invest in acceptances.

An easy way to get some idea of the general level of rates on bankers' acceptances and to see how they compare with yields on competing instruments is to check the "Money Rates" quotes in *The Wall Street Journal*. Rates on bankers' acceptances are normally quoted for maturities of 30, 60, 90, 120, and 180 days. Some dealers quote rates in 8ths of 1%, but rate quotes to 2 decimal points are also common.

Since payment on acceptances is guaranteed by both the accepting bank and the ultimate borrower, investing in acceptances exposes an individual to minimal risk. An investor can use bankers' acceptances as collateral for a bank loan. Also, if his need for cash is really pressing, chances are that the accepting bank will be willing to buy back the acceptance early.

To sum up, bankers' acceptances are an unknown, but at times very attractive, investment for the small investor.

Money Market Funds

5

A mutual fund is a device through which investors pool funds to invest in a diversified portfolio of securities. The investor who puts money into a mutual fund gets shares in return and becomes in effect a part owner of the fund. Professional guidance is provided by an outside management company, which charges a fee equal to some small percentage of the fund's total assets. Perhaps best known to investors are mutual funds which invest almost exclusively in common stocks. Some of these funds have growth and long-term capital gains as their primary objective; others seek high and consistent dividend income. There are also a wide variety of mutual funds that invest in bonds, which we shall discuss in Chapter 15.

In the mid-1970s when money market rates soared above time deposit rates offered by banks and thrifts, the stage was set for the birth of a new breed of mutual funds—funds that were able to offer investors high return as well as high liquidity by investing in high-yield, short-term debt securities. Mutual funds of this sort, known as *money market funds* (or simply *money funds*), first appeared in 1974. Exhibit 5-1 shows the spectacular growth of total net assets invested in money market funds and the number of funds between 1972 and June 30, 1986.

EXHIBIT 5-1 Total Net Assets and Number of Money Market Funds

Year end	All Money Market Funds Total Net Assets ($ millions)	All Money Market Funds Number of Funds	General Purpose Money Market Funds Total Net Assets ($ millions)	General Purpose Money Market Funds Number of Funds	Short-term U.S. Government Funds Total Net Assets ($ millions)	Short-term U.S. Government Funds Number of Funds	Tax-exempt Money Market Funds Total Net Assets ($ millions)	Tax-exempt Money Market Funds Number of Funds
June 30, 1986	$275,410	420	$171,051	212	$48,577	93	$55,782	115
1985	242,143	410	158,856	214	46,968	95	36,319	109
1984	232,824	391	166,146	203	43,039	93	23,639	95
1983	178,081	352	128,228	186	33,234	97	16,619	69
1982	236,062	310	182,435	174	39,785	93	13,842	43
1981	187,020	186	158,904	121	22,893	39	5,223	26
1980	77,461	122	67,157	84	8,143	25	2,161	13
1979	45,292	85	40,686	67	4,243	13	363	5
1978	10,360	59	9,067	50	1,262	7	31	2
1977	3,590	50	3,028	41	559	7	3	2
1976	3,306	40	2,971	34	335	6	—	—
1975	3,257	28	3,156	23	101	5	—	—
1974	2,205	16	2,178	14	27	2	—	—
1973	81	3	79	1	2	2	—	—
1972	0	2	0	1	0	1	—	—

SOURCE: Lipper Analytical Services, Inc.,—Fixed Income Fund Performance Analysis.

REASONS FOR THE GROWTH OF MONEY MARKET FUNDS

Money market funds were initially designed to meet the needs of the small investor, for whom investing in money market securities such as T bills, commercial paper, bankers' acceptances, and negotiable certificates of deposit is awkward. Such investing is difficult for several reasons. As we explained in Chapters 3 and 4, minimum denominations are high. Buying securities and rolling them over involves more work than some people care to experience, and having a bank or broker take over that job, although more convenient, usually entails high transaction costs. Also, for some instruments, yields on small denominations are lower than those on large denominations. Finally, the investor with limited funds cannot reduce risk by diversifying across a mix of different money market securities.

None of these difficulties exist for the money market funds, which pool the resources of many investors. Because these funds handle large sums of money, high minimum denominations pose no problem. Transaction costs, in terms of both money and time spent per dollar invested, are minuscule. Finally, money market funds are able to buy a wide range of securities, thereby reducing credit risk to a negligible level.

TYPES OF MONEY MARKET FUNDS

Money market funds can be classified into three categories: general purpose money market funds, U.S. government short-term funds, and tax-exempt money market funds. The average weighted maturity of all three types of funds is generally less than 120 days.[1]

General purpose money market funds invest in a wide range of good quality money market instruments that we discussed in Chapters 3 and 4, as well as other instruments such as letters of credit and corporation notes. Exhibit 5–2 shows the range in characteristics of general purpose money market funds as of June 30, 1986. Most funds in this group restrict maturities to less than 1 year. The average maturity

---

[1]The principal reason for this is the price risk of longer maturities. Also, money market funds want to maintain a fixed price, usually of $1 per share. To do so, a certain accounting convention must be used. The Securities and Exchange Commission (SEC) will allow a fund to use this accounting convention if average maximum maturity of the fund's portfolio is less than 120 days.

EXHIBIT 5-2 Range Characteristics of 151 General Purpose
Money Market Instrument Funds (as of June 30, 1986)

	Highest	Lowest	Average
12-month yield (%)	7.8%	5.6%	6.7%
Average portfolio maturity (days)	112	1	35
Total net assets ($ millions)	$18,152	$0.2	$909
Number of holdings	651	1	81
Portfolio structure (percent of total net assets):			
U.S. Treasury bills, notes, repos	100%	–0–	8%
U.S. government agencies	85	–0–	2
Bank certificates of deposit:			
Total	99	–0–	18
Foreign banks (note)	99	–0–	2
Bankers' acceptances	97	–0–	7
Commercial paper	101	–0–	57
Letters of credit	57	–0–	2
Corporation notes	69	–0–	–0–
Other assets	22	–0–	–0–

Note: 106 of the 151 funds did not hold any foreign bank certificates of deposit, while 7 funds held such paper to the extent of 25% or more of total portfolio value.

SOURCE: Lipper Analytical Services, Inc., *Portfolio Analysis Report of Fixed Income Funds.*

for most general purpose money market funds ranges from 30 to 40 days.

U.S. government short-term funds invest in U.S. Treasury securities and U.S. government agency issues.[2] The average maturities of funds in this group is about 40 days.

Tax-exempt money market funds invest in short-term municipal securities. As we shall explain in Chapter 11, municipal securities are exempt from federal income taxes. Consequently, the interest from investing in tax-exempt money funds is also exempt from federal income taxes. The yield is lower than the other two taxable types of money market fund categories, reflecting the federal income tax exemption.

Exhibit 5-1 shows the growth of the three categories of money market funds. The largest category, in terms of both total net asset value and number of funds, is the general purpose money market funds category.

---

[2]U.S. government agency securities are discussed in Chapter 10.

INVESTING IN A MONEY MARKET FUND

Money market funds do not accept deposits; they sell shares—typically, $1 per share. An initial minimum dollar investment is necessary. The minimum varies from fund to fund but generally it is less than $1,000. Money market funds do not issue share certificates. Instead, they send out periodic statements showing deposits, withdrawals, and dividends credited to the investor's account. Exhibit 5-3 is an example of a periodic statement.

To invest money in a money market fund, simply write or call the fund (most have toll-free numbers) to get a prospectus and application form. The SEC requires that a prospectus be sent to you—and you should read it. It explains exactly how the fund operates: on what terms it accepts investors' funds, how funds can be withdrawn, what investments can be made by the fund, who manages the fund, the management company's fee, and how operating expenses are divided between the management company and the fund itself.

Once you have the application form, you can invest in the fund by simply filling it out and mailing it with a check. After a fund account is opened, additional investments to the account can be made. The minimum amount is determined by the fund; for many funds it is $100.

All funds calculate dividends daily on outstanding shares and credit the accumulated total to the investor's account periodically, usually at the end of each month. The dividends credited to an investor's account buy him more shares, unless he has elected to withdraw accrued earnings.

Initially, some money market funds were *load* funds. That is, some of the money invested went to pay a commission to the broker who sold the fund. Today, however, *no-load* funds are the rule. Therefore, no commission is charged when shares of a money market fund are purchased or sold.

WITHDRAWING FUNDS

For liquidity, money market funds can not be beat, since withdrawals can be made anytime on demand and without penalty. Withdrawal practices vary somewhat from fund to fund but generally withdrawals can be made in several different ways. First, the investor can simply write the fund and ask them to send a check. Some funds require that

---

EXHIBIT 5-3 Sample Periodic Statement from a Money Market Fund

---

THE**Vanguard**GROUP
A member of
OF INVESTMENT COMPANIES

Vanguard
MONEY MARKET TRUST
FEDERAL PORTFOLIO

VANGUARD MARKETING
CORPORATION

FOR ACCOUNT SERVICE
CALL TOLL FREE:
1-800-662-CREW

TAX IDENT. OR SOC. SEC. NO.
ACCOUNT NO.   ALPHA

WHEN WRITING TO VANGUARD, PLEASE INCLUDE YOUR FUND NAME AND ACCOUNT NUMBER AND MAIL TO: VANGUARD FINANCIAL CENTER • P.O. BOX 2600 • VALLEY FORGE, PA 19482

CONFIRM DATE	TRADE DATE	TRANSACTION	DOLLAR AMOUNT OF TRANSACTION	SHARE PRICE	SHARES THIS TRANSACTION	TOTAL SHARES OWNED
		BEGINNING BALANCE				1,000.000
7/01	6/30	INCOME REINVEST	3.70	1.00	3.700	1,003.700
7/09	7/09	SHARES PURCHASED	2,244.12	1.00	2,244.120	3,247.820
8/01	7/31	INCOME REINVEST	15.78	1.00	15.780	3,263.600
9/03	8/31	INCOME REINVEST	19.92	1.00	19.920	3,283.520
9/09	9/06	CK-WRITING REDEMPTION 1003	705.00	1.00	705.000	2,578.520
10/01	9/30	INCOME REINVEST	15.87	1.00	15.870	2,594.390
10/02	10/02	SHARES PURCHASED	769.80	1.00	769.800	3,364.190
10/02	10/01	CK-WRITING REDEMPTION 1004	312.98	1.00	312.980	3,051.210
10/10	10/08	CK-WRITING REDEMPTION 1006	316.00	1.00	316.000	2,735.210
10/31	10/31	SHARES PURCHASED	769.80	1.00	769.800	3,505.010
11/01	10/31	INCOME REINVEST	16.73	1.00	16.730	3,521.740
11/01	10/31	CK-WRITING REDEMPTION 1005	330.00	1.00	330.000	3,191.740
11/08	11/07	CK-WRITING REDEMPTION 1007	450.00	1.00	450.000	2,741.740
11/18	11/18	SHARES PURCHASED	762.41	1.00	762.410	3,504.150
11/18	11/15	CK-WRITING REDEMPTION 1008	316.00	1.00	316.000	3,188.150
11/22	11/21	CK-WRITING REDEMPTION 1011	569.11	1.00	569.110	2,619.040
12/02	11/30	INCOME REINVEST	16.40	1.00	16.400	2,635.440
12/10	12/09	CK-WRITING REDEMPTION 1012	288.83	1.00	288.830	2,346.610
12/11	12/11	SHARES PURCHASED	769.80	1.00	769.800	3,116.410

YOUR DISTRIBUTION OPTION IS			SHARES YOU NOW OWN		
INCOME DIVIDENDS	CAPITAL GAINS	CERTIFICATE SHARES HELD BY YOU •	UNISSUED SHARES HELD BY AGENT •		TOTAL SHARES OWNED
REINVEST	REINVEST		3,116.410		3,116.410

		PAID THIS CALENDAR YEAR				
(1) TOTAL DIVIDENDS AND OTHER DISTRIBUTIONS	(2) INCOME DIVIDENDS	(3) ORDINARY TAXABLE INCOME	(4) TAX-EXEMPT INCOME	(5) AMT. OF (2) QUALIFYING FOR EXCLUSION	(6) LONG TERM CAPITAL GAINS DISTRIBUTION
88.40	88.40				

---

the investor's signature on a written withdrawal request be guaranteed by a commercial bank or by a member firm of a national securities exchange. This is especially likely if the check is to be made payable to a third party.

A second way to make a withdrawal is for the investor to request that the fund deposit money directly into his account at a commercial bank designated on his application form. Requests for such transfers can be made by mail, phone, or telex. If the size of the sum being transferred is large or the date when the money will be needed is uncertain, it may be worthwhile for the investor to wait until the day before the money is needed and then request the fund to wire money to his bank. At the cost of a few dollars, this approach avoids any unnecessary loss of interest.

A third method of withdrawing funds is by writing a check. Most money market funds have set up an arrangement with a commercial bank under which the investor is supplied with checks and can make withdrawals and execute payments simply by drawing a check against that bank. Generally the check has to be for some minimum amount—$250 or $500. When the check is presented to the bank against which it is drawn, that bank covers it by redeeming the required number of shares in the investor's fund account. (With this sort of fund, "shares" seem very much like interest-bearing demand deposits.)

Note that if you invest in a fund offering this sort of service, there is no reason for keeping just savings dollars in the fund. Money accumulated to make an anticipated tax payment or to pay for a vacation or some other anticipated expense can easily be parked in such a fund. Also if your income is high, even some of your living expense money might be put into a fund. Consider for example an individual who receives each month a sizeable pay check, which he uses over the month to cover family living expenses. He might deposit a large proportion of this check in a money market fund and then write checks against the fund to his checking account as he needed money; also he could pay large bills simply by writing checks against the fund. Note that on all checks written against the fund, the investor gets the advantage of the *float;* that is, he continues to earn interest on his money in the fund until his check against the fund clears, a process which can take anywhere from a few days up to 10. Keeping money in a savings account that pays day-of-deposit-to-day-of-withdrawal interest doesn't permit you to take advantage of the float, and getting money out of a savings account is less convenient—a trip to the bank or a several-day-turnaround-wait from the time you send in your passbook with a withdrawal slip to the time you get a check from your savings institution.

Finally we should mention that, for the investor who wants regular cash payments, money market funds will typically set up a systematic withdrawal plan. Under such a plan, a requested dollar amount is automatically paid to the investor monthly, quarterly, or annually. A fund may require that an individual have some minimum investment in the fund before it agrees to make such payments.

ACCOUNTING PROCEDURES

When the money fund industry was new, different people with different ideas and sometimes different objectives came to the SEC with their proposals for setting up a money market mutual fund. One would say, "We are going to account this way for capital gains and losses," and another would say, "We are going to account that way," and so on. Since every proposal looked reasonable, the upshot was that the SEC responded with an OK in each case. Thus was born a new class of institutions, with each firm comprising it using one of four different accounting methods.

Most money funds mark their portfolios to market daily, a sound practice but one that raises the question of how capital gains and losses, realized and unrealized, should be treated—as net income, or as a change in net asset value, etc. Some mark-to-market funds that wanted a steady income stream choose to reflect any realized or unrealized capital gains or losses as changes in the net asset value of their shares. Other funds that wanted to maintain a constant net asset value choose to include realized and unrealized gains and losses in their daily dividends. Still other funds that wanted a constant net asset value (for example, because they sold their fund to bank trust departments, municipal bodies, and other institutions that could assume no risk of capital loss) took the straight-line-accrual approach in accounting. Such funds make it a practice to hold money market instruments in which they invest to maturity, they do not mark their portfolios to market daily, and the dividends they credit each day to investors equals the average yield on all securities in the fund's portfolio.

A fourth approach, which seems to be the direction in which the industry is headed, is to run what is called a *penny rounded* fund. Such a fund sets net asset value at $1 initially. It then marks its portfolio to market and reflects capital gains or losses in the net asset value of its shares. However, these funds round their net asset value to the nearest penny, i.e., to the second decimal place. This means that their net asset value could deviate from $1 only if a tremendous change occurred in market values. On a yield basis, penny rounded funds are almost equivalent to the amortized-cost funds.

While each of the four accounting schemes sketched above seems reasonable and can be defended as achieving some desirable objective, the existence of differences in the way money funds report net income can and does on some days distort by hundreds of basis points comparisons of current yield among different funds.

To minimize distortions caused by accounting differences, an investor comparing several funds should look at what is called in the industry a *hypothetical:* If $1,000 were put in each fund and left there for one month, what rate of return would each fund have yielded the investor. The Lipper Analytical Services quotes the yields paid by different money funds on such a basis.

MONEY MARKET FUNDS VERSUS MMDAs

On December 14, 1982, Congress authorized banks and thrifts to create a money market deposit account (MMDA) that would be "directly equivalent to and competitive with money market mutual funds." As is the case with CDs, institutions are free to pay any interest rate they like on MMDAs. Unlike CDs, however, MMDAs have no maturity dates. The interest rate varies with some money market benchmark; therefore, as is the case with money market funds, a set yield is not guaranteed. The depositor may write checks against the balance in his MMDA.

The institution issuing the MMDA establishes the minimum balance, the maximum number of withdrawals per month that it will grant to account holders, and the charge for each check written. Although a MMDA in an institution that has federal deposit insurance is safe, the same is true for short-term government funds. However, there are several drawbacks of MMDAs compared to money market funds that invest in short-term government funds.

First, the minimum balances are generally higher than for many short-term government funds. If the balance for a MMDA falls below the minimum specified by the institution, the rate that is paid on the account will revert to the lower rate paid on regular savings accounts. For most money market funds, if the balance in the fund falls below the minimum balance necessary to open the account, the investor is given time to make up the deficiency. In the interim, the investor is not hit with rate penalties. Second, MMDAs give the investor limited check-writing privileges and limit the number of transfers that can be made to a regular checking account. Fees for any additional checks, transfers, or withdrawals may be high. In addition, there is the inconvenience of going to the bank to transfer or withdraw funds. Generally, there is no restriction on the number of checks that can be written on a money market fund, and there is no charge for writing a check. Most money market funds do, however, impose a lower limit on the dollar amount of checks written—usually $500.

ASSET MANAGEMENT ACCOUNTS

Most brokers offer their clients an in-house money market fund or some other money market fund in which clients may park investment proceeds, funds temporarily withdrawn from the market, or new funds awaiting investment in stocks and bonds. Merrill Lynch came up with the brilliant idea that, if some bells and whistles were added by a broker, such an account would generate a big number of large, new accounts. The name Merrill Lynch gave to its new account, introduced in 1979, was *Cash Management Account*. Not to be outdone by Merrill Lynch, other brokerage firms followed with similar accounts (for example, the E. F. Hutton Asset Management Account, Dean Witter Active Assets Account, Paine Webber Resource Management Account, and Smith Barney Vantage Account, to name a few).

These accounts are commonly referred to as asset management accounts. The bells and whistles on this type of account, which requires a specified minimum deposit of cash and/or securities and generally charges an annual fee, are (1) a checking account, (2) a periodic, usually daily, sweep of monies coming from a client's brokerage account into his asset management account, and (3) a credit card with a line of credit equal to the full amount by which any securities the client has deposited with the brokerage firm could be margined.[3] All cash that accumulates in an asset management account from dividends on stocks owned, interest on bonds, and proceeds from the sale or redemption of securities is automatically invested in a money market fund linked to the account or in some cases an insured savings account program. Many brokerage firms that offer asset management accounts give the customer a choice of three money market funds—a general purpose money market fund, a short-term U.S. government money market fund, or a tax-exempt money market fund. Merrill Lynch's Cash Management Account also allows the customer to invest idle funds in an insured savings program.

The fees, minimum investment, and extra features vary. For example, at the time of this writing, Merrill Lynch's Cash Management Account requires a minimum investment of $20,000 while the E. F. Hutton Asset Management Account has a minimum investment of $10,000. The annual fee for both of these accounts, which offer a free credit card, is $50 and $80, respectively. Some asset management ac-

---

[3]Margin is explained in Chapter 7.

counts impose a lower fee if a credit card is not included. For example, the Paine Webber Resource Management Account (minimum investment of $15,000) and the Smith Barney Vantage Account (minimum investment of $20,000) charge an annual fee of $100 for an account with a credit card but less if no credit card is issued ($60 in the case of Paine Webber and $40 in the case of Smith Barney). Even within a brokerage firm, a customer may have a choice of asset management account. For example, for those customers who find an asset management account attractive, but do not have enough capital to open a Cash Management Account, Merrill Lynch has a Capital Builder Account. This account offers many of the advantages of the Cash Management Account but only requires $5,000 in cash and/or securities to get started. However, there are fewer choices for investing idle cash in a Capital Builder Account.

To compete with wide-service, one-stop-shopping brokers, banks have in recent years offered brokerage service on the limited terms regulators permit. One bank that has gone far in this area is Citibank. It offers a Citibank Focus Account with features similar to those of asset management accounts offered by brokerage firms. Mutual funds also have started offering asset management accounts.

RISK, LIQUIDITY, AND RETURN

In evaluating money market funds, as with any other security, the investor should consider risk, liquidity, and return.

Liquidity

So far as liquidity is concerned, we have already seen that money market shares offer close to if not 100% liquidity. The only caveat with respect to liquidity is that somewhere in the fine print, every fund's prospectus contains a statement to the effect that redemptions of fund shares for cash may be suspended during any period in which the New York Stock Exchange is closed (other than for normal holidays); in which transactions on that exchange are restricted; or in which an emergency, as determined by the SEC, exists. The reason for the suspension clause is that with markets closed or trading restricted, it would be impossible for the fund to sell securities or to determine the value of its assets.

It is interesting to note that even when the money market fund industry was faced with withdrawals of 25% of its funds in 1983, it was still capable of satisfying redemptions quickly.

Risk

So much for liquidity; let's turn now to risk. The first risk that probably comes to mind for the investor is the risk of mismanagement or fraud. What would stop the manager of a $500 million fund from making shaky loans to business friends (the way the Teamsters pension fund has been accused of doing) or from grabbing $10 million from the till and going off on a vacation in the South Pacific.

As far as shaky loans are concerned, read the prospectus. The investment restrictions require that the management company invest the fund's assets in a diversified portfolio of liquid, low-risk securities. The management company, moreover, has to live up to the promises made in the prospectus because it is regulated by the SEC as well as by the state security commissions of all the states in which its shares are sold.

The management company cannot dip its fingers into the till—in plain English, steal the fund's money. All transfers of money to the fund are made into an account at a *custodial* bank and all payments by the fund are also made from this account. Thus the management company itself is never in a position to touch any of the fund's cash. The only fund money it ever sees is the payment it gets from the fund for its services. Of course, there is still the possibility that someone at the custodial bank might embezzle a few million dollars, but insurance and the bonding of bank employees protect the fund from any loss in that eventuality, just as they protect the bank's ordinary depositors.

The second source of risk likely to trouble the investor in a money market fund is the possibility that his fund might invest in securities of a firm that goes bankrupt and does not pay off its creditors. This source of risk is real *but* the investor has strong safeguards working to protect him. Money market funds concentrate almost all their investments in just a few instruments: T bills, CDs, bankers' acceptances, and commercial paper. On T bills the risk of loss due to failure of the issuer is zero. On large denomination CDs, it is probably almost zero since in all recent bank failures, regardless of the cause (mismanagement, foreign exchange speculation, and so on), the FDIC has fully protected all CD holders *and* it is likely to continue to do so. Because of the double guarantee of payment, risk on bankers' acceptances is also very low; in fact to date no investor in such acceptances has sustained a loss of principal. In the case of commercial paper, risk can be a factor but most funds restrict their investments to top-rated, minimal-risk paper.

Because of the high quality of the securities acquired by money market funds, the risk of capital loss due to the failure of issuers of securities is negligible for the investor. Moreover, since all funds hold a highly diversified portfolio (generally restricting their holdings of the debt securities of any one issuer to a small percentage of their total assets), the failure of one issuer would result in a relatively minor loss to the fund's investors.

To these remarks, one caveat should be added. Obviously, there are high-risk, high-yield, short-term securities around. And there may be an aggressive fund that invests in such securities in order to earn high yields and attract money fast. To protect against putting money into such a fund, *never* invest in a money market fund before you read their prospectus and check what securities they hold in their portfolio. If there is a lot of commercial paper in the portfolio, ask about its rating. Also stick to funds that invest in instruments you understand; there are some instruments that we have not discussed and in which a few funds have invested. If you follow these precautions, you will have *no* cause to lose sleep over the risk of capital loss. Generally money market funds have very conservative portfolios, so your only job is to make sure that if there is one shaky apple in the barrel, you don't invest in it.

Even after all we've said, if you're still concerned with the risk of capital loss due to defaults, restrict your investment to U.S. government short-term funds.

Return

An investor putting money into a money market fund can expect to get a rate of return below the rate yielded by securities in which the fund invests.

Since money market rates are extremely volatile, so too are the yields paid by money market funds. For example, between September 1984 and September 1985, the yield range for general purpose money market funds was 7.25 to 11.08%. The individual investing in a money market fund cannot expect a steady yield, but most of the time he can expect to do better than the steady yield offered on a regular savings account. Also, having an account at a money market fund makes it much easier, as noted above, to keep every spare dollar invested. Money market funds generally return higher yields than MMDAs. For example, during the September 1984 to September 1985 period, the yield range for MMDAs was 6.70 to 9.78% compared to 7.25 to 11.08% for general purpose money market funds.

Since the yields available from U.S. Treasury and agency issues are less than those of privately issued money market instruments of the same maturity, the yield on U.S. government short-term funds is less than that of general purpose money market funds, typically between .2 to .5% less.

The yields on tax-exempt money market funds are lower than the two other types of money market funds since the interest is exempt from federal income taxes. Consequently, when comparing the yield on a taxable money market fund with a tax-exempt money market fund, it is necessary to compare yields on either a pre-tax or an after-tax basis. To do so, an investor must determine his marginal tax rate (see Chapter 1). The formulas below can then be used to compare yields.

When comparing yields on an after-tax basis, the following formula should be used:

> After-tax yield on a taxable money market fund
> = Pre-tax yield on a taxable money market fund ×
> (1 − Marginal tax rate)

For example, for an investor who estimates his marginal tax rate to be 28%, the after-tax yield on a taxable money market fund that pays 10% is computed as follows:

> After-tax yield on a taxable money market fund
> = .10 × (1 − .28)
> = .10 × .72
> = .072 or 7.2%.

A yield on a tax-exempt money market fund that is greater than 7.2% would offer the investor a higher after-tax yield.

Alternatively, the comparison can be made on a pre-tax basis. The formula to determine the pre-tax yield for a tax-exempt money market fund is:

Pre-tax yield for a tax-exempt money market fund

$$= \frac{\text{Yield on a tax-exempt money market fund}}{(1 - \text{Marginal tax rate})}$$

Once again, considering our investor faces a 28% marginal tax rate, suppose that the yield on a tax-exempt money market fund is 7.2%. The pre-tax yield for this investor, then, is 10%, as shown below:

Pre-tax yield for a tax-exempt money market fund

$$= \frac{.072}{(1 - .28)} = .10 \text{ or } 10\%.$$

This investor would be better off buying a tax-exempt money market fund if the yield on taxable money market funds is less than 10%.

SELECTING A FUND

Currently there are many money market funds you might consider. In selecting one, the first step is to cross off your list of candidates all funds that charge a load—if there are any around. Note also that some funds accept investments only from institutional (financial and nonfinancial corporate) clients.

The next and single most important step in selecting a fund is to read carefully the prospectus and examine the composition of the portfolio. Make sure the fund in which you invest puts its money into top-grade securities.

Yield, of course, is another important consideration. It might seem that the logical way to choose between equally appealing funds is on the basis of which offers the highest yield. There is nothing wrong with this approach, but there are some inherent difficulties in comparing yields.

As we have seen in previous chapters, yields on some money market instruments consistently top those on others, with the size of the spread varying over time. In particular, T bills yield less than negotiable CDs, which yield less than commercial paper. Bearing this in mind, the investor might conclude that he would surely get a better yield from a fund investing heavily in commercial paper than from a fund investing exclusively in, say, negotiable CDs. This is not necessarily so.

What yield a money market fund pays depends on two factors: what return it earns on its portfolio *and* how much of that return goes to cover the management fee and operating expenses. Management fees, which are clearly stated in each fund's prospectus, generally run from 0.5 to 1%. Each fund's prospectus also states what expenses the management company will pay and what expenses the fund will bear. Since there is variability not only in management fees but also in the allocation of expenses between the management company and the fund, it is impossible to determine from the prospectus alone which funds operate at minimum cost to the investor.

The only feasible approach is to look at the income statements and balance sheets of various funds over a recent period and calculate for each what amount of total interest income went for expenses and the management fee. In a well-managed fund, the annual management fee plus operating costs should represent no more than 1% of total assets.

Because operating and management expenses vary from fund to fund, picking the fund with the highest-yielding portfolio is not a failsafe way for the investor to obtain maximum yield. A fund that invests heavily in commercial paper but had high expenses might, for example, yield over time less than a fund that invested only in CDs but incurred lower operating expenses.

For the investor determined to compare yields, the important figures are the actual daily yields (or monthly averages of such yields) paid by different funds on share accounts. However, even here we find a caveat. Comparisons of yields paid by funds in the recent past may be a misleading indicator of how their yields are likely to compare in the future. The reasons for this are several. First, some funds use the cost basis in calculating yield; others use the market-value approach. When money market rates are falling, the market-value approach will lead to higher yield figures than the cost-basis approach; but when rates are rising, the opposite will be true. Second, if two funds both use the cost-basis approach but fund A holds securities with a longer average maturity than fund B does, fund A's yield will look better than B's when money market rates are falling, but poorer when rates are rising.

Comparing yields is a tricky business. In order to do so, the investor will probably have to request additional information from the funds he is considering, since many do not include in their brochures any detailed information on recent operating results or on the composition of their portfolios.

EXHIBIT 5-4   Top Performing Consumer Money Funds by 30-Day Average Yield

---

Assets ($Mill)	Fund	30-Day Average Yield as of 3/4/86
$ 259.6	Lehman Management Cash Res.*	7.83
2.5	PRO Money Fund/Prime Port.*	7.75
560.2	Summit Cash Reserves	7.60
34.0	Flex-Fund M.M.F.*	7.56
4,626.6	Kemper Money Market	7.56
304.5	Trinity Liquid Assets Trust	7.56
11,904.5	Merrill Lynch Ready	7.53
17,330.8	CMA Money Fund	7.51
25.4	Newton Money Fund*	7.51
97.2	Counsellors Cash Reserve*	7.50

---

*Manager currently absorbing a portion of fund expenses
SOURCE: *Donoghue's MONEYLETTER,* March 1986—Second Issue, Vol. 7, No. 6. Reprinted with permission.

A consumer-oriented newsletter, *Donoghue's MONEYLETTER,* published twice a month by The Donoghue Organization, shows the top-performing money market funds available to individual investors.[4] A sample table from this publication, which costs $87 per year, is shown as Exhibit 5-4. The yields reported are based on calculations performed by the fund according to the specifications requested by The Donoghue Organization so that the yields are comparable and consistent.

Besides safety and yield, another important consideration in comparing funds is convenience. The minimum denomination required on various sorts of transactions varies from fund to fund. Some funds offer check-writing privileges (an important convenience), others do not. Also, some funds charge for the check-writing service, while others do not. To make sure you get the services you want without paying unnecessary fees, check carefully what features each fund offers and determine which fund best suits your needs.

As you can imagine, investing in a money market fund calls for a little homework.

---

[4]The Donoghue Organization, Inc., P.O. Box 540, Holliston, MA 01746.

SUMMARY

Money market funds offer the investor several advantages over direct investment in money market instruments: there is less bother to the investor, greater liquidity, and greater safety due to diversification. There are, however, possible disadvantages. An individual who has a large amount of money and who is willing to sacrifice some liquidity, may find he can get a better rate by investing directly in money market instruments. Also, income received from a taxable money market fund is subject to full state and federal taxes on income. In contrast, income from investments in T bills and certain other short-term federal securities is not subject to state income taxes. The importance of the latter consideration obviously depends on the investor's marginal tax rate.

Some Fundamentals about Notes and Bonds

6

In the last five chapters we focused primarily on certificates of deposit and the major money market securities. In this chapter we shift focus to another broad group of securities: Treasury notes and bonds, federal agency securities, state and municipal securities, and corporate notes and bonds. Some of these securities are short in maturity, but many have original maturities measured not in days or months, but in years or even decades. Generally notes are medium-term securities (although some notes are issued with short maturities); bonds are long-term securities.

Most of the instruments discussed in the following chapters are interest-bearing, negotiable, *long-term* securities—a species we have not encountered so far. Before we say anything about the specific securities available, let's take a quick look at the characteristics of such securities, the way changes in interest rates affect their market value, and related considerations that the thoughtful investor should bear in mind.

COUPON SECURITIES

Bonds and other interest-bearing, negotiable debt securities are all issued with a fixed *face value* —the face value being the amount that the issuer promises to pay the bondholder at some stated maturity date. The minimum denomination on corporate bonds (the minimum face value in which the bond is issued) is typically $1,000. For municipal bonds, it is typically $5,000. On other notes and bonds, it may run to $5,000, $10,000, $25,000, or larger.

If a bond matures 10 years after the date of issue, it is said to have an *original* maturity of 10 years. Six months after issue, its *current* maturity (also termed *time to maturity* or *term to maturity*) has fallen to 9 1/2 years. Once a bond is outstanding, its current maturity (or *time to call*) is of crucial importance in determining the security's market value.

All interest-bearing securities carry a stated *coupon rate*—this rate being the annual rate of interest that the issuer promises to pay the bondholder on the face value of the security. For example, if a bond with a $1,000 face value carries a 6% coupon, this means that the issuer promises to pay the bondholder $60 of interest each year.

Notes and bonds are issued in *registered* form and *bearer* or *coupon* form. An issuer with $5 million of bearer bonds outstanding obviously does not know where to send interest when the payment date comes along. Consequently, such securities carry *coupons,* one for each interest due date. When that date arrives, the bearer clips the appropriate coupon from the bond (or has his bank do it for him) and sends the coupon to the issuer's paying agent, who in turn makes the required payment. Generally, interest payments are made semiannually on coupon securities. Because bonds carry coupons, the return paid on face value is called the *coupon rate,* or more simply the *coupon.*

Bonds with a short current maturity are referred to in the trade as *short coupons* or *short bonds,* those with an intermediate current maturity (say, 2 to 7 years) as *intermediate coupons,* and those with a still longer current maturity as *long coupons* or *long bonds.* We will use this jargon, since it saves a lot of verbiage.

A bond buyer is naturally interested in the chance of default on any bond he buys. Bond issuers secure their promise to pay interest and principal on their bonds in various ways. U.S. Treasury securities are backed by the full faith and credit of the government. Some federal agency issues have this same backing on a *de jure* basis, others on a *de facto* basis. Municipal securities may be backed by the full faith, credit, and taxing power of the issuing body or by revenue from specified sources. Corporate securities may be backed by a lien on some piece of property (mortgage bonds) or simply by the general earning power of the issuing corporation. We look more closely at backing, risk, and bond ratings in later chapters.

Call and Refunding Provisions

Once a long-term bond issue is sold, the issuer might choose to redeem it early. For example, if long-term interest rates fell, the borrower could reduce his interest costs by *refunding* his loan, that is, by paying off outstanding high-coupon bonds and issuing new lower–coupon bonds. The issuer might also want to redeem bonds early to free collateral for some other use or because cash flow from operations exceeded expectations.

For the investor, early repayment on a bond is almost always disadvantageous. The reason is that a bond issuer will rarely be tempted to repay early when interest rates are rising, a time when it would be to the bondholder's advantage to get his funds out of the issuer's bond and into something else paying a higher return. On the other hand, early payment looks attractive to the issuer when interest rates are falling, a time when it is to the investor's advantage to keep funds invested in the issuer's relatively high-coupon bonds.

To protect investors making long–term commitments of their funds against frequent refundings by borrowers out to minimize interest costs, most bonds contain call and refunding provisions. A bond issue is said to be *callable* when the issuer has the option to repay part or all of the issue early by paying some specified redemption price to bondholders. Most bonds offer some call protection to the investor. Some are noncallable for life (NCL). Others are noncallable for some number of years (5, 10, or 15) after issue. An industrial bond that is not callable until 1990 would be denoted as NC90 on a dealer's quote sheet. In contrast, a government bond maturing on May 15, 1998, but callable in 1993, would have its maturity date written as 5/15/1998-93.

Besides call protection, many bonds offer refunding protection. Typically, long-term industrial bonds are immediately callable *but* offer 10 years of protection against calls for refunding. Such a bond is referred to as *callable except for refunding purposes*. Refunding protection through 1990 would be indicated on a dealer's quote sheet as NR90.

Generally investors and dealers place more emphasis on refunding protection than on call protection. However, the investor should check both provisions, since a bond that is NR for 10 years might be called at any time for purposes other than refunding. Obviously call and refunding protection are of the greatest importance to an investor who buys bonds when interest rates are at a peak, and the disadvantage of a subsequent call would be greatest.

Call provisions usually specify that the issuer who calls a bond must pay the bondholder a price above the face value. This *call premium* frequently equals the coupon rate on early calls and then diminishes to zero as the bond approaches maturity. Call provisions vary considerably from one type of issue to another and should be carefully checked by the investor. During recent periods of rising interest rates and credit crunches, borrowers have, not surprisingly, had to offer increasingly generous call protection to sell long–term bonds.

Convertible Bonds

Some corporate bonds contain a provision permitting the holder to convert his bonds at his option into the issuing company's common stock. *Convertible* bonds are often "junior" grade securities, that is, securities whose claim on the issuer's assets is subordinate to those of other creditors. The conversion provision always permits conversion between the issuer's bonds and common stock on some fixed exchange ratio. The deciding factor for the buyer of a convertible is the hope that the common stock of the company whose bonds he holds will rise in value, thereby permitting him to gain either through a rise in the price of his bond or through exercise of the conversion privilege.

Conversion provisions are written in many variations. Some permit conversion at any time on a fixed conversion ratio. In others the exchange ratio may vary over the life of the bond, or the conversion privilege may be limited to certain periods of the bond's life.

A convertible security can really be thought of as a double security: an ordinary bond plus an option to buy common stock. As such, its value consists of two parts. First, there is the underlying *investment value*—the price that the bond would command stripped of its conversion privilege. This part of the value is determined by the credit worthiness of the issuer, by the bond's coupon and current maturity, and (as explained below) by the prevailing level of interest rates. The second part of the convertible bond's value is the *premium above investment value* that investors are willing to pay for the conversion feature (i.e., for the implied stock option). Because of their two-part value, prices of convertible bonds respond over time not only to changes in interest rates as other bonds do, but also in a direct and volatile way to changes in the fortunes of the issuing company and the price of its common stock. More about convertibles in Chapter 13.

Bond Prices

Bond prices are quoted in slightly different ways depending on whether the bond is selling in the new-issue or the secondary market. When new corporate, federal agency, and municipal bonds are first issued, the price at which they are offered to investors is normally quoted as a *percentage* of face value. To illustrate, the new issue of Credithrift Financial Corporation announced in Exhibit 6–1 was offered at a price of 99.70% which means that the investor had to pay $99.70 for each $100 of face value. This percentage price is often called the bond's *dollar price,* a term that makes little sense but has nevertheless stuck. The security described in Exhibit 6–1 carries a 10 1/4% coupon but was offered at a price below par, so its actual yield over time was slightly greater than the coupon rate. We get into the relationship of yield to price and coupon rate below.

Once a bond is issued and trading in that issue moves to the secondary market, prices are also quoted on a percentage basis but always in 32ds for government and federal agency securities and in 8ths, 4ths, halves for corporate securities and municipal *dollar bonds,* i.e., those municipal securities that are quoted on a dollar basis.[1] Exhibit 6–2 reproduces by way of illustration a few quotes on Treasury notes posted by a large primary dealer on June 28, 1985. The second bid price is 101.14, which means that this dealer was willing to pay $101 14/32 ($101.4375) per $100 of face value for that issue.[2]

The main reason for dollar pricing of bonds is that it makes bonds with different denominations directly comparable in price. Also, quoting bonds at so many dollars per $100 of face value, instead of as so many dollars per $1,000, takes a lot of numbers off of dealers' quote sheets, which need all the compacting they can get.

Once a bond moves into the secondary market and onto dealers' quote sheets, it is identified by issuer, coupon rate, and maturity.

---

[1] Most municipal securities are quoted on a yield basis, as noted in Chapter 11.

[2] In the case of Treasury securities, the value following the decimal indicates the number of 32ds.

EXHIBIT 6-1

New Issue / October 31, 1985

$100,000,000

Credithrift Financial Corporation

10¼% Senior Notes due November 1, 1992

Price 99.70% and accrued interest from November 1, 1985

Salomon Brothers Inc

Shearson Lehman Brothers Inc.		**Alex. Brown & Sons** Incorporated
Donaldson, Lufkin & Jenrette Securities Corporation	**E. F. Hutton & Company Inc.**	**Kidder, Peabody & Co.** Incorporated
Prudential-Bache Securities	**Wertheim & Co., Inc.**	**Dean Witter Reynolds Inc.**

SOURCE: Salomon Brothers Inc

Treatment of Accrued Interest in Bond Pricing

There's another wrinkle with respect to bond pricing. Typically bond interest is paid semiannually to the bondholder on the coupon dates. This means that a bond's value will tend to rise by the amount of interest accrued as a payment date approaches and fall thereafter by the amount of the payment made. Since bonds are issued on every business day and consequently have coupon dates falling all over the cal-

EXHIBIT 6-2 U.S. Treasury Note Quotations, June 28, 1985

Coupon	Maturity	Bid	Asked	Yield to Maturity	Yield Value 1/32	Accrued Interest	Publicly Held (billion dollars)
13⅛	August 15, 1985	100.23	100.24	7.07	.2253	48.221685	6.00
9¾	January 31, 1987	101.14	101.15	8.73	.0212	39.861878	9.00
10½	August 15, 1988	102.18	102.20	9.50	.0116	38.577348	5.75
13¾	May 15, 1992	115.14	115.15	10.53	.0059	16.440217	9.01
10⅛	May 15, 1993	98.15	98.17	10.40	.0060	12.105978	4.75

endar, the effect of accruing interest on the prices of different bonds would, if incorporated into dealer quote sheets, make price comparisons between different bonds extremely difficult.

To get around this problem, bond prices in the new-issue and secondary markets are always quoted as some percentage of face value *plus* accrued interest. For example, if you buy a $1,000 bond quoted at 100 with an 8% coupon 3 months before its coupon date, you pay a *principal price* of $1,000 plus $20 of accrued interest. The accrued interest is determined as follows. First, the semiannual interest is found. In our example, since the coupon rate is 8%, the dollar interest is $80 ($1,000 × .08). Semiannual interest is then $40. Since the seller held the bond for 3 of the 6 months, the seller is entitled to one half of the $40, or $20. You will recover the $20 paid to the seller when you receive the $40 semiannual coupon payment in 3 months.

As another example, suppose you buy a 6% coupon bond with a face value of $1,000 for 90 1/2, 4 months before its coupon date. You will pay $915 as shown below:

$$
\begin{array}{lcl}
\text{Price of 90 1/2} & = & .905 \\
\times \quad \text{Face value} & = & \times\ \$1{,}000 \\
\hline
\text{Principal price} & = & \$\ 905 \\
\end{array}
$$

Coupon interest = .06 × $1,000 = $60
Semiannual interest = $30

Accrued interest for 2 months $= \dfrac{2}{6} \times \$30 = \$10$

Total proceeds you must pay = Principal price + Accrued interest
= $905 + $10 = $915

There are bonds in which no accrued interest is paid. This occurs when the issuer of the bond is in default of principal or interest payments.[3] In such cases the bond is said to be quoted *flat*.

EFFECT OF CHANGING INTEREST RATES ON BOND PRICES

As noted in later chapters, the way in which notes and bonds are issued varies somewhat depending on the issuer. Currently the U.S. Treasury sells new note and bond issues at auction. In contrast, new

---

[3]This also occurs when the interest on a bond is contingent upon sufficient earnings by the issuer. Such bonds are called *income bonds*

federal agency, state and municipal, and corporate issues are generally distributed through *underwriting syndicates,* that is, groups of securities dealers and banks who buy up new security issues directly from the issuer and then resell them to investors. Firms that engage in underwriting are frequently referred to as *investment bankers.* The term is misleading because an investment banker need not be a bank; in fact most are not. A bank, however, acts as an investment banker whenever it underwrites federal agency and municipal issues; banks are barred by the Glass-Steagall Act of 1933 from underwriting corporate issues. A bank that participates in underwriting and makes markets in various note and bond issues is also referred to as a *dealer bank.*

An organization issuing new notes or bonds through a syndicate attempts, with the aid of its investment banker, to set the coupon on its issue in line with current market yields on similar securities. Doing so enables the syndicate to sell the security being issued to investors at a price close to full face value—at or near *par.*

Discounts and *premiums* on new issues are, however, not uncommon. A $1,000 bond that is sold at issue for $1,010 carries a $10 premium. Why would anyone pay $1,010 for a $1,000 IOU? The answer is that a security issued at a premium carries a coupon that is slightly higher than the yield available on comparable outstanding issues. Consequently *if* it were sold at par, each $1 invested in the new security would yield more interest income than $1 invested in a similar outstanding security. Thus the new security is worth more than $1 per $1 of face value; it commands a price above par. (If you don't understand, read on; the discussion below will clear up this point.) In contrast, a security issued at a discount carries a coupon that is low relative to yields on comparable securities; for this reason it has to be priced below par to sell. The whys and wherefores of discounts and premiums at issue are something we will get into later. For the moment, let's concentrate on what determines the market price of an interest-bearing security once it is issued.

After all of a new issue is sold out by the syndicate that offers it, trading in the issue passes from the *new-issues market* to the *secondary market.* The secondary market is an over-the-counter market made by securities dealers; that is, by firms that typically act as a principal in security transactions, buying for their own account and selling from inventory. Dealers post bid and asked prices at which they are prepared to buy and sell the different issues for which they are market makers. An investor wanting to buy an outstanding issue gets it from a dealer, and an investor seeking to sell outstanding securities likewise sells to a dealer.

Generally the dealer's objective is to earn a modest profit by selling any security he buys at a price slightly higher than the price at which he bought it. Thus the dealer's bid price for any security (the price at which he is willing to add that security to his inventory) is determined by how much he thinks he can resell the security for—its worth to investors. What a given security is worth to investors at any point in time depends on how high current market yields are on issues of comparable risk and maturity.

To illustrate what is involved, let's work through a simple example. Suppose a new 15-year bond with an 8% coupon is issued at par. Six months later the Fed tightens monetary policy, and the yield on comparable securities rises to 8.5%. Now what is our 8% security worth? Since the investor who pays a price equal to par for this "seasoned issue" is going to get only an 8% return, while 8.5% is available elsewhere, it is clear that the security is now worth less than full par.

Yield to Maturity

To determine how much less, we have to introduce a new concept—*effective yield*. Whenever an investor buys a coupon security at a *discount* and holds it to maturity, he receives a two-part return on his investment: the promised interest payment *plus* a capital gain. The capital gain arises because the security that the investor bought at a price below par is redeemed at maturity for full face value. The investor who buys a coupon issue at a *premium* and holds it to maturity also receives a two-part return: interest payments due plus a capital *loss* equal to the amount of the premium paid.

For dollars invested in a coupon issue that sells at a discount or premium, it is possible to calculate the overall or effective rate of return received, which is the rate that the investor earns on his dollars when both interest received *and* capital gains (or losses) are taken into account. Naturally, an investor choosing between securities of similar risk and maturity will do so, not on the basis of coupon rates, but on the basis of effective yields, referred to in the financial community as *yield to maturity* in the case of coupon securities.

To get back to our example, it is now clear that once rates rise to 8.5% in the open market, our security with an 8% coupon has to be priced at a discount sufficiently great so that its yield to maturity equals 8.5%. Figuring out just how many dollars of discount this requires involves complicated calculations. Dealers used to use bond tables but most have now switched to preprogrammed calculators. Pulling out an HP 80 (a Hewlett Packard calculator that makes fast work of bond problems), one can determine in a few seconds that with interest rates at 8.5%, our $1,000 bond with an 8% coupon and a 14 1/2-year current maturity has to sell at $958.77 (a discount of $41.23) in order to yield 8.5% to maturity.

Current Maturity and Price Volatility

Without the aid of bond tables or an HP 80, it should be obvious to the reader that a capital gain of $41.23, which is what the investor in our discounted 8% bond would realize if he held it to maturity, is going to raise effective yield more, the faster this gain is realized (the shorter the current maturity of the security). Conversely, this capital gain will raise effective yield less, the more slowly it is realized (the longer the current maturity of the security).[4]

But if this is so, then a 0.5% rise in the yield on comparable securities will cause a much larger fall in price for a security with a long current maturity than for a security with a short current maturity. In other words, the discount required to raise a coupon security's yield to maturity by 0.5% is greater, the longer the security's maturity. Conversely, a 0.5% fall in yields will force an outstanding security with an 8% coupon to a premium—the premium being greater, the longer the security's current maturity.

As these observations suggest, when prevailing interest rates change, prices of long bonds respond much more dramatically than prices of short bonds. Exhibit 6-3 shows how sharp the contrast is. For a $1,000 bond carrying an 8% coupon, it shows the relationship between *current* maturity and the discount that would prevail if the yield on comparable securities rose to 8.5% or to 10%.[5] It also plots the premium to which a $1,000 bond with an 8% coupon would be

---

[4] If you don't see this, just think—somewhat imprecisely—of the capital gain as a certain number of dollars of extra interest paid out in yearly installments to the investor as his security matures. Clearly, the shorter the security's current maturity, the higher these extra annual interest installments will be, and consequently the higher the overall yield to the investor.

[5] *Comparable securities* are securities that have the same current maturity and carry the same risk of default by the issuer.

EXHIBIT 6-3 Premiums and Discounts at which a $1,000 Bond with an 8% Coupon Would, Depending on Current Maturity, Sell if Market Yields on Comparable Securities Were 6%, 8.5%, or 10%.

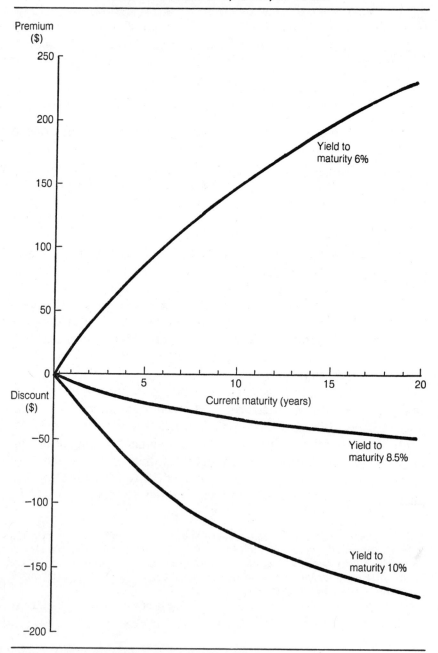

driven if the rate on comparable securities fell to 6%, depending on current maturity.

Coupon and Price Volatility

The volatility of a bond's price in the face of changing interest rates also depends on its coupon. The *lower* the coupon, the *greater* the percentage change that will occur in a bond's price when rates rise or fall. To illustrate, consider two bonds with 10-year current maturities. Bond A has a 10% coupon, Bond B a 5% coupon. Both bonds are priced to yield 10%. Suppose now that interest rates on comparable securities rise to 15% (the big credit crunch arrives). Bond A will fall in price by 25.49; since it was initially priced at 100, that works out to be a 25.49% fall in value. Bond B's dollar price drops from 68.84 to 49.81—a 19.81 fall, which equals a 28.78% loss of value. The reason for the greater percentage fall in the price of the low-coupon bond is that capital appreciation represents a greater proportion of promised income (capital appreciation plus coupon interest) on the low coupon than on the high coupon. Therefore, for the low–coupon bond's yield to maturity to rise 5 percentage points, its price has to fall relatively *more* than that of the high–coupon security.

Price Volatility and the Yield Value of 1/32d

Prices of government and federal agency securities, all of which are very actively traded, are quoted in 32ds. The greater the change in yield to maturity that results from a change in price of 1/32, the less volatile the issue's price will be in the face of changing interest rates. As a result, dealers generally include on their quote sheets for such securities a column titled *Yield Value 1/32*. Looking back at Exhibit 6–2, we see that the yield value of 1/32 on Treasury notes maturing on August 15, 1985, was .2253 which means that a fall in the bid price on this security from 100.23 to 100.22 (a 1/32 fall) would have raised yield to maturity by .2253%, from 7.07 to 7.29%. The yield value of 1/32 drops sharply as current maturity lengthens. Thus on notes maturing on May 15, 1992, the yield value of 1/32 was only .0060, indicating that these notes would have had to fall in value by approximately 38/32 for their yield to rise .2253%.

Current Yield

So far we have focused on yield to maturity, which is the yield figure always quoted on coupon securities. When the investor buys a bond, he may also be interested in knowing what rate of return interest payments per se will give him on the principal he invests. This measure of yield is referred to as *current yield*.

To illustrate, consider our earlier example of an 8% coupon bond selling at $958.77 to yield 8.5% to maturity. Current yield on the bond would be: ($80/$958.77) × 100 or 8.34%. On a discount bond, current yield is always less than yield to maturity, while on a premium bond it exceeds yield to maturity.

Liquidity of Long Coupons

The discussion above has important implications with respect to the liquidity and riskiness of investments in long coupons. A liquid security is one that can be converted into cash promptly at small or no loss of value. Whenever interest rates fluctuate sharply (as they have in recent years), wide swings occur in the prices of long bonds, with the result that the liquidity of these securities is sharply diminished. Put another way, for an individual who is *not* certain to be a hold-until-maturity investor, interest rate fluctuations mean that an investment in long coupons (especially those with low coupons) carries a much greater risk of capital loss if interest rates rise, than does an investment in a short-term debt security. Of course, holding long bonds also exposes the investor to a greater possibility of capital gain if interest rates fall, than does holding short bonds. The latter observation is certainly of considerable interest to speculators. However, to the long-term investor who is aware of the upward trend that interest rates have displayed over the last three decades, this possible source of gain on long coupons may appear to offer small compensation for the probably much greater risk of capital loss. The risk on bond investments due to possible fluctuations in interest rates is referred to as the *price risk*.

In recent years long-term interest rates have fluctuated much less than short-term rates. This contrast in behavior somewhat mitigates the effect of general ups and downs in interest rates on the prices of long coupons. However, it remains true that the prices of these securities do fluctuate substantially over time.

As long as we are on the topic of liquidity, there is one other general comment. While there is much variability from security to security, generally markets for long and intermediate coupons are much *thinner* than markets for short-term securities; that is, trading volume is much smaller in these markets than in the money market. Because of this, the marketability of long coupons is less than that of money market instruments, which is reflected in the fact that the spread between dealers' bid and asked prices is wider for long coupons than for bills and short bonds (which in effect trade in the money market). To the extent that a long coupon means decreased marketability, it also implies a corresponding decrease in liquidity.

Marketability and liquidity also vary considerably from one sector to another of the bond market. For example, corporate and municipal issues are a heterogeneous mix of relatively small issues that are all traded much less actively than governments. In the markets for these securities, it is sometimes difficult to move size without moving price. Also, dealers' quote spreads are much larger on such securities than they are on governments, ranging up to 2 or 3 points.

FIGURING BOND YIELDS

Dealer's quote sheets always contain a column in which current bid prices are expressed on a yield to maturity basis. Thus the modest bond investor does not have to work through bond tables or buy an expensive electronic calculator to make yield calculations.[6] However, it is conceivable that you might want to make such a calculation. If so, there is an approximation formula that gives adequate results. For a bond selling at a discount:

Yield to maturity

$$= \frac{\text{(Annual coupon interest)} + \text{(Discount/years to maturity)}}{\text{(Market price} + \text{par)}/2}$$

To test this formula, apply it to our earlier example. There we showed that a $1,000 bond with an 8% coupon and a 14 1/2-year current maturity would have to sell at a discount of $41.23 to yield 8.5% to maturity. Plugging all but the last of these numbers into the above approximation formula, we find that a $1,000 bond with an 8% cou-

---

[6]A consumer caveat: Lots of calculators are capable of solving interest rate problems, but only the most expensive are preprogrammed to do bond yield calculations. Don't buy one before making sure it does all the tricks you want.

pon and a 14 1/2-year current maturity selling at $958.77 will yield 8.46% to maturity, only 0.04% off from the true answer.

For a bond selling at a premium, the formula is:

Yield to maturity
$$= \frac{(\text{Annual coupon interest}) - (\text{Premium/years to maturity})}{(\text{Market price} + \text{par})/2}$$

SUMMARY OF INVESTMENT CHARACTERISTICS OF NOTES AND BONDS

We've bombarded you with a great deal of information about the investment characteristics of notes and bonds. Before we move on to give you more of the fundamentals that you will need to make intelligent decisions when purchasing these securities, let's recap the important investment characteristics that we covered in this chapter.

First, the most common measure for the return that an investor might be expected to earn from buying a bond and holding it to maturity is the yield to maturity. The yield to maturity takes into consideration the amount and timing of the coupon payments and any capital gain or loss that will be realized at maturity. When investors talk about the "yield" of a bond, they usually mean the yield to maturity. (One of the things that we will see in the next chapter is that the yield to maturity is far from a perfect measure of the potential return from buying a bond.)

Second, a fundamental property of a bond is that its price moves in the opposite direction of the change in yields required on comparable securities. That is, if yields on comparable bonds rise (fall) because interest rates in the economy change, the price of a bond will fall (rise). The investment implication is that if you have to sell a bond before its maturity date, you will not be certain of what price you will receive. The selling price depends on what has happened to interest rates since you purchased the bond.

Third, although the price of a bond will move in the opposite direction of the change in interest rates required on comparable securities, the price volatility of a bond depends on two characteristics of a bond: current maturity and coupon rate. For a given coupon rate, the longer the current maturity, the greater the price volatility of a bond. For a given current maturity, the lower the coupon rate, the greater the price volatility of a bond. Consequently, investors who purchase long-term, low-coupon bonds are exposed to the greatest price risk.

More Fundamentals about Notes and Bonds

7

In Chapter 6 we examined the principal characteristics of bonds and some determinants of bond prices. This chapter continues with fundamentals: reasons for differences between yields among securities, the reinvestment rate, original-issue deep-discount bonds, floating-rate and adjustable-rate notes, and speculating in bonds.

REASONS FOR DIFFERENCES BETWEEN YIELDS AMONG SECURITIES

If you peruse *The Wall Street Journal* or a dealer's quote sheet, it is clear that there is no single, going yield on bonds and notes. Quite to the contrary—at any one point in time, yields are quite different among securities. What are the primary factors that cause these differences in yields?

Default Risk

First, there are differences in the *risk* (perceived or real) of default. Default risk is the risk that the issuer will default in the contractual payment of interest and principal. U.S. Treasury obligations are considered to be free of default risk. For a given current maturity, the yield of a Treasury obligation establishes the floor yield that other taxable bonds must offer in the market. The greater the default risk, the greater the yield over a Treasury obligation of the same current maturity.

For issuers in which there is default risk, investors rely on the quality ratings assigned by commerical rating companies such as Moody's, Standard & Poor's, Duff & Phelps, and Fitch Investors Service to gauge the degree of default risk as well as independent credit evaluations by the research departments of some major investment banking firms.[1] The commercial rating companies are private concerns. They receive their fees from the issuers who request ratings. The acceptance of these ratings by investors depends on the reliability that the rating company has demonstrated. Historically, such ratings have proved to be valid, but they are not foolproof indicators of default risk. An excellent recent illustration of this is the Washington Public Power Supply System (WPPSS) bonds. In the early 1980s, both Moody's and Standard & Poor's gave these bonds their highest ratings. While these ratings were in effect, WPPSS sold over $8 billion in long-term bonds. By July of 1983, WPPSS defaulted on its Projects 4 and 5 bonds.

The timely review of ratings outstanding is believed to be one of the greatest difficulties facing both investors and the rating companies. A commercial rating company may have as many as 20,000 ratings outstanding. Consequently, a substantial delay may occur between published reviews of ratings. The concern of investors that the rating companies may not closely monitor their ratings once they are assigned can be illustrated with the case of an obligation (a construction loan note) of the Oklahoma Housing Finance Agency. When this debt obligation defaulted on June 1, 1982, it still had the highest quality rating assigned by both Moody's and Standard & Poor's.

Marketability

Another important consideration to investors is the marketability of a security. Any security that is quoted continually by a dealer is a marketable security, since there is a market for it. However, investors

---

[1]The ratings assigned by two of these commercial rating companies, Moody's and Standard & Poor's, will be discussed when we describe municipal bonds in Chapter 11 and corporate bonds in Chapter 12.

want to know much more than that; they want to know how good the market is.

The chief indication of marketability is the size of the spread between an issue's bid price and asked price. The dealer lives off the difference, which is called the *dealer's spread*. Two factors determine the size of the dealer's spread. First is the size of the trading volume for the issue. Generally, the greater the trading volume, the lower the spread. The second factor is the number of bonds that you are considering buying or selling. For example, the dealer's spread for $2 million of an issue (2,000 bonds with a par value of $1,000) will be substantially less than the dealer's spread for a transaction involving $2,000 (two bonds with a par value of $1,000). The easiest and most direct way to learn the size of the dealer's spread for the number of bonds you are considering acquiring is to ask a broker-dealer to tell you the bid price and asked price.

The greater the marketability of an issue, the more investors are willing to pay for an issue. This translates into a lower potential yield relative to otherwise comparable bonds.

Tax Factors

Tax aspects also influence yield spreads. Although the subject of taxes will be covered in the next chapter, here we focus our attention on the federal taxation of interest income. The interest income from Treasury and corporate debt obligations are subject to federal income taxes. This is not true for the interest income from state and local government debt, commonly called *municipals*. Because interest income on municipals is exempt from federal income taxes, investors are willing to accept a lower yield than that on otherwise comparable taxable debt obligations. Consequently, yields on municipals are lower than that on taxable debt obligations.

Call Protection

In the previous chapter we explained that one of the provisions in the contract between the issuer and the bondholder might be that the issuer will have the right to redeem all or part of the issue before the maturity date. This provision is referred to as a call provision. It is an advantage to the issuer but a disadvantage to the investor since issuers will call an issue when market yields have declined and force the investor to reinvest the proceeds at the prevailing lower yield.

To induce investors to purchase a callable bond when it is first offered, the issuer must offer a yield above that of otherwise comparable noncallable bonds. After the initial offering, a callable bond will continue to be priced so that its yield is greater than that of noncallable bonds that are otherwise comparable. How much of a premium investors will require for accepting the risk that a particular issue will be called depends on investors' expectations of the level of future interest rates in comparison to the coupon rate. If investors expect interest rates to decline sufficiently below the coupon rate so that the issuer will find it beneficial to call the issue, they will demand a substantial premium over the yield on otherwise comparable noncallable bonds. On the other hand, if interest rates are expected to rise, or not fall appreciably below the coupon rate on the issue, the yield premium will be negligible. Consequently, the higher the coupon rate, the more likely it is that interest rates will fall below the coupon rate and the greater the risk that the issue will be called.

Maturity and the Yield Curve

Default risk, marketability, taxation, and call protection, however, still do not reveal the whole story of yield spreads. For example, why do Treasury obligations selling at par value produce different yields even though they are all riskless, may have the same call protection, and have the same marketability? The explanation for such spreads largely lies in the *yield curve.*

Investors value liquidity and are willing to pay for it by accepting reduced yield. For reasons explained in the previous chapter, a security's liquidity is greater (lower price volatility) the shorter its current maturity. Therefore, short coupons and money market instruments normally yield less than long coupons. As noted in Chapter 3, if we plot the relationship between maturity and yield for securities on which the risk of default is identical, we get a *yield curve.* Exhibit 7–1 is an example of a yield curve on November 29, 1984, for Treasury securities; new-issue, A-rated public utilities; and new-issue, A-rated industrial bonds. Notice that the yield curve is *upward sloping.*

Although the yield curve is normally upward sloping, it does not have to be that way. As noted in earlier chapters, investors' and borrowers' expectations with respect to where interest rates are headed also influence the shape of the yield curve. If the general expectation is that interest rates are going to rise, investors will seek to keep their

EXHIBIT 7-1   Yield Curve—November 29, 1984

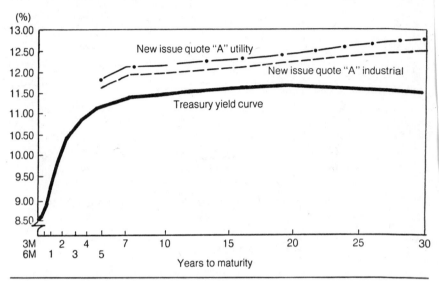

SOURCE: Paine, Webber Fixed Income Research.

money in short coupons to avoid getting locked into low-yield long bonds. Borrowers, on the other hand, will try to lengthen the maturity of their outstanding debt in order to lock in prevailing low rates for as long as possible. Both responses tend to force short-term rates down and long-term rates up, thereby accentuating the slope of the yield curve. Consequently, when the yield curve is upward sloping, longer-term bonds will yield more than otherwise comparable shorter-term bonds.

People, of course, can expect interest rates to fall. When this is the case, investors respond by buying long coupons in the hope of locking in a high yield. In contrast, borrowers are willing to pay extremely high, short-term rates while they wait for long rates to fall so that they can borrow long-term more cheaply. The net result of both responses is that when interest rates are expected to fall, the yield curve (or at least some part of it) may be inverted, with short-term rates above long-term rates. Exhibit 7–2 depicts the yield curve on September 3, 1981, when people anticipated a fall in rates. Note that for the Treasury yield curve, after a current maturity of approximately one year is reached, the slope of this curve becomes sharply negative.

EXHIBIT 7–2   Yield Curve—September 3, 1981

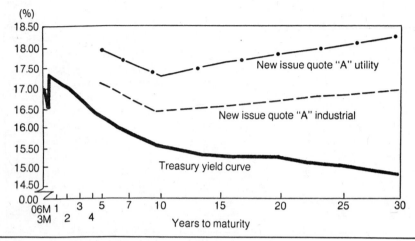

SOURCE: Paine, Webber Fixed Income Research.

If, inspired by our yield curves, you start poring over dealer quote sheets on governments, you are bound to discover some very out-of-line yields. The reasons for this are varied.[2] At the short end of the market, yields on certain issues may be low relative to others because these issues mature on a tax or dividend date when corporations need cash. In the case of Treasury note issues, those with $1,000 minimum denomination are actively bid for by small investors and therefore tend to yield less than similar issues with higher minimum denominations. Also some government bonds (*flower bonds* to the trade) are acceptable at par in payment of federal estate taxes when owned by the decedent at the time of death. These bonds, which all currently sell at substantial discounts, have yields much lower (2, 3, or 4 percentage points depending on maturity) than those on straight government bonds.[3]

---

[2]One trivial reason may be a mistake in the quote sheet. These are typically compiled daily in great haste with the result that errors do creep in. For this reason, such sheets often have a footnote disclaimer to the effect that the quotes are believed to be reliable but are not "guaranteed."

[3]Flower bonds are discussed in more detail in Chapter 9.

THE REINVESTMENT RATE

In Chapter 6 we introduced the idea of yield to maturity. For any bond, yield to maturity gives the average, annual rate of return earned through coupon interest *and* changes in capital value on *the funds initially invested* in the bond, assuming the bond is held to maturity. On coupon securities, yield to maturity does *not* normally measure the rate of growth of the combined value of principal invested plus interest received, that is, the rate of growth of the investor's capital.

To see why, let's work through a quick example. Suppose an investor puts $1,000 into a 2-year bond that has an 8% coupon and pays interest annually, to keep things simple. At the end of the first year, the investor gets $80 of interest. At the end of the second year, he gets $1,080—$1,000 of principal and $80 of interest. If he spends the first $80 of interest, then at the end of the 2-year period, he will be left with $1,080. The average annual rate of growth of his capital will have been 3.92%, even though yield to maturity on his bond was and is 8%. Alternatively, if he reinvests the first $80 of interest in a 5% savings account, at the end of the 2 years he will have $1,164, and the average annual rate of growth of his capital will be 7.89%. To get an annual average rate of growth of capital equal to 8%, he must *reinvest* his first $80 of interest at 8%; in that case at the end of the 2 years he will have $1,166.40. Note also that if our investor manages to reinvest his first $80 of interest at a rate above 8%, then the average annual rate of growth of his capital will exceed 8% by a small margin.

All this would be interesting but not of vital importance to an individual choosing which bond to invest in, if bonds all sold at par; but that is not the case. When interest rates rise, seasoned low-coupon bonds fall to a discount; and when interest rates fall, seasoned high-coupon bonds rise to a premium. Thus an individual buying a bond at a given point in time is likely to face a choice between a variety of bonds, all offering similar yields to maturity but selling at quite different prices. In this case the question arises: *in terms of rate of capital growth,* what is the better buy—a bond selling at a discount, a bond selling at par, or a bond selling at a premium? The answer hinges on the probable *reinvestment rate.*

To illustrate, let's assume that the investor, *who is interested in growth of capital and who consequently plans to reinvest coupon interest,* is faced with a choice between (1) a new-issue, 20-year, noncallable bond offered at par with an 11% coupon and (2) a seasoned, noncallable bond with a current maturity of 20 years that carries a 5% coupon and is currently selling for 51.86 (which implies an 11% yield to maturity). Suppose that this investor believes that interest rates will, on average, be lower in the future, perhaps substantially lower. In which bond should he invest?

Since our investor is interested in the growth of capital, he should, in choosing between the two bonds, focus on the dollar sum to which his capital *plus* accumulated interest earnings will grow at the end of the 20-year investment period. This sum, known as his investment's *future value,* will equal (1) the principal repayment he will receive at maturity *plus* (2) accumulated coupon interest *plus* (3) interest on coupon interest *at the reinvestment rate.* Clearly, to determine which bond offers the greater future value per dollar invested, our investor has to make some assumption as to the probable reinvestment rate.

Suppose that our investor concludes, after a careful study of inflation rates, government policy, and economic trends, that he will probably be able to invest any interest he receives at 8% on the average. He works with a single 8% figure, not because he expects the reinvestment rate will be a steady 8% but because he can't realistically hope to predict semiannual ups and downs in interest rates for 20 years.

Then, assuming for the moment that no taxes are imposed on interest income or capital gains, the future value of each $100 he invests today in the 11% bond is $627.52. In contrast, the future value of $100 invested today in the 5% bond is $648.78, a significantly larger figure. Moreover, the future value of $100 invested today in a 2.5% bond having a current maturity of 20 years and priced to yield 11% to maturity would be $687.08, almost 10% more than the future value of $100 invested in the 11% coupon. The differences in future value occur because the higher the coupon on the bond purchased, the more interest the investor will receive and the more he will have to reinvest at the relatively low 8% reinvestment rate.

The clear lesson of our example is that *when the anticipated reinvestment rate is less than current bond yields, a high-coupon bond selling at par is a poorer buy than a deep-discount bond.* A bond selling at a premium (one with an 11 + % coupon in our example) would be an even worse buy. To complete our example, note that if our investor had been able to capture an 11% reinvestment rate, the future value of $100 invested in *any one* of the bonds available to him would have been $851.33, a substantially larger sum than that obtained on any of these bonds when only an 8% reinvestment rate is available.

Effect of Taxes on Yield

The above example neglects taxes.[4] If our investor is holding an issue on which interest income is taxable, tax payments will reduce the amount of coupon interest he has available to reinvest. (Whether the investor uses other funds to pay taxes on bond interest is irrelevant, since doing so reduces his ability to invest the funds available to him from other sources.) In the case of discount issues, taxes on capital gains will decrease the future value of any sum invested by the amount of the taxes that have to be paid on the capital gain realized at maturity.

To see just how taxes affect our example above, let's assume that our taxpayer faces a 30% marginal tax rate. On an investment in the 11% coupon, taxes on interest would reduce the future value of a $100 investment to $469.26. In the case of the 5% coupon, taxes on interest and on the capital gain realized at maturity would reduce the future value of $100 invested today to $498.79. With no taxes on interest or capital gains, the future value of $100 invested in the discount bond exceeds by 3.5% the future value of $100 placed in the 11% bond. When taxes are taken into account, the differential widens to 6.18%. *Obviously the greater the investor's marginal tax rate, the greater the inherent advantage of market-created, deep-discount bonds when the reinvestment rate is low; also the greater the disadvantage of bonds selling at a premium.*

By market-created, deep-discount bond we mean a bond that was originally sold at or near par and has subsequently declined to a deep discount because of a dramatic rise in interest rates. *Original-issue, deep-discount bonds,* on the other hand, are sold at a deep discount when issued. We shall discuss these bonds in the next section. When we discuss taxes in the next chapter, we shall see why there is an inherent disadvantage to certain original-issue, deep-discount bonds the greater the investor's marginal tax rate.

The extra advantage that the market-created, deep-discount security offers when taxes are taken into account results from two factors. First, taxes have to be paid yearly on the coupon interest received

---

[4]The obvious and not so obvious ins and outs of taxation on bond income are discussed in the next chapter.

from either bond. However, the increases that occur in the value of the discount bond as it approaches maturity are not taxed until the bond matures and these gains are realized. Thus, the discount bond acts as a sort of tax shelter, postponing taxes on one element of the discount bond's overall yield until the bond matures. The second advantage of the discount bond is that the portion of its overall yield that comes in the form of a capital gain is taxed at the lower capital gains rate.[5]

The projected reinvestment rate could of course exceed the current yield on bonds. In that case it is the high-coupon bond that has the advantage, assuming that interest on the bond is tax exempt. If interest on the bond is not tax exempt, then the higher the tax bracket of the investor, the smaller the advantage of investing in the high-coupon bond, even when the anticipated reinvestment rate is high. In fact, in the latter situation for the high-tax-bracket investor, the market-created, deep-discount bond may still be the better buy. (If fine calculations of this sort seem worthwhile to you, given your situation, be prepared to buy an electronic calculator preprogrammed to make bond yield calculations.)

ORIGINAL-ISSUE, DEEP-DISCOUNT BONDS

The implication of the discussion of the reinvestment rate is that the yield to maturity measure of a bond's potential return is meaningful only if the entire coupon payment can be reinvested at a yield equal to the yield to maturity. When interest rates are high and are expected to fall, it is unlikely that coupon payments can be reinvested at the prevailing yield to maturity. The problem of reinvesting the coupon payment at an interest rate equal to the yield to maturity is reduced by buying market-created, deep-discount bonds.

When interest rates were at an historic high, professional money managers became much more aware of the reinvestment problem. At the same time, the cost of borrowing for issuers of even the highest quality rating was expensive. To reduce the cost of borrowing to issuers, investment bankers designed issues to make them more attractive to investors. One of these innovations was the *original-issue, deep-discount bond,* which are bonds that (when initially issued) carry a

---

[5]At this writing, Congress is considering tax legislation that will eliminate the preferential tax treatment afforded certain types of capital gain.

coupon interest rate that is considerably less than the prevailing yield to maturity. As a result, these are offered at a deep discount from par value.

The first original-issue, deep-discount bonds offered by a corporation in the U. S. came from Martin Marietta Corporation.[6] Its 7% coupon, 30-year bonds were offered to the public in March 1981 at a price equal to $53.835 per $100 of par value for a yield to maturity of 13.25%. Originally, the company planned to sell only $150 million of the bonds; however, the popularity of the offering made Martin Marietta's management increase the size of the offering from $150 to $175 million.

Later that month, General Motors Acceptance Corporation became the first high-grade finance company to offer original-issue, deep-discount bonds. Other corporate issuers quickly jumped on the bandwagon. According to The First Boston Corporation, an investment banking firm, in the first 5 months of 1982 approximately 40%, or $4 billion, of all new issues of publicly sold corporate bonds were original-issue, deep-discount bonds.[7]

To get some idea of the cost savings of this type of financing to the issuer, consider two issues offered by Archer Daniels Midland Company on May 12, 1981. Both issues matured on May 15, 2011, and were given the same investment grade quality rating by Moody's. The original-issue, deep-discount bonds, which carried a 7% coupon rate, were priced at $46.25 per $100 of par value to offer a yield to maturity of 15.35%. The other issue was a 16% coupon bond that was sold slightly below par to offer a yield to maturity of 16.08%. Thus, the original-issue, deep-discount bond was sold at a cost savings of .71 percentage points (71 basis points).

Zero-Coupon Notes and Bonds

The ultimate in corporate original-issue, deep-discount securities was brought to the public marketplace on April 22, 1981. J. C. Penney Company, Inc. issued $200 million of notes due May 1, 1989. The

---

[6]There were new offerings of moderate discount bonds sold prior to the Martin Marietta issue.

[7]Edward P. Foldessy and Jill Bettner, "Tax Break Involving 'Zero-Coupon' Bonds Is Attacked by Treasury, Backed by Issuers," *The Wall Street Journal,* May 19, 1982, p. 56.

issue, which did not carry any coupon interest at all, gave birth to the innovation called *zero-coupon securities.* The J. C. Penney zero-coupon notes were offered at a price of $33.427 per $100 of par value, which meant a 14.25% yield to maturity. The holder of this note receives the entire interest at maturity as measured by the difference between the redemption value of $100 and $33.427.

Today, there are many types of zero-coupon notes and bonds available to the investor. In addition to the zero-coupon securities issued by corporations, there are various types of zero-coupon securities issued by municipalities, commonly referred to as *compound interest bonds* or *municipal multipliers.* These are discussed in Chapter 11. Although the Treasury has not issued zero-coupon obligations, there are zero-coupon instruments in which a U.S. Treasury obligation is the underlying obligation. These are discussed in Chapter 9.

The primary advantage of a zero-coupon obligation is that the investor is not faced with the problem of reinvesting the coupon payments at an interest rate less than the yield to maturity when the bond is purchased. Therefore, assuming that an investor holds the security until maturity and the issuer does not default, the pre-tax yield to maturity is the yield to maturity at purchase. While the problem of coupon reinvestment is reduced with original-issue, deep-discount bonds with mini-coupon payments and market-created, deep-discount bonds, it is not eliminated. With zero-coupon notes and bonds it is eliminated.

Along with the advantages of zero-coupon notes and bonds come the disadvantages that investors should recognize. First, as we will explain in the next chapter, the federal income tax law requires that the owner of a zero-coupon note or bond must pay taxes that accrue each year even though no interest is actually paid. This means that there is a negative cash flow from holding a zero-coupon note or bond. Because of this, zero-coupon securities should be purchased only for portfolios in which no taxes must be paid, such as IRA and Keogh plans, and by individuals who are faced with very low marginal tax rates.

A second disadvantage is that zero-coupon securities have greater price risk than coupon bonds of the same current maturity—the result is poor liquidity. This follows from our discussion in the previous chapter that the lower the coupon rate, the greater the price volatility. You can't buy a note or bond with a coupon rate lower than zero! This is not a problem if an investor plans to hold the issue to maturity. On the other hand, the greater price volatility of zero-coupon securities compared to otherwise comparable coupon securities makes them attractive for an investor who wishes to speculate on the movement of interest rates.[8]

Because there is no problem with the reinvestment of coupon payments, at certain times and for certain issuers some investors may be willing to pay more for a zero-coupon security than otherwise comparable coupon securities. This action drives up the price of these securities and lowers their yield. Thus, the third disadvantage of investing in zero-coupon securities is that there is a potential sacrifice of yield. This also applies to market-created, deep-discount bonds and mini-coupon, original-issue, deep-discount bonds.

Finally, remember that when a zero-coupon security is purchased, the yield is locked in over the maturity of the obligation. If interest rates go down, that locked-in yield will look good. However, if interest rates go up, the investor is stuck with what may be an unattractive yield.

FLOATING-RATE AND ADJUSTABLE-RATE NOTES

So far we've discussed notes and bonds that have a coupon rate that is fixed until the maturity date or, in the case of zero-coupon securities, make no periodic coupon payments. With floating-rate notes and adjustable-rate notes, the coupon rate changes at prescribed intervals of time. The new coupon rate is based on the interest rate on a predetermined investment medium, such as the average yield on a category of Treasury obligations. Another feature of some floating-rate notes and adjustable-rate notes is that an option is granted to the investor to require the issuer to redeem the issue at par prior to maturity. This option is referred to as a *put* option. Some issuers allow the investor to "put" the issue only at prescribed times; others allow the investor to put the issue at any time. The advantage of the put feature is that the issue will trade around par value despite a rise in market interest rates since the investor could sell the notes back to the issuer at par, even if the market price is less than par.

Floating-rate notes first hit "the Street" with a flourish in 1974 when Citicorp (the holding company behind the First National City Bank of New York, now Citibank) sold $650 million of them, largely

---

[8]Strategies for speculating in bonds are discussed later in this chapter.

to small investors. This innovative issue was greeted with a great deal of enthusiasm and was rapidly imitated by other corporate issuers, financial and nonfinancial. The reason for investors' enthusiasm was that interest rates had been and were still rising rapidly at the time of the issue, with the result that many investors expected to get a minimum of a 10% return for a long time. Instead, rates started dropping in the fall of 1974 and the 10% initial return on early issues soon shrank to 7% and less. For many investors who bought floating-rate notes in 1974 and hung on to them, the investment was a big mistake. By buying fixed-rate, intermediate debt obligations they could have locked up high coupon rates for a number of years and thereby done better.

Because of a lack of investor interest, only a few floating-rate issues were issued by domestic corporations between 1974 and 1979. By the 1980s, however, a new generation of floating-rate notes were created. These differed from those issued earlier in that many had the put feature and had more frequent coupon adjustments. Financial institutions found floating-rate notes particularly attractive because these investments more closely matched the floating-rate nature of some of their liabilities. The new generation of floating-rate notes were also viewed as more defensive holdings because of their reduced price volatility and because they provided an enhanced short-term return.

Adjustable-rate notes also have a coupon rate that changes periodically, the distinguishing features being the benchmark upon which the coupon is based and the frequency with which the coupon rate is changed. The term floating-rate notes means that the coupon rate is based on some short-term interest rate index and the coupon rate changes more than once a year. Although there is no uniform investment vehicle to which floating-rate notes are pegged, the most common benchmarks for notes issued by U.S. corporations are the prime rate, commercial paper rate, 91-day Treasury bill auction rate, 3-month Treasury bill secondary market rate, 6-month Treasury bill auction rate, 6-month Treasury bill secondary market rate, 3-month London Interbank Offer Rate (LIBOR), and the 12-month LIBOR.

The term adjustable-rate or variable-rate notes is generally reserved for issues with a coupon rate that is based on a longer-term index; moreover, the coupon rate is redetermined no more than once a year. For example, in November 1980 General Motors Acceptance Corporation sold a 10-year adjustable-rate note with a coupon rate fixed at 13.45% for two years but adjusted annually thereafter. The adjustable coupon rate is pegged to the rate available on 10-year Treasury obligations.

There are issues that do not fall neatly into either the floating-rate or adjustable-rate category. An example of such an issue is the Gulf Oil Corporation Variable/Fixed Rate Debentures due June 1, 2009. The benchmark for this issue is a long-term Treasury obligation. However, the coupon rate is set twice a year. There is also another interesting feature of this issue. If certain conditions are met, the issue will automatically become a fixed-rate obligation with a coupon rate of 8.375%. This feature is known as a "drop/lock" feature.[9]

Advantages and Disadvantages of Floating-rate Notes

Investors who anticipate that interest rates over a particular period of time will be higher on average than they are today will find floating-rate notes attractive. Floating-rate notes that have a put feature and frequent resetting of the coupon rate can be viewed as short-term investments and, therefore, competitive with money market funds (described in Chapter 5) and rolling over T bills and commercial paper.

There is no definite answer as to whether an investment in floating-rate notes will provide an investor with a yield that is better or worse than alternatives such as investing in a fixed-rate intermediate-term security or rolling over funds in short-term high-quality instruments. As we noted earlier, investors would have been better off in 1974 investing in fixed-rate intermediate-term securities rather than floating-rate notes. However, consider a person who had funds to invest on January 1, 1980, for five years until December 31, 1984. Based on an index constructed by Ryan Financial Strategy Group, an investment in floating-rate notes would have outperformed a strategy of investing in 6-month CDs and rolling them over every 6 months and a strategy of buying a 5-year Treasury security.

SPECULATING IN BONDS

Most people tend to think of the bond market as a rather staid place for investors whose principal concern is preservation of capital. This is the case most of the time, especially in long coupons. However, the bond market also gets its share of speculation.

---

[9]Richard S. Wilson, "Domestic Floating Rate and Adjustable Rate Debt Securities," in *Floating Rate Instruments: Characteristics, Valuation, and Portfolio Strategies,* ed Frank J. Fabozzi (Chicago, Ill.: Probus Publishing, 1986).

Buying Bonds on the Margin

A lot of speculation in securities involves either short sales or margin purchases. For example, an investor who expected interest rates to rise and bond prices consequently to fall, might be tempted to short bonds. If interest rates did fall substantially and rapidly, he would make money doing so. In practice, however, shorting bonds is rarely done by small investors. One reason is that borrowing small quantities of the securities shorted might prove difficult. A second and more compelling consideration is that shorting bonds is an expensive form of speculation because the short seller has to pay out of his own pocket all coupon interest that accrues during the period that the short sale is outstanding.

While shorting bonds is not common, individual investors can and do buy government notes and bonds on the margin. When interest rates are expected to fall, this form of speculation offers interesting possibilities to those who are willing to accept substantial risk.

Buying bonds on the margin operates much like buying stock on the margin, but in some respects it is more attractive. On purchases of stocks and convertible bonds, the Fed sets margin requirements that vary over time but generally range from 50% on up. On purchases of government bonds, however, the Fed does not and is not authorized to set margin requirements. Individual brokerage houses establish their own in-house margin requirements on purchases of governments, but typically these are quite low, 10% being a common figure. Another advantage of buying bonds on the margin is the low transaction costs. Buying $100,000 of government bonds on the margin might cost $50 in commissions, whereas buying the same amount of stock could easily cost $1,000 in commissions—more or less depending on the price at which the purchased stock was trading. Still another advantage of buying bonds on the margin is that bond prices are likely to start rising at a point in the business cycle when stock prices are still falling, and the classic risky stance—going long in common stocks—is not a promising route to wealth.

To illustrate the speculative gains available by buying bonds on the margin, let's work through an actual example. Suppose that an investor decided in early February 1986 that interest rates were going to decline by at least 150 basis points. Being an individual who acts on his beliefs, he buys on the margin $100,000 of 7 7/8 Treasury bonds maturing in February 2000. The bonds are priced at 89.625 (asked price), so his purchase price costs $89,625 ($100,000 × .89625); he also has to pay about $3,280 in accrued coupon interest from the last coupon payment of August 18, 1985, to the time of purchase. However, the accrued interest will be recovered in about 2 weeks when the February 18, 1986, coupon payment is made. A commission of $50 must also be paid. To buy the bonds, our investor puts down 10% of the purchase price ($8,963 = $89,625 × .10) plus accrued interest plus the purchase commission. He borrows the remaining principal ($80,622 = $89,625 − $8,963). Two and a half months later interest rates have, in fact, fallen and yield to maturity on our investor's bond has declined from 9.21% to 7.36%, which correspond to a rise in price from 89.625 to 102.8125 (bid price). Our investor decides that the time has come to sell out. How has he done?

His $80,622 loan probably would have cost him no more than 11% per annum. This works out to a total interest bill of about $1,849. During the same period, he has recouped the accrued interest he paid to purchase the bonds; in addition, he received 2 weeks in coupon interest in February and about 2 months of coupon interest when he sells the bonds, for a total coupon interest return of about $1,641. Obviously his investment has involved a *negative carry,* to the tune of $208 ($1,641 − $1,849). Our investor, however, was out for big capital gains and he got them—$13,188 worth before commissions. If we throw in a $50 commission on the sale, his total gain after net interest and commissions equals $12,880 ($102,813 minus $50 purchase commission minus $50 sale commission minus $208 in net interest cost minus the purchase price of $89,625). Omitting the accrued interest that had to be paid to purchase the bonds since it was recovered two weeks later, the net gain of $12,880 on an investment of $9,013 translates into a 143% return on investment for a 2½ month period. Had our investor simply purchased the bond for cash, his total dollar return after commissions would have been $1,382 ($10,281 plus $164 coupon interest minus $50 purchase commission minus $50 sale commission minus the $8,963 purchase price); the return on investment would have been 15%. Not bad for a 2 1/2 month return, but nowhere near the 143% return by buying the bonds on the margin.

An investor who is tempted to speculate on a rise in bond prices should bear in mind what was said in Chapter 6 about the volatility of bond prices. The *longer* a bond's current maturity and the *lower* its coupon, the *more* a change in interest rates will cause its price to move. Thus a long-maturity, deep-discount bond is the best medium for speculative margin purchases.

The investor should also bear in mind some of the dangers inherent in this sort of speculation. Falling interest rates will cause the price of his bonds to rise (which is what he is hoping for) *but* rising interest rates will cause their price to fall. The investor can take some small solace from the fact that a 1 percentage point fall in rates will cause his bond to rise in price by slightly more than a 1 percentage point rise in rates will cause it to fall. But still, should the investor miscalculate and buy while interest rates are still rising, he may soon be faced with margin calls, which if not met, will result in his position being sold out at a loss. Moreover, even a small adverse movement in rates would cause a large percentage loss on his investment because debt leverage is going to work as hard against him if rates rise as it does for him when rates fall. The investor should also bear in mind that movements in interest rates and bond prices may be hard to predict.

Junk Bonds

Another way to speculate in the bond market is to buy *junk bonds,* which is "the Street's" familiar term for bonds that have low credit ratings and look risky or that (worse still) are in default.[10] There are both corporate and municipal junk bonds. In the corporate bond market, securities that fall into the junk bond classification are issued by companies that include:

1. Young, growing firms that lack the strong balance sheet profile of many established corporations but often have attractive income statements, adequate financial measurements, and lots of future promise.
2. Companies that have fallen on hard times and may be in default or near default.
3. Established firms whose financial ratios neither measure up to the strengths of investment grade corporations nor possess the weaknesses of companies on the verge of bankruptcy.[11]

On bonds that have begun to look risky but are still paying interest, yields can reach impressive levels. For example, in November 1975, when President Ford said he would veto any bailout for New

---

[10]Junk bonds are classified by "the Street" as debt instruments rated below investment grade (Ba1 and lower by Moody's and BB+ and lower by Standard & Poor's). Bond ratings for municipal and corporate bonds are discussed in Chapters 11 and 12, respectively.

[11]Richard S. Wilson, *High Yield Bonds,* speech to the 1986 Fixed Income Coordinators Seminar, Marlowe, England, April 8, 1986.

York City, tax-exempt Big Mac bonds (Municipal Assistance Corporation of New York) carrying a 9.25% coupon and due in 1990 sank to 72, which implied a yield to maturity of 13%. Or, to take another example, in January 1975, W. T. Grant was obviously a troubled company; as a result, its 4 3/4s of 1987, which were rated Ba, were quoted at 23—a yield to maturity of 26.67%.

Because of these high yields, investors and dealers in junk bonds often refer to such bonds as *high-yield* securities. That sounds more attractive than *junk,* but the latter euphemism in no way alters the fact that junk bonds (*high yielders*) are a risky investment.

The people who buy junk bonds are essentially speculators. They are gambling that the market has undervalued the bonds; that is, that the issuer's condition is not sufficiently bad to warrant the low value placed by the market on its securities or that the issuer's condition is likely to improve perceptibly in the near future.

The junk buyer who guesses right can, of course, make big money. For example, if you had bought Big Mac 9.25% bonds at 72 in November 1975, you would have seen them rise to 81 within 1 month for a gain of 13% (accrued interest not included). In hindsight, buying W. T. Grant bonds in January 1975 would also have been a good idea, since they were up to 41 by July for a 78% gain in value!

Junk, of course, can go down as well as up. It is risky stuff, which is why the yields are so high. W. T. Grant's fortunes, unfortunately, darkened after July 1975, and by November those Grant bonds that were selling at 41 and rated B in July, were in default, rated Caa, and trading flat at 13.

Of course, junk bonds do default. What has been the default experience of bonds? One recent study by Altman and Nammacher found that the average default rate in the 1970 to 1984 period on all publicly issued bonds was .15%.[12] For low rated bonds (junk bonds), the default rate was 2.24%. The same study found that investors were rewarded for accepting the greater default risk. Specifically, Altman and Nammacher found that for the period December 31, 1977, to December 31, 1983, a portfolio of junk bonds would have resulted in an annual compound return spread of over 580 basis points over a portfolio of long-term government bonds. These findings support an earlier study by Hickman which suggested that junk buyers may be right

---

[12]Edward I. Altman and Scott Nammacher, "The Default Rate Experience on High-Yield Corporate Debt," *Financial Analysts Journal,* July–August 1985, pp. 25–41.

on the average.[13] He found that during the period 1900 to 1943, the market tended to consistently *undervalue* corporate bonds at or near the date of default. As a result, investors who bought the bonds at issue and sold at default suffered extremely heavy losses, while investors who purchased at default fared very well on the average.

This, of course, should not be taken to mean that it is necessarily a good idea for you to invest in a couple of issues of junk. Both the Altman-Nammacher and Hickman studies show what happened on the average over many issues. Not every junk bond included in their sample eventually paid more than it traded for at default; and if you buy junk, you might just pick such an issue. At most, these studies suggest that a *diversified* portfolio of junk should do well, assuming that past experience is a good predictor of the future. We suggest that if you want to invest in junk bonds to increase yield, you consider doing so through bond funds so that diversification can be achieved. Bond funds are discussed in Chapter 15.

SUMMARY

In this chapter we have discussed the reasons why the yields on bonds differ—differences in default risk, marketability, taxation, call protection, and current maturity. We also explained a pitfall of the yield to maturity measure that an investor should recognize. If the interest rate at which the coupon payments can be reinvested is less than the yield to maturity, the actual yield that will be realized by the investor will be less than the yield to maturity. The problem of reinvesting the coupon payments can be mitigated by buying market-created, deep-discount bonds or original-issue, deep-discount bonds. A special type of original-issue, deep-discount bond, which completely eliminates the problem of reinvesting coupon payments and thereby locks in the yield to maturity if held to maturity, is the zero-coupon bond. For the investor who expects that interest rates will rise, floating-rate notes with frequent coupon adjustments and a put feature can be purchased as an alternative to money market instruments and money market funds. Two ways of speculating in the bond market are buying bonds on the margin and buying junk bonds.

---

[13]W. Braddock Hickman, *Corporate Bond Quality and Investor Experience* (Princeton, N.J.: Princeton University Press, 1958). For an update of the Hickman study, see John D. Fitzpatrick and Jacobus T. Severiens, "Hickman Revisited: The Case for Junk Bonds," *The Journal of Portfolio Management,* Summer 1978, pp. 53–57.

Federal Income Tax Considerations when Buying and Selling Bonds

8

As we have stressed throughout this book, investors are interested in after-tax, not pre-tax yields. Thus, it is necessary to understand the basic provisions of the tax code in order to make intelligent investment decisions. In this chapter, we walk you through those key provisions.

SOME DEFINITIONS

Gross Income, Adjusted Gross Income, and Taxable Income

Investors often use the term *income* in a very casual way. The Internal Revenue Code (IRC), however, provides a more precise definition of income. The IRC distinguishes between gross income, adjusted gross income, and taxable income. *Gross income* is all income that is subject to income tax. For example, interest income and dividends are subject to taxation. However, there is a statutory exemption for interest from certain types of debt obligations, as explained later in this chapter. For such obligations, interest income is not included in gross income.

Adjusted gross income is gross income minus certain business and other deductions. *Taxable income* is the amount on which the tax liability is determined. It is found by subtracting the personal exemption allowance and other permissible deductions (other than those deductible in arriving at adjusted gross income) from adjusted gross income.

Tax Basis of a Capital Asset, Capital Gain, and Capital Loss

The IRC provides for a special tax treatment on the sale or exchange of a capital asset. Bonds, money market instruments, and shares of bond funds (discussed in Chapter 15) would qualify as capital assets in the hands of a qualified owner. In order to understand the tax treatment of a capital asset, the tax *basis* of a capital asset must first be defined. In most instances the *original basis* of a capital asset is the investor's total cost on the date it is acquired. The *adjusted basis* of a capital asset is its original basis increased by capital additions and decreased by capital recoveries.

The proceeds received from the sale or exchange of a capital asset are compared to the adjusted basis to determine if the transaction produced a capital gain or capital loss. If the proceeds exceed the adjusted basis, the investor realized a *capital gain;* on the other hand, a *capital loss* is realized when the adjusted basis exceeds the proceeds received by the investor.

INTEREST INCOME

Interest received by an investor is included in gross income, unless there is a specific statutory exemption indicating otherwise. Therefore, if an investor purchases $10,000 in face value of a corporate or Treasury bond that has a coupon rate of 12%, the investor expects to receive $1,200 per year. If that amount is actually paid by the issuer in the tax year, it is included in gross income.

Interest received on debt issued by any state or political subdivisions thereof, the District of Columbia, any possession of the U.S., and certain local and urban agencies operating under the auspices of the Department of Housing and Urban Development is not included in gross income.

Interest paid on debt issued by the U.S. government is exempt from income taxation by state and local governments but not from federal income taxes. Interest income by U.S. territories, the District of Columbia, and certain local urban agencies operating under HUD is also exempt from all state and local income taxes. Most states exempt the interest income from its own debt obligations, its agencies, and its political subdivisions from its state and local income taxes. States may exempt the interest income from obligations of other states and political subdivisions. State income tax treatment is discussed further in Chapter 11.

A portion of the income realized from holding a bond may be in the form of capital appreciation, rather than interest income. The tax treatment of the income component that represents capital appreciation differs depending on when the bond was issued. Prior to the The Deficit Reduction Act of 1984, any capital appreciation that did not represent original-issued discount (to be discussed later) was generally treated as a capital gain. As explained later in this chapter, at the time of this writing, the IRC provides for favorable tax treatment for certain capital gains. The 1984 act still allows this tax treatment for bonds issued on or prior to July 18, 1984; however, for bonds issued after that date, part of the capital appreciation will be treated as ordinary income. The tax treatment of income from holding a bond will have a major impact on the after-tax return realized by an investor. Because of the importance of distinguishing between income in the form of a capital gain (or loss) and interest income, the investor must be familiar with certain rules set forth in the IRC. These rules are given later in this chapter.

Accrued Interest

Usually, bond interest is paid semiannually. As we explained in Chapter 6, the interest earned by the seller from holding the bond until the disposal date is called *accrued interest*. For example, if a corporate bond whose issuer promises to pay $60 on June 1 and December 1 for a specified number of years is sold on October 1, the seller is usually entitled to accrued interest of $40 ($60 × 4/6) for the 4 months that the seller held the bond.

Let us look at the tax position of the seller and the buyer, assuming that our hypothetical bond is selling for $900 in the market and that the seller's adjusted basis for this bond is $870. The buyer must pay the seller $940, $900 for the market price plus $40 of accrued interest. The seller must treat the accrued interest of $40 as interest income. The $900 is compared to the seller's adjusted basis of $870 to determine whether the seller has realized a capital gain or capital loss. Obviously, the seller has realized a capital gain of $30. When the buyer receives the December 1 interest payment of $60, only $20 is included in gross income as interest income. The basis of the bond for the buyer is $900, not $940.

Not all transactions involving bonds require the payment of accrued interest by the buyer. As explained in Chapter 6, such bonds are quoted flat. This occurs when the issuer of the bond is in default of principal or interest or the interest on the bonds are contingent on sufficient earnings of the issuer. The acquisition price entitles the buyer to receive the principal and unpaid interest for both past scheduled payments due and accrued interest. Generally, for bonds quoted flat, all payments made by the issuer to the buyer are first considered as payments to satisfy defaulted payments or unpaid contingent interest payments and accrued interest before acquisition. Such payments are treated as a return of capital. As such, the proceeds reduce the cost basis of the bond. On the other hand, accrued interest after the acquisition date is considered interest income when received.

For example, suppose the issuer of a corporate bond is in default of two scheduled interest payments of $60 each. The interest payments are scheduled on April 1 and October 1. The bond is sold for $500 on August 1. Assume that on October 1 of the year of acquisition the issuer pays the bondholder $120. The buyer would treat the payment as a return of capital of $120, since it represents the two defaulted interest payments. Hence the adjusted basis of the bond is $380 ($500 − $120) and is not considered interest income. Suppose that two weeks later the issuer pays an additional $60 to the bondholder. This payment must then be apportioned between accrued interest before the acquisition date of August 1 and accrued interest after the acquisition date. The latter is $20, since the bond was held by the buyer for 2 months. Thus $40 of the $60 payment reduces the adjusted basis of $380 prior to the second payment to $340 and is not treated as interest income. The $20 of accrued interest since the acquisition date is treated as interest income.

Bond Purchased at a Premium

When a bond is purchased at a price greater than its redemption value at maturity, the bond is said to be purchased at a premium. For a taxable bond purchased at a premium, the investor may elect to amortize the premium ratably over the remaining life of the security. In the case of a convertible bond selling at a premium, however, the amount attributable to the conversion feature may not be amortized. The amount amortized reduces the amount of the interest income that will be taxed. In turn, the basis is reduced by the amount of the amortization.

For a tax-exempt bond, the premium *must* be amortized. Although the amount amortized is not a tax-deductible expense since the interest is exempt from taxation, the amortization reduces the original basis.

For example, suppose on January 1, 1981, an investor purchased *taxable* bonds for $10,500. The bonds have a remaining life of 10 years and a $10,000 redemption value at maturity. The coupon rate is 7%. The premium is $500. The taxpayer can amortize this premium over the 10-year remaining life. If so, the amount amortized would be $50 per year ($500 ÷ 10).[1] The coupon interest received of $700 ($10,000 × .07) would then be effectively reduced by $50 so that $650 would be reported as interest income. At the end of 1981, the first year, the original basis of $10,500 is reduced by $50 to $10,450. By the end of 1985 the bond would be held for 5 years. The adjusted basis would be $10,250 (10,500 − $250). If the bond is held until retired by the issuer at maturity, the adjusted basis would be $10,000, and consequently there would be no capital gain or loss realized. If the investor does not elect to amortize the premium, the original basis is not changed. Consequently, at maturity the investor would realize a capital loss of $500.

Had our hypothetical bond been a tax-exempt bond, the premium would have had to be amortized. The coupon interest of $700 would be tax exempt, and the amortization of $50 would not be a tax-deductible expense.[2] Instead, the basis would be adjusted each year.

---

[1]There is a method that provides the precise value of the amount that should be amortized each year. This is known as the constant-yield (or scientific) method. However, this method provides lower amortization in the earlier years than the straight-line method of amortization used in the example. Consequently, the straight-line method is preferred for taxable bonds if the taxpayer elects to amortize the premium.

[2]In the case of tax-exempt bonds, the scientific method of amortization would be preferred, since the adjusted basis would be higher than if the straight-line method were used. Consequently there would be a greater capital loss or smaller capital gain if the bonds were sold before maturity.

Bond Purchased at a Discount

A bond purchased at a price less than its redemption value at maturity is said to be bought at a *discount*. The tax treatment of the discount depends upon whether the discount represents *original-issue discount* or a bond that was not sold at an original-issue discount but is purchased in the secondary market at a market discount.

Original-issue Discount Bonds. When bonds are issued, they may be sold at a price that is less than their redemption value at maturity. Such bonds are called original-issue discount bonds. The difference between the redemption value and the purchase price is the original-issue discount. Each year a portion of the original-issue discount must be amortized (accrued) and included in gross income. There is a corresponding increase in the adjusted basis of the bond.

The tax treatment of an original-issue discount bond depends on its issuance date. For obligations issued prior to July 2, 1982, the original-issue discount must be amortized on a straight-line basis each month and included in gross income based on the number of months the bond is held in that tax year. For obligations issued on or after July 2, 1982, the amount of the original-issue discount amortized is based on the constant-yield method (also called the effective or scientific method) and included in gross income based on the number of days in the tax year that the bond is held. With this method for determining the amount of the original-issue discount to be included in gross income, the interest for the year is first determined by multiplying the adjusted basis by the yield at issuance. From this interest, the coupon interest is subtracted. The difference is the amount of the original-issue discount amortized for the year. The same amount is then added to the adjusted basis.

To illustrate the tax rules for original-issue discount bonds, consider a bond with a 4% coupon rate (interest paid semiannually) maturing in 5 years that was issued for $7,683 and has a redemption value of $10,000. The yield to maturity for this hypothetical bond is 10%. The original-issue discount is $2,317 ($10,000 − $7,683). Suppose that the bond was purchased by an investor on the day it was issued, January 1, 198X. First, assume that this hypothetical bond was issued prior to July 2, 1982. The investor is required to amortize the original-issue discount of $2,317 on a straight-line monthly basis. Since there are 60 months to maturity, the prorated monthly interest on a straight-line basis is $38.62 ($2,317 ÷ by 60). Since the hypothetical bond is assumed to be purchased on January 1, the annual interest that must be reported from the amortization of the original-issue discount *each year* is $464 ($38.62 × 12). The total interest reported each year from holding this bond is $464 plus the coupon interest of $400 ($10,000 × .04). Exhibit 8-1 shows the amortization of the original-issue discount for each 6-month period. Notice that, if the bond is held to maturity, there is no capital gain or loss since the adjusted basis will equal the redemption value of $10,000. If the bond is held for 2 years and 6 months, in the third year the investor reports $232 ($38.62 × 6) of interest income from amortization of the original-issue discount. The adjusted basis is $8,844. If the proceeds from the sale of the bond exceed $8,844, the investor realizes a capital gain. A capital loss is realized if the proceeds from the sale are less than $8,844.

Suppose instead that the bond was issued after July 2, 1982. The constant-yield method is used to determine the amortization and the adjusted basis. The procedure is as follows. Each 6 months, the investor of this hypothetical bond is assumed to realize for tax purposes 5% of the adjusted basis. The 5% represents 1/2 of the 10% yield to maturity. The original investment is the purchase price of $7,683. In the first 6 months the bond is held, the investor realizes for tax purposes 5% of $7,683, or $384. The coupon payment for the first 6-month period that the bond is held is $200. Therefore, $184 ($384 − $200) is assumed to be realized (although not received) by the investor. This is the amount of the original-issue discount amortized. The amount that will be reported as gross income from holding this bond for 6 months is $200 in coupon interest plus the $184 of the original-issue discount amortized. The adjusted basis for the bond at the end of the first 6 months will equal the original-issue price of $7,683 plus the amount of the original-issue discount amortized, $184. Thus, the adjusted basis is $7,867.

Let's carry this out for one more 6-month period. If the bond is held for another 6 months, the amount of interest that the investor is expected to realize for tax purposes is 5% of the adjusted basis. Since the adjusted basis at the beginning of the second 6-month period is $7,867, the interest is $393. The coupon interest for the second 6 months is $200. Therefore, the amount of the original-issue discount amortized for the second 6-month period is $193 ($393 − $200). The $393 reported for holding the bond for the second 6 months is $200 in coupon interest and $193 in amortization of the original-issue dis-

---

EXHIBIT 8-1 Amortization Schedule for an Original-issue Discount Bond Issued Prior to July 2, 1982

Characteristics of hypothetical bond:
Coupon	= 4%
Interest payments	= semiannual
Issue price	= $7,683
Redemption value	= $10,000
Years to maturity	= 5
Yield to maturity	= 10%
Original-issue discount	= $2,317
Monthly amortized market discount	
(straight-line method)	= $38.62
6-month amortized market discount	= $232
Basis at time of purchase	= $7,683

		For the Period		
Period Held (years)	Adjusted Basis*	Gross Income Reported	Coupon Interest	Original-issue Discount Amortized
0.5	$ 7,916	$432	$200	$232
1.0	8,148	432	200	232
1.5	8,380	432	200	232
2.0	8,612	432	200	232
2.5	8,844	432	200	232
3.0	9,076	432	200	232
3.5	9,308	432	200	232
4.0	9,540	432	200	232
4.5	9,772	432	200	232
5.0	10,000	432	200	232

---

*Adjusted basis at the end of the period. The adjusted basis is found by adding $232 to the previous period's adjusted basis.

count. The adjusted basis at the end of the second 6-month period is $8,060—the previous adjusted basis of $7,867 plus $193. If this bond, which was assumed to be purchased on January 1, 198X, is sold on December 31, 198X, interest income would be $777, consisting of $400 of coupon interest and $377 of the original-issue discount amortized. If this bond is sold on December 31, 198X, for $8,200, there would be a capital gain of $140, the difference between the sale proceeds of $8,200 and the adjusted basis of $8,060.

Exhibit 8–2 shows the amount of the original-issue discount that must be reported as gross income for each 6-month period that the bond is held and the adjusted basis at the end of the period. Notice that amortization is lower in the earlier years, gradually increasing

---

EXHIBIT 8-2   Amortization Schedule for an Original-issue Discount Bond Issued after July 2, 1982

Characteristics of hypothetical bond:
 Coupon   = 4%
 Interest payments = semiannual
 Issue price   = $7,683
 Redemption value = $10,000
 Years to maturity = 5
 Yield to maturity = 10%
Original-issue discount   = $2,317
Basis at time of purchase = $7,683
Amortization based on constant-yield method

| | | *For the Period* | | |
Period Held (years)	Adjusted Basis*	Gross Income Reported†	Coupon Interest	Original-issue Discount Amortized‡
0.5	$ 7,867	$384	$200	$184
1.0	8,060	393	200	193
1.5	8,263	403	200	203
2.0	8,476	413	200	213
2.5	8,700	424	200	224
3.0	8,935	435	200	235
3.5	9,182	447	200	247
4.0	9,441	459	200	259
4.5	9,713	472	200	272
5.0	10,000	486	200	286

*Adjusted basis at the end of the period. The adjusted basis is found by adding the original-issue discount amortized for the period to the previous period's adjusted basis.
†The gross income reported is equal to the coupon interest for the period plus the original-issue discount amortized for the period.
‡By the constant yield method, it is found as follows:
 (Adjusted basis in previous period × .05) − $200

over the life of the bond on a compounding basis. For the pre-July 2, 1982, rules, the dollar amortization is constant each year. Note also that, if a bond is sold after 2.5 years, the adjusted basis is $8,700 using the constant-yield method but $8,844 (see Exhibit 8–1) using the straight-line method. The constant-yield method results in a greater capital gain.

The 1984 act requires the holders of original-issue discount tax-exempt bonds to amortize the original-issue discount using the constant-yield method. However, the amount of the original-issued discount amortized is not included as part of gross income because all interest is exempt from federal income taxes. The amount of the original-issue discount is added to the adjusted basis.

The original-issue discount rules do not apply to two cases. The first is the case of Series EE savings bonds, which we discuss in Chapter 9. The holders of these bonds may elect to have the original-issue discount on these bonds taxed when the bonds are redeemed rather than having the accrued interest taxed annually. The second exception is for non-interest-bearing obligations such as T bills and other taxable money market instruments that we described in Chapter 4, with no more than 1 year to maturity. When these obligations are held by investors who report for tax purposes on a *cash* rather than an accrual basis, the discount is not recognized until redeemed or sold. However, there are restrictions on the deductibility of interest to carry such obligations, as explained later in this chapter.

There are two more points you should be familiar with when dealing with original-issue discount bonds. First, if an original-issue discount bond is sold before maturity, subsequent holders must continue to amortize the original-issue discount. The second point to keep in mind is that an investor may have to pay taxes on interest included in gross income but not received in cash. *Consequently, original-issue discount obligations are unattractive for portfolios of individual investors subject to taxation.*

Bond Purchased at a Market Discount with no Original-issue Discount. When a bond is purchased at a market discount and there is no original-issue discount, the tax treatment depends on whether the bond was issued on or prior to July 18, 1984, or after. For bonds issued before that date, any capital appreciation is treated as a capital gain. If there is a loss, it is a capital loss. For example, suppose that the hypothetical bond used to illustrate the original-issue discount rules is not an original-issue discount bond. Instead, suppose that the bond was issued 25 years ago at par ($10,000) and 20 years later the price of the bond declined to $7,683 because of a rise in interest rates. If this bond is purchased by an investor for $7,683 and sold 2.5 years later for $9,000, the investor will realize a capital gain of $1,317. No amortization of the discount is required even though a portion of the capital appreciation really represents a form of interest.

The 1984 act changed the tax treatment for *taxable* bonds issued after July 18, 1984. Any capital appreciation must be separated into a portion that is attributable to interest income (as represented by bond amortization) and a portion that is attributable to capital gain.[3] The portion representing interest income is taxed as ordinary income when the bond is sold. This is called *accrued market discount*. Unlike original-issue discount, the amount of the market discount that represents interest income (that is, bond amortization) is not taxed until the bond is sold. Accrued market discount can be determined using either the straight-line method or the constant-yield method.

Exhibit 8–3 shows the tax consequences for 5 assumed selling prices for the hypothetical bond that has been used in the examples above. The results are shown for bonds issued before and after July 18, 1984. The results are also shown for the constant-yield and straight-line methods.

Two implications are evident from Exhibit 8–3. First, from a tax perspective, taxable bonds issued before July 18, 1984, and selling at a discount will be more attractive than bonds issued after that date and selling at a discount. This will be reflected in the market price of those bonds. Consequently, investors that are in low marginal tax rates will find that they may be overpaying for bonds issued before July 18, 1984. The second implication is that it is not in the best interest of the investor to select the straight-line method to compute the accrued market discount because the capital gain will be lower than if the constant-yield method is elected.

Because of the difference in the tax treatment of original-issue discount bonds and market discount bonds, prior to purchase the investor should check the type of bond and when it was issued.

CAPITAL GAIN AND LOSS TREATMENT[4]

Once a capital gain or capital loss is determined for a capital asset, there are special rules for determining the impact on adjusted gross income.

To determine the impact of transactions involving capital assets on adjusted gross income, it is first necessary to ascertain whether the sale or exchange has resulted in a capital gain or loss that is long term or short term. The classification depends on the length of time the capital asset is held by the investor. For capital assets acquired after

---

[3]The elimination of favorable tax treatment for capital gains will render the distinction between capital gains and interest income unimportant.

[4]See note 3.

EXHIBIT 8-3   Tax Treatment of Market Discount Bond for 5
Assumed Selling Prices

Characteristics of hypothetical bond:
   Coupon   = 4%
   Interest payments = semiannual
   Bond price   = $7,683
   Redemption value = $10,000
   Years to maturity = 5
   Yield to maturity   = 10%
Market discount   = $2,317
Basis at time of purchase   = $7,683
Bond sold after 2.5 years

Bond issued before July 18, 1984

Sale Price	Accrued Market Discount	Capital Gain (loss)
$9,500	$ 0	$1,817
9,000	0	1,317
8,700	0	1,017
7,683	0	0
7,000	0	(683)

Bond issued after July 18, 1984, with amortization based on constant-yield method

Sale Price	Accrued Market Discount	Capital Gain (loss)
$9,500	$1,017	$ 800
9,000	1,017	300
8,700	1,017	0
7,683	1,017	(1,017)
7,000	1,017	(1,700)

Bond issued after July 18, 1984, with amortization based on straight-line method

Sale Price	Accrued Market Discount	Capital Gain (loss)
$9,500	$1,161	$ 656
9,000	1,161	156
8,700	1,161	(144)
7,683	1,161	(1,161)
7,000	1,161	(1,844)

June 22, 1984, the general rule is that if a capital asset is held for 6 months or less, the gain or loss is a short-term capital gain or loss.[5] A long-term capital gain or loss results when the capital asset is held for 1 day more than 6 months, or longer. For capital assets acquired before June 22, 1984, the holding period for a long-term capital gain is 1 day more than 1 year.

Second, all short-term capital gains and losses are combined to produce either a *net short-term capital gain* or a *net short-term capital loss*. The same procedure is followed for long-term capital gains and losses. Either a *net long-term capital gain* or a *net long-term capital loss* will result.

Third, an overall *net capital gain* or *net capital loss* is determined by combining the amounts in the previous step. If the result is a net capital gain, the entire amount is added to gross income. However, net long-term capital gains are given preferential tax treatment. A deduction is allowed from gross income in determining adjusted gross income. The permissible, deduction is 60% of the excess of net long-term capital gains over net short-term capital losses.[6] Exhibit 8-4 provides 6 illustrations of the treatment of a net capital gain.

If there is a net capital loss, it is deductible from gross income. The amount that may be deducted, however, is limited to the lesser of (1) $3,000 (but $1,500 for married taxpayers filing separate returns), (2) taxable income without the personal exemption and without capital gains and losses minus the zero bracket amount, and (3) the total of net short-term capital loss plus half the net long-term capital loss. The third limitation is the so-called $1 for $2 rule and is the basic difference between the tax treatment of net short-term capital losses and net long-term capital losses. The former is deductible dollar for dollar, but the latter requires $2 of long-term capital loss to obtain a $1 deduction.

Because of the difference in the tax treatment of net long-term capital losses and net short-term capital losses, the order in which

---

[5]An exception to this general rule applies to wash sales. A wash sale occurs when "substantially identical securities" are acquired within 30 days before or after a sale of the securities *at a loss*. In such cases, the loss is not recognized as a capital loss. Instead, the loss is added to the basis of the securities that caused the loss. The holding period for the new securities in connection with a wash sale then includes the period for which the original securities were held.

[6]A capital gain deduction taken by an individual could result in a minimum tax liability.

EXHIBIT 8-4   Tax Treatment of a Net Capital Gain

			Illustration Number			
	(1)	(2)	(3)	(4)	(5)	(6)
1. Net long-term capital gain (loss)	$35,000	$35,000	$35,000	$ 0	($ 3,000)	($ 8,000)
2. Net short-term capital gain (loss)	(15,000)	15,000	0	15,000	15,000	15,000
3. Net capital gain: Increase in gross income	20,000	50,000	35,000	15,000	12,000	7,000
4. Excess of net long-term capital gain over net short-term capital loss	20,000	35,000	35,000	0	0	0
5. Capital gains deduction (60 percent of line 4)	(12,000)	(21,000)	(21,000)	0	0	0
6. Increase in adjusted gross income (line 3 minus line 5)	8,000	29,000	14,000	15,000	12,000	7,000

these losses are deductible in a tax year are specified by the Treasury. First, net short-term capital losses are used to satisfy the limitation. Any balance to satisfy the limitation is then applied from net long-term capital losses using the $1 for $2 rule. Any unused net short-term or net long-term capital losses are carried over on a dollar-for-dollar basis.[7] When they are carried over, they do not lose their identity but remain either short term or long term. These losses can be carried over indefinitely until they are all utilized in subsequent tax years.

Exhibit 8–5 provides 10 illustrations of the net capital loss deduction rule. In the illustrations it is assumed that taxable income as defined in (2) above is greater than $3,000, and the taxpayer, if married, is not filing a separate return.

DEDUCTIBILITY OF INTEREST EXPENSE INCURRED TO ACQUIRE OR CARRY SECURITIES

Some investment strategies involve the borrowing of funds to purchase or carry securities. Although interest expense on borrowed funds is a tax-deductible expense, the investor should be aware of the following three rules relating to the deductibility of interest expense to acquire or carry securities.

First, there are limits on the amount of current interest paid or accrued on debt to purchase or carry a market discount bond. It is limited by the amount of any income from the bond. Any interest expenses that remain can be deducted in the current year only to the extent that they exceed the amortized portion of the market discount. The amount of the interest expense that is disallowed can be deducted either (1) in future years if there is net interest income and an election is made or (2) when the bond is sold.

To illustrate this limitation, suppose that interest expense incurred to carry a market discount bond is $500 for the current year, the coupon interest from that bond is $200, and the amortized portion of the market discount is $140. The investor is entitled to deduct $200 (the amount of the coupon interest). In addition, since the remaining interest expense of $300 ($500 − $200) exceeds the amortized portion of the market discount of $140 by $160, an additional $160 may be deducted. Thus, the total interest expense that may be deducted in the

---

[7]However, in determining the amount of the net capital loss deduction in a future tax year, the $1 for $2 rule applies.

EXHIBIT 8-5 Tax Treatment of a Net Capital Loss

	(1)	(2)	(3)	(4)	(5)	(6)	(7)	(8)	(9)	(10)
						Illustration Number				
1. Net long-term capital gain (loss)	$ 0	($7,000)	($ 7,000)	($7,000)	($3,000)	($4,000)	$6,000	($4,000)	($12,000)	$ 4,000
2. Net short-term capital gain (loss)	(5,000)	0	(5,000)	(2,000)	(1,000)	0	(7,000)	1,000	2,000	(14,000)
3. Net capital loss	5,000	7,000	12,000	9,000	4,000	4,000	1,000	3,000	10,000	10,000
4. Capital loss deduction*	3,000	3,000	3,000	3,000	2,500	2,000	1,000	1,500	3,000	3,000
5. Long-term capital loss carryover	0	1,000	7,000	5,000	0	0	0	0	3,000	0
6. Short-term capital loss carryover	2,000	0	2,000	0	0	0	0	0	4,000	7,000

*Assumes that the taxpayer (1) is not married or if married is not filing a separate return and (2) has taxable income without the personal exemption and without capital gains and losses minus the zero bracket amount greater than $3,000.

current year is $360. The $140 can be deducted in future years if it does not exceed the limit or when the bond is sold.

There is an exception to the above rule. An investor can elect to have the amortized portion of the market discount taxed each year. In that case, the entire interest expense to purchase or carry the bond is tax deductible in the current year. For example, if an investor elects to include the $140 of amortized market discount as gross income in the current year, he may deduct the $140 as current interest expense.

Second, the IRC specifies that interest paid or accrued on "indebtedness incurred or continued to purchase or carry obligations, the interest on which is wholly exempt from taxes," is not tax deductible. It does not make any difference if any tax-exempt interest is actually received by the taxpayer in the taxable year. In other words, interest expense is not deductible on funds borrowed to purchase or carry tax-exempt securities. The nondeductibility of interest expenses also applies to debt incurred or continued in order to purchase or carry shares of a regulated investment company (e.g., mutual fund) that distributes exempt interest dividends.

Finally, there is also a limitation on investment interest deductions equal to $10,000 plus investment income.

Treasury Notes and Bonds

9

In Chapter 3 we talked about T bills, which are non-interest-bearing, discount securities always issued with an original maturity of 1 year or less. In addition to bills, the Treasury issues marketable notes and bonds that are interest-bearing securities. These are referred to as Treasury coupon securities. Since 1982, zero-coupon securities backed by Treasury securities have been sold. In this chapter, we shall discuss Treasury coupon securities and zero-coupon Treasury derivative securities.

ATTRACTIONS TO INVESTORS

Treasury coupon securities offer the investor several attractive features. Although they yield less than corporate bonds of comparable maturity and coupon, they expose him to zero credit risk. The dealer spreads on Treasury notes and bonds are the smallest in the bond market. Another advantage of Treasury coupon securities is that interest income earned on them is *not* subject to state and local income taxes. A final attraction is the wide range of these securities available.

TREASURY NOTES

Treasury notes are coupon securities that may be issued with a maturity of not more than 10 years but not less than 2 years. Interest is paid semiannually. Notes are available in registered, bearer, and book entry form. When the Treasury wants to encourage individuals to invest in a new note issue, it may set the minimum denomination at $1,000.[1] At other times it sets it at $5,000. Notes are also available in $10,000, $100,000, and $1 million denominations. The note market is a wholesale market, except for sales to individuals and small portfolio managers, who typically buy to hold to maturity. Treasury notes are not callable.

TREASURY BONDS

Treasury bonds have an original maturity of more than 10 years and are issued in registered, bearer, and book entry form. They come in denominations of $1,000, $5,000, $10,000, $50,000, $100,000, and $1 million.[2] The bond market, like the note market, is largely a wholesale market in which institutions buy and sell.

Treasury notes are not callable, but many government bond issues outstanding are callable. Generally, the call date is 5 years before maturity. On old low-coupon issues, the call provision is of small importance, but new high-coupon issues might conceivably be called someday.

U.S. SERIES EE SAVINGS BONDS

Although the focus of this chapter is on marketable Treasury notes and bonds, let's take a quick look at a nonmarketable security issued by the U.S. government that under the right circumstances might be attractive for you. For many years, nonmarketable bonds offered such poor yields relative to other investments that they were not attractive investment outlets. However, to attract investors, the Treasury now offers a nonmarketable bond, the Series EE savings bond, that has several attractive features.

---

[1] The $1,000 denomination has not been available on most Treasury note issues with a maturity of less than 4 years since the latter part of 1974.

[2] The $500 denomination was eliminated on bonds issued after mid-1971.

Series EE bonds pay no coupon interest. Instead, they are purchased for 50% of the face value. The interest rate on the bond is reset every 6 months, each May and November. The interest rate that is set for the next 6 months is equal to 85% of the average yield on 5-year Treasury obligations. There is no ceiling imposed on the interest rate. If the bond is held at least 5 years, you will receive the face value and possible more. The minimum return that you earn if you hold the bond at least 5 years is currently guaranteed to be 7.5%. However, if the average periodically adjusted rate set by the Treasury while you held the bond exceeds 7.5%, the bonds will be redeemed for an amount in excess of the face value. The Treasury compounds the investment at the average adjusted rate to determine the redemption value.

For example, if a Series EE bond was purchased in April 1983, the average annual rate for the first 4 semiannual periods since the time of purchase was 9.77%. The final rate that the Treasury will pay depends on what happens in the last 6 semiannual periods. But in no case can it fall below 7.5%. If a Series EE bond was purchased in June 1983, the average rate for the first 3 semiannual periods was 9.32%.

If you redeem a Series EE bond before the fifth year, you will not receive the guaranteed 7.5% minimum rate nor the average of the periodically adjusted rate. Instead, you will receive a rate of 5.5% compounded semiannually after 1 year, increasing by .25% each 6 months. You can not redeem the bond in the first 6 months, except in an emergency.

In addition to the more competitive yield they now offer, Series EE bonds also have other attractive features. First, they present no default risk. Second, there is no risk that you will receive less than the amount you invested even if interest rates increase. Third, when they are purchased and redeemed there is no commission. (They can be purchased from banks and savings institutions, the Federal Reserve banks or through payroll deduction plans.)

And finally, they offer a tax advantage in addition to the exemption from state and local income taxes offered by any U.S. Treasury security. The advantage is that you have an option as to how the accrued interest earned on the bond will be taxed. The earned interest can be reported annually and thereby taxed annually. Alternatively, tax on the earned interest can be deferred until *you elect* to redeem the bond. You can choose to hold the bond for more than 5 years, accumulating interest at a minimum of 7.5%. This option combined with the tax deferral option allows those nearing retirement to postpone re-deeming the bond until retirement when their marginal tax bracket may be lower.

The Treasury imposes an annual limit on the amount of Series EE bonds that may be purchased by an individual in a calendar year. The limit is $30,000 in *face* amount. This means no more than $15,000 may be invested in a calendar year.

PRICE QUOTATIONS

Exhibit 9–1 is an excerpt from *The Wall Street Journal* showing Trea-sury note and bond price quotations. The coupon rate, year of matu-rity, and month of maturity are indicated in the first 3 columns, re-spectively. When an issue is callable, 2 years will be indicated in the "*Mat.*" column. The first year is the year in which the Treasury may begin to call the issue. The second year is the year of maturity. The *n* appearing after the month indicates that the issue is a Treasury note. The *p* after the month denotes a Treasury note for which nonresident aliens are exempt from withholding taxes.

The bid and asked price quotations are expressed as a percentage of par value. For example, the asked price of the first issue listed in the excerpt on Exhibit 9–1, the Treasury bond that matures April 1992 with a coupon rate of 11¾%, referred to as the "11¾s of April 1992," is 121.27. The "27" following the decimal point represents 27/32, or .84375% of par. For a $10,000 par value, the asked price is $12,184.38 ($10,000 × 1.2184375).

On dealer quote sheets, the decimal form to represent the number of 32ds is not used. Instead, the number of 32ds is shown after a hy-phen. For example, 121 and 27/32 would be expressed as 121-27. A plus sign following the number of 32ds means that 1/64 is added to the price. Exhibit 9–2 gives the decimal equivalent of each 8th, 16th, 32d, and 64th.

The last column, "*Yld.*," is the yield to maturity for a noncallable issue. For an issue that is callable and selling at a discount, the yield to maturity is shown. When the callable issue is selling at a premium over par value, the yield shown is the yield to first call. Yields are based upon the asked price.

The prices quoted in *The Wall Street Journal* are representative midafternoon, over-the-counter quotations supplied by the Federal Reserve Bank of New York City. They are based on transactions of $1

EXHIBIT 9-1 Excerpt from *The Wall Street Journal* Showing Quotations on Treasury Bonds and Notes (Monday, April 14, 1986)

Rate	Mat. Date	Bid	Asked	Bid Chg.	Yld.
11¾s,	1992 Apr	121.19	121.27	+ .13	7.20
13¾s,	1992 May n	131.11	131.15	+ .13	7.26
10⅜s,	1992 Jul p	115.15	115.19	+ .13	7.23
4¼s,	1987-92 Aug	90.20	91.20	+ .12	5.85
7¼s,	1992 Aug	101.14	101.30	+ .9	6.87
9¾s,	1992 Oct p	113.3	113.7	+ .12	7.17
10½s,	1992 Nov n	116.25	117.1	+ .13	7.20
8¾s,	1993 Jan p	108.19	108.23	+ .14	7.10
4s,	1988-93 Feb	90.26	91.26	+ .16	5.45
6¾s,	1993 Feb	98.18	99.18	+ .9	6.83
7⅞s,	1993 Feb	103.30	104.14	+ .10	7.05
10⅞s,	1993 Feb n	119.11	119.15	+ .14	7.22
7⅜s,	1993 Apr p	101.30	102	+ .19	7.01
10⅛s,	1993 May n	115.23	115.27	+ .13	7.23
7½s,	1988-93 Aug	101.6	101.22	+ .13	6.71
8⅝s,	1993 Aug	108.8	108.16	+ .14	7.12
11⅞s,	1993 Aug n	125.26	126.2	+ .15	7.23
8⅝s,	1993 Nov	108.11	108.19	+ .12	7.14
11¾s,	1993 Nov	125.16	125.24	+ .14	7.27
9s,	1994 Feb	110.13	110.21	+ .11	7.20
4⅛s,	1989-94 May	90.16	91.16	+ .8	5.44
13⅛s,	1995 May p	134.20	134.28	+ .12	7.33
8¾s,	1994 Aug	109.13	109.21	+ .16	7.19
12⅝s,	1994 Aug p	132.12	132.20	+ .14	7.33
10⅛s,	1994 Nov	117.20	117.28	+ .19	7.29
11⅝s,	1994 Nov	126.27	127.3	+ .18	7.32
3s,	1995 Feb	90.16	91.16	+ .8	4.16
10½s,	1995 Feb	120.9	120.17	+ 1.5	7.31
11¼s,	1995 Feb p	125.6	125.14	+ .19	7.29
10⅜s,	1995 May	119.28	120.4	+ .12	7.30
11¼s,	1995 May p	125.16	125.24	+ .19	7.32
12⅝s,	1995 May	134.7	134.15	+ .11	7.35
10½s,	1995 Aug p	121.7	121.24	+ .22	7.32
9½s,	1995 Nov p	115.11	115.19	+ .24	7.22
11½s,	1995 Nov	127.31	128.7	+ .7	7.35
8⅞s,	1996 Feb p	111.25	111.29	+ .23	7.17
7s,	1993-98 May	97.3	97.19	+ .20	7.30
3½s,	1998 Nov	90.16	91.16	+ .10	4.39
8½s,	1994-99 May	107.3	107.19	+ .23	7.24
7⅞s,	1995-00 Feb	102.26	103.10	+ .17	7.36
8⅜s,	1995-00 Aug	107.1	107.9	+ .27	7.29
11¾s,	2001 Feb	137.24	138	+ 1.2	7.47
13⅛s,	2001 May	150.3	150.11	+ .31	7.50
8s,	1996-01 Aug	104.15	104.31	+ .30	7.31
13⅜s,	2001 Aug	152.16	152.24	+ 1.1	7.52
15¾s,	2001 Nov	174.9	174.19	+ 1.27	7.54
14¼s,	2002 Feb	160.15	160.23	+ .11	7.59
11⅝s,	2002 Nov	137.25	138.1	+ 1.4	7.56
10¾s,	2003 Feb	130.1	130.9	+ .25	7.54
10¾s,	2003 May	130.3	130.11	+ .27	7.56
11⅛s,	2003 Aug	133.28	134.4	+ .24	7.56

SOURCE: Reprinted by permission of *The Wall Street Journal*,

million or more. Consequently, the prices quoted are not necessarily the price at which an investor can purchase or sell a particular issue.

BUYING AND SELLING TREASURY NOTES AND BONDS

The investor may purchase an outstanding Treasury note or bond in the secondary market or purchase a new issue. Outstanding or seasoned issues may be acquired through banks and brokers. A new issue

EXHIBIT 9-2 Decimal Equivalents

8ths	16ths	32ds	64ths	Decimal Equivalent	8ths	16ths	32ds	64ths	Decimal Equivalent
			1	.015625				33	.515625
		1	2	.031250			17	34	.531250
			3	.046875				35	.546875
	1	2	4	.062500		9	18	36	.562500
			5	.078125				37	.578125
		3	6	.093750			19	38	.593750
			7	.109375				39	.609375
1	2	4	8	.125000	5	10	20	40	.625000
			9	.140625				41	.640625
		5	10	.156250			21	42	.656250
			11	.171875				43	.671875
	3	6	12	.187500		11	22	44	.687500
			13	.203125				45	.703125
		7	14	.218750			23	46	.718750
			15	.234375				47	.734375
2	4	8	16	.250000	6	12	24	48	.750000
			17	.265625				49	.765625
		9	18	.281250			25	50	.781250
			19	.296875				51	.796875
	5	10	20	.312500		13	26	52	.812500
			21	.328125				53	.828125
		11	22	.343750			27	54	.843750
			23	.359375				55	.859375
3	6	12	24	.375000	7	14	28	56	.875000
			25	.390625				57	.890625
		13	26	.406250			29	58	.906250
			27	.421875				59	.921875
	7	14	28	.437500		15	30	60	.937500
			29	.453125				61	.953125
		15	30	.468750			31	62	.968750
			31	.484375				63	.984375
4	8	16	32	.500000	8	16	32	64	1.000000

may be purchased at auction, or through banks and some brokers. An advantage of purchasing an issue in the secondary market is that the investor has a wider choice of maturities; also, the investor may find a discount security that is more attractive than a current issue.

Buying in the Secondary Market

Very little trading in Treasury notes and bonds occurs on organized exchanges. The New York Stock Exchange lists a few issues, and the American Stock Exchange (AMEX) offers odd-lot trading in a few others, but neither exchange moves much volume. The real secondary market is the dealer-made market. In this market, huge quantities of notes and bonds are constantly being traded under very competitive conditions and at very small margins. For the investor, this means that there is always an active liquid market in which to buy and sell outstanding issues.

Since notes and bonds have long maturities, the effect on yield of a small purchase commission is minimal, and avoiding it should not be an important consideration for the investor. An investor who decides to acquire a security with a long current maturity should be sure to get a dealer's quote sheet from a banker or broker and study what is available. An investor should not expect every banker or broker to be keenly aware of what is available or to be necessarily able or willing to advise as to what securities best fit the investor's needs.

Settlement on a round-lot transaction is usually the next business day for coupon issues. In the dealer market round-lot transactions are those involving securities that have a par value of $1 million or multiples thereof. Arrangements for settlement other than the next business day can also be made. For example, "cash" settlement requires settlement the same day, and a "skip-day" settlement delays settlement until 2 business days following the day of trade. Securities that have been auctioned but not yet issued are traded on a when-issued basis. For odd-lot government transactions, settlement is the next business day following the trade.

Buying a New Issue at Auction

For a new issue the cheapest method of acquisition is to buy through auction. To sell new notes and bonds, the Treasury currently relies on auctions carried out by the Federal Reserve System.

Under the *yield-bid* system used to auction notes and bonds, the Treasury announces what amount of securities it is going to issue, when they will mature, and what denominations will be available. Competitive bidders bid yield to 2 decimal points (e.g., 8.53) for specific quantities of the new issue. After bids are received, on the basis of both the bids and the amount it wishes to borrow, the Treasury determines the stop-out bid. It then sets the coupon on the security to the nearest ⅛ of 1 percent necessary to make the average price charged to successful bidders equal to 100.00 or less. Once the coupon on the issue is established, each successful bidder is charged a price (discount, par, or premium) for the securities; the price is determined so that the yield to maturity on a bidder's securities equals the bidder's yield bid. Noncompetitive bids are also accepted for amounts up to $1 million. The noncompetitive bidder pays the average price of the accepted competitive tenders.

There are three ways to ascertain when an issue is coming out: (1) look for an announcement in *The Wall Street Journal* or the financial section of major metropolitan dailies, (2) telephone the Federal Reserve Bank 24-hour information number on scheduled auctions, or (3) request that the Federal Reserve bank in the district in which you reside place your name on its mailing list for note and bond issues.

The Treasury follows a regular schedule for the auctioning of Treasury notes and bonds. Two-year notes are auctioned on a monthly basis, a week or so before the end of each month. The 3-year and 10-year notes and the 30-year bonds are generally auctioned the second month of every quarter (in February, May, August, and November). In the last month of each quarter (in March, June, September, and December), the Treasury usually auctions 4-year and 7-year notes. Typically, the 5-year notes are auctioned after the 3-, 10-, and 30-year Treasuries and before the 4- and 7-year maturities.

Once an issue is announced, an investor can get a good idea of the yield at which it will be sold by consulting quotes on Treasury issues of comparable maturity. Unless something dramatic happens between the announcement and the auction, the yield on comparable securities will be very close to what the investor will get. To submit a competitive or noncompetitive bid, a tender offer must be obtained from a Federal Reserve bank.

If an investor is not in touch with the pulse of the market, the investor's best bet is to submit a noncompetitive bid. By doing so, the investor agrees to accept the average yield and equivalent price based upon the competitive tenders that have been accepted by the Treasury. Usually, the Treasury accepts all noncompetitive tenders; hence the investor does not risk the rejection of the bid by the Treasury, as would be the case in a competitive tender in which too high a yield is specified. Moreover, the investor avoids the risk of bidding a yield that is so low that he will be paying too high a price for the issue (given interest rate conditions prevailing at the time).

Redemption or Sale of Treasury Notes and Bonds

When an issue matures, it can be redeemed at a Federal Reserve bank. There is no service charge for redeeming an issue. Alternatively, an issue may be redeemed through a commercial bank or securities dealer, which may impose a charge. A maturing issue may be used to tender a bid for a new Treasury issue.

The Treasury obligations discussed in this section are marketable securities. Therefore they can be sold prior to maturity at the prevailing market price. The services of a commercial bank or securities dealer are required to sell a security in the secondary market.

FLOWER BONDS

There are a number of Treasury bonds that have a favorable tax treatment for federal estate tax purposes. When tendered for payment of federal estate taxes these bonds are valued at par value regardless of their market price. Thus, if $100,000 of par value of these special bonds is held in an individual's portfolio who has died and the deceased's estate owes $100,000 of federal estate taxes, these bonds can be tendered to satisfy the tax liability. It doesn't make a difference if the market price of the bonds at the time that they are tendered is only $50,000. However, any gain realized at the time of the holder's death is taxed as a capital gain.

These bonds are nicknamed "flower bonds" because they are suggestive of funerals. Flower bonds were issued by the Treasury between 1953 and 1963. The following Treasury issues are flower bonds.

Coupon Rate	Maturity
4¼%	August 15, 1987–92
4	February 15, 1988–93
4⅛	May 15, 1989–94
3½	February 15, 1990
3	February 15, 1995
3½	November 15, 1998

Since these bonds carry a coupon rate between 3 and 4¼%, they sell at a discount (that is, below par). For example, on April 14, 1986, the 3% coupon issue due on February 1995 had an asked price of 91.16 (91 16/32) or 91.50% of its par value. Thus, $100,000 of par value of these bonds had a market value of $91,500 but could be used to satisfy a $100,000 federal estate tax liability. In fact, the only reason for holding flower bonds is for federal estate tax planning purposes. The yields on these bonds reflect this feature and consequently are lower than the yields on similar maturity Treasury bonds. For example, the 10½% coupon issue due in February 1995 was priced to yield 7.31% on April 14, 1986. The flower bond maturing in February 1995 was priced to yield only 4.16%.

The redemption of flower bonds at par value in order to pay federal estate taxes is subject to conditions imposed by the Treasury Department. These conditions include the following:

1. At the time of the decedent's death, the bonds must actually be owned by the decedent.
2. The par value plus accrued interest of the issues tendered may not exceed the amount of the federal estate taxes. When the denomination does exceed the federal estate tax liability, a denominational exchange is permitted.
3. The decedent's representative must submit the securities to the Division of Securities of the Treasury Department at least 3 full weeks before the date credit for redemption is sought.

ZERO-COUPON TREASURIES

In August of 1982, Merrill Lynch, banking on the idea that Treasuries packaged as zeros could lure into long-term government bonds many investors who would not otherwise buy them, came up with an idea of how to do this packaging: buy long bonds, put them into an irrevocable trust with a bank, and issue receipts against all coupon payments and the principal repayment that the Treasury is scheduled to make. Packaging a Treasury long bond this way creates a series of zero-coupon Treasuries, one maturing on every coupon date including the final principal repayment date.

Although the investment vehicles created are not issued by the U.S. Treasury, the obligations of the trust—future coupon payments and principal values—are collateralized by U. S. Treasury securities. Other investment banking firms followed suit by creating their own zero-coupon Treasury derivative securities using the same procedure. For example, in August 1982, Salomon Brothers marketed its "Certificates of Accrual on Treasury Securities" (CATS). The two largest originators are Salomon Brothers (CATS) and Merrill Lynch (TIGRs).

In August 1984, the Treasury announced its Separate Trading of Registered Interest and Principal of Securities (STRIPS) program. This program allows the stripping of designated Treasury issues for purposes of creating zero-coupon Treasury securities. The zero-coupons created are the direct obligations of the U.S. government. The securities would be book entry securities. This means that the securities are not represented by an engraved piece of paper that is sent to the buyer. Instead, evidence of ownership is maintained in computerized records at the Fed. The first STRIPS were offered in February 1985.

In this chapter, the term "zero-coupon Treasuries" refers to the trademarks (such as CATS and TIGRs) and securities resulting from the Treasury's STRIPS program.

As we explained in Chapter 7, zero-coupon notes and bonds have the advantage of eliminating reinvestment risk. That is, you can lock in the yield to maturity at the time of purchase. Since there is no default risk with zero-coupon Treasuries, you can put this investment on automatic pilot—there are no coupons to reinvest and no need to check if the issuer's credit quality has changed. Remember, however, they should only be held in a tax-exempt retirement plan because of the tax disadvantage of zero-coupon instruments discussed in Chapter 8.

Some brokers and financial advisors who have recommended that their clients purchase zero-coupon Treasuries have failed to point out that there is substantial price volatility for long-term zero-coupon Treasuries. For example, according to one story in *The Wall Street Journal* (June 1, 1984) a denizen of Los Angeles purchased about $100,000 of 20-year zero-coupon Treasuries. In 4 weeks, the market value of these securities declined to $78,000. This poor fellow, according to the *Journal,* thought he was buying a money market instrument that didn't fluctuate in value. Although he worked in the real estate area, he claimed he was misled by his broker.

As we explained in Chapters 6 and 7, the lower the coupon rate, the greater the price volatility. And a zero-coupon is the lowest coupon you can get. Consequently, there is more interest rate risk with zero-coupon Treasuries than for conventional Treasury coupon obligations of the same maturity. What is distressing is that there are financial advisors who are not aware of this characteristic of zero-coupon Treasuries. Even one sales manager of a large brokerage firm according to the *Journal* article admitted that she did not realize that zero-coupon Treasuries have greater interest rate risk than conventional Treasuries with similar maturities. That's why we dwelled earlier on the risks associated with investing in bonds. You won't be trapped, for example, by a statement in a promotional piece that states that zero-coupon Treasuries are "one of the safest investments available."

Although zero-coupon Treasuries are still subject to considerable interest rate risk, you may decide that you want to accept that risk. If you plan to hold them in a tax-exempt portfolio until maturity, you won't care about the risk.

One potential disadvantage of a zero-coupon Treasury that you should be aware of is the potential lower yield to maturity compared to coupon Treasury securities. When zero-coupon Treasuries were first issued in August of 1982, the yield to maturity on these investments for maturities of 9 to 10 years was 20 basis points less than that of Treasury coupon issues with the same maturity. This doesn't seem like a high price to pay for the elimination of reinvestment risk. For the longer maturities, however, the yield sacrifice was as much as 1%. However, by May 1, 1985, the yield on 9- to 10-year zero-coupon Treasuries was 25 basis points greater than that on same maturity Treasury issues; for longer maturities the yield gain on zero-coupon Treasuries was as much as 50 basis points. Obviously there was no longer any yield sacrifice for the elimination of reinvestment risk. To the contrary, investors were demanding a higher yield on stripped Treasuries relative to coupon Treasuries of identical maturities.

RISK, RETURN, AND LIQUIDITY

Because of the huge volume of Treasury notes and bonds outstanding and the high level of trading activity in these securities, notes and bonds are extremely liquid in the sense of marketability, although marketability does decrease slightly for very long bonds in which trading is lighter than in other issues and on which dealer's bid-ask spreads are consequently wider.

The investor should be aware, however, that prices of long-term coupons do fluctuate considerably over time (see Chapter 6), which decreases the liquidity or increases the price risk—whichever way you want to put it—of investments in long coupons. In this respect it should also be noted that government securities tend to respond to economic developments with more volatility in price than do those of other long-term securities, such as municipals. This makes sense since changes in Treasury financing needs and switches in Fed policy all have an immediate and direct impact on the market for governments. Also, banks and other institutions that are directly affected by any switch in Fed policy are active participants in the market for governments, making frequent adjustments in their portfolios there. While price risk is high on long-term governments, the risk of default is naturally zero.

Except for periods when a sharp break in interest rates is anticipated and the yield curve is consequently negatively sloped, yield is typically greater the longer the current maturity. Thus notes and bonds generally offer higher returns than bills. A natural question is: How much higher? Since the slope of the yield curve changes over time, it is impossible to give a precise answer to this question. In fact, because of the volatility of rates in recent years, it is impossible to give even meaningful average figures.

While short-term rates sometimes exceed long-term rates, going long-term gives the investor the opportunity to lock in a high yield for a long period of time by buying low coupon Treasuries or, if taxes are not a consideration, zero-coupon Treasuries. Yields on 3-month bills can fall 3 percentage points (300 basis points) in a single month, so for the investor in bills the reinvestment rate can be a great unknown.

An individual for whom long-term securities might be an appropriate investment faces some difficult and important choices with respect to maturity and type of security in which to invest (government, corporate, or municipal). Some of the important considerations with respect to the maturity choice are discussed in Chapter 6.

Federal Government
Agency Securities

$$10$$

The market for securities of federal government agencies and sponsored corporations (known on "the Street" as simply *agencies*), while smaller than that of governments, has, in recent years, become an active and important sector of the bond market.[1] In this chapter, federal agency securities are discussed.

ATTRACTION TO INVESTORS

Federal agencies are attractive to a wide range of investors for a number of reasons. First, most agency issues are backed either *de jure* or *de facto* by the federal government, so the credit risk attached to them is zero or negligible. Second, many agency issues offer the tax advantage that interest income on them, like interest on governments, is exempt from state and local income taxation. A third advantage of many agency issues is good marketability. Note, however, that agency issues are smaller in size than Treasury issues, so they do not have the same degree of marketability Treasury issues do.

---

[1] In this chapter, the securities of federal government agencies and sponsored corporations are simply referred to as federal agency, or just agency, securities.

Normally, agencies trade at some spread to Treasury issues of the same maturity. This spread varies considerably depending on supply conditions and the tightness of money. In recent years, some agency issues with a 2-year maturity have offered investors a yield advantage over governments that ranged from 3 to 87 basis points. For agencies with a 10-year maturity, the yield advantages has ranged from 7 to 134 basis points. Until recently, the spread at which agencies trade in relation to governments appears primarily to have reflected differences in marketability. In recent years, yield spreads between otherwise comparable agencies and governments have reflected the financial problems faced by the agency. For example, in 1985 investors in securities of the Federal Farm Credit System (discussed below) saw the yield on these securities rise substantially above those on governments due to the financial difficulties faced by the system. The spread between 1985 and early-1986 varied with the prospects of congressional approval of a bailout measure for the system.

AGENCY SECURITIES ISSUED

Among the agencies still issuing securities to the public, practices and types of securities issued vary considerably. One can, however, make a few generalizations. Each federal agency establishes a fiscal agent through which it offers its securities, all of which are negotiable. Agency issues are not sold directly to investors by these fiscal agents. Instead they are sold through a syndicate of dealers, who distribute the agency's securities to investors and participate in making a secondary market for these securities.

Agency securities come in varying forms: short-term notes sold at a discount and interest-bearing notes and bonds. Agency bonds are frequently issued with the title *debenture*. Any bond is an interest-bearing certificate of debt. A mortgage bond is a bond secured by a lien on some specific piece of property. A debenture is a bond secured only by the general credit of the issuer.

Interest on agency securities and principal at maturity are usually payable at any branch of the issuing agency, at any Federal Reserve bank or branch, and at the Treasury. Agency bonds are typically not callable.

Like Treasury securities, agency securities are issued under the authority of an act of Congress. Therefore, unlike private offerings, they are exempt from registration with the Securities and Exchange

Commission (SEC). Typically agency issues are backed by collateral in the form of cash, U.S. government securities, and the debt obligations that the issuing agency has acquired through its lending activities. A few agency issues are backed by the full faith and credit of the U.S. A number of others are guaranteed by the Treasury or supported by the issuing agency's right to borrow funds from the Treasury up to some specified amount. Finally, there are agency securities with no direct or indirect federal backing.

Housing Credit Agencies

The major federal agencies still offering securities differ considerably in mission and method of operation, so we have organized our survey of them by function: first the mortgage-related agencies and then the farm credit agencies.

The four major mortgage-related agencies are the Federal Home Loan Banks, the Federal National Mortgage Association, the Government National Mortgage Association, and the Federal Home Loan Mortgage Corporation. Only the first is discussed here. The others are discussed in Chapter 14.

Federal Home Loan Banks. Behind the nation's commercial banks stands the Federal Reserve System, which regulates member banks, acts as a lender of last resort, and otherwise facilitates a smooth operation of the banking system. Behind the nation's S&Ls stands a somewhat similar institution, the *Federal Home Loan Bank System*. The FHLB, created in 1932, is composed of 12 regional banks and a central board in Washington.

S&Ls, savings banks, and insurance companies may all become members of the FHLB system; federally chartered S&Ls are required to do so. Currently about 3,400 S&Ls belong to the FHLB system; these S&Ls hold over 98% of the total assets of all S&Ls in the country.

The Federal Home Loan banks are owned by the private S&Ls that are members of the system, just as the 12 Federal Reserve banks are owned by their member banks. The private ownership, however, is only nominal since the FHLB, like the Fed, operates under federal charter and is charged by Congress with regulating member S&Ls and with formulating and carrying out certain aspects of government policy with respect to the savings and loan industry. Thus the Federal Home Loan banks are in fact an arm of the federal government.

In addition to overseeing member S&Ls, the FHLB also lends to member S&Ls just as the Fed lends to commercial banks. Here, however, the similarity ends. The Fed obtains money to lend to banks at the discount window by monetizing debt. The Federal Home Loan banks have to borrow the money they lend to member S&Ls. Most of the money S&Ls provide to home buyers comes from their depositors. The FHLB lends to member S&Ls primarily to augment this source of funds. In a nutshell, the FHLB borrows money in the open market, then relends it to S&Ls, which in turn either relend it again to home buyers or, in recent years, use it to offset deposit outflows. One purpose of this involved operation is to aid S&Ls with a temporary liquidity problem.

The main security issued by the FHLB is *consolidated bonds,* "consolidated" referring to the fact that the bonds are the joint obligation of all 12 Federal Home Loan banks. FHLB bonds have a maturity at issue of 1 year or more, pay interest semiannually, and are not callable. They are issued in book entry form and are now sold in minimum denominations of $10,000 and thereafter $5,000 multiples. FHLB bonds often appear on dealers' quote sheets as *FHLB notes.* The FHLB used to issue short-term, interest-bearing notes, but it switched some time ago to the sale of discount notes to raise short-term money. These discount notes have a minimum denomination of $100,000 and maturities under 1 year.

FHLB securities are backed by qualified collateral in the form of secured advances to member S&Ls, government securities, insured mortgages, etc. FHLB securities are *not* guaranteed by the U.S. government. However, they are the obligation of the FHLB system, which plays a key federal role in regulating and assisting the S&L industry. Given this role and the importance of the S&L industry to the economy, it is inconceivable that the U.S. government would ever permit the FHLB to default on outstanding securities.

Interest income from FHLB securities is subject to full federal taxes, but is specifically exempt from state and local taxation.

Farm Credit Agencies

The production and sale of agricultural commodities require large amounts of credit. So, too, does the acquisition by farmers of additional land and buildings. To assure an adequate supply of credit to meet these needs, the government has put together over time the Farm

Credit Administration. This administration, which operates as an independent agency of the U.S. government, oversees the Federal Farm Credit System, which operates in all states plus Puerto Rico. Under this system, the country is divided into 12 farm credit districts. In each of these, there is a Federal Land Bank, a Federal Intermediate Credit Bank, and a Bank for Cooperatives, each supplying specific types of credit to qualified borrowers in its district. To obtain funds, these 37 banks plus a Central Bank for Cooperatives all issue securities through a common fiscal agency in New York City.

Before discussing the obligations of the Bank for Cooperatives, Federal Land Banks, and Federal Intermediate Credit Banks, let's first discuss the Consolidated Systemwide obligations of the Federal Credit Banks.

Consolidated Systemwide discount notes and bonds of the Farm Credit Banks were first introduced in January 1975 and August 1977, respectively. These obligations are the secured joint and several obligations of the 37 Farm Credit Banks. The smallest denomination for the discount notes is $50,000 and is issued in bearer form. The maturities on these obligations range from 5 to 270 days. Consolidated Systemwide bonds are issued each month with maturities of 6 and 9 *months*. About 6 times a year, longer-term bonds are issued. For maturities of less than 13 months, they are issued in multiples of $5,000. For longer maturities, bonds are issued in multiples of $1,000. Bonds are issued in book entry form. Interest income from Consolidated Systemwide discount notes and bonds is subject to full federal income taxation but is specifically exempt from state and local income taxes.

Banks for Cooperatives. The 12 district Banks for Cooperatives, organized under the Farm Credit Act of 1933, make seasonal and term loans to cooperatives owned by farmers, engage in purchasing farm supplies, provide business services to farmers, and market farm output. These loans may provide working capital or finance investments in buildings and equipment. The Central Bank for Cooperatives participates in large loans made by individual district banks. Initially the Banks for Cooperatives were owned by the U.S. government. Since 1955, however, government capital has been replaced by private capital, and ownership is now private.

The major means by which the Banks for Cooperatives finance new loans is through the sale of consolidated collateral trust debentures (*co-ops*). These debentures, which are not callable, are typically offered to investors once a month. They are available in bearer and book entry form, and the smallest denominations available are $5,000 and $10,000; however, new issues are available in book entry form in multiples of $1,000. Many recent issues have had an original maturity of 6 months and pay interest at maturity, but longer-term (2 to 5 years) co-ops have also been issued.

All debentures issued by the Banks for Cooperatives must be secured by acceptable collateral in the form of cash, Treasury securities, and notes or other obligations of borrowers from the banks. Also, each bank is examined at least annually by the Farm Credit Administration. Obligations of these banks are not, however, guaranteed either directly or indirectly by the U.S. government. Nevertheless, given the semiofficial status of the Banks for Cooperatives and the government's high degree of concern for agriculture, it seems unlikely, to say the least, that the government would permit these banks to default on their securities.

Interest income from debentures issued by the Banks for Cooperatives is subject to full federal income taxation but is specifically exempt from state and local income taxes.

Federal Land Banks. The 12 Federal Land Banks were organized under the Federal Farm Loan Act of 1916. These banks extend first mortgage loans on farm properties and make other loans through local Federal Land Bank (FLB) associations. Mortgage loans must be made on the basis of appraisal reports and may not exceed 65% of the appraised value of the mortgaged property. Maturities on FLB loans may run from 5 to 40 years, but most have original maturities of around 20 years. Although the Federal Land Banks were set up under government auspices, all government capital in these banks has been replaced by private capital, and they are now owned by the FLB associations, which in turn are owned by the farmers who have obtained FLB loans through these associations.

The Federal Land Banks obtain funds to lend out primarily by issuing Consolidated Federal Farm Loan bonds and by occasional short-term borrowings between bond issues. Since 1963, all FLB bond issues have been noncallable. These securities range in maturity from a few years to 15 years. Most have an original maturity of longer than 1 year. Securities with a maturity of less than 5 years are available in bearer and book entry form. Those with a maturity of more than 5 years are also available in registered form. Interest on FLB bonds is payable semiannually. The smallest denominations available are $1,000, $5,000, and $10,000. All new issues, however, are available in book entry form only, in multiples of $1,000.

S&Ls are placed in an uncomfortable position whenever interest rates rise because the nature of their business is to borrow short and lend long. Federal Land Banks are in a somewhat similar situation since maturities on the loans they extend tend to be longer than the original maturities of the bonds they issue. To avoid the danger inherent in this position, Federal Land Banks now write only *variable-rate* mortgages. This approach enables them to keep loan income in line with borrowing costs whether interest rates rise or fall.

FLB bonds must be backed with collateral in the form of cash, Treasury securities, or notes secured by first mortgages on farm properties. Federal Land Banks are examined at least annually by the Farm Credit Administration. Their securities are not guaranteed either directly or indirectly by the U.S. government. However, their semiofficial status makes it extremely unlikely that the government would ever permit default on their securities.

Income from FLB bonds is subject to full federal income taxation but is exempt from state and local income taxation.

Federal Intermediate Credit Banks. The 12 Federal Intermediate Credit Banks (FICB) were organized under the Agricultural Credit Act of 1923. Their job is to help provide short-term financing for the seasonal production and marketing of crops and livestock and for other farm-related credit purposes. These banks do not lend directly to farmers. Instead they make loans to and discount agricultural and livestock paper for various financial institutions that lend to farmers.[2] These institutions include commercial banks, production credit associations organized under the Farm Credit Act of 1933, agricultural credit corporations, and incorporated livestock loan companies. Originally, Federal Intermediate Credit Banks were government-owned, but like the other farm credit banks discussed above, today their ownership is wholly private.

Although FICBs are authorized to borrow from commercial banks and to rediscount agricultural paper with the Fed, the principal source of their funds is monthly sales of consolidated collateral trust debentures. These debentures are available in bearer and book entry

---

[2]*Discounting agricultural paper* means buying up farmers' loan notes at a discount.

form and come in denominations of $5,000, $10,000, $50,000, $100,000, and $500,000. New issues are available in book entry form only, in multiples of $1,000. The Federal Intermediate Credit Banks are authorized to issue securities with a maturity of up to 5 years, but many of their obligations are issued with 9-month maturities with interest payable at maturity. Farmers may order and purchase FICB securities directly from the production credit associations of which they are members. Otherwise FICB securities are sold through dealers, as in the case of other agency securities.

FICB debentures are backed by collateral in the form of Treasury securities, other farm credit agency securities, cash, and the notes, discounted obligations, and loans that these banks acquire through their lending activities. Federal Intermediate Credit Banks are regularly examined by the Federal Farm Credit Administration. Their securities are not guaranteed by the government, but as in the case of the institutions discussed above, their semiofficial status offers considerable assurance to the investor that the government would not permit default on FICB debentures.

Interest income on FICB debentures is subject to full federal income taxation but exempt from state and local income taxation.

PRICE QUOTATIONS

Exhibit 10–1 is an excerpt from *The Wall Street Journal* of Federal Home Loan Bank securities quotations. The price quotation convention is the same as that for Treasury securities. That is, the bid and asked price quotations are expressed as a percentage and the value after the decimal (or hyphen) represents the number of 32ds.

BUYING AND SELLING AGENCY SECURITIES

The cheapest way to buy agency securities, and the best way if you buy short-term issues, is to buy at issue through a syndicate member. The syndicate handling a new agency issue always sells the securities at par and with no commission. The syndicate makes its profit on the selling concession (roughly $3 per $1,000 of face value), which it is granted by the issuing agency. Because of the tendency for new agency issues to be priced generously and consequently presold, if you want to buy agency securities at issue, you should get in your subscription for whatever quantity you wish to buy *before* the pricing announce-

---

EXHIBIT 10-1 Excerpt from *The Wall Street Journal* Showing Quotations on Federal Home Loan Bank Securities (Monday, April 14, 1986)

Fed. Home Loan Bank

Rate	Mat	Bid	Asked	Yld	Rate	Mat	Bid	Asked	Yld
9.15	4-86	99.31	100.3	5.53	9.15	7-88	104.18	105.2	6.71
10.25	4-86	100.2	100.5	4.40	11.63	8-88	109.18	110.10	6.81
11.70	4-86	100.5	100.8	2.55	9.45	8-88	105.14	105.22	6.79
8.75	5-86	100.5	100.9	6.12	11.40	10-88	109.30	110.10	6.88
15.50	5-86	101.2	101.7	4.72	9.55	10-88	106.1	106.7	6.83
7.50	6-86	100.5	100.6	6.39	8.90	11-88	104.19	104.25	6.86
8.25	7-87	100.14	100.17	6.19	14.20	11-88	116.18	116.30	6.98
15.35	7-86	102.9	102.15	6.10	10.70	12-88	108.27	109.7	6.89
7.80	7-86	100.9	100.10	6.54	11.38	1-89	110.14	110.30	6.97
14.60	8-86	102.24	102.30	6.18	8.30	2-89	103.16	103.18	6.90
16.40	9-86	104.14	104.20	5.68	10.80	2-89	109.8	109.24	6.98
12.25	9-86	102.11	102.16	6.42	15.10	2-89	119.28	120.12	7.11
10.80	10-86	102.3	102.8	6.43	7.45	3-89	101.9	101.11	6.94
8.30	10-86	100.30	101.1	6.30	14.25	4-89	118.18	118.30	7.18
11.00	11-86	102.13	102.18	6.63	10.20	5-89	108.6	108.18	7.08
11.30	11-86	102.24	102.29	6.35	14.13	7-89	119.6	119.22	7.26
9.88	12-86	102.6	102.10	6.44	12.50	9-89	115.6	115.22	7.27
13.25	12-86	104.12	104.18	6.49	14.55	9-89	121.6	121.22	7.31
8.65	1-87	101.11	101.15	6.66	11.55	11-89	112.20	113.4	7.35
10.10	2-87	102.30	103.4	6.64	11.20	1-90	112.2	112.14	7.36
10.45	2-87	102.30	103.4	6.65	11.90	3-90	114.28	115.8	7.37
11.05	2-87	103.20	103.26	6.41	9.50	6-90	107.8	107.20	7.35
11.05	3-87	104.1	104.5	6.43	9.75	7-90	108.2	108.18	7.37
11.10	3-87	103.23	103.30	6.72	12.50	9-90	118.6	118.22	7.48
11.25	3-87	104	104.6	6.59	10.30	9-90	110.6	110.18	7.46
7.65	5-87	101	101.16	6.23	13.70	11-90	123.6	123.22	7.52
9.63	5-87	103.5	103.11	6.45	10.90	12-90	112.22	113.6	7.51
13.00	5-87	106.14	106.30	6.43	8.70	12-90	104.24	105	7.42
8.45	6-87	101.31	102.5	6.53	9.10	1-91	106.16	106.20	7.42
10.30	6-87	103.28	104.12	6.42	11.88	2-91	116.28	117.12	7.53
11.35	7-87	105.10	105.22	6.63	7.75	3-91	101.11	101.13	7.40
13.30	7-87	107.20	108	6.67	11.10	8-91	114.8	114.24	7.69
7.60	8-87	101	101.12	6.52	11.75	9-91	117.10	117.26	7.68
12.63	8-87	107.8	107.20	6.58	11.40	12-91	116.4	116.20	7.73
9.38	9-87	103.19	103.25	6.59	11.45	2-92	116.20	117.4	7.75
12.05	10-87	107.11	107.23	6.75	11.70	4-92	118.8	118.24	7.75
12.15	10-87	107.7	107.19	6.74	10.35	8-92	112.22	113.2	7.60
8.70	11-87	102.31	103.3	6.64	10.85	10-92	115.6	115.22	7.74
10.65	11-87	105.19	105.31	6.67	11.10	11-92	116.12	116.28	7.78
11.30	11-87	106.18	106.30	6.68	10.70	1-93	114.26	115.10	7.75
8.05	12-87	102.2	102.4	6.70	9.50	1-93	109.8	109.12	7.69
10.63	1-88	106.8	106.20	6.60	10.75	5-93	115.22	116.6	7.74
8.45	1-88	102.30	103	6.62	11.70	7-93	120.20	121.4	7.83
10.20	3-88	105.30	106.14	6.61	11.95	8-93	122.4	122.20	7.84
11.90	3-88	109.6	109.18	6.64	7.38	11-93	98.12	99.4	7.53
10.15	4-88	106.6	106.18	6.64	12.15	12-93	123.30	124.14	7.86
10.38	4-88	106.18	106.30	6.66	12.00	2-94	124.14	124.30	7.71
10.15	5-88	106.12	106.24	6.66	10.00	6-95	113.20	114	7.83
8.80	6-88	103.29	104.3	6.76	10.30	7-95	115.18	116.2	7.83
10.80	6-88	107.22	108.6	6.72	8.10	3-96	102.4	102.8	7.77
					7.88	2-97	100.2	100.26	7.76

ment is made. Determining approximately what coupon the new issue will carry is not difficult; all you need do is to look up *yields to maturity* on comparable securities on a dealer's quote sheet or in *The Wall Street Journal*. Or you can ask the selling dealer to estimate the probable coupon; the dealer's informed guess is sure to be quite close to the mark.

Selling syndicates usually include in their membership several securities dealers with nationwide sales organizations and a number of major money market banks. If it is not convenient to deal with a syndicate member, you can order agency issues from your bank, which in turn will purchase them through its correspondent bank. The latter route is likely to involve a charge equal to that on the purchase of Treasury securities. In this respect, it is worth noting that agency issues are a surprisingly unknown commodity to some small bankers. Consequently, if you intend to buy through a small bank, plan to know exactly what you want.

You can also buy outstanding agency issues in the secondary market. Such purchases can be made through any bank or securities dealer. On small purchases in the secondary market, the seller will charge a fee or commission. The commission will depend in part on how many hands the securities being purchased have to pass through. A dealer bank that trades agencies might charge only $25, whereas a suburban bank or broker who had to go through a bank to obtain agency securities might charge $35 or more. Such charges naturally reduce yield to the investor, especially if the amount purchased is small or the maturity short. Thus, unless the secondary market has something especially attractive to offer (say, a desired maturity or a deep-discount bond for the long-term investor) buying at issue is preferable.

Agency securities can always be sold before maturity through any bank or securities dealer. The investor making such a sale will incur a sales charge comparable to the charge on the purchase of Treasuries. As a comparison of the quotes in Exhibit 10-1 and Exhibit 9-1 of the previous chapter shows, spreads between bid and ask prices are slightly wider for agency issues than for governments, so the argument for being a hold-until-maturity investor is even stronger in the case of short-term agencies than for governments.

RISK, LIQUIDITY, AND RETURN

With respect to the risk and liquidity of agency securities, most of what we said in earlier chapters about U.S. Treasury securities applies. Agencies are actively traded and consequently have good marketability. However, on short maturities, because of purchase and sales commissions, you should attempt to buy at issue and hold to maturity. Long-coupon agencies, like long-coupon Treasuries, fluctuate considerably in price over time as interest rates rise and fall. This price variability makes long agencies less liquid or more risky than short agencies. Risk of default is zero on all federal agency issues backed by the full faith and credit of the U.S. government. Most other federal agency issues possess *de facto* government backing so the actual risk of default is negligible to zero on them, too.

The return on agencies is typically slightly more than on governments, which makes them especially attractive to the conservative investor. Corporate issues (discussed in Chapter 12) offer still higher yields, but at the expense of at least some small risk of default.

The exemption of interest income on many agencies from state and local income taxes may be an important consideration for some investors.

Municipal Securities

The term *municipal securities* is used in blanket fashion by "the Street" to denote all debt securities issued by state and local governments and their agencies. The ranks of the latter include school districts, housing authorities, sewer districts, municipal-owned utilities, and authorities running toll roads, bridges, and other transportation facilities.

Municipal securities are issued for various purposes. Short-term notes are typically sold in anticipation of the receipt of other funds— taxes or proceeds from a bond issue, for example. Their sale permits the issuer to cover seasonal and other temporary imbalances between expenditure outflows and tax inflows. In contrast, the sale of long-term bonds is the principal way state and local governments finance the construction of schools, housing, pollution control facilities, roads, bridges, and other big-ticket items. Bond issues are also used to fund long-term budget deficits arising from current operations, as opposed to capital projects.

The most important advantage of municipal securities to the investor is that interest income on them is exempt from federal income taxes.[1] Interest income on municipal bonds issued within territories of

---

[1] As explained later in this chapter, state and local tax treatment varies from state to state.

the U.S. and bonds issued by certain local housing and urban renewal agencies operating under HUD are exempt from both federal and state taxes in *all* states.

Prior to the 1970s, municipal bonds were viewed second only to U.S. government bonds in safety. The financial crisis faced by New York City in 1975, however, made it evident that the so-called legal protection that investors thought municipals had could be withdrawn under political pressure. The change in the federal bankruptcy law in 1979 reinforced investor concerns about the safety of municipal bonds because the revised law made it easier for municipalities to seek protection from bondholders by filing for bankruptcy. The Reagan administration's cutbacks in federal grants and aid programs were also viewed as a factor that would reduce the safety of certain municipal bonds. Consequently, one must carefully examine the default risk before purchasing a municipal bond.

The distribution of outstanding municipal securities among investor groups differs sharply from those of federal and federal agency securities. Since the single most important advantage of municipals for the investor is their federal tax exemption, the groups who hold these securities are those who benefit the most from this exemption. The three investor groups that have dominated the municipal securities market are commercial banks, property and casualty insurance companies, and households (retail investors). Although these three investor groups have dominated the market since the mid-1950s, the relative participation by each category has shifted.

Retail investor participation in the municipal securities market has fluctuated widely since 1972. With some interruptions, retail investors' market share had been trending downward; however, in 1981 the trend was reversed and individual investors are now the largest holders of municipal bonds. Commercial banks are the second largest holders of municipal securities. Commercial bank participation in the municipal market peaked during the early-1970s and since that time has been trending downward. Declining profitability and lower tax liabilities apparently are the primary reasons for this reduced participation. By the end of 1982, property and casualty insurance companies were the third largest holders of tax-exempt securities. Purchases of municipal securities by property and casualty insurance companies are primarily a function of their underwriting profits and investment income. Life insurance companies and pension funds hold few municipals; the exemption is of little importance to them because of their low tax rates.

GENERAL CHARACTERISTICS OF MUNICIPAL SECURITIES

Our general description of bond characteristics in Chapters 6 and 7 fits municipal bonds quite accurately. Such securities are issued with a fixed value and coupon; they pay interest semiannually; they mature on a given date; and they may or may not contain call and refunding provisions.

Municipals used to be issued in minimum denominations of $1,000. However, the minimum denomination on most large issues has been raised to $5,000. The main reason for this increase is that handling and storing bonds in $1,000 denominations was expensive and awkward for both underwriters and large investors.

Municipal bonds used to be issued either as bearer bonds or in registered form. As their name implies, bearer bonds are negotiable by anyone who holds them. Attached to bearer bonds are coupons that investors clip and submit for payment. Issuers send coupon payments to whomever submits the coupon for payment. With registered bonds, the holder's name is registered with the issuer. The issuer will only send registered bondholders principal and interest payments. There are no coupons attached to registered bonds—interest payments are sent directly to bondholders. Effective July 1, 1983, all new municipal bonds must be issued in registered form.

On some municipal issues, all bonds mature at the same time. These bonds are known as *term bonds*. Currently, most municipal issues are *serial bonds*. On a serial issue, maturities are staggered, with some of the bonds maturing each year after issue up to some maximum number of years—10, 20, 30, or more. When the issuer is financing a capital project that it expects to pay for gradually (as the owner of a mortgaged home pays for his house year by year), serial bonds provide a convenient way of matching debt structure with the flow of funds that the issuer anticipates will be available to pay off principal.

GENERAL OBLIGATION AND REVENUE BONDS

There are basically two different types of municipal bond security structures. The first type is the general obligation bond, and the second is the revenue bond.

General obligation bonds are debt instruments issued by states, counties, special districts, cities, towns, and school districts. They are secured by the issuer's general taxing powers. Usually, a general obligation bond is secured by the issuer's unlimited taxing power. For smaller governmental jurisdictions such as school districts and towns, the only available unlimited taxing power is on property. For larger general obligation bond issuers such as states and big cities, the tax revenues are more diverse and may include corporate and individual income taxes, sales taxes, and property taxes. The security pledges for these larger issuers are sometimes referred to as *full faith and credit obligations.*

Additionally, certain general obligation bonds are secured not only by the issuer's general taxing powers to create revenues accumulated in the general fund, but from certain identified fees, grants, and special charges, which provide additional revenues from outside the general fund. Such bonds are known as being *double barreled* in security because of the dual nature of the revenue sources.

Not all general obligation bonds are secured by unlimited taxing powers. Some have pledged taxes that are limited as to revenue sources and maximum property-tax-millage amounts. Such bonds are known as *limited-tax general obligation bonds.*

The second basic type of security structure is a revenue bond. Such bonds are issued for either project or enterprise financings—the bond issuer's pledge to the bondholders the revenues generated by the operating projects financed. Below are examples of the specific types of revenue bonds that have been issued over the years.

Airport Revenue Bonds

The revenues securing airport revenue bonds usually come from either traffic-generated sources—such as landing fees, concession fees, and airline apron-use and fueling fees—or lease revenues from one or more airlines for the use of a specific facility such as a terminal or hangar.

College and University Revenue Bonds

The revenues securing college and university revenue bonds usually include dormitory room rental fees, tuition payments, and sometimes the general assets of the college or university as well.

Hospital Revenue Bonds

The security for hospital revenue bonds is usually dependent on federal and state reimbursement programs (such as Medicaid and Medicare), third-party commercial payers (such as Blue Cross and private insurance), and individual patient payments.

Single-Family Mortgage Revenue Bonds

Single-family mortgage revenue bonds are usually secured by the mortgages and mortgage loan repayments on single-family homes. Security features vary but can include Federal Housing Administration (FHA), Federal Veterans Administration (VA), or private mortgage insurance.

Multifamily Revenue Bonds

These revenue bonds are usually issued for multifamily housing projects for senior citizens and low-income families. Some housing revenue bonds are secured by mortgages that are federally insured; others receive federal government operating subsidies, such as those under section 8, or interest-cost subsidies, such as those under section 236; and still others receive only local property tax reductions as subsidies.

Industrial Development and Pollution Control Revenue Bonds

Bonds have been issued for a variety of industrial and commercial activities that range from manufacturing plants to shopping centers. They are usually secured by payments to be made by the corporations or businesses that use the facilities.

Public Power Revenue Bonds

Public power revenue bonds are secured by revenues produced by electrical operating plants. Some bonds are for a single issuer who constructs and operates power plants and then sells the electricity. Other public power revenue bonds are issued by groups of public and private investor-owned utilities for the joint financing of the construction of one or more power plants. This last arrangement is known as a *joint power* financing structure.

Resource Recovery Revenue Bonds

A resource recovery facility converts refuse (solid waste) into commercially saleable energy, recoverable products, and a residue to be landfilled. The major revenues for a resource recovery revenue bond usually are (1) the "tipping fees" per ton paid by those who deliver the garbage to the facility for disposal; (2) revenues from steam, electricity, or refuse-derived fuel sold to either an electric power company or another energy user; and (3) revenues from the sale of recoverable materials such as aluminum and steel scrap.

Seaport Revenue Bonds

The security for seaport revenue bonds can include specific lease agreements with the benefiting companies or pledged marine terminal and cargo tonnage fees.

Sewer Revenue Bonds

Revenues for sewer revenue bonds come from hookup fees and user charges. For many older sewer bond issuers, substantial portions of their construction budgets have been financed with federal grants.

Sports Complex and Convention Center Revenue Bonds

Sports complex and convention center revenue bonds usually receive revenues from sporting or convention events held at the facilities and, in some instances, from earmarked outside revenues such as local motel and hotel room taxes.

Student Loan Revenue Bonds

Student loan repayments under student loan revenue bond programs are sometimes 100% guaranteed either directly by the federal government—under the Federal Insured Student Loan program (FISL) for 100% of bond principal and interest—or by a state guaranty agency under a more recent federal insurance program, the Federal Guaranteed Student Loan program (GSL). In addition to these two federally backed programs, student loan bonds are also sometimes secured by the general revenues of the specific colleges involved.

Toll Road and Gas Tax Revenue Bonds

There are generally two types of highway revenue bonds. The bond proceeds of the first type are used to build specific revenue-producing facilities such as toll roads, bridges, and tunnels. For these pure enterprise-type revenue bonds, the pledged revenues usually are the monies collected through the tolls. The second type of highway bond is one in which the bondholders are paid by earmarked revenues outside of toll collections, such as gasoline taxes, automobile registration payments, and driver's license fees.

Water Revenue Bonds

Water revenue bonds are issued to finance the construction of water treatment plants, pumping stations, collection facilities, and distribution systems. Revenues usually come from connection fees and charges paid by the users of the water systems.

HYBRID AND SPECIAL BOND SECURITIES

Though possessing certain characteristics of general obligation and revenue bonds, some municipal bonds have additional security structures that are unique. These are described below.

Insured Bonds

In addition to being secured by the issuer's revenues, insured bonds are backed by insurance policies written by commercial insurance companies. The insurance, usually structured as an insurance contract, is supposed to provide prompt payment to the bondholders if a default occurs. These bonds are discussed in more detail later in this chapter.

Refunded Bonds

These are bonds that may have been issued originally as general obligation or revenue bonds but are now secured by an "escrow fund" consisting of obligations that are sufficient for paying the bondholders. *They are among the safest of all municipal bonds if the escrow is structured as a "pure escrow."*

Lease-backed Bonds

Lease-backed bonds are usually structured as revenue-type bonds involving annual rent payments. In some instances, the rental payments may only come from earmarked tax revenues, student tuition payments, or patient fees. In other instances, the underlying lessee governmental unit is required to make annual appropriations from its general fund.

Letter of Credit-backed Bonds

Some municipal bonds, in addition to being secured by the issuer's cash flow revenues, also are backed by commercial bank letters of credit. In some instances, the letters of credit are irrevocable and, if necessary, can be used to pay the bondholders. In other instances, the issuers are required to maintain investment quality worthiness before the letters of credit can be drawn upon.

Life Care Revenue Bonds

Life care bonds are issued to construct long-term residential facilities for older citizens. Revenues are usually derived from initial lump-sum payments made by the residents.

Moral Obligation Bonds

A moral obligation bond is a security structure for state-issued bonds; it indicates that if revenues are needed for paying bondholders, the state legislature involved is legally authorized, though not required, to make an appropriation out of general state tax revenues.

Municipal Utility District Revenue Bonds

These are bonds that are usually issued to finance the construction of water and sewer systems as well as roadways in underdeveloped areas. The security is usually dependent on the commercial success of the specific development project involved, which can range from the sale of new homes to the renting of space in shopping centers and office buildings.

Tax Allocation Bonds

These bonds are usually issued to finance the construction of office buildings and other new buildings in formerly blighted areas. They are secured by property taxes collected on the improved real estate.

"Troubled City" Bailout Bonds

There are certain bonds that are structured to appear as pure revenue bonds but in essence are not. Revenues come from general purpose taxes and revenues that otherwise would have gone to a state's or city's general fund. Their bond structures were created to bail out underlying general obligation bond issuers from severe budget deficits. Examples are the New York *Municipal Assistance Corporation for the City of New York Bonds* (MAC) and the state of Illinois *Chicago School Finance Authority Bonds*.

Federal Savings and Loan Insurance Corporation-backed Bonds

In this security structure, the proceeds of a bond sale were deposited in a savings and loan association that, in turn, issued a CD. The CD was insured by the FSLIC up to a limit of $100,000 of combined principal and interest for each bondholder. The savings and loan association used the money to finance low- and moderate-income rental housing developments. While these bonds are no longer issued, there are billions of dollars of these bonds in the secondary market.

"Territorial" Bonds

These are bonds issued by United States territorial possessions such as Puerto Rico, the Virgin Islands, and Guam. The bonds are tax-exempt throughout most of the country. Also, the economies of these issuers are influenced by positive special features of the United States corporate tax codes that are not available to the states.

MUNICIPAL NOTES

Tax-exempt debt issued for periods ranging not beyond 3 years is usually considered to be short term. Below are descriptions of some of these debt instruments.

Tax, Revenue, Grant, and Bond Anticipation Notes: TANs, RANs, GANs, and BANs

These are temporary borrowings by states, local governments, and special jurisdictions. Usually, notes are issued for a period of 12 months, though it is not uncommon for notes to be issued for periods as short as 3 months or as long as 3 years. TANs and RANs (also known as TRANs) are issued in anticipation of the collection of taxes or other expected revenues. These are borrowings to even out the cash flows caused by the irregular flows of income into the treasuries of the states and local units of government. BANs are issued in anticipation of the sale of long-term bonds.

Construction Loan Notes: CLNs

CLNs are usually issued for periods up to 3 years to provide short-term construction financing for multifamily housing projects. The CLNs generally are repaid from the proceeds of long-term bonds, which are provided after the housing projects are completed.

Tax-exempt Commercial Paper

This short-term borrowing instrument is used for periods ranging from 30 to 270 days. Generally, the tax-exempt commercial paper has back-stop commercial bank agreements, which can include an irrevocable letter of credit, a revolving credit agreement, or a line of credit.

In this book we shall refer to both municipal bonds and municipal notes simply as municipal bonds.

NEWER MARKET-SENSITIVE DEBT INSTRUMENTS

As explained earlier, municipal bonds are usually issued with one of two debt retirement structures or a combination of both. Either a bond has a "serial" maturity structure (where a portion of the loan is retired each year), or it has a "term" maturity (where the loan is repaid on a final date). Usually, term bonds have maturities ranging from 20 to 40 years, and retirement schedules (which are known as sinking funds) that begin 5 to 10 years before the final term maturity.

Because of the sharply upward sloping yield curve that has existed in the municipal bond market since 1979, many investment bankers have introduced innovative financing instruments priced at short or intermediate yield levels. These debt instruments are intended to raise money for long-term capital projects at reduced interest rates. Below are descriptions of some of these more innovative debt structures.

Zero-coupon Bonds

As explained in Chapter 7, a zero-coupon bond is a bond that is issued at a deep discount from par. The interest income is the difference between the maturity value and the purchase price. In the case of a zero-coupon municipal bond, this difference is treated as interest income, not a capital gain, and therefore the income is exempt from federal income taxes. Thus, unlike a zero-coupon taxable bond, there is no federal income tax disadvantage from buying a zero-coupon municipal bond.

A variation of the zero-coupon bond, known as *compound interest bond* or *municipal multiplier,* was introduced to allow municipal issuers to circumvent restrictions on the amount of par value that they were legally permitted to issue. This type of bond is issued at par and does actually have interest payments. However, the interest payments are not distributed to the holder of the bond until maturity. Rather, the issuer agrees to reinvest the undistributed interest payments at the bond's yield to maturity when it was issued. For example, suppose that a 10%, 10-year bond with a par value of $5,000 is sold at par to yield 10%. Every 6 months, the maturity value of the bond is increased by 5% of the maturity value of the previous 6 months. So at the end of 10 years, the maturity value of the bond will be $13,267. In contrast, a 10-year zero-coupon bond priced to yield 10% would have a maturity value of $5,000 but would be issued for $1,884.

Usually, zero-coupon municipal bonds are callable in 15 years. Unlike a coupon municipal, the call price cannot be stated as a percent of the par value. Instead, the call price is based on the *compounded accreted value* (CAV) of the issue at each possible call date. The CAV is the value of the bond at the call date if the bond grew by its yield to maturity when issued. To the CAV is added a premium for each possible call date that is determined by the issuer when the bond is first issued.

Put or Option Tender Bonds

A *put* or *option tender* bond is one in which the bondholder has the right to return the bond at a price of par to the bond trustee prior to its stated long-term maturity. The put period can be as short as 1 day and as long as 10 years. Usually, put bonds are backed by either commercial bank letters of credit in addition to the issuer's cash flow revenues, or entirely by the cash flow revenues of the issuers.

Super Sinkers

A *super sinker* is a specifically identified maturity for a single-family housing revenue bond issue in which all funds from early mortgage prepayments are used to retire bonds. A super sinker has a long stated maturity but a shorter, albeit unknown, actual life. Because of this unique characteristic, investors have the opportunity to realize an attractive return when the municipal yield curve is upward sloping on a bond that is priced as if it had a maturity considerably longer than its anticipated life.

Variable-rate Notes

Variable-rate notes have coupon rates that change on a weekly or monthly basis. The coupon rate may be tied to one of various indexes such as T bill rates, the weekly *Bond Buyer Index,* the *J. J. Kenney Municipal Index,* or the prime rate. When a variable-rate note also has a put feature, it is called a *variable-rate demand note.*

DEFAULT RISK

Most investors rely on credit ratings and written reports provided by rating services or underwriters in assessing the default risk of a municipal issuer. There are several commercial rating companies. We shall discuss the two dominant companies in the credit rating business—Moody's and Standard & Poor's (S&P).

Moody's municipal bond rating system grades the investment quality of municipal bonds in a 9-symbol system that ranges from the highest investment quality, which is Aaa, to the lowest credit rating, which is C. The respective 9 alphabetical ratings and their definitions are as follows:

Rating	*Definition*
Aaa	Best quality; carry the smallest degree of investment risk.
Aa	High quality; margins of protection not quite as large as the Aaa bonds.
A	Upper medium grade; security adequate but could be susceptible to impairment.
Baa	Medium grade; neither highly protected nor poorly secured—lack outstanding investment characteristics and sensitive to changes in economic circumstances.
Ba	Speculative; protection is very moderate.
B	Not desirable investment; sensitive to day-to-day economic circumstances.
Caa	Poor standing; may be in default but with a workout plan.
Ca	Highly speculative; may be in default with nominal workout plan.
C	Hopelessly in default.

Municipal bonds in the top four categories (Aaa, Aa, A, and Baa) are considered to be investment-grade quality. Additionally, bonds in the Aa through B categories that Moody's concludes have the strongest features within the respective categories are designated by Aa1, A1, Baa1, Ba1 and B1, respectively.

The municipal note rating system used by Moody's is designated by 4 investment-grade categories of Moody's Investment Grade (MIG). They are MIG-1 (best quality), MIG-2 (high quality), MIG-3 (favorable quality), and MIG-4 (adequate quality).

S&Ps municipal bond rating system grades the investment quality of municipal bonds in a 10-symbol system that ranges from the highest quality, which is AAA, to the lowest credit rating, which is D. Bonds within the top 4 categories (AAA, AA, A, and BBB) are considered by S&P as being investment-grade quality. The respective 10 alphabetical ratings and definitions are as follows:

Rating	*Definition*
AAA	Highest rating, extremely strong security.
AA	Very strong security; differs from AAA in only a small degree.
A	Strong capacity but more susceptible to adverse economic effects than two above categories.
BBB	Adequate capacity but adverse economic conditions more likely to weaken capacity.
BB	Lowest degree of speculation; risk exposure.
B	Speculative; risk exposure.
CCC	Speculative; major risk exposure.
CC	Highest degree of speculation; major risk exposure.
C	No interest is being paid.
D	Bonds in default with interest and/or repayment of principal in arrears.

S&P also uses a plus (+) or minus (−) sign to show relative standing within the rating categories from AA to BB. The municipal note rating system used by S&P is the same as that used for bonds, ranging from AAA to D.

Although there are many similarities in how Moody's and S&P approach credit ratings, there are certain differences in their respective approaches as well. For example, with respect to the rating of general obligation bonds, Moody's seems to focus on the debt burden and budgetary operations of the issuer, while S&P focuses largely upon the issuer's economic environment. Another example is the difference in their treatment of state general obligation bonds versus local government general obligation bonds. S&P seems to make a distinction between state and local issuers, viewing state general obligation bonds as sufficiently stronger than those of their respective underlying jurisdictions. S&P has never given a rating below A to a state. Moody's, on the other hand, applies the same debt- and budget-related concerns to state general obligation bonds as it does to general obligations bonds issued by counties, school districts, towns, and cities, and has even assigned ratings below A to state general obligation bonds.

What we said in earlier chapters about the commercial rating companies bears repeating here. Although they have been for the most part reliable indicators of credit quality, they are not foolproof—ask investors who purchased WPPSS bonds in 1980, when the bonds received investment-grade ratings, and who watched the issue default in 1983. And ask investors who purchased New York City general obligations bonds in 1973, when the rating companies upgraded the bonds to investment-grade quality, and who watched the issue default in 1975.

ISSUING PROCEDURES

As explained in Chapter 12, when a corporation issues a new bond to the public, the Securities Act of 1933 requires that the issuer file a prospectus with the SEC. The prospectus must contain material information about the corporation and the particular issue. The prospectus is generally reviewed by the SEC prior to the issuance of the bonds. A prospectus must be furnished to prospective buyers of the issue.

The equivalent of the prospectus for a municipal offering is the *official statement*. The official statement is not subject to the review of the SEC or any other government agency. Instead, if the issuer prepares an official statement or a more abbreviated offering circular, a copy must be filed with the Municipal Securities Rulemaking Board and a copy must be distributed to potential investors.

Issuers of municipal bonds obtain their authority to issue such securities from the state constitution or statutes. In some cases this authority is limited, and a favorable vote by the electorate may be necessary before bonds can be issued and sold.

The legality of every municipal bond issued must be approved by an attorney. Typically such opinions are obtained from one of a number of recognized firms of bond attorneys who specialize in municipal law. The popular notion is that much of the legal work done in a municipal bond issue is boiler plate in nature, but from the bondholder's point of view, the legal opinions and document reviews should provide the ultimate security provisions. This is crucial because, if all else fails, the bondholder may have to go to court to enforce his security rights. Therefore, the integrity and competency of the lawyers who review the documents and write the legal opinions that are usually summarized and stated in the official statements are very important.

Underwriting

A substantial number of municipal obligations are brought to market each week. A state or local government can market its new issue by offering them publicly to the investing community or by placing them privately with a small group of investors. When a public offering is selected, the issue is usually underwritten by investment bankers and municipal bond departments of commercial banks. Public offerings may be marketed by either competitive bidding or direct negotiations with underwriters. When an issue is marketed via competitive bidding, the issue is awarded to the bidder submitting the lowest bid.

Most states mandate that general obligation issues be marketed via competitive bidding; however, this is generally not required for revenue bonds. Usually state and local governments require that a competitive sale be announced in a recognized financial publication, such as *The Bond Buyer,* which is the trade publication of the municipal bond industry. *The Bond Buyer* also provides information on upcoming competitive sales and most negotiated sales, as well as the results of the sales of previous weeks.

When an underwriter purchases a new bond issue, it relieves the issuer of two obligations. First, the underwriter is responsible for the distribution of the issue. Second, the underwriter accepts the risk that investors might fail to purchase the issue at the expected prices within the planned time period. The second risk exists because the underwriter may have incorrectly priced the issue and/or because interest rates have risen, resulting in a decline in the value of unsold securities held in inventory. The underwriter spread (that is, the difference between the price it paid the issuer for the issue and the price at which it reoffered the issue to the public) is the underwriter's compensation for undertaking these risks as well as for other services it may have provided the issuer. For example, in the case of negotiated offerings, there is the value of the origination services provided by the underwriter. Origination services represent the structuring of the issue and planning activities surrounding the offering.

THE SECONDARY MARKET

Although municipal bonds are not listed and traded in formal institutions, as are certain common stocks and corporate bonds on the New York and American stock exchanges, there are very strong and active billion-dollar secondary markets for municipals that are supported by hundreds of municipal bond dealers across the country. Markets are maintained in local issues by regional brokerage firms, local banks, and by some of the larger brokerage firms and banks, many of whom have investment banking relationships with the issuers. Buying and selling decisions are often made over the phone and through municipal bond brokers. For a small fee these brokers serve as intermediaries in the sale of large blocks of municipal bonds among dealers and large institutional investors. These brokers are primarily located in New York City and include Chapdelaine & Company, Drake & Company, the J. J. Kenny Company, and Titus & Donnelly, Inc., among others.

In addition to these brokers and the daily offerings sent out over *The Bond Buyer's* "munifacts" teletype system, many dealers advertise their municipal bond offerings for the retail market in what is known as *The Blue List*. This is a 100+ -page booklet which is published every weekday by the Standard & Poor's Corporation. In it are listed state municipal bond and note offerings and prices.

In the municipal bond market, an odd lot of bonds is $25,000 (5 bonds) or less in par value for retail investors. For institutions, anything below $100,000 in par value is considered an odd lot. Dealer spreads—the difference between the dealer's bid and ask prices—depend on several factors. For the retail investor, the dealer spread can range from as low as ¼ of 1 point ($12.50 per $5,000 of par value) on large blocks of actively traded bonds to 4 points ($200 per $5,000 of par value) for odd-lot sales of an inactive issue. The average spread for retail investors seems to be around 2 points ($100 per $5,000 of par value). For institutional investors, the dealer spread rarely exceeds ½ of 1 point ($25 per $5,000 of par value).

Price Quotes

As noted in previous chapters, government and agency securities are always quoted in terms of dollar prices (which are really percentages). In the case of municipals—all general obligation (GOs) and many revenue bonds—the normal practice in the secondary market is to quote not dollar prices but *yield*. A price quote in terms of yield is referred to as a *basis price,* a practice which makes sense since price is being quoted in terms of basis points of yield.

The one exception to the rule that municipals are quoted in yield is what are called *dollar bonds*. These are actively traded revenue bonds quoted in dollar prices. There is no rule for which way revenue issues are quoted. The practice simply develops to quote certain issues in terms of dollar prices. Prices of a number of dollar bonds are quoted in *The Wall Street Journal,* but the paper quotes no GO issues.

On issues subject to call and quoted in terms of yield, the question naturally arises whether the quote should be in terms of *yield to call* or *yield to maturity.* The normal practice is to quote yield to maturity whenever the security is selling at a discount; that is, when market rates are above the security's coupon and call seems unlikely. Note in this situation that if call occurred, it would actually raise yield to maturity. When a municipal is selling at a premium, yield is quoted in terms of yield to call.

BUYING AND SELLING MUNICIPALS

A glance at the back pages of *The Wall Street Journal* will show that new municipal issues are constantly being issued through dealer syndicates. Announcements in national publications cover only the tip of the iceberg, so to speak, since many other new issues that are too small to attract a national market are also constantly being offered.

One way to buy municipals is to watch public announcements and, when an issue comes along that is attractive in terms of rate and maturity, put in an order with one of the firms distributing the issue. A list of syndicate members is always included in the announcement of a new issue. For federal agency issues, any subscription, once accepted, will be honored. In the case of municipals, first come first served is not necessarily the rule. An investor who puts in an order for $5,000 of a given maturity of a new serial issue may have his order knocked out by an order for all bonds of that maturity from a large institutional investor.

One advantage in shopping the new-issue market is that under syndicate pricing rules, all orders—large and small—have to be filled at the syndicate offering price. Thus on purchases of a new issue from a syndicate member, there is no sales commission.

The investor interested in municipals should also shop the secondary market. As we noted, prices on popular revenue bonds are quoted in *The Wall Street Journal,* but prices of GOs are not. To shop the secondary market, the investor has to call a bank or broker and find out what they have available in the maturity and quantity he wants. If the dealer happens to have an appropriate small lot on the shelf, he may actually price it more favorably (say, to yield 30 basis points more) than he would price a big block of the same issue. The reason is not generosity. Banks, insurance companies, and other institutional investors want large blocks, not odd lots, so an odd lot is hard to sell. Another consideration is that if interest rates rise and the market goes "under water," the dealer will have to cut price more on a small piece than on a large piece to move it.

Apart from bits and pieces, dealers are likely to offer small lots out of inventory at the quoted asked price plus some commission to cover the cost of writing the sales ticket. This is really a break-even service, and the price the dealer offers is likely to depend on whether he thinks a small sale now could lead to more profitable business later.

Except for the individual who buys on the speculation that the price of the bond he is acquiring will rise, the investor in municipals should plan to hold to maturity. The reason is that dealers are loath to buy hard-to-sell odd lots; consequently they bid as much as $10 less per $1,000 of face value for an odd-lot amount than for a round-lot amount. On a sale of $5,000 of bonds, this differential works out to be a $50 sales charge, a sum large enough to significantly reduce the investor's return.

EXHIBIT 11-1 Yield Levels and Ratios (early February 1984 and November 21, 1985)

	February 1984			November 21, 1985		
Issue	Municipal Yield	Treasury Yield	Yield Ratio	Municipal Yield	Treasury Yield	Yield Ratio
3 year AAA G.O.	6.25%	10.75%	.58	5.60%	8.75%	.64
5 year AAA G.O.	6.90	11.40	.60	6.25	9.17	.68
10 year AAA G.O.	8.00	11.60	.69	7.10	9.60	.74
30 year AAA G.O.	9.00	11.75	.77	8.25	9.94	.83

SOURCE: Merrill Lynch, *Bond Market Comment* 8, no. 2 (January 11, 1985) and *Bond Market Comment* 8, no. 47 (November 22, 1985).

RISK, LIQUIDITY, AND RETURN

An investor thinking of buying municipals should do so only after carefully evaluating risk, liquidity, and return.

Return

Because of the tax-exempt feature of municipal bonds, the yield is less than that on Treasuries with the same maturity. Exhibit 11-1 shows the yield levels and the ratio of municipal yields to Treasury yields for four market sectors on February 1984 and November 21, 1985. As can be seen, the yield ratio changes over time.

Before buying municipal bonds, an investor must determine whether his present and *expected future* tax brackets are sufficiently high enough to warrant purchasing municipal bonds for his portfolio. Some brokerage firms publish tables showing for each tax bracket the "equivalent taxable yield" from owning a municipal bond. The equivalent taxable yield is the yield an investor would have to earn before taxes on a taxable bond in order to produce an equivalent after-tax yield offered on a municipal bond. By comparing the equivalent taxable yield to the yield offered on taxable bonds of the same credit rating and maturity, an investor can determine if municipal bonds will enhance a portfolio's after-tax return.

The following formula can be used to approximate the equivalent taxable yield:

$$\text{Equivalent taxable yield} = \frac{\text{Tax-exempt yield}}{(1 - \text{marginal tax rate})}$$

For example, suppose an investor in the 30% marginal tax bracket is considering the acquisition of a municipal bond that offers a tax-exempt yield of 7%. The equivalent taxable yield is 10%, as shown below.

$$\text{Equivalent taxable yield} = \frac{.07}{(1 - .30)} = .10$$

When a brokerage firm offers a municipal bond, it usually provides two yield measures. The first is the yield to maturity. For example, in mid-November of 1984, Fairfax County, Virginia, 4.90s general obligation bonds due October 1, 1992, sold for 76.25% of par for a yield to maturity of 9.25%. The second is the yield to maturity assuming a certain capital gains tax. The reason for this second yield measure is that only the interest, not the capital gain from holding a municipal bond, is exempt from federal income taxes. For certain municipal bonds purchased at a discount from par, there is a potential capital gains liability if the bond is held to maturity. Since the maximum capital gains tax at the time of this writing is 20%, yield to maturity after a 20% capital gains tax is quoted. In the case of the Fairfax, Virginia, general obligation bonds, although the yield to maturity was 9.25%, the yield after an assumed 20% capital gains tax was 8.73%.

An investor also must decide whether to purchase an in-state or an out-of-state issue. The Dade County, Florida, general obligation bond, for example, is an in-state bond if the holder of the bond resides in Florida but an out-of-state bond for all holders of the bond who do not reside in Florida. An important factor in the decision to buy an in-state or out-of-state bond is state and local taxes on investment income and personal property.

The tax treatment at the state and local levels varies. There are three types of tax that can be imposed—an income tax on coupon income, a tax on realized capital gains, and a personal property tax. Only six states do not impose at least one of these taxes on individuals.

For those states that do impose at least one type of income tax, the tax treatment depends on whether the investor owns a municipal bond of an in-state issuer or an out-of-state issuer. Several states do not levy a tax on any coupon interest from municipal bonds, whether the issuer is in-state or out-of-state. Most states give favorable treatment to in-state issuers by exempting coupon interest paid by such issuers, but tax the coupon interest of out-of-state issuers. However, there are states that levy an income tax on coupon interest regardless of whether it is an in-state bond or an out-of-state bond.

In many states where the coupon interest is exempt if issued by an in-state issuer, the same exemption will not apply to capital gains involving municipal bonds. For example, in California, New York, and Virginia, coupon interest from in-state issuers is exempt while capital gains from the disposal of an in-state bond are subject to tax. New Jersey and Pennsylvania exempt both coupon interest and capital gains when the issuer is in-state.

Alabama, Florida, Georgia, Indiana, Kansas, Kentucky, Michigan, North Carolina, Ohio, Pennsylvania, and West Virginia each have a personal property tax applicable to municipal bonds. The rate varies from $1 to $5 per $1,000 of par value (or in some cases market value). There are some states, such as Ohio, in which the annual income of the municipal bond held is the basis for the property tax.

As a result of the difference in state taxes, strong investor demand for in-state issuers in states with high income taxes (for example, New York, Massachusetts, and California) will reduce yields relative to bonds of issuers located in states where state and local taxes are not important considerations (for example, Illinois, Florida, and New Jersey). In states where there is a high individual maximum tax rate, purchasing in-state bonds may still be the most prudent investment strategy. However, some investors who buy in-state municipal bonds to benefit from state and local tax exemptions pay too much, in terms of yield give-up, to purchase bonds of these in-state issuers. Other investors exhibit extreme reluctance to purchase issues from issuers outside of their state or region. This in-state parochialism tends to decrease relative yields on bonds whose issuers are from states in which investors exhibit this behavior.

The yield on a municipal bond is also determined by the number of years remaining to maturity. The yield curve depicts the relationship at a given point in time between yields and maturity for bonds that are identical in every way except maturity. Three hypothetical yield curves are possible. When yields increase with maturity, the yield curve is said to be *normal* or have a *positive slope*. Therefore, as investors lengthen their maturity, they require a greater yield. It is also possible for the yield curve to be "inverted," meaning that long-term yields are less than short-term yields. If short-, intermediate-, and long-term yields are roughly the same, the yield curve is said to be *flat*.

In the taxable bond market, it is not unusual to find all three shapes for the yield curve at different points in the business cycle.

However, in the municipal bond market, the yield curve is typically normal or upward sloping. Consequently, in the municipal bond market, long-term bonds offer higher yields than short- and intermediate-term bonds.

Another characteristic of the municipal bond yield curve is that yield spreads between maturities are usually wider in the municipal bond market than maturity spreads in the taxable market. This means that potential rewards are increased by lengthening maturity in the municipal bond market compared to the taxable bond market.

All other factors constant, the greater the credit risk perceived by investors, the higher the return expected by investors. Exhibit 11–2 shows general obligation municipal bond yields for the weeks of November 14 and November 21, 1985, as well as 52-week highs and lows by credit quality and maturity. As can be seen from Exhibit 11–2, the spread between municipal bonds of different credit quality is not constant. Reasons for the change in spreads are (1) the outlook for the economy and its anticipated impact on issuers, (2) federal budget financing needs, and (3) municipal market supply and demand factors. During periods of relatively low interest rates, investors sometimes increase their holdings of issues of lower credit quality in order to obtain additional yield. This narrows the spread between high-grade and lower-grade credit issues. During periods in which investors anticipate a poor economic climate, there is often a "flight to quality" as investors pursue a more conservative credit-risk exposure. This widens the spread between high-grade and lower-grade credit issues.

Another factor that causes shifts in the spread between issues of different quality is the temporary oversupply of issues within a market sector. For example, a substantial new-issue volume of high-grade state general obligation bonds may tend to decrease the spread between high-grade and lower-grade revenue bonds. In a weak market environment, it is easier for high-grade municipal bonds to come to market than for weaker credits. Therefore, it is not uncommon for high grades to flood weak markets at the same time that there is a relative scarcity of medium- and lower-grade municipal bond issues.

Liquidity

Because of the heterogeneity of municipal issues and the small size of many issues, municipal securities are traded much less actively than governments. Reflecting this, dealer's bid-asked spreads on even the most actively traded issues are relatively wide. All these factors make

EXHIBIT 11-2 Yields by Credit Quality and Maturity

New general obligations	Superior Investment Quality				High Investment Quality				Medium Investment Quality				Low Investment Quality			
	November 1985		52 Week		November 1985		52 Week		November 1985		52 Week		November 1985		52 Week	
	11/21	11/14	High	Low	11/21	11/14	High	Low	11/21	11/14	High	Low	11/21	11/14	High	Low
1 year	5.00	5.00	6.00	4.50	5.10	5.20	6.10	4.55	5.20	5.40	6.20	4.00	5.40	5.40	6.75	5.40
2 years	5.60	5.25	7.00	6.25	5.75	5.45	7.25	5.45	5.90	5.65	7.50	5.65	6.65	6.65	7.75	6.65
3 years	6.25	6.50	7.50	6.25	6.45	6.70	7.60	6.45	6.65	6.90	7.75	6.65	7.65	7.65	8.50	7.25
7 years	6.75	7.00	8.10	6.75	6.90	7.10	8.75	6.90	7.10	7.35	8.40	7.10	8.15	8.15	9.25	8.15
10 years	7.10	7.50	8.60	7.10	7.25	7.60	8.80	7.25	7.40	7.80	9.55	7.40	8.75	8.90	9.75	8.50
15 years	7.80	8.05	9.45	7.80	8.00	8.15	9.60	8.00	8.25	8.40	9.75	8.25	9.12	9.27	10.25	8.55
20 years	8.15	8.35	9.80	8.15	8.25	8.40	9.95	8.25	8.40	8.60	10.10	8.40	9.25	9.40	10.50	8.63
25 years	8.20	8.40	9.85	8.20	8.35	8.50	10.00	8.35	8.50	8.75	10.15	8.50	9.37	9.52	10.75	9.37
30 years	8.25	8.40	9.90	8.25	8.40	8.50	10.05	8.40	8.50	8.75	10.25	8.50	9.50	9.65	10.89	9.50

SOURCE: Merrill Lynch, *Bond Market Comment* 8, no. 47 (November 22, 1985).

municipals less liquid than governments. The investor should also realize that for some small local issues, there is likely to be no resale market outside the issuing locality, and even there the market may be thin to nonexistent.

The market for municipals responds less dramatically to changes in economic conditions and government policy than does the market for governments. This is not to say that the market does not respond at all. Changes in Fed policy, by altering the willingness of banks to hold municipals, directly affect the municipal market. Combined with other factors, such as the tendency for investors to shop different markets, this causes yields on municipals to rise and fall with other rates. Naturally, prices of municipals fluctuate in response to changes in current market yields. Moreover, because municipals have such long maturities, rising interest rates can force them in to large discounts. The investor who contemplates putting money into long-term municipals should realize that such an investment can turn out to be quite illiquid or, to put it another way, can expose him to a considerable price risk. Unless an investor is convinced that interest rates are at historic highs, he should not buy long-term municipals with the intention of selling them several years hence.

A final factor to bear in mind is that for reasons explained in Chapter 6, discount municipals display more price volatility than full-coupon municipals.

Risk

The investor who puts money into municipals exposes himself not only to the price risk noted above, but also to the risk of default by the issuer. While in the past investing in municipal bonds has been considered second in safety only to that of U.S. debt, there have now developed among many investors ongoing concerns about the credit risks of municipal bonds. This is true regardless of whether the bonds have been given high investment-grade credit ratings by the commercial rating companies.

The first reason for this concern results primarily from the New York City, billion-dollar financial crisis in 1975. The financial crisis sent a loud and clear warning to municipal bond investors in general that regardless of the supposedly ironclad protections for the bondholder, when issuers such as large cities have severe budget-balancing difficulties, the political hues, cries, and financial stakes of public-employee unions, vendors, and community groups may be dominant forces in the budgetary process.

This reality was further reinforced by the new federal bankruptcy law, which took effect on October 1, 1979, and which makes it easier for municipal bond issuers to seek protection from bondholders by filing for bankruptcy.

The second reason for increased concern with default risk came from the proliferation in the municipal bond market of innovative financing techniques for securing new bond issues. In addition to the more traditional general obligation bonds and toll road, bridge, and tunnel revenue bonds, there are now more nonvoter-approved, innovative, and legally untested security mechanisms. What distinguishes these newer bonds from the more traditional general obligation and revenue bonds is that there is no history of court decisions and other case law that firmly establishes the rights of the bondholders and the obligations of the issuers. For the newer financing mechanisms, it is not possible to determine the probable legal outcome if the bond securities are challenged in court.

Investor concerns over bonds secured by legally untested structures is perhaps most recently shown in the troubled bonds of the Washington Public Power Supply System (WPPSS). Both of the major commercial rating companies gave their highest ratings to these bonds in the early 1980s. One of them, Moody's, had given the WPPSS Projects 1, 2, and 3 bonds its very highest credit rating of Aaa and the Projects 4 and 5 bonds its rating of A-1. This latter investment-grade rating is defined as having the strongest investment attributes within the upper-medium grade of credit worthiness. The other major commercial company, Standard & Poor's, also had given the WPPSS Projects 1, 2, and 3 bonds its highest rating of AAA and the Projects 4 and 5 bonds its rating of A+, which is comparable to Moody's A-1 rating. While these high-quality ratings were in effect, WPPSS sold over $8 billion in long-term bonds. By 1984, Moody's had no ratings on any of the bonds. Standard & Poor's only rated the defaulted Projects 4 and 5 bonds. Its rating was D.

The third reason for concern over municipal bonds, and one that began with the first electoral victory of President Reagan in 1980, is the impact that the scaling down of federal grants and aid programs will have on the credit worthiness of both general obligation and revenue bonds. As an example of the change in federal funding policies, in December 1981 the president signed into law an extension of the Clean Water Act of 1970. Among other changes, the new amendments reduce the total federal contribution to local waste treatment programs from $90 billion projected under the old law to $36 billion. Additionally, after October 1, 1984, the federal matching contribution to local sewerage construction projects declined from 75% to 55% of the costs. Over the previous 20 years, many state and local governments had grown dependent on this and other federal grant programs as direct subsidies to their own capital construction and operating budgets. These federal grants had provided indirect subsidies to their local economies as well.

The fiscally conservative federalism can be expected to continue through the 1980s. The Reagan election victories in 1980 and 1984 can be seen as an electoral message from the American people that they want a major change in federal-state financial relationships. The passage of the 1982 Tax Equity and Fiscal Responsibility Act, with its reduction in hospital aid, is but an example of these changes. With the continued support from a broad-based, fiscally conservative, national, political constituency, we can expect the process of scaling-down federal aid to state and local governments to continue. The increased population growth in the more conservative Sun Belt regions of the country would indicate a further strengthening of this electoral base for fiscal conservatism. What this means for investors in municipal bonds is that many general obligation and revenue bond issuers may undergo serious financial stresses as the federal grant and aid reductions are implemented over the coming years.

The fourth reason for investor concern is that the American economy is undergoing a fundamental change, which is resulting in a decline of the durable goods sector of the economy. This decline has widespread implications for whole regions of the country. Many general obligation and revenue bond issuers can be expected to undergo significant economic deterioration that could negatively impact their tax collections and wealth indicators such as personal income, bank deposits, retail sales, and real property valuations. An example of this would be in the state of Illinois, where the basic structure of employment is shifting away from higher-paying manufacturing jobs to lower-paying trade and service jobs. This shift in employment is a long-term negative factor in the rate of growth of personal income and the state's general fund revenues.

Municipal Bond Insurance

Municipal bond insurance is a contractual commitment by an insurance company to pay the bondholder any bond principal and/or coupon interest that is due on a stated maturity date, but has not been paid by the bond issuer. Once issued, this municipal bond default insurance usually extends for the term of the bond issue, and it cannot be canceled by the insurance company. A one-time insurance premium (generally paid at the time of original bond issuance) is paid for the insurance policy and is nonrefundable.

The bondholder or trustee who has not received payments for bond principal and/or coupon interest on the stated due dates for the insured bonds must notify the insurance company and surrender to it the unpaid bonds and coupons. Under the terms of the policy, the insurance company is obligated to pay the paying agent sufficient monies for the bondholders. These monies must be enough to cover the face value of the insured principal and coupon interest that was due but not paid. Once the insurance company pays the monies, the company becomes the owner of the surrendered bonds and coupons and can begin legal proceedings to recover the monies that are now due it from the bond issuer.

Municipal bond insurance has been available since 1971. Some of the largest and financially strongest insurance companies in the U.S., as well as smaller monoline insurance companies, are participants in this industry. By mid-1985, approximately 25% of all new municipals were insured. The following companies are some of the major municipal bond insurers as of 1986:

American Municipal Bond Assurance Corporation (AMBAC)
Bond Investors Guaranty Insurance Company (BIGIC)
Financial Guaranty Insurance Corporation (FGIC)
Municipal Bond Insurance Association (MBIA)

At the time of this writing, all of these have ratings of AAA from Standard & Poor's, and two of them (FGIC and MBIA) also have ratings of Aaa by Moody's.

In general, although insured municipal bonds sell at yields lower than they would without the insurance, they tend to have yields substantially higher than Aaa/AAA-rated noninsured municipal bonds.

Corporate Bonds

12

We treat corporate bonds last, not because they are relatively unimportant, but simply because it seemed logical to deal with all types of government obligations first. Corporate bonds are issued in order to provide the issuer with long-term debt financing. Beyond that, it becomes difficult to generalize because there are substantial differences among the major issuers and among their purposes in borrowing.

Corporate bonds are classified into four groups: public utilities, transportations, industrials, and banks and finance companies. Finer breakdowns are often made to create more homogeneous groupings. Public utilities are subdivided into electric power companies, gas distribution companies, water companies, and telephone companies. Transportations are subdivided into airlines, railroads, and trucking companies. Industrials are the catchall class, and the most heterogeneous of the groupings with respect to investment characteristics. Industrials include all kinds of manufacturing, merchandising, and service companies.

GENERAL CHARACTERISTICS

Corporate bonds have the same general characteristics as the other bonds we have discussed. They have a fixed face value, pay interest semiannually according to a fixed coupon rate, and mature on some specified date. Both bearer and registered issues are available; however, in recent years corporations have issued bonds only in registered form.

The minimum denomination on most issues is $1,000. In common parlance, a corporate bond is assumed to have a face value of $1,000 unless otherwise explicitly specified. A dealer who says he has five bonds to sell means five bonds each of $1,000 face amount.

Historically, corporate bonds, because of the long-term nature of the capital needs they finance, have had quite long maturities—25 to 30 years. In 1970, however, utility firms started a trend toward shorter maturities by issuing five-years bonds. The reason for the switch was the high level of interest rates which led some borrowers to believe that they could reduce long-term interest costs by borrowing short and refunding later. Unfortunately for these borrowers, the trend to shorter maturities began just as interest rates hit their 1970 highs. Thereafter, rates did fall, but by the time the first short bonds were coming due, rates had risen to new historic highs, with the result that 5 years later these short issues appeared to have been an expensive miscalculation for their issuers.

The following example illustrates the trend in shortening maturities. In 1974, the average maturity of new corporate bond issues was 20 years. By 1980, the average maturity had fallen to 18 years, and by 1984, to 15 years. This shortening of maturities reflects the fact that investors wanted shorter maturities because interest rates had become so volatile.[1]

Any bond is simply a debt contract between the issuer and the bondholder. The promises of corporate issuers and the rights of investors who buy them are set forth in contracts called *bond indentures*. If bondholders were handed the complete indenture, they would have trouble understanding the legalese, and even greater difficulty determining whether the corporate issuer was keeping all the promises made. These problems are resolved for the most part by bringing in a corporate trustee as a third party to the contract. The indenture is made out to the corporate trustee as a representative of the interests of bondholders.

---

[1]Richard S. Wilson, *Bond Market Comment,* 8, no. 3 (New York: Merrill Lynch, Fixed Income Research Department, January 18, 1985).

A corporate trustee is a bond or trust company with a corporate trust department and officers who are experts in performing the functions of a trustee. In legal practice, the indenture is made out to the trustee, who acts in a fiduciary capacity for investors who own a bond issue. This is no small task. The corporate trustee must, at the time of issue, authenticate the bonds—that is, keep track of all the bonds sold and make sure that they do not exceed the principal amount authorized by the indenture. He must then be a watchdog for the bondholders, seeing to it that the issuer complies with all the covenants of the indenture. We will describe some of these covenants below.

It is important that corporate trustees be competent and financially responsible. There is a federal statute, the Trust Indenture Act, requiring that for all corporate bond offerings in the amount of more than $5 million sold in interstate commerce, there must be a corporate trustee. The indenture must include adequate requirements for performance of the trustee's duties on behalf of bondholders; there must be no conflict of business interests for the trustee; and there must be provision for reports by the trustee to bondholders. If a corporate issuer fails to pay interest or principal, the trustee must declare a default and take any action necessary to protect the rights of bondholders.

Corporate bond issues vary a great deal with respect to the provisions securing the issue as well as call and refunding practices. Consequently, careful attention to the terms of the indenture are especially important for the corporate bond buyer.

MEANS OF SECURING BOND ISSUES

Shylock demanded a pound of flesh as his security. Investors who buy corporate bonds don't go that far, but they do like some security. A bond's indenture spells out precisely how the issue is secured beyond the general credit standing of the issuer.

Mortgage bonds are always secured by a lien on property, equipment, or other real assets. The specific terms of individual mortgage bonds vary considerably. If you read *The Wall Street Journal,* you may have seen an advertisement for "$50,000,000 Metropolitan Edison, First Mortgage Bonds, 9% series, due December 1, 2008." That title tells you that the issuer has granted the bondholders a first-mortgage lien on nearly all of its properties. This lien, which is a legal right to sell mortgaged property to satisfy unpaid obligations to bondholders, protects holders of the issue.

Often first-mortgage bonds are issued in series with bonds of each series secured equally by the same first mortgage. The title of the bond issue mentioned above includes "9% Series," which tells you that the issue is one of a series. Many companies, particularly public utilities, have a policy of financing part of their capital requirements continuously by long-term debt. They want some part of their total capitalization in the form of bonds because the cost of such capital is ordinarily less than that of capital raised by sale of stock. So, as a principal amount of debt is paid off, they issue another series of bonds under the same mortgage. As they expand and need a greater amount of debt capital, they can add new series of bonds. It is a lot easier and more advantageous to issue a series of bonds under one mortgage and one indenture than it is to create entirely new bond issues with different arrangements for security.

When a bond indenture authorizes the issue of additional series of bonds with the same mortgage lien as those already issued, the indenture imposes certain conditions that must be met before the additional series may be issued. Bondholders do not want their security impaired; these conditions are for their benefit. It is common for a first-mortgage bond indenture to provide that property acquired by the issuer subsequent to granting the first mortgage lien shall be subject to the first-mortgage lien. This is termed the *after-acquired clause.* Then the indenture usually permits the issue of additional bonds up to some specified percentage of the value of the after acquired property, such as 60%. The other 40%, or whatever the percentage may be, must be financed in some other way. This is intended to assure that there will be additional assets with a value significantly greater than the amount of additional bonds secured by the mortgage. Another customary kind of restriction on issue of additional series is a requirement that earnings in an immediately preceding period must be equal to some number of times the amount of annual interest on the new series plus interest on all outstanding series. Still another common provision is that additional bonds may be issued to the extent that earlier series of bonds have been paid off.

You seldom see a bond issue with the term *second mortgage* in its title. The reason is that this term has a connotation of weakness. Sometimes companies get around that difficulty by using such words as *first and consolidated mortgage bonds, first and refunding,* or *general and refunding.* Usually this language means that a bond issue is secured by a first mortgage on some part of the issuer's property, but by a second or even third lien on other parts of its assets. A general and refunding mortgage bond generally is secured by a lien on all the company's property *subject* to the prior lien of first-mortgage bonds.

Some companies do not own fixed assets or other real property and so have nothing on which they can give a mortgage lien to secure bondholders. Instead, they own securities of other companies; they are *holding companies* and the other companies are *subsidiaries.* To satisfy the desire of bondholders for security, they pledge stocks, notes, bonds, or whatever kinds of obligations they own. These assets are termed *collateral* bonds.

Collateral trust indentures contain a number of provisions designed to protect bondholders. Generally, the market or appraised value of the collateral must be maintained at some percentage of the amount of bonds outstanding. The percentage is greater than 100 so that there will be a margin of safety. If collateral value declines below the minimum percentage, additional collateral must be provided by the issuer. There is almost always provision for withdrawal of some collateral provided other acceptable collateral is substituted.

Collateral trust bonds may be issued in series in much the same way that mortgage bonds are issued in series. The rules governing additional series of bonds require that adequate collateral must be pledged, and there may be restrictions on the use to which the proceeds of an additional series may be put. All series of bonds are issued under the same indenture and have the same claim on collateral.

Many years ago the railway companies developed a way of financing purchase of cars and locomotives called *rolling stock,* that enabled them to borrow at just about the lowest rates in the corporate bond market. Railway rolling stock has for a long time been regarded by investors as excellent security for debt. This equipment is sufficiently standardized that it can be used by one railway as well as another. And it can be readily moved from the tracks of one railroad to those of another. There is generally a good market for lease or sale of cars and locomotives. The railroads have capitalized on these characteristics of rolling stock by developing a legal arrangement for giving investors a legal claim on it that is different from, and generally better than, a mortgage lien.

The legal arrangement is one that vests legal title to railway equipment in a trustee, which is better from the standpoint of investors than a first-mortgage lien on property. A railway company orders some cars and locomotives from a manufacturer. When the job is finished, the manufacturer transfers the legal title to the equipment to a trustee. The trustee leases it to the railroad that ordered it and at the same time sells *equipment trust certificates* in an amount equal to a large percentage of the purchase price. Money from sale of certificates is paid to the manufacturer. The railway company makes an initial payment of rent equal to the balance of the purchase price, and the trustee gives that money to the manufacturer. Thus the manufacturer is paid off. The trustee collects lease rental money periodically from the railroad and uses it to pay interest and principal on the certificates. These interest payments are known as dividends. The amounts of lease rental payments are worked out carefully so that they are enough to pay the equipment trust certificates. At the end of some period of time, such as 15 years, the certificates are paid off, the trustee sells the equipment to the railroad for some nominal price, and the lease is terminated.

The beauty of this arrangement from the viewpoint of investors is that the railroad does not legally own the rolling stock until all the certificates are paid. In the event the railroad does not make the lease rental payments, there is no big legal hassle about foreclosing a lien. The trustee owns the property and can take it back because failure to pay the rent breaks the lease. The trustee can lease the equipment to another railroad and continue to make payments on the certificates from new lease rentals. It is significant that even in the worst years of depression, railways have paid their equipment trust certificates, though they did not pay bonds secured by mortgages.

Although the railway companies developed the equipment trust device, it has also been used by companies engaged in providing other kinds of transportation. The trucking companies, for example, finance purchase of huge fleets of trucks in the same manner; air transportation companies use this kind of financing to purchase transport planes; and international oil companies use it to buy the huge tankers that bring oil across the oceans.

After all the emphasis upon security, you might think that Shylock-minded investors would not buy bonds without something to secure them. But not so! Investors often buy large issues of unsecured bonds just as they buy first-mortgage bonds. These unsecured bonds are termed *debentures*. However, investors generally get higher rates of interest on debentures than on well-secured bonds, or they get the privilege of converting them into common stock of the issuer.

Debenture bonds are not secured by a specific pledge of designated property, but that does not mean that they have no claim on property of issuers or on their earnings. Debenture bondholders have the claim of general creditors on all assets of the issuer not pledged specifically to secure other debt. And they even have a claim on pledged assets to the extent that these assets have value greater than necessary to satisfy secured creditors. In fact, if there are no pledged assets and no secured creditors, debenture bondholders have first claim on all assets along with other general creditors.

These unsecured bonds are sometimes issued by companies that are so strong financially and have such a high credit rating that to offer security would be gilding the lily. Such companies can simply turn a deaf ear to investors who want security and still sell their debentures at relatively low interest rates. But debentures are sometimes also issued by companies that have already sold mortgage bonds and given liens on most of their property. These debentures rank below the mortgage bonds or collateral trust bonds in their claim on assets, and investors may regard them as relatively weak. This is the kind that bears the higher rates of interest.

Even though there is no pledge of security, the indentures for debenture bonds contain a variety of provisions designed to afford some protection to investors. Frequently the amount of a debenture bond issue is limited to the amount of the initial issue. This limit is to keep issuers from weakening the position of debenture holders by running up additional unsecured debt.

You might think that debenture bonds have about the weakest possible claim on assets and earnings of a corporate issuer, but that is not so. Some companies have issued *subordinated debenture bonds*. The term *subordinated* means that such an issue ranks after secured debt, after debenture bonds, and often after some general creditors in its claim on assets and earnings. Owners of this kind of bond stand last in line among creditors when an issuer fails financially.

Because subordinated debentures are so weak in their claim on assets, issuers would have to offer a very high rate of interest unless they also offer some special inducement to buy the bonds. The inducement is an option to convert bonds into stock of the issuer at the discretion of bondholders. If the issuer prospers and the market price of its stock rises substantially in the market, the bondholders can convert bonds to stock worth a great deal more than they paid for the bonds. This conversion privilege may also be included in the provisions of debentures that are not subordinated. Convertible securities are discussed in the next chapter.

It used to be thought that security provisions of bonds were extremely important. This is less true today for three reasons. First, bankruptcies of various types of firms have made it clear that mortgage backing for a bond is of little value to the investor if the mortgaged assets are specialized equipment that cannot be used profitably. The resale value of such equipment may be only a fraction of its cost and of the mortgage bond indebtedness. A second consideration is that in cases where bonds in default are backed by a lien on property that could be converted to alternative uses (consequently with a potentially high resale value), the courts have been loath to permit bondholders to exercise their lien, leaving little or nothing for junior creditors. Instead, they have preferred reorganization of the bankrupt companies under which all existing claims were liquidated in exchange for new claims against the reorganized company. The mortgage lien is important, though, because it gives the mortgage bondholders a very strong bargaining position relative to other creditors in determining the terms of a reorganization. Finally, in the case of government-regulated companies providing vital services, the government may require a firm in bankruptcy to continue to operate at a loss, even though doing so is to the detriment of the company's creditors—the Penn Central Railroad being a case in point.

Because of the limited value of security pledges, there is a growing tendency today to protect bondholders with various *protective covenants*. For example, a bond's indenture may specify that dividend payments must be limited if certain minimum standards with respect to the size of retained earnings or working capital are not met. Or, there may be a provision limiting the portion of current earnings that may be used to pay dividends. Provisions that specify a minimum amount of working capital give the corporate trustee early warning of deterioration of the issuer's financial strength. In such instances, the corporate trustee must watch the issuer's balance sheet and, upon the issuer's failure to maintain the minimum amount of working capital, take appropriate action to protect the interests of the bondholders. Sinking fund provisions discussed below give the bondholder added security. The investor, however, should realize that such provisions do not guarantee that an issue will never go into default, nor is the absence of the provisions necessarily a sign of weakness. Top-grade borrowers such as AT&T are so well known and trusted by the market that they can forego such provisions without impairing investor confidence in their issues. The situation is not unlike that of an individual trying to borrow at a bank. If his credit is average, he has to put up collateral. If his credit is unquestioned, he can obtain a *signature loan* simply by writing his name on a loan note.

Sometimes a corporation may guarantee the bonds of another corporation. The terms of the guarantee may call for the guarantor to guarantee the payment of interest and/or principal. For example, the debentures of Exxon Pipeline Company due 2004 are unconditionally guaranteed by Exxon Corporation and as such carry the triple-A ratings of its guarantor. There may be more than one corporate guarantor. Each guarantor may be responsible not only for its pro rata share, but the entire amount guaranteed by the other guarantors. For example, the joint venture of Gulf Oil and Texaco, called Pembroke Capital Company, is guaranteed by the two partners.

Recently, the concept of insured bonds that has been so successful in the municipal bond market has been introduced in the corporate bond market. Banks, insurance companies, and investment bankers are forming corporate-bond insurance companies to guarantee the principal and interest payments of issuers. Insured corporate bonds are rare, being limited to high-quality companies that cannot get a top credit rating because they are too small, or limited to issues that have unusual or complicated provisions unpopular with investors. But some observers believe that as much as 10 to 20% of corporate bonds may eventually be insured. Most of the corporate bonds that will be insured are expected to be short-term bonds.[2]

Regardless of whether a bond is guaranteed by a related corporation or by a corporate-bond insurance company, the issue is not free of default risk. The safety of a guaranteed or insured bond depends upon the financial capability of the guarantor or insurer.

PROVISIONS FOR PAYING OFF BONDS

Corporate bonds, as opposed to municipal bonds, are typically term rather than serial issues; that is, they run for a term of years and then become due and payable. Term bonds may be paid off prior to the

---

[2]Ann Monroe, "Triple-A Corporate Bond, Now Scarce, Is Making a Comeback as Insured Debt," *The Wall Street Journal,* June 14, 1985, p. 34.

maturity date by use of a *sinking fund* or by an optional *call feature,* both of which are described in the bond indenture. In the case of convertible bonds, the subject of the next chapter, the bonds may be converted to or exchanged for another security prior to maturity.

The sinking fund provision requires that the issuer make annual payments into a sinking fund. Those last two words are often misunderstood to mean that the issuer accumulates a fund in cash, or in assets readily sold for cash, that is used to pay bonds at maturity. It had that meaning many years ago, but too often the money supposed to be in a sinking fund was not all there when it was needed. In modern practice there is no fund, and *sinking* means that money is applied periodically to redemption of bonds before maturity. Corporate bond indentures require the issuer to retire a specified portion of an issue each year. This kind of provision for repayment of corporate debt may be designed to liquidate all of a bond issue by maturity date, or it may be arranged to pay only a part of the total by the end of the term. If only a part is paid, the remainder is called a *balloon maturity.*

The issuer may satisfy the sinking-fund requirement in one of two ways. A cash payment of the face amount of the bonds to be retired may be made by the corporate debtor to the trustee. The latter then calls the bonds by lot for redemption. They may be selected randomly by serial number. Owners of bonds called in this manner turn them in for redemption; *interest payments stop at the redemption date.* Alternatively, the issuer can deliver to the trustee bonds with a total face value equal to the amount that must be retired. The bonds are purchased by the *issuer* in the open market. This option is elected by the issuer when the bonds are selling below par. Some corporate bond indentures, however, prohibit the open market purchase of the bonds by the issuer.

The issuer is granted a special call price to satisfy any sinking-fund requirement. If the bonds were originally sold at par, the sinking-fund price is that par value. If they were issued at a price greater than par, the sinking-fund call price generally starts at the issuance price and scales down to par as the issue approaches maturity.

Sinking-fund provisions provide the investor with additional security because they force some financial discipline upon the issuer. On the other hand, such provisions have the disadvantage of placing the investor in a position where his bond may be called at any time, in particular at a time when interest rates are low and currently available bonds are less attractive than the called bond. The call price on a bond retired for sinking fund purposes is typically lower than the price the issuer would have to pay if the whole issue were called.

Industrial issues almost always include sinking-fund provisions. Finance companies, on the other hand, almost always do not. The inclusion or absence of a sinking-fund provision in public utility debt obligations depends upon the type of public utility. Pipeline issues almost always include sinking-fund provisions, whereas telephone issues do not. For electrical utilities a "blanket" sinking-fund requirement is generally included.

Some corporate obligations are arranged so that specified principal amounts become due on specified dates. Such issues are called *serial bonds*. Equipment trust certificates, discussed earlier, are structured as serial bonds. The advantage of a serial bond issue from the investor's point of view is that the repayment schedule will match the decline in the value of the equipment used as collateral. Hence, default risk is reduced. In addition, the potential investor can select from a spectrum of maturity dates.

Bonds may be called for other than sinking-fund purposes. Provisions for such calls and for refunding calls are common on corporate bond issues and should be studied carefully by the investor, particularly if he feels that he is investing at a time when long-term interest rates are at a peak. Calls other than for sinking-fund purposes are most likely to occur and are more detrimental to the investor during periods when market yields fall below the coupon on the bond he holds.

These provisions typically deny the issuer the right to redeem bonds during the first 5 or 10 years following the date of issue if the proceeds for the redemption come from lower cost funds obtained with issues ranking equal or superior to the redeemed debt. This type of redemption is called *refunding*. However, while most long-term issues have these refunding bars or prohibitions, they are usually immediately callable, in whole or in part, if the source of funds is from other than lower-interest-cost money. Such sources may include retained earnings, the proceeds from a common stock sale, or funds from the disposition of property.

Many shorter- to intermediate-term bonds and notes are not callable for the first 3 to 7 years (in some cases, not callable for the life of the issue). Thereafter, they may be called for any reason. Bond market participants often confuse refunding protection and call protection. Call protection is much more absolute in that bonds cannot be redeemed for any reason. Refunding restrictions only provide protection against one type of redemption.

Long-term industrial issues generally have 10 years of refunding protection but are immediately callable. Electric utilities most often have 5 years of refunding protection although, during times of high interest rates, issues with 10 years of refunding protection have been sold. Long-term debt of the former members of the Bell Telephone System have 5 years of call protection.

As a rule, corporate bonds are callable at a premium above par. Generally, the amount of the premium declines as the bond approaches maturity. The initial amount of the premium may be as much as 1 year's interest or as little as interest for half a year.

When less than the entire issue is called, the specific bonds to be called are selected randomly or on a pro rata basis. If the bonds selected on a random basis are bearer bonds, the serial number of the certificates is published in *The Wall Street Journal* and major metropolitan dailies. Such information can also be found in *Moody's Bond Survey.*

BOND RATINGS

On corporate bonds, as on municipal issues, there is a risk of default. The investor has a legitimate and compelling need to compare the quality of available issues before he buys. Corporate bonds, like municipals, are a heterogeneous mix of securities emanating from different issuers and carrying different provisions. However, investors would find making such quality comparisons a difficult and time-consuming task if they had to do it themselves. Fortunately, they do not, since all large corporate issues marketed nationally are rated by at least one of the well-known commercial rating companies—Standard & Poor's, Moody's, Duff & Phelps, and Fitch. (As in the case of municipal issues, the corporate issuer willingly pays to have his issue rated because the issue may not be saleable without a rating.) In addition, several investment banking firms perform more timely credit analysis of issues for their clients.

In the rating of corporate bonds, as in the rating of municipals, the principal question concerns the issuer's predicted ability to make timely payments of interest and principal. In the case of corporate issuers, much of the analysis underlying the rating focuses on (1) the character of the industry in which the issuer operates (Is it growing or stagnant, cyclical or steady?); (2) the strengths and weaknesses of the issuing firm within the industry (Does the firm have adequate access to raw materials? How good is its physical plant?); (3) the specific nature of the collateral provisions and/or other pledges given in the indenture; and (4) recent and probable future trends in the issuer's balance sheet and income statement. With respect to the last factor, special attention is often given to earnings coverage, that is, the ratio of earnings before interest and tax payments to interest charges on all debt or, if sinking-fund charges are mandatory, to such payments plus interest charges.

Evaluating all these factors and determining what they imply about the issuer's ability to meet interest and principal payments on its debts is a difficult and involved operation, one in which opinions can differ and some subjective evaluation inevitably enters. Ratings are put together by committees of people, not ground out by computers. Thus the ratings of the commercial rating companies do differ on some individual issues; and issues that hold top ratings when first issued do sometimes end in default. Nevertheless, investor confidence in the ratings is high, in part because their track record is good. Studies of past experience reveal that bond default rates have been consistently and substantially lower for top-rated issues than for lower-rated issues.[3]

Ratings on individual corporate issues, like those on municipals, are constantly being revised up or down in light of changes in the fortunes of particular industries and individual firms within these industries. As we explained in Chapter 7, however, one problem with the rating companies has been the lag in altered ratings based on changes in circumstances of the issuer. The ratings assigned by each of the four commercial rating companies are summarized in Exhibit 12–1.

ISSUING PROCEDURE

Because of some rather flagrant abuses that occurred in the 1920s and the considerable losses sustained by investors as a result of the stock market crash of 1929 and the ensuing depression, the climate was ripe in the 1930s for some substantial securities reform legislation. The result was the Securities Act of 1933 and the Securities Exchange Act of

---

[3]See, in particular, W. Braddock Hickman, *Corporate Bond Quality and Investor Experience,* National Bureau of Economic Research (Princeton University Press, 1958).

EXHIBIT 12-1 Bond Ratings

	Duff & Phelps	Fitch	Moody's	Standard & Poor's	Definition
High grade	1	AAA	Aaa	AAA	The highest rating assigned to a debt instrument indicating an extremely strong capacity to pay principal and interest. Bonds in this category are often referred to as *gilt edge securities.*
	2–4	AA	Aa	AA	High-quality bonds by all standards with strong capacity to pay principal and interest. These bonds are rated lower primarily because the margins of protection are not as strong as those for Aaa and AAA.
Medium grade	5–7	A	A	A	These bonds possess many favorable investment attributes, but elements may be present which suggest a susceptibility to impairment given adverse economic changes.
	8–10	BBB	Baa	BBB	Bonds regarded as having adequate capacity to pay principal and interest, but certain protective elements may be lacking in the event of adverse economic conditions which could lead to a weakened capacity for payment.

Speculative	11–13	BB	Ba	BB	Regarded as having only moderate protection of principal and interest payments during both good and bad times.
	14	B	B	B	Generally lack characteristics of other desirable investments. Assurance of interest and principal payments over any long period of time may be small.
Default	15	CCC	Caa	CCC	Poor quality issues that may be in default or in danger of default.
	16	CC	Ca	CC	Highly speculative issues; often in default or possessing other marked shortcomings.
Default	17		C		The lowest rated class of bonds. Can be regarded as extremely poor in investment quality.
		C		C	Rating given to income bonds on which no interest is being paid.
		DDD, DD,D		D	In default with principal and/or interest payments in arrears. Extremely speculative and should be valued only on the basis of their value in liquidation or reorganization.

Adapted from *Bond Guide* (New York: Standard & Poor's Corporation, monthly); *Bond Record* (New York: Moody's Investors Services, Inc., monthly); *Rating Register* (New York: Fitch Investors Service, Inc., monthly) Reprinted by permission.

SOURCE: Frank K. Reilly, *Investment Analysis and Portfolio Management,* 2nd ed. (Hinsdale, Ill.: Dryden Press, 1985), Table 17–2, pp. 510–11.

1934. The protection that these acts provide for the investor is now taken for granted, their provisions being viewed as normal and reasonable in the U.S. These acts are, however, unusual in that most foreign countries have never passed comparable legislation.

The Securities Act of 1933 was concerned primarily with the issue of new securities. Its principal purposes were (1) to ensure that full disclosure of pertinent information was made to investors and (2) to prohibit misrepresentation and other forms of fraud in the distribution of securities.

To obtain full disclosure the act requires that before a new issue is sold, a registration statement be filed with the Securities and Exchange Commission (SEC).[4] This statement includes information on the issuer, its officers and directors, its capitalization, the purpose of the financing, the terms of the underwriting, income statements and balance sheets for the issuer, and certain legal agreements. The act also requires that a *prospectus* containing information from the first part of the registration statement on the issuer's finances and on other factors of vital interest to investors be distributed to prospective buyers of the issue during the initial distribution and a 90-day period thereafter. Because of this requirement, newspaper announcements of new issues always contain the phrase: "This announcement is neither an offer to sell nor a solicitation of an offer to buy these securities. The offer is made only by the Prospectus."

Registration of a security with the SEC is no guarantee that it will turn out to be a good investment. The SEC does not pass on the investment quality of securities registered with it. It does, however, require that a waiting period of at least 20 days be observed between registration and sale. During this time, the Commission examines the registration statement to check that all information has been fully and accurately disclosed. On large issues, while the Commission is doing its work, it is common practice to issue a preliminary prospectus containing all information required except the offering price and coupon. A preliminary prospectus must be stamped *preliminary* in red ink, which has led to the nickname *red herring*. The purpose of a red herring is to give the underwriters participating in the distribution of a new issue information on which they can engage in a pre-issue selling

---

[4] Actually, not all new issues are subject to registration with the SEC. New issues not exceeding an amount specified by the SEC may be exempted by the Commission. Also, intrastate issues and issues not offered publicly for sale are exempt.

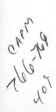

effort. Such efforts permit the selling syndicate to locate investor interest in the new issue, which in turn enables the syndicate to sell out the issue rapidly once it is cleared by the SEC and final pricing terms are set.

One problem that arises for the SEC in deciding what and how much information must be included in a prospectus is that full disclosure of the operations of a modern corporation may result in the investor being given so much information in such an indigestible form that reading the prospectus actually informs him of very little. On the other hand, requiring that the prospectus be written in a summary and comprehensible form poses the danger of inadequate disclosure and possible misrepresentation.

Prospectuses are generally written in anything but informal English, and they are full of standard disclaimers. Ray Garrett, ex-SEC chairman, parodied one for an airplane manufacturer as follows:

> There can be no assurance that a heavier-than-air machine can be made to fly, or that if it can, anyone will want to buy one, or if someone wants to buy one, he will be willing to pay enough to make production profitable.

Or better still, General Eisenhower's message to the D-day troops as filed with the SEC:

> The officers who planned this assault, including myself, have never before planned anything like this. In fact, I have never commanded any troops in combat. The airborne and other methods being employed have never before been tried by our Army. The weather forecast is only slightly favorable and such forecasts have a high degree of unreliability. Therefore, there is no assurance that any of you will reach Normandy alive, or, if you do, that you can secure the beach.[5]

All this is funny and a bit discouraging, but whatever shortcomings registration may have, the process has served to force broader disclosure and to get more information into the hands of investors.

Underwriting

Like municipals, corporate bonds are distributed by underwriting syndicates and for much the same reason. The issues are small in size

---

[5]Reprinted with permission of *The Wall Street Journal,* © Dow Jones & Company, Inc., October 23, 1975. All rights reserved.

relative to the market and heterogeneous in character, with the result that underwriters are needed to obtain a broad market.

In the market for corporate new issues, however, underwriting practices differ somewhat from those in the market for municipals. Generally, municipal new issues are sold to underwriters through competitive bidding. In the case of corporate new issues, competitive bidding is rare. The normal practice is to have a negotiated sale. First, the issuer chooses an investment banking firm and agrees upon a selling concession; this may range from less than ½ point for a top-grade issue sold in a good market to 1½ or even 1¾ points for a Baa issue sold in a poor market.

Once the underwriter is chosen, the issuer and the underwriter decide upon the terms and timing of the new issue. To the issuing corporation, this arrangement offers an important advantage, namely, that in formulating the terms of its issue, it can rely on the investment banker's wide knowledge of the bond market and close contact with current conditions in that market. The offsetting disadvantage is that the underwriting concession may be greater than the cost at which the issue could have been sold through competitive bidding. For firms that make frequent trips to the capital market for new funds, it is normal to have a continuing relationship with a single investment banker.

Besides helping the issuer to design his issue and prepare a registration statement, the investment banker also assumes responsibility for the distribution of the issue. This is done through an underwriting syndicate, which the investment banking firm typically heads. Such syndicates do not have a continuing life; they are formed for individual issues and terminate when the issue has been distributed. The members of the syndicate receive from the underwriting spread a commission on the bonds they sell—¼ to ⅜ of a point.

Because the normal practice is for the underwriter to buy up the issue at a fixed price from the issuer (except on marginal issues which may be sold on a "best efforts" basis), the underwriting group assumes a considerable price risk which they attempt to minimize through a quick sellout. As noted above, this is the major purpose of soliciting preliminary interest with a *red herring*.

Generally there is some lag—4 to 5 days—between the sale and the actual issuance of corporate bonds. During this period the bonds trade on a *when as and if issued* basis, which means that the seller promises to deliver the bonds ordered by the buyer *when as and if* the bonds are actually issued. The *if* part of this clause might seem unnecessary given all the preparation, including registration, that precedes the actual sale of an issue. However, the clause has a real purpose—to protect the seller against last-minute complications that can and sometimes do prevent final issuance. To pick a classic example, in 1974 AT&T offered $600 million of notes and debentures through Salomon Brothers, a leading investment banking firm. A few days before scheduled delivery, when the issues were almost sold out, the Justice Department, thinking that the sale had been completed, filed sweeping antitrust charges against AT&T. As a result of these charges, the SEC demanded that AT&T amend or revise its registration statement and give buyers at least 1 day to reconsider their purchase commitments. These demands could have been met, but disaffection for the issue spread among prospective buyers, and AT&T finally withdrew the issue at considerable cost and inconvenience to itself, the selling syndicate, and also the many institutional investors who had liquidated old bonds as part of an intended swap for the new AT&T issue.

One wrinkle that is common in corporate placements but uncommon in government agency and municipal securities (except for government-guaranteed ship financing bonds and certain municipal revenue bonds) is *direct placements*. In a direct placement the bonds being issued are never offered publicly for sale. Instead, they are placed with one or several large institutional buyers, such as insurance companies and pension funds.

Direct placements may be worked out directly between the issuer and the buyer, or they may be worked out with the aid of an investment banking firm, which offers the issuer advice and helps locate buyers for the issue. In the case of a direct placement, the investment banking house can approach only a limited number of buyers to avoid having the SEC view the issue as a public offer—just how many buyers is one of those undefined numbers but it obviously grows with the size of the issue. Generally, direct placements are not rated unless the buyer requires it, for example, if he is required to invest in securities carrying some minimum rating.

THE SECONDARY MARKET

Once a corporate issue has been distributed, trading in it passes to the secondary market. The principal secondary market for corporate bonds is a dealer-made, over-the-counter market. This market, in which probably 95% of all trading occurs, is similar to those that exist for governments and municipal securities and is made in many cases by the same dealers, the main exception being dealer banks who are barred from underwriting or making markets in corporate bonds. The other 5% of secondary trading in corporate bonds occurs on organized stock exchanges. The New York Stock Exchange lists a large number of corporate bonds; the American Stock Exchange lists a much smaller number. On both exchanges, a high proportion of listed bonds are convertibles. Generally, trading on the exchanges is in small lots. Almost all small-lot trading in bonds listed on the NYSE occurs on that exchange because of the *rule of 10*. This exchange rule requires dealers who are members of the NYSE to execute trades in listed bonds on the exchange whenever the trade is for 9 bonds or less.

Buying and Selling Corporate Bonds

In buying governments, agencies, and municipals, you can go to either a bank or a broker. If you want to buy corporate bonds, your trip has to be to a broker. There are a large number of dealers in the corporate bond market. Many of the most important shops, Salomon Brothers and The First Boston Corp., to name two, deal with only institutional customers—pension funds, life insurance companies, and other large business investors. The individual who wants to buy corporates has to go to a firm with a retail business, any brokerage house at which he would normally trade stocks.

While individuals have been buying an increasing number of bonds in recent years, the volume of bond trades by individuals is still minuscule compared with their stock trades. As a result, the investor may find that some retail brokers are not very enthusiastic or informed about bonds. The typical broker is a fount of information about stocks because being informed about and proffering free advise on stocks is a competitive device used by brokers to attract customers and earn commissions. For bonds, however, low trading volume and low commissions make such effort less worthwhile.

Nevertheless, it is helpful to buy through a broker who knows bonds. To find such a broker, your best bet is probably to start with a firm that has extensive retail operations and is also active as an underwriter and dealer in corporate and other bonds. Call the firm and ask for an account executive who *has* customers trading bonds. If you are lucky, you will find someone who can offer you the help and information you would expect if you were trading stocks.

There are essentially two sources of bonds to the investor: the new-issue market and the secondary market, which trades seasoned issues.

Shopping the new-issues market restricts the investor's choice somewhat but offers him the advantage that he can buy there at no commission. The seller earns his profit from the underwriting spread and is required to sell to all customers at the offering price. One way to shop the new-issues market is to watch announcements and, when you see an appealing issue, call your broker and put in an order. This approach, while it works much of the time, may lead to disappointments, since corporate issues are sometimes presold. The tombstone announcements published when a new issue is priced and offered for final sale are published even if a new issue has been presold, since a published announcement is required as a matter of legal record (see Exhibit 12–2).

Rather than watch for tombstone announcements, you can check the weekly publication *Moody's Bond Survey* for information about proposed offerings. A sample page from that publication is shown as Exhibit 12–3. In addition to providing information about proposed offerings, Moody's provides summary information about the issue and issuer such as the business of the issuer, how the issuer will use the proceeds, the quality rating of the issue as assigned by Moody's, denominations available, the form of the security (registered or bearer), exchange options, security for the bonds, guarantees, call provisions, sinking-fund requirements, restrictions on management, and statistical highlights about the issuer. Exhibit 12–4 is a sample write-up of a new offering taken from this publication. *Creditwatch,* published weekly by Standard & Poor's, provides similar information. Both of these publications are usually carried by local libraries.

Probably the best approach if you want to buy a new issue is to call your broker and tell him roughly what you want—say, an Aa or better industrial issue with a 15-year maturity. If your broker is alert, he should be able to suggest an appropriate new issue in short order and before it is announced in the paper. Of course, he will not be able to tell you the exact coupon the issue will carry, but he can give you a good estimate of what the coupon will be and he can supply you with a red herring prospectus. That is enough information for you to determine whether you are interested in the issue and whether you want to put in an order for the issue, provided that the actual coupon has a value of at least a certain predetermined percentage.

EXHIBIT 12-2 Announcement of a Corporate Bond Offering

This announcement is neither an offer to sell nor a solicitation of an offer to buy these securities.
The offer is made only by the Prospectus Supplement and the related Prospectus.

New Issue / April 25, 1986

$100,000,000

Florida Power & Light Company

First Mortgage Bonds, 9⅛% Series due May 1, 2016

Price 100% and accrued interest, if any, from May 1, 1986

Copies of the Prospectus Supplement and the related Prospectus may be obtained
in any State in which this announcement is circulated only from such of the
undersigned as may legally offer these securities in such State.

Salomon Brothers Inc

Goldman, Sachs & Co.

Merrill Lynch Capital Markets

The First Boston Corporation   Morgan Stanley & Co.   Shearson Lehman Brothers Inc.
                                Incorporated

Bear, Stearns & Co. Inc.   Alex. Brown & Sons
                                                        Incorporated

Daiwa Securities America Inc.   Deutsche Bank Capital   Dillon, Read & Co. Inc.
                                 Corporation

Donaldson, Lufkin & Jenrette   Drexel Burnham Lambert
Securities Corporation   Incorporated

E. F. Hutton & Company Inc.   Kidder, Peabody & Co.   Lazard Frères & Co.
                               Incorporated

The Nikko Securities Co.   Nomura Securities International, Inc.   PaineWebber
International, Inc.   Incorporated

Prudential-Bache   L. F. Rothschild, Unterberg, Towbin, Inc.
Securities

Smith Barney, Harris Upham & Co.   Swiss Bank Corporation International
Incorporated   Securities Inc.

UBS Securities Inc.   Wertheim & Co., Inc.

Dean Witter Reynolds Inc.   Yamaichi International (America), Inc.

First Equity Corporation   Raymond, James & Associates, Inc.
of Florida

In shopping the secondary market, you have a lot more choice. One advantage of shopping the secondary market is that you may be able to pick up some very attractive deep-discount bonds there. As we noted, a large number of bonds are listed on the NYSE and the AMEX and there are hundreds more unlisted bonds traded in the dealer-made, over-the-counter market. Leading newspapers publish daily a record of prices at which NYSE-listed bond issues were traded on the preceding business day. Exhibit 12–5 shows part of the record of trading in NYSE bond issues on a randomly selected day.

The first task is to identify corporate issuers. Most of us can read "ATT" to mean American Telephone and Telegraph Company, but what is the name of the issuer abbreviated to "Bally"? You may have to refer to one of the bond-rating booklets published monthly by one of the commercial rating companies to get the full name. The particular bond issue is indicated by the interest rate and year of maturity; thus, "ATT 7s01" means an issue bearing interest at 7% and due in the year 2001. In the next column reading from left to right is the current yield on the issue. *Notice that this is not the yield to maturity.* In some instances you find the letters *cv* instead of current yield. The letters mean that the bond is *convertible.* The conversion option affects market price and distorts current yield. Sometimes the letter *f* appears in the column for current yield. This means that the bond is *traded flat;* that is, a purchaser does not have to pay a seller accrued interest from the bond's last interest payment date to date of purchase. All other bonds are traded with accrued interest. Bonds traded flat are in default, or for some other reason the next interest payment is particularly uncertain. Looking to the right, you see a number that indicates the total volume of trading in an issue during the day. Scan that column and you see that trading in some issues has been only 5 or 10 bonds and that many listed issues do not appear in this table of prices because there was no trading during the day. Then you come to the high, low, and closing prices for the day. For some issues these three numbers are all the same, which usually means that only one transaction took place during the day. In the last column is the net change in closing price on the day of the report relative to the closing price on the most recent previous day the bond issue was traded.

Commissions on purchases of listed corporate bonds run quite low: for bonds with a maturity of more than 7 years, it is $10 per bond for the first 5 bonds and $5 per bond thereafter; on shorter

EXHIBIT 12-3

7340 • *Moody's Bond Survey*

Transportation

New Offering

American Airlines, Inc.
Sub. Debenture 6¼s with Warrants, 3/1/1996

Rating	Amount (Mill.)	Call Price	Offering Price	Yield Current	Maturity
Baa2	$200.0	[1]	[2]	...	...

[1] The debentures are redeemable, in whole or in part, at American's option, at any time on or after March 1, 1988, at par plus accrued interest. The warrants are redeemable, in whole or in part, at AMR's option, on or after March 1, 1988, if the closing price of AMR common stock has equalled or exceeded 115% of the then effective exercise price of the warrants for at least 20 trading days within a period of 30 consecutive trading days ending within 15 days prior to the notice of redemption. Any such redemption of warrants will be at $50 per warrant for the 12 month period beginning March 1, 1988, and at declining prices thereafter, to March 1, 1996. [2] $1,000 per unit.

Details: The debentures and warrants were offered on March 7, 1986, in units consisting of one debenture of $1,000 principal amount and one warrant to purchase 16.19 shares of AMR Corporation common stock ($1 par) through Morgan Stanley & Co. Incorporated and Salomon Brothers Inc. The issue was priced to the company at $990 per unit.

The debentures and warrants will be issued in fully registered form, and will not be separately transferrable until after June 16, 1986, or on an earlier date to be determined by the underwriters.

The debentures and warrants will be dated March 1, 1986. Interest will be payable semiannually, on September 1 and March 1, beginning September 1, 1986, to holders registered as of the August 15 or the February 15 preceding the interest payment date.

craft at lease terminations. Also at such date, approximately $870 million had been authorized by AMR and its subsidiaries, including American, for aircraft modifications, spare parts and equipment, and for additional airport and office facilities and equipment, of which approximately $650 million was expected to be expended during 1986. AMR and American intend to fund such expenditures with internally generated funds and through debt and lease financings.

Fixed Charge Coverage: Consolidated for AMR:

	1985	1984	1983	[1] 1982	1981
[2] Actual	...	3.29	2.84	2.54	...	1.14

[1] Earnings were inadequate to cover fixed charges by $46,117,000 for the year ended December 31, 1982. [2] As outlined in the prospectus, earnings represent consolidated earnings before income taxes and extraordinary item and fixed charges (excluding interest capitalized). Fixed charges consist of interest and the portion of rental expense deemed representative of the interest factor.

Security: The debentures will be direct, unsecured obligations of American Airlines. They will be subordinate in right of payment to the full principal of the principal of, premium, if any, and interest on all senior debt.

Original Issue Discount: The debentures may be issued at an original issue discount. Initial and subsequent holders will be required to report, for federal income tax purposes, a ratable share of the discount as ordinary income each year.

Business: AMR is the parent company of American Airlines, Inc., which accounted for approximately 96% of AMR's consolidated operating revenues and expenses in 1985.

American is one of the largest United States airlines, serving 130 airports in 39 states, the District of Columbia, Bermuda, Canada, the Caribbean, France, West Germany, Great Britain, Mexico, and Puerto Rico. American's leading nonstop routes in 1985, in terms of revenue passenger miles, were those between Los Angeles and

Application will be made to list the debentures on the New York Stock Exchange, and AMR intends to make application to list the warrants on NASDQ.

Quality & Rating: Medium grade; **Baa2**.

The rating of the subordinated debentures of American Airlines, Inc., is based on the airline's strong liquidity, superior financial performance relative to its peers, and its premier market position. American's two-tier wage structure has allowed the airline to implement an aggressive expansion plan, and it plans to establish new hubs at Nashville, Tennessee, Raleigh/Durham, North Carolina, and San Juan, Puerto Rico.

American's nationwide route structure, combined with its frequent-traveler program and computerized reservation system, give it a strong fundamental advantage. Considering its present high cost position, the major challenge facing the airline is to maximize the differential between yields and costs. However, this process may be aggravated by industrywide fare discounting due to the cash-flow pricing techniques of weaker carriers, strategies to maintain or increase market share, and American's increased exposure to low-fare airlines.

Although American will dedicate a substantial part of its financial resources to a major aircraft-acquisition program, we expect the company to be able to maintain its financial flexibility even as industrywide pricing discipline fails.

Purpose: The net proceeds from the sale of the debentures and warrants will be added to the working capital of American and AMR, respectively, and will be available for general purposes, among which may be the financing of capital expenditures by American or other subsidiaries of AMR, including the acquisition by American of aircraft and related equipment. At December 31, 1985, payments expected to be made by American during 1986 aggregate approximately $970 million for purchase of aircraft and related equipment, including the purchase of 22 Boeing 727 air-

New York; Dallas/Fort Worth (DFW) and New York; DFW and Honolulu; New York and San Juan; Chicago and Los Angeles; Honolulu and Los Angeles; DFW and Los Angeles; New York and San Francisco; Chicago and San Francisco; and DFW and London. During the year ended December 31, 1985, American's scheduled commercial flights averaged over 1,056,000 airplane miles daily. In 1985, American's passenger service and its freight operations accounted for approximately 85.1% and 2.8% of its total operating revenues, respectively. In the same period, American's domestic and Canadian flights accounted for 92.0% of its total passenger revenues, Caribbean and Mexican flights accounted for 4.9%, and European flights accounted for 3.1%.

Common Statistics per Share: AMR

	[1] 1986	1985	1984	1983	1982	1981
Earnings	...	$5.94	$4.37	$4.79	−$1.00	$1.21
Dividends	...	0	0	0	0	0
Price Range:						
High	53½	50¾	41¼	39⅛	25¾	21⅝
Low	39¼	33½	24¼	18½	9¼	8⅝

[1] For the first quarter through March 3, 1986.

Capitalization: Consolidated for AMR and adjusted for the application of the proceeds from sale of the units (dollars in thousands):

	Pro Forma December 31, 1985	% of Total
[1] Short-term debt	$143,231	3.2
Long-term debt	1,993,725	44.8
Total debt	$2,136,956	48.0
Preferred stock	88,621	2.0
[2] Common & surplus	2,217,914	50.0
Total	$4,443,491	100.0

[1] Includes $99,660,000 current maturities of long-term debt and $43,565,000 of capitalized lease obligations. [2] Includes 58,681,000 common shares ($1 par) and 2,971,000 preferred shares outstanding.

EXHIBIT 12–3 *(concluded)*

March 17, 1986

Statistical Highlights AMR (dollars in millions):

	1985	1984	1983	1982	1981	1980
Gross revenue.........	$6,131	$5,354	$4,763	$4,177	$4,109	$3,821
Operating profit	537	368	281	9	72	− 86
Operating margin	8.8%	6.9%	5.9%	0.2%	1.1%	− 2.3%
[1] Net income	$346	$234	$228	− $20	$47	$76
Interest coverage						
(times)...............	...	3.4x	2.4x	0.7x	1.1x	− 0.3x
Retained cash flow...	...	$621	$538	$210	$258	$193
Net capital expend...	...	429	490	403	516	417
RCF/Net capex	...	144.8%	109.7%	52.0%	49.3%	46.2%
Total debt..............	...	$1,650	$1,624	$1,617	$1,625	$1,364
Total capital...........	...	3,657	3,285	2,645	2,656	2,280
Debt/capital...........	...	45.1%	49.4%	61.1%	63.2%	59.8%
RCF/debt...............	...	37.6	33.1	13.0	15.3	14.1
Return on sales	...	4.4	4.8	− 0.5	12	− 2.0
Return on equity	...	13.2	14.9	− 2.1	2.1	−
						18.9
Return on capital	...	6.4	6.9	− 0.7	0.7	− 6.6
Load factor............	...	62.6	65.0	63.3	61.4	60.4
Breakeven load factor ..	...	57.1	60.4	63.7	60.5	62.8
Yield/RPM	...	18.81c	11.39c	11.04c	12.13c	11.12c
[2] Yield x load factor	...	7.39x	9.40x	6.99x	7.45x	6.72x
[2] Op. rev./ASM	...	8.67c	8.64c	8.15c	8.67c	7.95c
[2] Op. cost/ASM.....	...	8.09	8.17	8.19	8.57	8.39

---

[1] Net results include the following net extraordinary items: 1984, $3.6 million; 1983, $78 million; 1982, $130.5 million; 1981, $28.7 million, and 1980, $57 million.
[2] Calculated by Moody's.

---

maturities it is $5 per bond. Some brokerage houses, however, impose minimum commissions in the range of $20 per trade. On unlisted bonds that the broker has in inventory, the commission on a buy order may be zero because the seller makes his profit on his bid-asked spread.

Generally speaking, it is a wise practice to stick to listed bonds. The reason is liquidity. Prices on over-the-counter issues that are not too actively traded can take tumbles quite out of line with what happens to the market in general. Thus, the investor who buys unlisted bonds may be inviting an unnecessary liquidity problem. You can determine whether a new issue is going to be listed before you buy. The listing is something the issuer typically applies for and pays for before a new issue is offered for sale.

Corporate bonds can be sold through your broker at the same commission rates at which they are bought.

EXHIBIT 12–4

STANDARD & POOR'S CREDITWEEK

enhancement. However, meaningful improvement in key indicators of bondholder protection depends importantly on the company's ability to complete Hope Creek in a timely fashion and responsive ratemaking treatment in the pending rate case.

Barbara Walicke (212) 208-1656
Michael Puleo (212) 208-1844

Wisconsin Power & Light Co.

$38 million first mortgage bonds due 1991
To be sold, mid-May, Goldman Sachs & Co.
Rated 'AA+'; outstanding ratings affirmed

Rationale: S&P assigns an 'AA+' rating to Wisconsin Power & Light Co.'s proposed issue of $38 million first mortgage bonds. Ratings are affirmed on all publicly outstanding senior debt at 'AA+', preferred stock at 'AA', and commercial paper at 'A-1+' (*Credit Bulletin, Apr. 28*). Approximately $303 million of debt is outstanding. The ratings reflect prospects for continued strength in overall measures of creditor protection. Expectations of moderate growth in demand, coupled with hefty capacity margins, should obviate the need for additional base load generating capacity through the balance of the century. Meanwhile, prospective construction expenditures, primarily for additions and improvements to existing facilities, should continue to be fully manageable and funded almost entirely from internally generated sources. Pretax coverage of interest charges, earnings quality, and return on equity remain quite strong and may strengthen further as last summer's rate relief is fully realized. Revenues are derived largely from the residential and commercial sectors, providing some insulation from economic cyclicality. The utility continues to pursue diversification and, as of year-end 1985, aggregate net assets of the nonutility subsidiaries were $7.5 million. Credit quality is expected to remain strong, given prospects for a continuation of healthy internal funds generation, solid earnings quality, and a conservative capital structure.

Regulation: Rate regulation in Wisconsin historically has been largely supportive of strong credit quality. However, recent changes in the makeup of the Public Service Commission could alter the tenor of regulation. The utility's last major rate hike of $17.4 million for electric, $0.6 million for gas, and $33,000 for water service became effective in August 1985. The order, which awarded about 58% of the total revised amount sought, was predicated upon a 14.5% return on equity. The bulk of the revenue shortfall was attributable to a lower rate of return, disallowance of certain labor costs, a lower inflation rate, denial of a cash return on construction work in progress (CWIP), and amortization of some nuclear fuel disposal costs.

Currently pending before the commission is an application filed on Dec. 30, 1985 for a $14.4 million electric, a $0.5 million gas, and a $0.6 million water rate increase based upon a $14.5% return on equity. A final decision is expected later this year.

Financial statistics	1985	1984	1983	1982
Gross cash flow (mil. $)	125.8	111.5	112.8	101.9
Net cash flow (mil. $)	85.7	74.1	78.4	70.4
Capital outlays (mil. $)	82.3	91.7	92.5	100.0
Net plant (mil. $)	780.7	550.2	544.9	553.9
CWIP (mil. $)	10.5	225.9	187.7	141.2
Total assets (mil. $)	976.7	925.1	881.2	833.9
Total capital (mil. $)	778.6	743.3	691.4	649.5
Short-term debt (%)	2.6	4.2	1.6	0.8
Long-term debt (%)	42.8	40.3	43.3	45.3
Preferred stock (%)	7.7	9.1	10.0	10.8
Common equity (%)	47.0	46.5	45.1	43.1
Cash flow/debt (%)	36.8	34.8	37.0	34.1
Cash flow/capital (%)	16.5	15.5	16.8	16.0
Net cash flow/capital (%)	11.3	10.3	11.7	11.1
Net cash flow/capital outlays (%)	104.2	80.8	84.7	70.4
Capital outlays/capital (%)	10.8	12.8	13.8	15.7
Current ratio (x)	1.22	1.01	0.95	0.98
Net plant/capital (%)	100.3	74.0	78.8	85.3
Net plant/debt (%)	221.2	166.5	175.4	185.0
CWIP/common equity (%)	2.9	65.4	60.2	50.5

Construction and finances: Following the early 1985 commercial operation of the 75%-owned Edgewater 5 coal-fired facility, construction of new generating capacity is not envisioned until the turn of the century. Construction will focus predominately on transmission and distribution projects and modifications to existing plants. Capital spending, including allowance for funds used during construction (AFDC), for the five years through 1990 are projected to total $412.4 million, of which $70.7 million is budgeted for this year. Potential adverse acid rain legislation could require additional expenditures. In view of a prospective moderate construction program, internal cash flow should continue to cover virtually all planned outlays. Pretax coverage of interest charges and return on equity remain strong. Responsive treatment in the pending rate case may permit an opportunity for further enhancement of key statistical measures. Additionally, earnings quality is excellent, with only minute AFDC accruals included in net income. A limited need for outside funds, together with a very strong equity base and high earnings quality, should continue to support a financial profile consistent with current ratings.

Barbara A. Walicke
(212) 208-1656

Income analysis	1985	1984	1983	1982
Revenues (mil. $)	588.9	575.5	555.5	512.5
Pretax operating income (mil. $)	131.1	122.7	113.9	124.1
Interest expense (mil. $)	24.0	28.9	27.8	30.6
Income taxes (mil. $)	49.0	46.6	50.1	49.9
AFDC (mil. $)	5.8	13.8	7.3	4.0
Net income (mil. $)	60.7	58.3	54.6	47.4
Preferred dividends (mil. $)	4.4	4.8	5.0	5.1
Pretax interest coverage (x)	5.57	4.64	4.76	4.17
Excluding AFDC (x)	5.33	4.16	4.50	4.04
Preferred dividend coverage (x)	4.17	3.55	3.58	3.19
Excluding AFDC (x)	3.99	3.18	3.38	3.09
Pretax return on capital (%)	17.57	18.66	19.77	20.10
Excluding AFDC (%)	16.81	16.73	18.68	19.47
Return on equity (%)	15.86	16.30	16.78	15.83
Excluding AFDC (%)	14.22	12.10	14.32	14.33
Pretax operating ratio (%)	77.7	78.7	79.5	75.8
Income tax rate (%)	44.7	44.4	47.9	51.3
AFDC/common earnings (%)	10.3	25.8	14.7	9.5
Payout ratio (%)	63.4	60.9	59.3	62.5

EXHIBIT 12-5 Trading on New York Stock Exchange (May 1, 1986)

CORPORATION BONDS
Volume, $39,120,000

Bonds	Cur Yld	Vol	High	Low	Close	Net Chg.
AMR 10¼06	10.4	2	99	99	99	...
Advst 9s08	cv	225	115	113	114¾	−1¼
AetnLf 8⅛07	8.6	10	95	95	95	+1¾
AlaP 9s2000	9.3	7	97¾	96⅞	96⅞	+½
AlaP 7¾s02	8.9	20	87¼	87⅛	87⅛	...
AlaP 8⅞s03	9.3	20	95¾	95¾	95¾	+⅜
AlaP 10⅞05	10.6	4	103	103	103	...
AlaP 10½05	10.2	9	103⅜	103⅜	103⅜	+½
AlaP 8¾07	9.3	17	94⅜	94⅛	94⅜	+1⅜
AlaP 9¼07	9.3	12	99	99	99	+⅛
AlaP 9½08	9.5	40	99¾	97⅛	99¾	+1⅛
AlaP 9⅝08	9.7	11	98¾	98¾	98¾	−¼
AlaP 12⅝10	11.6	6	109¼	109¼	109¼	−¼
AlaP 15¼10	13.6	96	112¼	112¼	112¼	...
AlaP 18¼89	16.9	42	108	107½	108	+1
AlskA 9s03	cv	10	114	114	114	−3
AlskH 16¼99	14.4	13	113	113	113	...
AlskH 17¾91	14.8	13	119¾	119¾	119¾	−1¼
AlskH 18⅜01	16.4	190	115	110⅜	111⅞	−3⅛
AlskH 15¼92	14.5	28	105	105	105	...
AlskH 12⅞93	12.3	10	105	105	105	+1
Alco 8½10	cv	10	113	113	113	−1½
AllgWt 4s98	6.8	3	59⅛	59⅛	59⅛	+⅝
Allgl 10.4s02	12.5	27	83⅞	83¼	83¼	−⅝
Allgl 9s89	9.8	4	91⅜	91⅜	91⅜	+⅞
AlldC 6.6s93	7.3	1	90¼	90¼	90¼	...
AlldC 7⅞96	8.2	25	96½	96½	96½	−1½
AlldC zr87	...	30	90⅞	90⅞	90⅞	...
AlldC zr92	...	16	58⅝	58⅜	58⅜	−⅝
AlldC zr96	...	40	43½	43	43	−1⅜
AlldC zr98	...	3	33½	33½	33½	+⅛
AlldC zr2000	...	45	27¾	27⅜	27¾	+⅛
AlldC d6s88	6.3	5	94⅞	94¾	94⅞	+⅛
AlldC d6s90	6.5	8	92½	92½	92½	+1¾
AlldC zr91	...	50	64	64	64	−1
AlldC zr95	...	50	44⅛	44⅛	44⅛	+⅛
AlldC zr05	...	5	17¾	17¾	17¾	+¼
AlldC zr09	...	65	13	13	13	+⅛
AlsCha 16s91	14.3	27	111½	111½	111½	...
Alcoa 7.45s96	8.2	1	91⅜	91⅜	91⅜	−⅛
AMAX 8½96	10.3	20	82⅝	82⅝	82⅝	...
AMAX 14¼90	13.3	60	107⅝	107⅜	107⅜	−¼
AMAX 14½94	13.2	46	110⅛	110	110	−⅝
AAirl 4¼92	5.6	4	76⅛	76	76	+¾
ABrnd 4⅝90	5.2	1	88⅛	88⅛	88⅛	+⅛
ABrnd 5⅞92	6.6	2	89⅜	89⅜	89⅜	+⅜
ACan 6s97	7.6	6	79⅛	79	79	−½
ACan 11⅜10	10.5	4	108	108	108	+1
ACan 13¼93	12.0	25	110½	110½	110½	+½
ACeM 6¾91	cv	10	67½	67½	67½	−2⅞
AExC 14¾92	12.4	17	119	119	119	...
AmGn 11s07	cv	3	210	210	210	+1
AHoist 5½93	cv	38	73	73	73	...
AmMed 9½01	cv	170	106	105	105	−1
AmMed 8¼08	cv	37	96¾	96½	96¾	...
AmMot 6s88	cv	4	89½	89¼	89½	+⅛
ASmel 4⅝88	5.1	1	90⅛	90⅛	90⅛	...
ATT 2⅝s86	2.6	5	99⅛	99⅛	99⅛	...
ATT 2⅞s87	3.0	17	96⅛	96⅛	96⅛	+⅛
ATT 3⅞s90	4.3	10	90	90	90	+½
ATT 8¾00	8.9	403	99⅛	98¾	98¾	−¼
ATT 7s01	8.0	152	87¾	87¼	87½	−¼
ATT 7⅛s03	8.1	40	87¾	87½	87¾	−¼
ATT 8.80s05	9.0	195	98½	97⅜	98⅛	+⅛
ATT 8⅝s07	9.0	60	96¾	96¼	96¼	−⅛
ATT 10⅜90	10.3	379	100¼	100⅛	100¼	...
Amfac 5¼94	cv	16	90	90	90	...
Amoco 6s91	6.5	15	92⅞	92⅜	92⅞	+1
Amoco 6s98	7.1	16	84⅝	84⅝	84⅝	−¼
Amoco 8¼89t	8.2	5	100½	100½	100½	+⅛
Amoco 7⅞07	8.6	30	92	92	92	+⅜
Amoco 14s91	12.6	70	111½	111	111	−¼
Ancp 13⅞02f	cv	19	100	99½	99½	−1½
Anhr 6s92	6.8	1	87⅝	87⅝	87⅝	−⅜
Anxtr 8¼03	cv	15	110	109	109	−½
ArizP 12⅛09	11.2	5	108⅝	108⅝	108⅝	...
ArmS 8.7s95	9.8	5	89	89	89	+1⅞
ArmS 9.2s00	11.0	5	84	84	84	...
Arms 8½01	10.8	5	78¾	78¾	78¾	+1¼
AshO 8.2s02	9.4	21	87	87	87	−½
AsCp 12⅜89	12.0	10	103¼	103¼	103¼	−¾
Atchsn 4s95	5.6	10	71¼	71¼	71¼	...
ARich 11⅜10	10.4	10	109	109	109	+1
ARich 13⅝11	11.8	35	115¼	115¼	115¼	...
ARch 11⅛15	10.5	100	106	106	106	−1
ARch 10⅜95	9.4	10	110¾	110¾	110¾	+1
AutDt 6½11	cv	109	107	106	106¼	−¾
AvcoC 5½93	cv	7	91	91	91	...
Avnet 8s13	cv	75	109	108	108	...
viBldU 10s09f	16.1	12	62	61¼	62	−⅞
Bally 6s98	cv	32	92⅛	92	92	−1
Bally 10s06	cv	109	104½	103	103	−1
B O 4½10A	cv	5	155⅛	155⅛	155⅛	...
BalGE 3s89	3.4	8	88⅛	88⅛	88⅛	−⅝
BalGE 8⅜06	9.0	25	92¾	92¾	92¾	−1
BalGE 9⅜08	9.3	5	101	101	101	+1
BalGE 16¾91	15.4	60	109	108½	109	...
BethSt 9s00	11.0	62	81¾	81⅝	81⅝	+⅜
BethSt 8.45s05	11.4	95	74¼	73⅝	74¼	+⅝
BethSt 8⅜01	11.1	54	75¾	75½	75½	...
Bevrly 7⅝03	cv	60	109½	109	109½	−½
Beverly zr03	...	12	28½	28⅜	28⅜	...
BigT 8½06	cv	72	97½	96½	97½	+½
Bowatr 9s09	cv	51	124½	122½	122½	−2¾
BrkUn 9⅛95	9.1	10	100½	100½	100½	−1
BrkUn 7⅞97	8.7	2	90½	90½	90½	+¾
BrkUn 8¾99	9.1	5	95⅞	95⅞	95⅞	−⅜
BwnSh 9¼05	cv	25	106	105½	105½	−1
Burllnd 8¾08	cv	13	108	107½	108	...
BurNo 12⅞05	11.3	39	113½	113½	113½	−1¼
Burro 11½10	10.2	5	113	113	113	+4¾
Burro 7¼10	...	197	106	105¼	105½	+¼
CBS 10⅞95	9.9	9	109½	109⅛	109½	+⅝
CIGNA 8s07	cv	10	109½	109½	109½	−½
CIT 9s91	9.0	4	100⅛	100⅛	100⅛	...
CIT 9⅝09	9.7	15	99½	99½	99½	+1⅜
CIT 15½87	14.0	10	110⅝	110⅝	110⅝	−¼
CapHd 12¾06	11.2	22	113½	113½	113½	+1
CaroT 7¾01	8.7	20	88¾	88¾	88¾	−⅜
CartH 9⅛08	10.0	10	91	91	91	+½
CatTr 5½00	cv	150	119	118	118	−½
CATS zr05-92	...	1	62¾	62¾	62¾	−¼
CATS zr11-94	...	20	49	49	49	+¾
CATS zr05-95	...	1	46	46	46	...
CATS zr11-96	...	50	43¼	42	42	−1⅜
CATS zr05-98	...	11	36¼	36¼	36¼	−2½
CATS zr11-99	...	1	32¾	32¾	32¾	...
CATS zr11-03	...	20	22	21⅝	22	−⅞
vjChtC d14¾02f	...	22	52¼	52¼	52¼	+1
ChsCp 6½96	cv	5	156⅛	154½	154½	−3½
CPoM 9s18	9.0	5	99⅞	99⅞	99⅞	+3½
CPoV 8⅜09	9.1	7	95	95	95	...
ChesbP 10⅝90	10.5	20	101⅜	101⅜	101⅜	...
ChvrnC 11¾88	10.8	69	108⅞	108⅞	108⅞	+¼
ChvrnC 12s94	10.4	27	116⅜	115½	115½	−½
ChvrnC 11s90	10.3	30	107¼	107⅛	107¼	+¼
Chvrn 8¾05	9.3	15	94	94	94	−1½
ChCft 15s99	14.1	15	106¾	106½	106½	−2⅜
Chrysl 8⅞95	9.3	6	95⅝	95⅝	95⅝	−⅞
Chryslr 8s98	8.9	31	89¾	89⅝	89¾	+⅛
ChryF 9s86	9.0	11	100	100	100	...
ChryF 13¼88	12.0	50	110½	110½	110½	...
ChryF 9⅜89	9.2	3	101¾	101¾	101¾	−¼
CirclK 8¾04	cv	15	123	123	123	−4
CirclK 8¼05	cv	248	121½	121	121½	+½
Citicp 8.40s89t	8.3	15	101½	101½	101½	...
Citicp 8.45s07	9.1	20	93	92½	93	+1¼
Citicp 8⅛07	9.1	10	89½	89½	89½	−1½
Citicp 8.4s98t	8.5	14	99¼	99	99¼	−⅛
Citicp 7.40s04t	7.5	3	98¼	98¼	98¼	+⅛
Citicp 12s90	11.2	2	106¾	105⅞	106¾	+⅞
Citicp 13.60s99	13.5	35	100⅝	100⅝	100⅝	...
Citicp 11⅞95	10.6	20	112	112	112	+1
CitSv 6⅛97	8.6	6	71	71	71	+½
CitSv 13⅞11	12.6	8	110½	110½	110½	−½
CitSvc zr86	...	103	95⅜	95¼	95⅜	+⅛
CitSvc zr87	...	100	87⅝	87⅛	87⅛	−⅜
CitSvc zr88	...	129	80½	79½	80½	+⅜
CitSvc zr89	...	99	72¼	71½	71⅞	−⅜
Claytn 7¾01	cv	4	125	125	125	...
ClevEl 3s89	3.5	1	86	86	86	+1
ClevEl 8¾05	9.7	30	90	89	90	+⅞
ClevEl 9⅛09	9.9	11	93⅜	93⅛	93⅜	+¼
ClevEl 9.85s10	10.1	10	98	98	98	...
ClevEl 8⅜11	9.9	4	85	85	85	...
Coleco 14⅜02	13.9	30	103½	103⅜	103⅜	−⅛
ColuG 9s94	9.2	28	99¼	98	98⅛	+1⅛
ColuG 7½97M	8.0	2	94	94	94	+4⅛
ColuG 7½97O	8.2	25	91⅛	91⅛	91⅛	+3⅛
Cmdis 8s03	cv	411	105¼	105¼	105¼	−¼
Cmdis 9.65s02	10.9	1	88¼	88¼	88¼	−1¼
CmlCr 8¾91	9.3	15	94⅜	94⅜	94⅜	+⅜
CmlCr 8.8s86	8.8	10	99⅞	99⅞	99⅞	+⅜
CmwE 7⅝03F	9.0	1	84½	84½	84½	−¼
CmwE 7⅝03J	8.9	9	85⅝	85½	85½	+⅛
CmwE 8s03	9.0	51	89	88⅞	89	+⅛
CmwE 9⅜04	9.5	10	99	98¾	99	+¼
CmwE 8⅛07J	9.1	10	89¾	89⅝	89¾	+½
CmwE 8¼07	9.2	1	89⅝	89⅝	89⅝	−1⅜
CmwE 9⅛08	9.4	50	96⅞	96⅞	96⅞	−1⅛
CmwE 14s91	13.2	58	106⅞	106¼	106⅜	−¾
CmwE 16s90	14.7	15	109⅛	109⅛	109⅛	...
CmwE 16¾11	14.7	37	113⅝	113¼	113⅝	...
CmwE 14¼92	12.7	13	112	111	112	+1½
CmwE 13s12	11.4	25	114½	114½	114½	...
Compq 9½05	cv	15	148	146½	148	+1
Cmpvsn 8s09	cv	30	83¼	83¼	83¼	−1¾
ConEd 4¼86	4.3	10	98 19/32	98 19/32	98 19/32	−13/32
ConEd 5s87	5.2	53	97	96¾	97	+¼
ConEd 9⅜00	9.4	9	100¼	100¼	100¼	−⅝
ConEd 7.9s01	8.5	9	92⅞	92⅞	92⅞	+⅝
ConEd 8.4s03	8.8	12	95⅛	95	95⅛	+⅛
ConEd 9⅛04	9.2	10	99	99	99	...
CnNG 7¾94	8.2	5	94¼	94¼	94¼	−⅞
CnNG 8⅛94	8.3	32	99	99	99	−1⅛
CnNG 9s95	9.1	11	99¼	99¼	99¼	...
CnNG 9¼95	9.2	1	100⅛	100⅛	100⅛	+⅛
CritAc 11.85s15	11.4	10	103½	103½	103½	...
Dana d5⅞06	cv	11	83½	83	83	−2¼
Dart 7½96	8.7	20	86⅜	86⅜	86⅜	−¼
Datpnt 8⅞06	cv	41	54¼	53¾	54¼	−¼
Dayc 5¾94	cv	1	100¼	100¼	100¼	−¾
Dayc 6s94	cv	10	106	106	106	...
DaytH 15¼91	14.6	7	105½	104½	104½	−¼
DaytP 8⅛01	9.3	2	87½	87½	87½	−1⅞
DaytP 8s03	9.3	1	86¼	86¼	86¼	−1¾
DaytP 10.7s05	10.4	25	103	103	103	...
DaytP 8½07	9.6	5	89	89	89	−1⅛
DaytP 17s91	15.7	25	108⅛	108	108⅛	+⅛
Deere 9s08	cv	185	107½	106½	106½	−1½
DeereCr 9.35s03	9.6	5	97	97	97	+½
DetEd 6s96	7.6	4	79	79	79	+¼
DetEd 6.4s98	8.1	10	79⅛	79⅛	79⅛	+½
DetEd 9s99	9.4	10	95½	95½	95½	...
DetEd 9.15s00	9.5	40	96½	95¼	96½	+1¾
DetEd 8.15s00	9.1	20	90	89½	89½	−½
DetEd 8⅛01	9.2	10	88⅝	88¼	88⅝	−⅜
DetEd 7⅜01	8.8	10	83½	83½	83½	+⅛
DetEd 7½03	9.1	30	82½	81⅜	82½	+¼
DetEd 9⅞04	9.9	13	100	100	100	...
DiaSh 8½08	10.3	30	82½	82½	82½	+3
Dow 8⅞2000	9.1	15	97½	97½	97½	+1
Dow 8.92000	9.2	25	96¾	96¾	96¾	−¼
Dow 8½s06	9.2	2	92¾	92¾	92¾	−⅛
duPnt 8.45s04	8.6	60	98¼	97	98¼	+1¼
duPnt 8½06	8.7	10	98¼	98¼	98¼	+¾
duPnt d6s01	7.6	55	78¾	78¾	78¾	...
duPnt 12⅞92	11.3	11	114	113⅞	113⅞	+⅜
DukeP 7¾03	8.6	10	90½	90½	90½	+1
DukeP 8⅛03	8.8	10	92½	92½	92½	−1
DukeP 9¾04	9.5	10	102⅛	102⅛	102⅛	...
DukeP 9½05	9.4	19	101½	100¾	100¾	−¾
DukeP 8⅜06	8.8	1	94⅞	94⅞	94⅞	−¾
DukeP 8⅛07	8.6	1	94½	94½	94½	+1⅞
DukeP 9⅜08	9.4	10	100	100	100	−1¼
DukeP 10⅛09	9.7	10	103⅞	103⅞	103⅞	...
DukeP 12s90	11.8	97	102¼	102	102	−¼
DuqL 9s06	9.7	11	93	91¾	93	+1⅛
DuqL 10⅛09	10.1	20	100	99⅞	99⅞	−½
DuqL 12¼10	11.5	10	106½	106½	106½	−1¼
ECL 9s89f	...	6	76½	76½	76½	−3½
EasAir 5s92	cv	1	59½	59½	59½	−½
EasAir 4¾93	cv	35	56½	55¾	55¾	−¾
EasAir 11½99	cv	63	85⅜	84	84	−1½
EasAir 11¾05	cv	100	89⅞	89	89⅞	−⅛
EasAir 17½97	15.8	10	111	111	111	−½
EasAir 16⅛02	15.2	12	106⅞	106⅛	106¼	...
EKod 8¼07	cv	554	112	110¾	111	−1½
Eaton 8½08	cv	22	117	117	117	−4½
Ekco 4.60s87	4.8	5	95½	95½	95½	+3¼
Englh 11¾05	10.8	3	109¼	109¼	109¼	...
Ens 7.65s98	8.7	10	88⅜	88⅜	88⅜	+⅜
Ens 10s01	cv	88	102	101	102	+¾
EqutR 9⅝95	9.4	10	102	102	102	−½
EqutR 9½06	cv	6	165¼	165¼	165¼	+¼
Equitc 10s04	cv	32	100¾	99	99	−½
Exxon 6s97	6.9	17	87	86⅛	86⅜	+¼
Exxon 6½98	7.3	108	88⅞	88½	88⅞	+⅜
ExxP 8⅞00	8.9	31	99¾	99½	99½	...
ExxP 8¼01	8.5	30	97	97	97	...
ExxP 5⅝97	6.9	5	81	81	81	+1
ExxP 6⅝98	7.7	15	85½	85½	85½	+2½
FedSt 10¼10	10.0	3	103	103	103	−2½
FinCpA 11⅞98	12.7	26	94¾	93¾	93¾	−1⅛
FinCp d11½02	cv	102	107½	107½	107½	...
Firest 9¼04	9.5	133	97¼	96¼	97¼	+¼
FstChi 7¾86	7.8	2	99 21/32	99 21/32	99 21/32	−11/32
FMerBc 13⅜92	12.5	24	110	110	110	+2
FtWis 8½96	8.9	20	95⅝	95⅝	95⅝	...
FisbCp 8½05	cv	2	106	106	106	...
FishF 6½94	cv	12	85	85	85	...
FleetFn 12½90	12.1	10	103	103	103	−¼
FleetFn 8½10	cv	10	136⅛	136⅛	136⅛	−1⅞
Flwr 8¼05	cv	11	120	120	120	−½
Ford 9¼94	9.1	17	101⅜	101⅜	101⅜	−⅜
Ford 14¼90	13.4	163	107	106⅛	106½	−½
FrdC 8⅞90A	8.9	4	100¼	100¼	100¼	−⅛
FrdC 8⅞90N	8.8	15	100⅝	100⅝	100⅝	+⅛
FrdC 8½91	8.5	15	100⅛	100	100	−¼
FrdC 7½91	7.6	34	98⅛	98	98⅛	+⅛
FrdC 8.7s99	8.9	12	97⅜	97⅜	97⅜	+⅛
FrdC 10½94	10.2	5	103⅛	103⅛	103⅛	−⅛
FrdC 9.7s00	9.7	7	102½	100½	100½	...
FrdC 9⅛01	9.1	38	99⅞	99⅞	99⅞	+2⅛
FrdC 8¼88	8.3	85	100¼	100	100	...
FrdC 8⅜01	9.0	10	93½	93½	93½	+½
FrdC 7⅞89	7.9	102	100	100	100	+⅛
FrdC 8⅞90	8.8	100	100⅜	100⅜	100⅜	−⅛
FreptM 10½14	cv	107	105¼	104¼	105	...
Fruf 5½94	cv	11	126½	125½	126½	−½
FrufF 8s87	8.0	50	99⅝	99⅝	99⅝	−⅛
Fuqua 9½98	10.2	16	93	92	93	+½
Fuqua 9⅞97	10.3	8	98	96	96	−1½
GTE 10½07	cv	345	109	108¼	108¼	−¾
GTE 10⅝95	9.4	39	112½	112	112½	+⅞
Gelco 14⅜99	13.7	37	107⅛	107	107⅛	+⅛
Gelco 14s01	cv	10	106⅝	106⅝	106⅝	−⅛

SOURCE: *The Wall Street Journal*, reprinted by permission.

RISK, LIQUIDITY, AND RETURN

Normally, the yield curve is upward sloping, which means that the longer the maturity, the higher the yield.[6] For this reason, corporate bonds usually yield more than shorter-term corporate debt securities. This higher yield as well as the opportunity to realize it for a long period of time are two important pluses if you are considering corporate bonds.

Just how much extra yield going long term is likely to be worth to you is hard to say. Yield spreads between short-term, medium-term, and long-term securities vary over the interest rate cycle, with the yield advantage offered by long-term securities being the smallest when interest rates are expected to fall, and the advantage of realizing a high rate long term being the greatest.

Corporate bonds carry a greater risk of default than either government or agency securities and consequently yield more at any maturity level. Part of the greater yield reflects not only credit risk, but (1) the greater bid-asked spread compared to government securities and (2) the fact that Treasuries are not taxed at the state and local levels while corporate bonds are. There is substantial variability of the corporate/government yield spread. Exhibit 12–6, which graphically portrays the yield spread between long-term AA public utilities and 20-year Treasuries, illustrates this volatility. During the 1950s, there were several occasions when the yield spread was as narrow as 25 basis points. In 1981, the yield spread was as wide as 275 basis points. The yield spread not only varies substantially, it also changes rapidly. A classic example is 1980, when within a 1 month span of time, the yield spread dropped by 100 basis points.[7]

Generally, the corporate/government yield spread is widest when credit is scarce and interest rates are high. There are several reasons for the wide spread at the top of the interest rate cycle. For one thing, investors tend to behave in a somewhat irrational way; they are less willing to trade safety for return when rates are high than when rates are low. (This phenomenon is referred to as a *flight to quality*.) Probably added to that is a feeling by investors that no matter what the rat-

---

[6]See Chapter 7.

[7]James L. Kochan, "Corporate-Treasury Yield Spreads: A Cyclical Analysis," in *The Handbook of Fixed Income Securities,* ed. Frank J. Fabozzi and Irving M. Pollack (Homewood, Ill.: Dow Jones-Irwin, 1987).

EXHIBIT 12-6

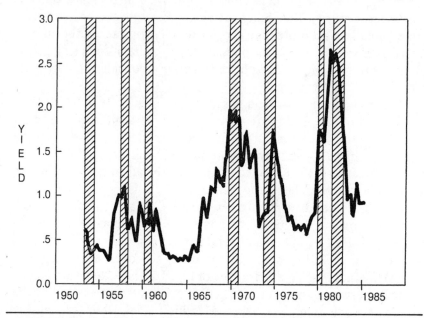

SOURCE: Frank J. Fabozzi and Irving M. Pollack, eds., *The Handbook of Fixed Income Securities,* 2nd ed. (Homewood, Ill.: Dow Jones-Irwin, 1987).

ing services say, bonds are a riskier investment at the peak of the business cycle—when interest rates are high and some decline in economic activity seems likely—than they are at other times.

Although the above discussion has focused on the yield spread between corporates and Treasuries, the same things can be said about the yield spreads between corporates of different quality ratings. Lower-quality-rated corporates offer a higher yield than higher-quality corporates. This is illustrated in Exhibit 12-7, which shows monthly corporate bond yield averages by quality rating from April 1980 to March 1986. The quality spreads reflect the same pattern as the corporate/government yield spread over the interest rate cycle.

Municipal securities, like corporate bonds, expose the investor to default risk. Municipals, however, have the additional advantage of being tax-exempt, with the result that top-grade corporate bonds yield substantially more than prime municipals. Whether that makes corporate bonds a better investment than municipals depends, of course, on your tax bracket.

Yields vary not only between corporate and other types of debt securities, such as Treasuries and municipals, and within a corporate category by quality, but also between the different categories of corporate bonds. (See Exhibit 12–7.)

There are other features that we have discussed throughout this book that impact the relative yield of corporate bonds. Zero-coupon corporate bonds tend to be priced more expensively, that is, to yield less than comparable, full-coupon corporate bonds because they eliminate reinvestment risk. Yet, despite this advantage, they should not be purchased for a portfolio that is subject to taxation.

The call feature also influences the relative yield of a corporate bond. A callable bond should yield more than an otherwise comparable noncallable bond. The size of the yield premium (i.e. the extra yield the investor wants for accepting call risk) depends upon several factors. Most important is the expectations of market participants for the course of future interest rates. If market participants expect interest rates to decline sufficiently below the coupon rate on the issue so that it would be economical for the corporate issuer to refund it, there will be a substantial premium between callable and noncallable bonds. On the other hand, if interest rates are anticipated to rise, or not fall appreciably below the coupon rate of the issue, the size of the yield premium will be negligible.

Last but not least, there are convertible bonds (the subject of the next chapter) whose prices and yield depend largely on the price of the underlying common stock and junk bonds (see Chapter 7) whose prices and yield depend on the changes in the financial strength of the issuer.

As far as liquidity is concerned, corporate bonds traded on the exchanges present no problems. Small amounts of these bonds can always be sold at the going market quotes. On corporate bonds, as on other bonds, there is a substantial price risk which increases with the length of current maturity. Since the extra return received for going very long is small, there is good argument for staying with shorter current maturities unless you are convinced that interest rates are at a long-term peak.

This point in our discussion is perhaps a good place to recall something we said earlier. In Chapter 6, we noted that at any point in time even experts differ on what they think interest rates are going to do in the short run. Predicting with any certainty where interest rates are going over the long run is simply impossible because there are so

EXHIBIT 12-7

Moody's Corporate Bond Yield Averages

	Av. Corp.	Corporate by Ratings				Corporate by Groups			Public Utility Bonds				Industrial Bonds				Railroad Bonds			
	Corp.	Aaa	Aa	A	Baa	P.U.	Ind.	R.R	Aaa	Aa	A	Baa	Aaa	Aa	A	Baa	Aaa	Aa	A	Baa
1980																				
Apr.	13.21	12.04	13.06	13.55	14.19	13.50	12.93	11.63	12.27	13.49	13.87	14.35	11.81	12.63	13.23	14.03	---	11.63	10.74	11.80
May	13.11	10.99	11.91	12.35	13.17	12.17	12.04	11.54	11.23	11.99	12.53	12.93	10.74	11.82	12.18	13.41	---	10.80	11.67	12.15
June	11.64	10.58	11.39	11.59	12.71	12.71	11.41	11.26	10.88	11.73	12.21	12.63	10.27	11.03	11.57	12.78	---	10.64	11.44	11.71
July	11.77	11.07	11.43	11.95	12.65	12.12	11.43	11.28	11.48	11.96	12.26	12.75	10.65	10.89	11.63	12.54	---	10.60	11.37	11.88
Aug.	12.33	11.64	12.09	12.44	13.15	12.82	11.84	11.36	12.10	12.73	12.96	13.50	11.17	11.45	11.93	12.79	---	10.53	11.50	12.04
Sept.	12.80	12.02	12.52	12.97	13.70	13.29	12.31	11.56	12.46	13.18	13.43	14.07	11.58	11.85	12.49	13.33	---	10.85	11.81	12.06
Oct.	13.07	12.31	12.68	13.05	14.23	13.53	12.60	11.72	12.79	13.33	13.58	14.43	11.83	12.02	12.51	14.03	---	10.99	12.03	12.13
Nov.	13.63	12.97	13.34	13.59	14.64	14.07	13.20	12.02	13.39	13.96	14.12	14.79	12.53	12.71	13.06	14.48	---	11.11	12.39	12.57
Dec.	14.04	13.21	13.78	14.03	15.14	14.48	13.60	12.22	13.62	14.37	14.63	15.29	12.79	13.18	13.43	14.98	---	11.31	12.58	12.76
1981																				
Jan.	13.80	12.81	13.52	13.83	15.03	14.22	13.37	12.42	13.31	14.03	14.26	15.30	12.31	13.01	13.39	14.76	---	11.40	12.69	13.17
Feb.	14.22	13.35	13.89	14.27	15.37	14.84	13.60	12.61	13.95	14.65	14.91	15.86	12.75	13.19	13.64	14.87	---	11.61	12.96	13.27
Mar.	14.26	13.33	13.90	14.47	15.34	14.86	13.66	12.72	13.85	14.61	15.14	15.83	12.81	13.19	13.80	14.84	---	11.96	12.91	13.39
Apr.	14.66	13.88	14.39	14.82	15.56	15.32	14.00	12.85	14.41	15.23	15.48	16.14	13.33	13.55	14.15	14.98	---	12.30	12.86	13.39
May	15.15	14.32	14.88	15.43	15.95	15.84	14.45	12.90	14.83	15.61	15.74	16.66	13.81	14.14	14.60	15.24	---	12.49	12.99	13.22
June	14.76	13.75	14.41	15.08	15.80	15.27	14.25	13.09	14.16	14.89	16.25	16.30	13.35	13.92	14.43	15.29	---	12.50	13.07	13.71
July	15.18	14.38	14.79	15.36	16.17	15.87	14.48	13.22	14.87	15.42	16.21	16.98	13.87	14.16	14.52	15.35	---	12.64	13.21	13.82
Aug.	15.60	14.89	15.42	15.76	16.34	16.33	14.87	13.50	15.41	16.14	16.58	17.19	14.36	14.69	14.94	15.48	---	12.77	13.60	14.13
Sept.	16.18	15.49	15.95	16.36	16.92	16.89	15.47	13.71	16.06	16.28	17.16	17.76	14.92	15.32	15.55	16.08	---	12.96	13.90	14.27
Oct.	16.20	15.40	15.82	16.47	17.11	16.76	15.64	13.88	15.83	16.28	17.21	17.71	14.97	15.35	15.73	16.50	---	13.01	14.17	14.45
Nov.	15.35	14.22	14.97	15.82	16.39	15.50	15.19	13.92	14.43	14.88	16.20	16.49	13.99	15.04	15.43	16.28	---	13.05	14.24	14.48
Dec.	15.38	14.23	15.00	15.75	16.55	15.77	15.00	13.84	14.52	15.23	16.29	17.02	13.93	14.77	15.21	16.07	---	13.07	14.09	14.37
1982																				
Jan.	16.05	15.18	15.75	16.19	17.10	16.73	15.37	14.10	15.79	16.48	16.83	17.83	14.57	15.01	15.54	16.36	---	13.52	14.24	14.53
Feb.	16.13	15.27	15.72	16.35	17.18	16.72	15.53	14.08	15.88	16.33	16.84	17.83	14.66	15.09	15.86	16.51	---	13.42	14.29	14.53
Mar.	15.68	14.58	15.21	16.12	16.82	16.07	15.29	14.00	15.05	15.57	16.50	17.16	14.09	14.85	15.73	16.47	---	13.22	14.11	14.62
Apr.	15.53	14.46	14.90	15.95	16.78	15.82	15.22	14.03	14.86	15.12	16.31	17.00	14.07	14.68	15.58	16.55	---	13.27	14.11	14.72
May	15.34	14.26	14.77	15.70	16.64	15.60	15.08	13.93	14.68	15.01	16.04	16.68	13.83	14.53	15.35	16.60	---	13.17	13.96	14.66
June	15.77	14.81	15.26	16.07	16.92	16.18	15.35	13.99	15.32	15.78	16.42	17.21	14.30	14.73	15.72	16.63	---	13.27	14.06	14.64
July	15.70	14.61	15.21	16.20	16.80	16.04	15.37	14.05	14.96	15.67	16.42	17.09	14.24	14.74	15.98	16.50	---	13.41	14.03	14.71
Aug.	15.06	13.71	14.48	15.70	16.32	15.22	14.88	13.90	13.98	14.71	15.83	16.37	13.43	14.25	15.56	16.28	---	13.27	13.61	14.81
Sept.	14.34	12.94	13.72	15.07	15.63	14.56	14.11	13.69	13.24	13.92	15.40	15.68	12.64	13.51	14.73	15.57	---	13.07	13.41	14.61
Oct.	13.54	12.12	12.97	14.34	14.73	13.88	13.19	13.08	12.42	13.21	14.79	15.10	11.81	12.73	13.88	14.35	---	12.28	12.75	14.21
Nov.	13.08	11.68	12.51	13.81	14.30	13.58	12.57	12.74	12.11	12.92	14.46	14.81	11.24	12.10	13.15	13.79	---	11.74	12.48	14.01
Dec.	13.02	11.83	12.44	13.66	14.14	13.55	12.48	12.60	12.32	12.76	14.43	14.69	11.34	12.12	12.88	13.58	---	11.42	12.63	13.75

1983–1986 Bond Yield Averages

Panel 1

1983								
Jan.	12.90	11.79	12.35	13.53	13.94	13.46	12.34	12.27
Feb.	13.02	12.01	12.58	13.52	13.95	13.60	12.43	12.13
Mar.	12.71	11.73	12.32	13.15	13.61	13.28	12.12	12.11
Apr.	12.44	11.51	12.06	12.86	13.29	13.03	11.84	11.90
May	12.30	11.46	11.95	12.68	13.09	13.00	11.59	11.62
June	12.54	11.74	12.15	12.88	13.37	13.17	11.90	11.78
July	12.73	12.15	12.39	12.99	13.39	13.28	12.18	12.07
Aug.	13.01	12.51	12.72	13.17	13.64	13.50	12.52	12.13
Sept.	12.91	12.37	12.62	13.11	13.55	13.35	12.46	12.04
Oct.	12.79	12.25	12.49	12.97	13.46	13.19	12.39	12.08
Nov.	12.93	12.41	12.61	13.09	13.61	13.33	12.54	12.35
Dec.	13.07	12.57	12.76	13.21	13.75	13.48	12.66	12.46
1984								
Jan.	12.92	12.20	12.71	13.13	13.65	13.40	12.63	12.41
Feb.	12.88	12.08	12.70	13.11	13.59	13.50	12.60	12.28
Mar.	13.33	12.57	13.22	13.54	13.99	13.66	13.00	12.54
Apr.	13.59	12.81	13.48	13.77	14.31	14.30	13.25	12.81
May	14.13	13.28	14.10	14.37	14.74	14.95	13.72	13.25
June	14.40	13.55	14.33	14.66	15.05	15.16	14.03	13.31
July	14.32	13.44	14.12	14.57	15.15	15.16	14.09	13.60
Aug.	13.78	12.87	13.47	14.13	14.63	14.29	13.61	13.82
Sept.	13.56	12.66	13.27	13.94	14.35	14.04	13.42	13.68
Oct.	13.33	12.63	13.11	13.61	13.94	13.68	13.10	13.44
Nov.	12.88	12.29	12.66	13.09	13.48	13.15	12.61	13.02
Dec.	12.74	12.13	12.50	12.92	13.40	12.96	12.51	12.69
1985								
Jan.	12.64	12.08	12.43	12.80	13.26	12.88	12.41	12.62
Feb.	12.66	12.13	12.49	12.80	13.23	13.00	12.32	12.38
Mar.	13.13	12.56	12.91	13.36	13.69	13.66	12.60	12.57
Apr.	12.89	12.23	12.69	13.14	13.51	13.42	12.37	12.60
May	12.47	11.72	12.30	12.70	13.15	12.89	12.04	12.39
June	11.70	10.94	11.46	11.98	12.40	11.91	11.48	11.81
July	11.69	10.97	11.42	11.92	12.43	11.88	11.49	11.63
Aug.	11.76	11.05	11.47	12.00	12.50	11.93	11.57	11.56
Sept.	11.75	11.07	11.46	11.99	12.48	11.95	11.55	11.54
Oct.	11.69	11.02	11.45	11.94	12.36	11.84	11.53	11.54
Nov.	11.29	10.55	11.07	11.54	11.99	11.33	11.23	11.35
Dec.	10.89	10.16	10.63	11.19	11.58	10.82	10.96	11.18
1986								
Jan.	10.75	10.05	10.46	11.04	11.44	10.66	10.83	10.86
Feb.	10.40	9.67	10.13	10.67	11.11	10.16	10.63	10.58
Mar.	9.79	9.00	9.49	10.15	10.50	9.33	10.24	10.05

Panel 2

1983								
Jan.	12.29	12.74	14.24	14.56	11.28	11.94	12.81	13.33
Feb.	12.48	13.02	14.26	14.61	11.54	12.14	12.77	13.27
Mar.	12.19	12.67	13.94	14.33	11.27	11.97	12.36	12.89
Apr.	12.00	12.43	13.61	14.07	11.03	11.69	12.11	12.52
May	12.01	12.44	13.50	14.05	10.91	11.46	11.86	12.12
June	12.23	12.64	13.64	14.16	11.25	11.66	12.12	12.57
July	12.69	12.86	13.58	14.01	11.61	11.93	12.41	12.76
Aug.	13.04	13.18	13.57	14.21	11.99	12.26	12.77	13.07
Sept.	12.85	13.04	13.42	14.10	11.87	12.19	12.80	12.99
Oct.	12.66	12.88	13.25	13.95	11.83	12.09	12.68	12.95
Nov.	12.82	12.97	13.38	14.12	12.00	12.25	12.79	13.10
Dec.	13.00	13.14	13.52	14.23	12.14	12.36	12.88	13.27
1984								
Jan.	—	13.02	13.39	14.05	12.01	12.39	12.85	13.24
Feb.	—	13.04	13.41	14.05	12.08	12.37	12.81	13.13
Mar.	—	13.66	13.87	14.56	12.57	12.78	13.21	13.42
Apr.	—	13.93	14.16	14.82	12.81	13.02	13.38	13.78
May	—	14.66	14.90	15.28	13.28	13.54	13.84	14.21
June	—	14.90	15.09	15.50	13.55	13.76	14.22	14.60
July	—	14.42	15.00	15.50	13.44	13.80	14.30	14.79
Aug.	—	13.67	14.43	14.79	12.87	13.26	13.82	14.48
Sept.	—	13.43	14.17	14.51	12.66	13.12	13.70	14.19
Oct.	13.00	13.38	13.80	14.17	12.42	12.85	13.42	13.71
Nov.	12.66	13.00	13.23	13.72	11.92	12.32	12.94	13.24
Dec.	12.49	12.76	13.11	13.46	11.76	12.23	12.72	13.34
1985								
Jan.	12.47	12.68	12.99	13.36	11.67	12.18	12.61	13.15
Feb.	12.61	12.87	13.08	13.44	11.64	12.10	12.51	13.00
Mar.	13.08	13.50	13.87	14.19	12.04	12.32	12.84	13.18
Apr.	12.77	13.17	13.61	14.11	11.67	12.22	12.71	12.90
May	12.18	12.65	13.12	13.62	11.26	11.95	12.28	12.68
June	11.17	11.68	12.13	12.66	10.71	11.24	11.83	12.14
July	11.18	11.55	12.07	12.70	10.74	11.29	11.77	12.17
Aug.	11.23	11.65	12.13	12.73	10.87	11.29	11.87	12.27
Sept.	11.27	11.68	12.13	12.72	10.86	11.24	11.85	12.24
Oct.	11.23	11.61	12.01	12.52	10.80	11.29	11.85	12.20
Nov.	10.71	11.10	11.49	12.04	10.38	11.03	11.58	11.93
Dec.	10.24	10.57	10.97	11.48	10.08	10.69	11.39	11.67
1986								
Jan.	10.14	10.44	10.79	11.24	9.95	10.47	11.27	11.63
Feb.	9.65	9.98	10.26	10.74	9.68	10.27	11.07	11.48
Mar.	8.75	9.16	9.48	9.91	9.23	9.82	10.81	11.08

Panel 3

1983					
Jan.	—	—	11.24	12.55	13.02
Feb.	—	—	11.12	12.34	12.93
Mar.	—	—	11.14	12.27	12.92
Apr.	—	—	11.11	12.00	12.58
May			10.91	11.68	12.28
June			11.26	11.89	12.19
July			11.69	12.04	12.48
Aug.			11.90	12.15	12.34
Sept.			11.86	12.06	12.22
Oct.			11.84	12.13	12.27
Nov.			12.14	12.36	12.54
Dec.			12.27	12.46	12.66
1984					
Jan.	—	—	12.22	12.42	12.59
Feb.	—	—	12.05	12.30	12.50
Mar.	—	—	12.30	12.55	12.75
Apr.	—	—	12.56	12.78	13.09
May			14.66	14.90	15.28
June			13.04	13.35	13.55
July			13.39	13.62	13.79
Aug.			13.54	13.87	14.05
Sept.			13.31	13.77	13.97
Oct.			12.94	13.56	13.83
Nov.			12.53	13.15	13.37
Dec.			12.22	12.77	13.09
1985					
Jan.			12.15	12.72	12.98
Feb.			12.10	12.38	12.66
Mar.			12.17	12.56	12.97
Apr.			12.08	12.55	13.17
May			11.94	12.32	12.92
June			11.26	11.95	12.21
July			11.05	11.81	12.03
Aug.			11.22	11.62	11.85
Sept.			11.23	11.61	12.05
Oct.			11.17	11.58	11.86
Nov.			10.95	11.39	11.70
Dec.			10.75	11.25	11.53
1986					
Jan.			10.45	10.88	11.24
Feb.			10.18	10.62	10.93
Mar.			9.74	9.98	10.42

Notes: See Moody's Bond Survey for a brief description and the latest published list of bonds included in the averages. Because of the dearth of Aaa-rated railroad term bond issues, Moody's Aaa railroad bond yield average was discontinued as of December 18, 1967. Moody's Aaa public utility average suspended from Jan. 1984 thru Sept. 1984. Oct. 1984 figure for last 14 business days only.

SOURCE: *Moody's Bond Record*, April 1986, p. 2.

many unknowns that might affect economic activity (changes in productivity, wars, formation of new international cartels, etc.). Even experts can make only an informed guess as to where rates will go over the long run. Nevertheless, one occasionally finds an "expert" predicting that rates *will* fall over the long run and that this is *the* moment to buy long bonds. Such a prediction means at most that the expert is willing to go out on a limb, in fact, he is already there!

Convertible Bonds

13

In Chapter 12, we discussed corporate bonds that are straight debt securities. As mentioned in Chapter 6, there are corporate bond issues that carry a conversion feature. The formulation of the conversion feature varies considerably from issue to issue, but all *convertible bonds* permit conversion of the issuer's bonds to a fixed number of shares of common stock. There are four examples of convertible bonds which we will use in our illustrations throughout this chapter: U.S. Steel's 5¾s of 2001, which are convertible into 15.936 shares of U.S. Steel common stock; Burlington Industries' 8¾s of 2008, which are convertible into 20.619 shares of Burlington Industries common stock; MidCon Corp.'s 10¼s of 2009, which are convertible into 23.809 shares of MidCon Corp. common stock; and Celanese's 4s of 1990, which are convertible into 10.87 shares of Celanese common stock.

The number of shares that an issue can be exchanged for is called the *conversion ratio*. For the U.S. Steel, Burlington Industries, MidCon Corp., and Celanese issues, the conversion ratios are 15.936, 20.619, 23.809, and 10.87, respectively. The conversion ratio may be fixed over the life of the issue or it may vary over time. In most cases, including the 4 convertibles described above, it is fixed over the life of the issue.[1]

The conversion privilege may be permitted for all or only some portion of the bond's life. Typically, the conversion privilege is for the life of the issue. An exception is Dana Corporation's 5⅞s convertibles due 2006 in which the conversion privilege expires on December 15, 1993.

There are some convertible bond issues that are exchangeable into common stock of firms other than the issuer.[2] For example, Ford Motor Credit's 4½s of 1996 are convertible into 24 shares of the common stock of the parent company, Ford Motor Company. There are a few issues that are exchangeable into more than one security. For example, General Cinema's 10s of 2009 are convertible into 3.333 shares of the common stock of R. J. Reynolds plus approximately 2.67 shares of the common stock of Sea-Land Corporation.

Any firm issuing new bonds obviously does so in order to obtain additional capital. When a conversion feature is added to a bond, the issuer's hope and intent are usually to obtain additional equity capital, as opposed to debt capital, over the long run. An immediate and direct way to do this would be to issue additional stock instead of bonds. The issuer, however, may feel that the price of its common stock is likely to rise over time and that a sale of common stock would therefore be more advantageous to the firm's current shareholders if postponed until that price rise had occurred. On a convertible bond, the conversion ratio is usually set so that the conversion is not profitable for the bondholder until the price of the issuer's common stock has risen significantly above the level at which it was trading at the time the bond was issued. Thus, issuing a bond with a conversion feature, in effect, gives the issuer the opportunity to raise equity capital today at tomorrow's stock prices—provided, of course, that the price of the issuer's shares does rise. In exchange for that opportunity, the issue pays interest until the bonds are converted.

Another, less common reason for issuing convertible bonds is that the issuing firm's position may be such that it has difficulty borrowing

---

[1]The conversion ratio is always adjusted proportionately for stock splits and stock dividends. For example, if the conversion ratio for a convertible bond is 20 and the issuer declares a 2-for-1 stock split (or equivalently a 100% stock dividend), the conversion ratio will increase to 40.

[2]Typically, this occurs as a result of name changes, mergers, or issuance of securities by subsidiaries.

at a reasonable interest cost unless it adds an *equity kicker* in the form of a conversion feature or attached *warrants*. The latter grants the bondholder the right to buy a given number of the issuer's common stock at some fixed price. Either feature sweetens the issuer's bonds by creating the possibility that the bondholder will eventually realize some capital gains in addition to receiving interest.

Depending on the investor's objectives, convertible bonds can offer a number of advantages. These can best be described after we investigate how the market values convertible bonds.

MARKET VALUATION OF CONVERTIBLES

The buyer of a convertible bond is really buying two distinct things: (1) a straight corporate bond *and* (2) a conversion privilege (the latter being in effect a set of implied stock purchase warrants). The value of the straight bond feature is referred to as the convertible's *investment value*. The investment value of any convertible can be determined by finding the price at which a nonconvertible bond of comparable risk and maturity is selling. For example, suppose that on July 1, 1985, MidCon Corp.'s convertible bond, 10¼s due on March 31, 2009, would have had to sell in the market for a yield of 12% if it was a nonconvertible issue. A straight bond with 23 years and 9 months to maturity and a coupon rate of 10¼% would sell for roughly $863 to yield 12%. Thus, $863 would be the investment value of the bond.

Convertible bonds frequently are junior-grade securities, subordinated to other debt in their claim on the issuer's assets. This subordination may, however, be masked by labeling the bonds *consolidated obligations* or some similar term. Thus, in determining the investment value of a convertible, it is important to check the precise terms of the indenture.

The value of the conversion feature, referred to as the bond's *conversion value*, equals the market value of the shares into which the bond can be converted. This is also frequently referred to as "parity." The conversion value of the four convertible bonds described at the beginning of this chapter based on a common stock price on July 5, 1985, follows:[3]

---

[3]The prices for the convertible bonds and underlying issues used in the illustrations of this chapter were obtained from Preston M. Harrington III and Bernie Moriarty, *Convertible Securities: Quarterly Statistical Report* (New York: Merrill Lynch Capital Markets, Securities Research Division, July 1985).

Issuer	Conversion Ratio	Common Stock Price July 5, 1985	Conversion Value
U.S. Steel	15.936	$ 27.250	$ 434.26
Burlington Ind.	20.619	27.375	564.45
MidCon Corp.	23.809	47.000	1,119.02
Celanese	10.870	123.875	1,346.52

The conversion value rises proportionately with the value of the issuer's common stock. This is depicted on Exhibit 13-1. For example, if the common stock price increases by 10% for U.S. Steel (from $27.25 to $29.975), the conversion value will increase by 10% (from $434.26 to $477.686).

The *market value* of a convertible (the price at which it trades) depends on both its investment value and conversion value (among other things). If the price of the issuer's common stock is extremely depressed, then the convertible will sell at or near its investment value if that is higher. At somewhat higher stock prices, the implied warrants in the conversion feature begin to assume value, and the bond will typically sell at some *premium above investment value.*[4]

If the price of the issuer's stock climbs still higher, it will eventually reach what we have dubbed in Exhibit 13-1 the *investment value conversion price,* that is, the price at which the market value of the shares for which the bond can be exchanged just equals the bond's current investment value. At this stock price, conversion value and investment value are equal. (See Exhibit 13-1.)

This does not mean that conversion is likely to occur. Instead, the convertible will typically sell at a *premium over conversion value* (or, simply a *conversion premium*). The premium over conversion value is usually expressed as a *percentage* of the conversion value, that is

$$\frac{\text{Market value}}{\text{Conversion value}} - 1$$

---

[4]The premium above the investment value is computed as follows:

$$\frac{\text{Market value}}{\text{Investment value}} - 1$$

To illustrate the computation, suppose that on July 5, 1985, the market price of the MidCon Corp. convertible was 124 (that is, $1,240 per $1,000 of par value). Assuming that its investment value is $863, the premium above the investment value is 44% as shown below:

$$\frac{\$1,240}{\$863} - 1 = .44 \text{ or } 44\%$$

EXHIBIT 13-1 Factors Determining the Market Value of a
Convertible Bond*

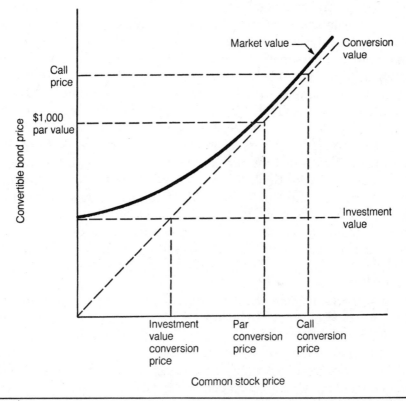

*The coupon on this bond is assumed to be below current market yields. If the reverse were true, investment value would exceed par value.

The premium over conversion value based on July 5, 1985, prices for the common stock and the convertible bond for our 4 convertible bonds is shown below:

Issuer	Conversion Value	Market Value	Premium over Conversion Value
U.S. Steel	$ 434.26	$ 642.50	47.6%
Burlington Ind.	564.45	875.00	55.0
MidCon Corp.	1,119.02	1,240.00	10.8
Celanese	1,346.52	1,346.52	0

Notice that although there is a premium over the conversion value for the first 3 issues, there is no premium for the Celanese convertible bond. The reason for the typical conversion premium (which, as Exhibit 13-1 shows, is likely to exist over a relatively wide range of share prices) is that from the investor's point of view, holding the convertible offers several advantages over holding the common stock.

One advantage is that interest income on the bond as a percentage of its market value will almost always exceed dividends on the stock as a percentage of its market value, the differential being greater for prices near the investment value conversion price than for prices above it. For example, the current yield on the convertible bond (annual dollar coupon divided by the market value of the convertible bond) on July 5, 1985, was 8.95% for the U.S. Steel issue, 10.0% for the Burlington Industries issue, and 8.27% for the MidCon Corp. issue. At the same time, the current yield on the underlying common stock was 3.67% for the U.S. Steel issue, 5.99% for the Burlington Industries issue, and 5.02% for the MidCon Corp. issue. Thus, for these 3 convertible bonds, holding the bond offers the investor more current income than holding the common stock. In the case of the Celanese convertible bond, the current yield on the common stock exceeded the current yield on the convertible bond by .52% (3.55% versus 3.03%).

A second advantage of the convertible is that it is more secure than the common stock. Dividends on the common can easily be cut or eliminated should the firm fall upon hard times, but failure to meet interest payments on outstanding bonds would force the firm into bankruptcy proceedings, under which assets would be liquidated and bondholders would have a first lien on assets.

A third advantage of the convertible has to do with the upside potential and downside risk. If a convertible bond is not selling at a premium too much over its conversion value, any further increase in the price of the common stock will result in an almost equal increase in the market value of the bond because it increases the conversion value of the bond. Thus a long position in the convertible bond offers almost the same upside potential as a long position in the common. With respect to downside risk, however, the convertible is more attractive. Should the price of the common fall, the conversion value and, consequently, the market value of the bond will also fall. However, the decline in the latter will be limited by the bond's investment value at the time of the decline, which sets a floor of sorts under which the market value of the convertible bond cannot fall. For example, suppose that by March 31, 1987, the common stock of MidCon Corp.

drops from $47 per share to $32 per share, a decline of 47%. An investor who owns the common stock will realize a 47% decline in his investment if he had to sell the common stock. The conversion value of the bond will decline from $1,119.02 to $761.88 (23.809 × $32). On the other hand, the investment value will depend on market yields for comparable risk and maturity bonds at the time. Listed below is what the investment value of MidCon Corp.'s convertible bond (10¼% coupon and 22 years to maturity as of March 31, 1987) would be for various market yields and the corresponding loss as a percentage of the market price on July 5, 1985 ($1,240):

Market Yield at Time	Investment Value	Realized Loss (%)
8.0%	$1,231.20	1%
9.0	1,118.90	10
10.0	1,022.10	18
11.0	938.30	24
12.0	865.40	30
13.0	801.70	35

For the above market yields, the loss is less than the 47% loss that occurs if the common stock is owned. In fact, if market yields are less than 7.8% on March 31, 1987, the investment value of the convertible bond would be greater than the current market price of $1,240, resulting in a gain rather than a loss.[5]

The inherent advantages of the convertible over the common stock (better current yield and less risk) explain why the convertible usually trades at a premium over conversion value before and after the *investment value conversion price* is reached. The size of the conversion premium, however, is likely to diminish as the stock price advances further and further above the investment value conversion price. This is so for several reasons. First, as the price at which the convertible trades increases, the differential between the percentage current return offered by the convertible bond and that offered by the common stock will become smaller. In the case of the Celanese con-

---

[5]It should also be noted that the conversion value acts as a cushion for the price of the convertible bond should market yields rise. For example, if the market yield on March 31, 1987, is greater than 13.6%, the investment value of the convertible bond would be less than the conversion value. The market value would have to equal at least the conversion value, otherwise investors would realize an arbitrage gain by buying the convertible bond and converting it.

vertible bond, for example, there is no premium over the conversion value because there is no current yield advantage to owning the convertible bond. Also, the higher the convertible bond trades above its investment value floor, its downside potential is greater and, consequently, it becomes riskier.

Exhibit 13–1 also shows something called the *par conversion price.* This stock price, referred to in bond indentures as simply *conversion price,* is the price at which the bond's face value just equals the market price of the shares into which it can be converted.[6] While a bond's *par* conversion price appears prominently in many discussions of convertibles, it is in fact of little significance to the investor unless he is managing a portfolio whose balance sheet is published publicly and on which discount bonds are valued at par.

As noted above, many firms that issue convertibles do so with the intent of eventually obtaining additional equity capital. Because of the inherent advantages of the convertible over the common stock, conversion might be quite slow even if the price of the common stock has risen substantially. A provision for call gives the issuer a way to force conversion. Once the price of the common stock rises above the level dubbed the *call conversion price* in Exhibit 13–1, the convertible's price necessarily exceeds its call price.[7] At this point, call by the issuer will force immediate conversion. Because of this, call will naturally wipe out any existing conversion premium. It will also result in a loss to the bondholder of all interest accrued since the last coupon payment. Due to the dangers of call, the conversion premium on

---

[6]The par conversion price is found as follows:

$$\frac{\text{Par value of convertible bond}}{\text{Conversion ratio}}$$

The par conversion price for the four convertible bonds used throughout this chapter is given below:

Issuer	Par Value	Conversion Ratio	Par Conversion Price
U.S. Steel	$1,000	15.936	$62.75
Burlington Ind.	1,000	20.619	48.50
MidCon Corp.	1,000	23.809	42.00
Celanese	1,000	10.870	92.00

[7]The call conversion price is found by dividing the current call price of the convertible bond by the conversion ratio.

bonds selling above their call price are generally small, and you should be wary of putting money into them.

There are some convertible issues that do have call protection. This protection can be either in the form of not allowing the issuer to redeem the issue prior to a specified date or not allowing the issuer to do this unless the stock price has increased by a predetermined percentage above the par conversion price. For example, the Burlington Industries convertible bond cannot be called prior to November 15, 1986. MidCon Corp.'s convertible bond cannot be called prior to March 31, 1987. National City Corp.'s 9½s of 2010 convertible bond cannot be called prior to January 1, 1988, unless the common stock trades at a premium of 50% above the par conversion price. Since the conversion ratio for this issue is 22.222, the par conversion price is $45 ($1,000/22.222). Consequently, if the common stock price trades at a price of at least $67.50 (1.50 × $45), the issue may be called before January 1, 1988.

One related caveat: It is easy for the casual investor to miss seeing call announcements. Thus, convertibles selling near or above their call price should be left with a broker who will keep careful track of such things.

INVESTING IN CONVERTIBLES

Diverse investment objectives lead investors to buy convertible bonds. The investor committed to bonds and other debt securities may acquire convertibles as a means of obtaining an equity kicker that may enlarge the return on his portfolio. Alternately, the investor who really wants to be in stocks may acquire convertible bonds as a conservative way of taking a position in the issuer's common stock. Finally, convertibles may be bought as a substitute for a warrants-plus-cash position or as part of a hedge operation in which the issuer's stock is sold short against the convertible. The first two strategies are discussed below. The third, which is really a form of speculation in stocks, falls outside the scope of this book.

If you, a *bond* investor, are tempted to invest in convertibles to obtain an equity kicker, be clearly aware of what you are doing. Whether you buy your convertible bond at issue or in the secondary market, you are likely to pay a premium over the investment value—usually a substantial one. Because of this premium, what you are really doing is (1) investing an amount equal to the convertible's investment value in bonds and (2) investing an amount equal to the premium over investment value in implied stock warrants. This description has the disadvantage of sounding less exciting than "picking up an equity kicker," but it has the offsetting advantage of highlighting some important things. First, you should never buy convertibles unless you want to acquire the stock of the issuing firm. Second, you should calculate the amount of your investment in implied warrants and ask yourself if you want to make an investment of that proportion in the equity market and if convertible bonds are the lowest-cost way to do so. Many investors feel that the equity kicker is costless because even if the issuer's common fails to raise in price, the bond will eventually be redeemed at par. However, the investor who buys a convertible bond (even at or below par) and holds it to maturity loses something, namely, the extra interest income he could have obtained by investing in a straight bond of the same quality and maturity—one that sold at no premium over investment value.

Because of the risk and return advantages of convertibles, an investment in convertibles as a substitute for an investment in *stock* can be quite attractive. For the small investor, this appeal is enhanced by the fact that substituting convertibles for stock will reduce transaction costs, since brokerage house commissions on bond trades are usually much lower per dollar invested than those on stock trades. Professional money managers of large funds are quick to pick up attractively priced convertibles as substitutes for stock. Consequently, the best opportunities for the individual investor are in small and more speculative issues which, because they are inappropriate for portfolios of many financial institutions, are likely to be priced on the low side.

While convertibles have undeniable advantages, they also have some drawbacks. The downside risk of investing in a convertible can easily be understated. One reason is that the investment value of a bond is subject to considerable fluctuation *up and down* over time due to changes in market yields. Consequently, the investment value of a convertible bond may have all the stability of a top-story elevator in constant operation. To make matters worse, tight-money periods, which are likely to crimp the value of the bond issuer's common (and, consequently, the conversion value of the convertible), are exactly when the convertible's investment value is likely to plummet as rates rise. Moreover, the same negative investor psychology which produces a downward trend in the price of the common may also decrease the convertible's conversion premium, which in turn will accentuate the effect of any fall in the price of the common on the price at which the convertible trades.

Anyone who buys convertibles as an alternative to stocks should also be aware that if a convertible is purchased at a premium over conversion value, the percentage increase in the convertible's value that results (assuming no change in the conversion premium) from an X percent increase in the price of the common stock will be something less than X percent. Consider, for example, the U.S. Steel convertible bond; it sold on July 5, 1985, at $642.50 and could be exchanged for 15.936 shares of common stock selling at $27.25. A 10.1% increase in price of the common stock from $27.25 to $30 would increase the conversion value of the convertible bond to about $478. Assuming the dollar premium over the conversion value, $208.24 ($642.50 − $434.26), does not change, the market value of the convertible bond would increase from $642.50 to $686.42. Thus, a 10.1% increase in the price of the common stock will increase the price of the convertible bond by 6.8%. In fact, the premium over the conversion value would probably decrease, resulting in an increase of less than 6.8%.

The tendency for a given percentage increase in the common stock to generate a smaller percentage increase in the price of the convertible bond is often described as the result of *deleveraging*. To understand the sense of this term, recall our discussion of debt leverage in Chapter 7. It is easy to see that if an investor leverages his stock position (i.e., buys stock on margin), the percentage return he earns on his investment will exceed the percentage change in the price of the stock. Taking a position in a stock through the purchase of a convertible bond selling at a premium over conversion value is just the opposite of a margin purchase— the investor puts down more money than the price at which the stock is actually selling. Hence, we have the term deleveraging.

To see how the investor is putting up more to purchase the stock, consider the price that an investor would pay by buying the convertible bond and then immediately exchanging the bond for the common stock. Suppose that on July 5, 1985, an investor purchased the U.S. Steel convertible bond at $642.50 and exchanged it for 15.936 shares of common stock of U.S. Steel. This means that the investor effectively paid $642.50 for 15.936 shares of common stock of U.S. Steel or $40.32 per share ($642.50/15.936).[8] Had this investor purchased

---

[8]The $40.32 per share is referred to as the *market conversion price*. In general, the market conversion price is found by dividing the market value of the convertible bond by the conversion ratio.

the common stock of U.S. Steel directly, he would have paid $27.25 per share. Thus, the investor paid a premium to buy the common stock.[9]

The decreased upside potential resulting from deleveraging is somewhat compensated for by the greater current return generally offered by the convertible. However, no matter how great this return advantage, wherever there is a conversion premium, there exists some *threshold value* of the stock; that is, once the stock rises above that value, an investment in the common would have yielded a greater overall return than an investment in the convertible. The Celanese convertible was past that threshold value on July 5, 1985. Since the current yield advantage assumes greater importance as the position is held longer, an investment in a convertible makes the most sense when the investor expects the rate of appreciation on the common stock to be modest and consequently invests with a long time horizon.

The reasonableness of conversion premiums on convertibles is often evaluated by the use of various "break-even ratios." Such ratios are relatively easy to calculate, but it is not clear that any of them provides an analytically significant measure of the desirability of investing in a convertible bond. A more informative method is to make intelligent estimates of what is likely to happen to the price of the common stock over time and compare that price with threshold prices of the common stock for different periods. This procedure calls for more thought and effort on the part of the investor.

Also, keep in mind that a convertible bond like any other bond is subject to default risk. There are very few convertible bonds that carry a credit rating greater than triple-B. This should not be disturbing for an investor who would otherwise have invested directly in the common stock. However, an investor who wants to invest in a bond, and feels that the current yield on a convertible is sufficiently attractive as a bond investment to justify investing in it, should clearly understand

---

[9]Notice that the premium over the conversion value in percentage terms can also be found using the market conversion price and the market price of the common stock, as follows:

$$\frac{\text{Market conversion price}}{\text{Market price of common stock}} - 1$$

For the U.S. Steel convertible issue, we have:

$$\frac{\$40.32}{\$27.25} - 1 = .47 \text{ or } 47\%.$$

that convertibles generally carry greater default risk than straight bonds selling at the same yield.[10]

One final note on taxes. The exchange of a convertible bond for the shares of the common stock of the same issuer is not a taxable event. However, as noted earlier, there are some convertible bonds that can be exchanged for common stock not of the issuer but of another corporation. In such cases, conversion may be taxable. That is, conversion will be treated for tax purposes as if the investor sold the convertible bond. Thus, the investor should check with the issuing company to determine if conversion will be a taxable event.

OBTAINING INFORMATION ABOUT CONVERTIBLE BONDS

As we explained in the previous chapters, there are several sources that can be used to obtain information about the provisions of a corporate bond. These same sources can be used to obtain information about the features of a convertible bond. Exhibits 13–2 and 13–3 are sample pages from *Moody's Bond Record* and *Standard & Poor's Corporation Bond Guide,* respectively.

---

[10]For example, the current yield on the Burlington Industries issue was 10% and the current yield on the MidCon Corp. was 8.27% on July 5, 1985. Relative to other bond yields at the time, these current yields were fairly attractive.

EXHIBIT 13-2

98   Acap-BAY   MOODY'S   BOND   RECORD

Convertible Bonds

(Where an issue is printed in bold type face such company also has straight debt securities outstanding. See pages 4-97.)

Issue	Int. Dates	Moody's Rating	Ann. S.F. Thous.	Curr. Call Price	Amt. Outs. Mill.	Conv. Price	Shs. $1,000 Deb.	Current Market Com.	Current Market Deb.	Deb. Curr.	Yield Mat.	Deb. Conv. Value	m Antic. Conv. Com. Price	1986 Price Range Com.	1986 Price Range Deb.	Lat. Ann. Per Earns j	Com. Ann. Div. Rate
Acapulco Y Los Arcos Rest c.s.d. 13.50 1996 ¹·	JAJ&O1	N.R. r	833-'87	110.38	.65	9.20	108.69	25%b	---	---	---	71	---	9% - 6%	95 - 95	0.75	0.10
AccuRay Corp. c.s.d. 5.50 1991 ¹·	J&D 1	N.R. r	900-'81	101.30	10.2	35.88	27.87	15	154b	5.8	3.5	151%	15%	26% - 22%	88 - 88	1.90	0.24
ACTION IND. INC. c.s.d. 9.00 1998	A&O 1	N.R. r	1,750-'89	105.00	1.95	9.87	101.32	16%	113%	7.9	7.7	102	18%	15 - 12	154 - 120	0.92	Nil
●Advest Group Inc. c.s.d. 9.00 2008	M&S 15	N.R. r	1,375-'94	107.80	27.5	16.42	60.90	4%	---	---	---	70%	---	16% - 12%	116% - 98%	0.71	0.13
Aeronca Inc. c.s.d. 12.50 1993	F&A1	N.R. r	None	109.00	9.82	5.88	170.21			---	---			5% - 3%	100 - 73	1.22	Nil
AFG INDUSTRIES c.s.d. 8.375 2005	A&O1	Ba3 r	3,000-'95	107.20	40.0	25.32	39.49	22%	---	---	---	89%	---	22% - 15%		1.41	Nil
Air Wis Services, Inc. c.s.d. 7.75 2010	J&D15	B1 r	1,750-'95	107.75	35.0	19.00	52.63	15%b	99b	7.8	7.8	79%	18%	15% - 11%	99 - 86	0.18	Nil
Airlit International c.s.d. 5.75 1987	Fe-30-74	Caa	1,100-'77	100.00	4.67	6.21	161.03	---	5b	flat	flat			% - %	5 - 5		Nil
Aland Corp. c.s.d. 6.50 1991	J&D 1	N.R. r	1.10%-'82	101.95	7.24	27.75	36.04			flat	flat					0.00	Nil
Alaska Air Grp. Inc. c.s.d. 7.75 2010	J&D 15	Ba3 r	2,250-'95	105.43	50.0	28.25	35.40	20%	97%b	7.9	8.0	73%	27%	21% - 15%	97% - 97%	2.10	0.16
●Alaska Airlines, Inc. c.s.d. 9.00 2003	M&N 15	Ba2 r	1,500-'93	107.20	35.0	18.13	55.17	20%	123	7.3	6.7	114%	22%	21% - 15%	126 - 106%	2.10	0.16
do c.s.d. 9.00B 2003	M&N15	Ba2 r	600-'93	106.30	35.0	18.13	55.17	20%	---	---	---	114%	---	21% - 15%	111 - ---	2.10	0.16
Alco Standard Corp. c.s.d. 9.00 2007	M&S30	Baa1r	2,500-'92	106.30	2.17	37.00	27.03	45%	121b	7.4	7.1	121%	44%	45% - 35%	121 - 111	3.38	1.24
do c.s.d. 8.50 2010	M31&S30	Baa1r	3,000-'95	107.65	0.53	43.50	22.99	45%	116%b	7.3	3.2	103%	50%	45% - 35%	116% - 104%	2.32	1.24
●Alexander's Inc. c.s.d. 5.50 1996	J&J 1	B2 r	1,000-'82	101.16	15.0	32.25	31.01	37%	120b	4.6		127%	38%	37% - 34%	122% - 113%	1.11	Nil
●ALLEGHENY BEVERAGE cv.sr.sub.deb. 9.50 2010	M&S1	B2	5%-'96	106.65	100	21.50	46.51	27%b	---	---	---	128%	---	29 - ---	131% - 131%	√0.44	0.40
Allied Artists Ind. c.s.d. 8.75 1987	J&D15	N.R.	5%-'77	100.97	0.91	2.25	444.44			---	---					---	Nil
do c.s.d. 8.75 1990	M&N15	N.R.	158-'80	100.00	2.17	2.25	444.44			---	---					---	Nil
●ALLIED STORES c.s.d. 4.50 1992	M&S15	A3 r	2,000-'78	100.50	0.53	22.25	44.94	37%	183	5.2	3.8	169	73%	38% - 33	183 - 167%	7.40	1.16
●do c.s.d. 9.50 2007	M&N1	A3 r	6,250-'94	106.65	111	40.00	25.00	37%	141	6.2	5.6	94		34% - 20	141 - 131	7.40	1.16
do c.s.d. 8.75 2009	J&J15	A3	6,250-'96	107.88	125	54.63	18.31	37%	---	flat	flat	68%	77	38% - 33	141 - 131	7.40	1.16
●ALTEC CORP. c.s.d. 15.00 1995 ·	A&O1	N.R. r	135-'85	106.70	2.66	1.20	833.33			---	---			34% - 20		1.81	0.60
America West Air. c.s.d. 7.75 2010	F&A1	B2 r	3,000-'99	107.75	60.0	13.50	74.07	76	65b	10.8	19.9	137		78% - 59%	71 - 60	√3.26	Nil
●AMERICAN CAN INTL. cv'gtd.deb. 4.75 1988	M&N 15	Baa1	None	None	30.0	55.42	18.04	6	61%	10.9	18.7	45%	8%	6% - 5%	59 - ---	5.06	2.90
●American Century Corp. c.s.d. 7.00 1990 ᵐ	A&O1	N.R. r	2,200-'82	100.75	1.67	13.09	76.39	68%	220%b	1.9	7.0	457	10%	6% - 5%	194% - 194%	0.15	Nil
do c.s.d. 6.75 1991	J&D15	N.R. r	None	101.88	8.41	17.56	56.95	42%	98	5.6	2.8	34%	33	69% - 50%	100 - 97	0.15	Nil
●American Express O/S cv.eurodeb. 4.25 1987	MAY 15	Aa2	875-72	100.00	40.0	15.04	66.49	42%	230%	4.8	3.0	230%	42%	42% - 33%	230% - 190	3.55	1.36
●AMERICAN GENERAL CORP. c.s.d. 5.50 1987 ·	M&S 1	N.R. r	None	102.75	1.90	18.33	54.55	42%	230b	4.8		230%	42%	42% - 33%	225 - 188	3.23	1.12
●do c.s.d. 11.00 2007 "	F&A7	N.R. r	None	"110.00	128	18.33	54.55							42% - 33%		3.23	1.12
●do c.s.d. 11.00 2008	M&N4	N.R. r	None	110.00	176	18.33	54.55							41% - 33%		3.23	1.12
American Hoist c.s.d. 4.75 1992 ·	J&D 1	B1 r	625-'78	100.25	0.58	15.66	63.86	10%	77b	7.1	10.1	64%	15%	10% - 9	73% - 70%	√1.38	Nil
do c.s.d. 5.50 1993	J&D 1	B1 r	900-'92	100.75	6.21	19.90	50.25	10%	94	12.5	12.8	50%	16	10% - 7%	94% - 88%	√1.19	Nil
●American Israeli Paper c.s.d. 11.75 1997	NOV 15	N.R. r	1,400-'90	100.00	13.3	17.07	58.58	11%	112	10.5	10.1	69%	16	12% - 7%	112 - 105	1.11	Nil
●American Maize-Prod. c.s.d. 11.75 2000 "	F&A 1	Ba2 r	2,000-'91	107.85	25.0	18.18	55.00	21%	109%	8.7	8.4	83%	26%	15% - 13%	111 - 103	1.92	0.52
●AMER. MEDICAL INTL. c.s.d. 9.50 2001	M&N15	A3	9,375-'91	107.60	125	24.37	41.03	21%	95%			87%	26%	22% - 18%	95% - 85%	1.94	0.72
●do c.s.d. 8.25 2008	A&O 1	A3	5,000-'93	107.01	67.6	40.00	25.00	30%	---	8.7	8.7	53%	38	22% - 18%		1.94	0.72
American Medicorp c.s.d. 5.50 1989 "·	A&O1	N.R. r	2,000-'80	100.00	0.17	37.86	26.41	%b	---					33% - 28%		2.19	0.76
American Midland Corp. c.s.d. 6.00 1987 ᵐ·	J&D15	N.R. r	1,125-'77	100.25	3.81			4%	91	6.6	10.2	63%	6%	4% - 2%	94% - 80	√0.01	Nil
●American Motors Corp. c.s.d. 6.00 1988	A&O1	N.R. r	2,100-'82	100.67	17.3	7.48	133.69	38%b	---	---	---	321%	---	40% - 35		0.04	Nil
American Nat'l. Hold. c.s.d. 8.50 1991	A&O 1	N.R. r	375-'84	100.00	1.53	11.90	84.03						6%			4.20	1.24

Bond	Int. Date	Rating	Redemption	Call Price		Price		Yld	Div
AMF INC. c.s.d. 5.00 1987 "	SEP 15	B3	None	5⅜'79	100.00	20.0	52.25	19.14	0.91 / Nil
AMFAC, Inc c.s.d. 5.00 1989	M&S 1	Ba3 r	1,750.·80		100.11	6	35.71	28.00	1.28 / Nil
do c.s.d. 5.25 1994	M&N 1	Ba3 r	1,750.·80		101.25	24.4	43.67	22.90	1.28 / Nil
Ampad Corp. c.s.d. 8.00 2010	F&A 1	Ba3 r	5%·95		108.00	25.0	21.38	46.77	1.11 / 0.40
Anacomp Int'l NV euro c.s.d. 9.00 1996 "	JAN 15	Ca	Ca		100.00	10.5	19.75	50.63	.002 / Nil
Anacomp, Inc. c.s.d. 13.875 2002	J&J 15	Ca	3,750.·92		100.00	23.2	17.50	57.14	0.02 / Nil
Andal Corp c.s.d. 5.50 1997 "	M&S 15	Caa	2,000.·82		102.00	12	22.50	44.44	0.16 / Nil
Andersen Group Inc. c.s.d. 10.50 2002	A&O 15	Caa	834.·93		109.45	9.98	16.17	61.84	1.23 / Nil
Anixter Bros, Inc. c.s.d. 8.25 2003	J&J 1	Baa3r	3,150.·93		105.78	42.0	27.45	36.43	0.48 / 0.14
Anthony Industries c.s.d. 11.25 2000	J&J 1	N.R. r	1,570.·91		102.27	22.0	16.34	61.20	1.02ª / 0.44
Apache Corp. c.s.d. 6.00 1990 "	J&J 1	N.R. r	Yes		100.80	0.74	21.00	47.62	3.21 / 1.80
Apollo Computer Inc. c.s.d. 7.25 2011	F&A 1	B2	2,400.·82		107.25	100	18.00	55.56	0.04ª / Nil
ARA SERVICES, INC. c.s.d. 4.625 1996 "	J&O 15	B2	5%·82		101.39	7.55	19.00	52.63	0.00 / Nil
Arlen Corp. c.s.d. 5.00 1986 "	J&O 15	Caa	None		100.80	0.85	34.80	28.73	0.25 / Nil
ARROW ELECTR. INC. c.s.d. 9.00 2003	F&A 1	B2	2,250.·93		106.75	30.0	88.42	11.31	2.00 / 0.20
Arwood Corp. c.s.d. 4.625 1987 "	J&O 15	N.R.	500.·78		100.13	1.00	15.00	66.67	3.94 / 2.60
ARX, Inc. c.s.d. 9.375 2005 "	M&S 15	B2	1,750.·95		109.38	25.0	33.33	30.00	1.05 / Nil
ASHLAND OIL, INC. c.s.d. 4.75 1993	F&A 15	Baa1r	3,500.·82		101.35	2.94	14.50	68.97	4.12 / 1.60
Astrex Inc. c.s.d. 9.50 2000	M&S 1	B3	15%·95		109.50	15.0	29.78	33.58	0.96 / Nil
Atlantic Research Corp. c.s.d. 8.00 2008	M&N 1	N.R.	1,500.·93		106.40	30.0	57.21	17.50	1.57 / Nil
Automatic Data Proc. c.s.d. 7.50 2010	F&A 15	A2	3.6%·96		106.75	100			2.14 / 0.68
do c.s.d. 6.50 2011	M&S 1	A2	3%·97		106.50	150	83.45	11.98	2.14 / 0.68
Avalon Corp. c.s.d. 7.00 1992 "	F&A 15	N.R. r	7.5%·82		102.50	5.82	25.00	40.00	0.00ª / 0.05
AVCO CORP. c.s.d. 5.50 1993	M318&N30	0a2 r	None		101.65	20.8		44.44	3.11 / 1.80
Aviation Group, Inc. c.s.d. 8.00 2003 "	J&O 15	N.R. r	1,875.·93		107.20	25.0	22.50		2.63ª / 1.10
Avnet, Inc. c.s.d. 8.00 2013	J&J 1	A2	4%·93		106.40	100	52.00	19.23	1.39 / 0.50
BALLY MFG. CORP. c.s.d. 6.00 1998	M&S 15	B1	7.5%·83		100.75	34.5	28.99	34.50	0.95 / 0.20
do c.s.d. 10.00 2006	J&O 1	B1	5,000.·91		108.66	100	32.68	30.60	0.95 / 0.20
BALT. & OHIO R.R. 1st con. 6.25 G 1997 "	J&J 1	A3	2,000.·83		102.87	0.13	9.54	104.82	2.07 / 1.16
do c.s.d. 4.50 A 2010	J&J 1	Baa2	None		101.50	8.75	100.00	37	2.07 / 1.16
BANK OF BOSTON CORP. c.s.d. 7.75 2011	J&J 15	A1	None		107.75	100	70.25	14.23	4.23ª / 1.32
BANK OF NEW ENG. CORP. cv cap.nts. 5.00 1994 "	M&N 1	N.R. r	None		101.25	0.23	53.03	18.86	6.39 / 2.28
BANK OF NEW YORK CO. c.s.d. 8.25 2010	J&J 1	A2	"105.78	150	"105.78	1.50	34.50	18.35	6.39 / 2.28
BANK OF VIRGINIA CO. c.s.d. 5.00 1997	M&N 1	N.R. r	None		101.75	0.22	19.50	51.28	3.05 / 1.12
BankAmer. Rlty. c.s.d. 6.75 1990	J&J 15	Baa1r	6.5%·84		101.13	0.86	14.00	71.43	2.29 / 2.40
do c.s.d. 9.50 2010	A&O 1	Baa1r	4,000.·91		106.33	0.68	17.44	57.34	2.29 / 2.40
do c.s.d. 9.50 2008	J&O 1	Baa1r	2,500.·94		107.60	50.0	31.00	32.26	2.29 / 2.40
Barringer Resources, Inc. c.s.d. 12.50 1996	J&O 1	N.R. r	470.·88		111.50	4.19	8.00	125.00	0.74ª / Nil
Basix Corp. c.s.d. 8.75 2005	M&N 1	B2	7.5%·95		"108.75	30.0	13.86	72.12	0.98 / 0.12
Baxter Trav. Lab. c.s.d. 4.375 1991 "	M&N 1	Baa1r	2,750.·81		100.75	5.0	9.50	100.50	0.85 / 0.40
do c.s.d. 4.75 2001	J&J 15	Baa1r	5,000.·86		101.75	34.2	11.72	85.32	0.85 / 0.40
BAY COL PROP. CO. c.s.d. 6.75 1991 "	M&N 15	N.R. r	"10%·81		101.88	0.54	21.00	47.62	0.18 / 0.20

¹Acq. by Restaurant Associates Industries. ²Form. Indust. Nucleonics. ³Due 6-15-87. ⁴Cv. into Alaska Group Com. ⁵Fr. 6-15-88. ⁶Cv into Apex Holding Co. com. ⁷Fr. 9-1-88. ⁸Acq. by Gulton Industries. ⁹Gtd. by American Can Co. ¹⁰Form. Amer. Century Trust.In process of liquidation. ¹¹Gtd.by & cv.into American Express Co. ¹²Exch. for com. Lincoln Amer. Corp. ¹³Also cv. into 12.24 shs. of $3.25 Jr. pfd. stk. thru 8-31-87. ¹⁴Fr. 2-7-87. ¹⁵Conv. into stk. and $2.75 Cum. conv. class A pfd. stk. ser. 1 of Creditthrift Fin'l. ¹⁶Fr. 2-7-87. ¹⁷Conv. into stk. at $0.335 per sh. ¹⁸Conv. into Class A com. ¹⁹Acq. by Humana, Inc. ²⁰Each $23.56 is conv. into $26.375 prin. amt. of 11.7% debs. ²¹Formerly Midland Resources. ²²Acq. by Minstar, Inc. ²³Gtd. by & cv. into Anacomp, Inc. ²⁴Form. National Kinney. ²⁵Form. 5.25. ²⁶Due 1-31-2000. ²⁷Plus stk. ²⁸Conv. into Continental Telecom com. ²⁹Co. is privately owned. ³⁰Conv. into $708.10 per thousand. ³¹Form. Arlen Realty & Devel. ³²Cv. into com. of Interlake Inc. ³³Formerly Aeroflex Labs. ³⁴Sk. ³⁵Formerly Tri-South Mtge. Inv. ³⁶Conv. $926 per $1,000 deb. ³⁷Acq. by Primark Corp. ³⁸Due 10-1-2013. ³⁹Exch. for CSX Corp. com. stk. based on last quoted sale price on stk. mrk. plus accrued int. on Ser. G bond & cash for fractional shs. ⁴⁰Form. New England Merchants Co. ⁴¹Fr. 7-1-88. ⁴²S.F. requirement met by conversion and purchases of deb. after 7/15/78. ⁴³Fr. 6-1-87. ⁴⁴Acq. by Amer. Hospital Supply Corp. ⁴⁵Now Bay Financial.

Notes: Moody's ratings are subject to change. Because of the possible time lapse between Moody's assignment or change of a rating and your use of this monthly publication, we suggest you verify the current rating of any security or issuer in which you are interested. For standard abbreviations and symbols, see page 3.

EXHIBIT 13-3

CONVERTIBLE BONDS

CONVERTIBLE BONDS Issue, Rate, Interest Dates and Maturity	S&P Quality Rating	B F o o d m	Outstdg. Mil.-$	Conv Ex- pires	Shares per $1,000 Bond	Price per Share	Div. Income per Bond	1986 RANGE Hi Lo	Curr Bid Sale($) Ask(Å)	Curr. Return	Yield to Mat	Stock Value of Bond	Conv. Parity	STOCK DATA Curr. Price P/E Ratio		Earnings Per Share Yr. End 1984 1985			V Last 1984 12 Mos u'l'n
Coeur d'Alene Mines..9¼s sJl 2005	B-	R	25.0	2005	52.91	18.90	.....	113⅛ 105½	109¼	8.68	8.48	71⅛	20⅝	13⅝	d Dc	0.20 Pd.10	d0.10	n/r
Cagnic Energy Sys......10⅞ s Fs31 2000	NR	R	15.00	2000	333.33	3.00	.....	104⅜ 79¾	100	10.2	10.2	100	3	3	d Jd	d0.39	*3.87	d0.43	n/r
Coleco Indus 11s Ms15 1989	B-	R	47.1	1989	72.73	13.75	.....	147½ 117	s145	7.59	7.25	143¾	19⅞	.19¾	d Dc	d4.95	*3.87 d3.87	*3.17
Comarco Inc............9⅜ s Ao15 2000	NR	R	10.0	2000	86.96	11.50	.....	121⅜ 109¾	121¼	8.01	7.25	121¾	14	14	22 Ja	20.57	P1.15 0.65	n/r
C.O.M.B. Co ....8⅞ s Ao15 2000	NR	R	27.0	2000	53.39	18.73	.....	112½ 101	112¾	7.91	7.45	97¾	21	18%	16 Dc	0.43	P1.15 1.15	1.12
Comcast Corp ....8⅜ s Fs15 2010	R	R	40.0	2010	48.38	20.67	5.81	130 104¾	124⅞	6.62	6.25	124½	25¼	25%	37 Dc	0.64	P0.70 0.70	0.70
Comdisco, Inc...........8⅜ s Fs15 2003	BB+	R	58.0	2003	41.10	24.33	6.58	108⅛ 85½	s108¾	7.37	7.13	89%	21⅛	21%	14 Sp	0.70	1.41 1.57	n/r
America Inc⁴ 5⅞ jd31 1992	BB+	R	16.3	1992	37.06	26.98	81.53	173¾ 142⅜	172	5.22	5.22	172½	46⅛	46%	14 Je	4.81	FA4.48 4.48	*4.30
Commercial Solv........4⅞ sJl 1991	BBB-	R	2.50	1991	Conv into $662.00	.....	74¾ 73¾	76	5.92	10.5	.....	.....	.34¾	14 Je	3.04	4.39 2.51	n/r
Comnusic's Corp Am ....8⅝ s jDl5 2007	CCC	R	20.0	2007	57.54	17.38	.....	53⅜ 42½	46¾	18.7	19.1	5%	8%	0.937	d Je	d1.18	d2.73 d3.07	n/r
Communications Ind.....9s sO15 2009	BB-	R	57.5	2009	Conv into 1193.77	.....	119 103¾	119	7.56	7.29	125	15⅜	.94½	10 Dc	8.46	9.08 9.08	n/r
COMPAQ Computer9¼s Jd 2005	BB	R	75.0	2005	86.96	11.50	12.32	145 122	s138	6.70	5.90	.....	25⅜	.14%	14 My	0.47	P0.97 0.97	0.90
Comprehensive Care ....7⅛ s Ao15 2010	BB+	R	46.0	2010	38.51	25.97	.....	99¾ 96¼	96¾	7.75	7.80	63⅜	25%	24%	5 My	0.53	P3.13 1.15	n/r
Computer Consols........7⅛ s Fs15 1998	BB+	R	80.0	1998	46.99	21.28	.....	67¾ 51½	s67¾	11.5	13.3	37⅜	14%	.33%	d Dc	0.54	P3.61 d3.61	n/r
Computer Sciences..6s mS15 1994	BB+	R	34.9	1994	37.04	27.00	.....	138¾ 116	123¾	4.85	2.83	123%	33%		21 Mr	2.02	Ex1.62 1.62	1.92
Computervision Corp ....8s jD 2009	R	R	110	2009	22.22	45.00	.....	82¾ 63¾	s82	9.76	9.99	35%	36%	.16¾	d Dc	Δ1.31	Pd.82 d2.82	n/r
Comserv Corp⁷ ....11s jJ 2002	CC	R	20.0	2002	68.97	14.50	.....	73 54¾	70	15.7	16.3	35	10%	4%	2 Dc	0.85	d3.00 2.98	n/r
Conductron Corp..9¼s Fs15 1996	CCC	R	13.0	1996	40.00	25.00	.....	66¾ 59	66	14.3	16.5	15	16%	3%	10 Dc	0.85	Δ1.65 1.65	n/r
Consol Oil & Gas(SerG)...8s Mn 2000	NR	R	0.99	2000	35.39	28.26	.....	No Sale	66	14.2	15.9	12	15%	3%	0 Dc	0.58	Δ0.27 0.27	n/r
Consol Oil&Gas(SerH)9s Jd 1994	NR	R	9.94	1994	70.77	14.13	.....	75 75	75	12.0	14.2	23%	10%	3%	0 Nv	0.58	Δ0.27 0.27	n/r
Consul Restaurants..13s mN 1992	NR	R	117.5	1992	160.00	6.25	.....	55¾ 41	47	.....	.....	34	3	2%	d My	Δ0.32	d3.32⅛ d3.44	n/r
Consul(Corp)Restaurants..10s mN 2003	NR	R	3.15	2003	51.28	19.50	.....	56 43	56	.....	18.5	10%	10%	2%	d My	Δ0.32	d3.32⅜ d3.44	n/r
Continental⁹ Airll..3⅜ s jJ 1992	D	R	17.4	1992	Common&Pfd¹²	.....	69¾ 42	69¾	.....	Flat	69%	.....	.20¾	d Dc	P2.49	P2.49 2.49	*1.81
Cont'l Inform Sys........9s jJ31 2006	B+	R	32.0	2006	51.61	19.375	.....	116 100	s114¾	7.84	7.55	95%	22¾	.18%	3 Fb	13 1.19	P1.47 1.47	n/r
Continental²⁰Telecom...5⅜s1A 1986	BBB+	R	1.31	8-1-86	43.63	22.91	78.53	115 109¾	130¾	4.01	24.5	130%	30	.30	9 Dc	0.27	P3.21 3.21	3.19
Cont'l Tel Ind Fin¹⁶ .....5⅞s Ma 1988	NR	C	7.18	1988	42.18	23.71	75.92	No Sale	126¾	4.35	.....	126%	30	.30	9 Dc	2.67	P3.21 3.21	*3.19
CooperVision Inc.......8⅜s Ms 2005	BB-	R	195	2005	36.43	27.45	14.57	118½ 105¾	s117	7.37	6.99	99%	32%	.27¼	10 Dc	1.30	1.69 1.75	n/r
Corning Glass Works....8⅞s jD 2007	A+	R	100	2007	26.23	38.125	36.72	145 106¾	s144¾	5.72	4.90	146%	55	.56	13 Dc	3.87	4.42 4.42	n/r
Corroon & Black⁷.......7⅜s jD 2005	A+	R	30.0	2005	17.86	56.00	23.22	123 98	112¾	6.69	6.39	112%	62%	.56	20 Dc	0.63	P3.15 3.15	n/r
Covington Techno²⁰....12¼s1A15 1994	NR	R	5.94	1994	148.15	6.75	.....	65 58	58	21.5	24.5	19%	3%	1.312	d Dc	0.27	q0.31	n/r
CP Nat¹ 12¼s ²QSep30 1998	BBB	R	6.84	1998	41.67	24.00	62.51	143¾ 108⅜	130¾	9.40	8.31	126%	31¼	.31¼	11 Dc	2.35	P2.90 2.90	*2.61
CP Nat¹ 11¼s Jd15 1999	BBB-	R	4.06	1999	41.67	24.00	62.51	143¾ 108⅜	130¾	8.64	7.58	130%	31¼	.31¼	11 Dc	2.35	P2.90 2.90	*2.61
CPT Corp...........10s mN15 2001	B-	R	37.3	2001	43.48	23.00	.....	83 76½	82⅜	12.1	12.5	25%	19	5%	d Je	1.05	d0.18 Nil	n/r
Crane Co⁷B¹ ....5s jJ 1994	BBB	R	12.21	1994	69.59	²14.37	111.34	337½ 257¾	327½	1.53	12.1	327%	47	.47	24 Dc	3.13	1.92 1.92	1.92
Crane Co(Sr)............8⅜s aO 2005	BBB+	R	75.0	2005	23.15	43.20	37.04	127 104⅜	s122¾	7.14	6.67	108%	52%	.47	24 Dc	3.13	1.92 1.92	n/r
Cray Research.......6⅛s Fa 2011	BBB	R	100	2011	11.90	84.00	.....	100 88½	100	5.65	5.49	83%	91%	.70½	28 Dc	1.53	2.49 2.49	2.49
Crestwood Realty Inv²¹...6⅜s aO 1990	A-	R	2.06	1990	Conv into $928.57	24.84	90 88½	90	7.50	5.50	.....	2%	.....	.....	d	.....	.....	n/r
Crestwood Realty Inv²¹...6⅜s jD 1991	A-	R	6.50	1991	Conv into $532.09	24.84	82 80	80¾	7.78	7.78	1%	3%	.....	.....	d	.....	.....	n/r
Crestwood Realty Inv²¹..7s aO 1997	A-	R	6.53	1997	Conv into $975	24.84	94½ 94½	94¾	7.41	10.9	67%	43%	.....	.....	d	.....	.....	n/r
Crime²⁰ Control⁰.........10s ⏎ 1997	NR	R	20.0	1997	58.34	17.14	24.84	52 51	52	.....	Flat	9%	10%	.1%	d Dc	d4.94	q2.00	n/r
Crown Zellerbach⁷B²⁷...9⅜s Mn 2009	BBB-	R	75.0	2009	24.84	40.25	24.84	111 103¾	s110¾	8.24	8.39	114¾	44%	.46¾	d Dc	2.61	Pd.56 1.56	n/r
Crystal Oil 11⅞s Ao15 2000	CCC	R	120.4	2000	49.50	20.20	.....	37½ 10¾	s12	.....	Flat	1%	2%	0.312	d Dc	Δ1.10	Pd.83 d2.83	n/r
Custom Energy Sys²⁸...15s Jd15 1997	NR	R	2.17	1997	140.00	7.143	25.38	60 48	50½	6.81	Flat	10%	3%	.4%	d Dc	d3.00	d2.81	n/r
Dana Corp 5¾s Jd15 2006	BBB	R	150	1993	19.83	50.43	25.38	86¾ 71½	s86¾	6.81	7.17	67%	43%	.34¾	12 Dc	3.40	2.95 2.95	0.82
Data-Design Labs.......12⅝s mN15 2000	A	R	19.9	2000	105.82	9.45	25.40	115¾ 101¾	108¾	11.2	11.0	75%	10%	.7%	13 Je	0.98	0.89 2.95	0.82

Uniform Footnote Explanations.—See Page XVI. Other: ¹Incl disc. ²Yr Dec'84 & prior. ³Into CIA. ⁴Was DETROITBANK. ⁵Due Nov 30. ⁶Subsid & data of Int'l Minerals & Chem.
⁷Sub&data of Pacific Telesis Gr. ⁸Int due 7-1-84,pd 7-31-84. ⁹Subsid & data of Texas Air. ¹⁰Default 1,1-83 Int. ¹¹Filed bankruptcy Chapt 11. ¹²Into 18.35 com&6.26 S3 Pfd of Texas Air.
¹¹12 Mo Feb'85,prior Fiscal. ¹²Was Cont'l Telephone. ¹³Was Cont'l Telecom. ¹⁴Offered outside U.S.;Pfd pay in U.S.S. ¹⁷Into Continental Telecom.
¹⁸Cv into&data of Owens Corning Fiberglas. ¹⁹Cv into Owens Corning Fiberglas. ²⁰Was Covington Bros. ²¹Option to rec int mthly. ²¹In certain events Co. option to lower price.
²¹Was MassMutual M&R inv. ²⁸Default 5-1-85 int. ²³Plan each for 11 3/4%SfSubCvDeb'90,com&wrrts. ²⁴Incl 1-84,pd 5-24-85. ²⁷James River plans acq;min $41 in stk. ²⁸Int due 12-15-84,pd 2-20-85.

Mortgage Pass-through Securities: Ginnie Maes, Fannie Maes, and Freddie Macs

14

So far, we've dealt with debt obligations that, barring a "call" or default, provide predictable cash flows. For a zero-coupon security (a debt obligation that does not make periodic interest payments), the cash flow is simply the value to be received at the maturity date. For a coupon-bearing debt obligation, the cash flow is the periodic coupon interest payments and the value at the maturity date. Adding to the uncertainty about the actual return that may be realized from investing in a coupon-bearing security is the uncertainty about the interest rate at which the interim coupon payments may be reinvested.

In this chapter, we'll introduce you to securities that represent an undivided interest in a pool of real estate mortgages. These securities (known as mortgage pass-through securities) have uncertain cash flows. As we shall see, there are pass-through securities that do not expose you to any risk of default. Moreover, they offer the opportunity for greater return than Treasury securities do, yet there is uncertainty about the return.

Most individual investors will not invest in pass-through securities directly because that requires an investment of about $25,000, although it may soon be possible to purchase certain pass-throughs in $1,000 denominations. Instead, most individuals will purchase mortgage pass-through securities via bond funds, the subject of Chapter 15. In this chapter, we'll explain the investment characteristics of pass-through securities.

MORTGAGES

The collateral behind a pass-through security is a pool of mortgages. Therefore, the first things we must define are mortgages and their cash flow characteristics.

Very few people purchase a home for cash. Instead, they borrow a major portion of the cost of the house from a bank, thrift, or other lender. A mortgage is a pledge of the house to secure the payment of the loan. The mortgage gives the lender (mortgagee) the right to foreclose on the loan and seize the property, all to ensure that the loan is paid off if the homeowner (mortgagor) fails to make the contracted payments.

Traditional Mortgages

The mortgage loan specifies the interest rate, the frequency of payment, and the number of years. A traditional mortgage has the following characteristics: (1) the term of the loan is fixed; (2) the interest rate is fixed for the term of the loan; and (3) the amount of the monthly mortgage payment is fixed for the term of the loan. Each monthly mortgage payment consists of (1) 1/12th of the fixed interest rate times the amount of the outstanding mortgage balance at the beginning of the previous month and (2) a repayment of a portion of the outstanding mortgage balance.

The difference between the monthly mortgage payment and the portion of the payment that is interest equals the portion that goes to reduce the outstanding mortgage balance. The monthly mortgage payment is designed so that after the last scheduled monthly payment is made, the amount of the outstanding mortgage balance is zero. That is, the loan is fully paid off.

To illustrate how the mortgage payments work for a traditional mortgage, consider a 30-year (360 month), $100,000 mortgage with a 10% interest rate. The monthly mortgage payment would be $877.57. Exhibit 14-1 shows how each monthly mortgage payment is split between interest and repayment of principal. In month 0, the mortgage balance is $100,000, the amount of the original loan. The mortgage payment for month 1 will include interest on the $100,000 borrowed for 1 month. Since the interest rate is 10%, the monthly interest rate is .0083333 (.10 divided by 12). Interest for month 1 is therefore $833.33 ($100,000 times .0083333). The difference between the monthly mortgage payment of $877.57 and the interest of $833.33 is the portion of the monthly mortgage payment that represents repayment of principal. Therefore, $44.24 of the mortgage payment for month 1 goes to reduce the mortgage balance.

The mortgage balance at the beginning of month 1 is then $99,955.76 ($100,000 minus $44.24). The interest for the second monthly mortgage payment is $832.96, the monthly interest rate (.008333) times the mortgage balance at the beginning of month 1 ($99,955.76). The difference between the $877.57 monthly mortgage payment and the $832.96 is $44.61, representing the amount of the mortgage balance paid off with that monthly mortgage payment. Notice that the last monthly mortgage payment is sufficient to pay off the remaining mortgage balance.

As Exhibit 14-1 clearly shows, *the portion of the monthly mortgage payment applied to interest declines each month and more goes to reducing the mortgage balance.* The reason is that as the mortgage balance is reduced with each monthly mortgage payment, the interest on the mortgage balance declines. Since the monthly mortgage payment is fixed, more of the payment is going to reduce the principal as time goes by.

The schedule shown in Exhibit 14-1 assumes that the homeowner will not prepay any portion of the mortgage balance prior to the scheduled due date. But homeowners in fact do prepay the entire mortgage balance prior to the maturity date. Prepayments occur for one of several reasons. First, homeowners pay off the entire mortgage balance when they sell their home. Second, if interest rates have dropped substantially since the time they obtained their mortgage, homeowners may find it beneficial to refinance (even after paying all closing costs) at a lower interest rate. Third, in the case of homeowners who can't meet their obligations, the property is repossessed and sold; the proceeds from the sale are used to pay off the mortgage. Finally, there are cases in which property is destroyed by a fire, and the insurance company pays off the mortgage; or a homeowner who has mortgage life insurance dies, and the proceeds from the policy are used to pay off the mortgage.

EXHIBIT 14-1 Amortization Schedule for a Traditional Mortgage

Mortgage loan: $100,000
Interest rate: .10
Term of loan: 30 years (360 months)

(1)	(2)	(3)	(4)	(5)	(6)
	Beginning	Monthly	Interest		Ending
	Mortgage	Mortgage	for	Principal	Mortgage
Month	Balance	Payment	Month	Repayment	Balance
1	$100,000.00	$877.57	$833.33	$44.24	$99,955.76
2	99,955.76	877.57	832.96	44.61	99,911.16
3	99,911.16	877.57	832.59	44.98	99,866.18
4	99,866.18	877.57	832.22	45.35	99,820.83
5	99,820.83	877.57	831.84	45.73	99,775.10
6	99,775.10	877.57	831.46	46.11	99,728.99
7	99,728.99	877.57	831.07	46.50	99,682.49
8	99,682.49	877.57	830.69	46.88	99,635.61
9	99,635.61	877.57	830.30	47.27	99,588.34
10	99,588.34	877.57	829.90	47.67	99,540.67
11	99,540.67	877.57	829.51	48.06	99,492.61
12	99,492.61	877.57	829.11	48.46	99,444.14
13	99,444.14	877.57	828.70	48.87	99,395.27
14	99,395.27	877.57	828.29	49.28	99,346.00
15	99,346.00	877.57	827.88	49.69	99,296.31
16	99,296.31	877.57	827.47	50.10	99,246.21
17	99,246.21	877.57	827.05	50.52	99,195.69
18	99,195.69	877.57	826.63	50.94	99,144.75
19	99,144.75	877.57	826.21	51.36	99,093.39
20	99,093.39	877.57	825.78	51.79	99,041.60
21	99,041.60	877.57	825.35	52.22	98,989.37
22	98,989.37	877.57	824.91	52.66	98,936.71
23	98,936.71	877.57	824.47	53.10	98,883.62
24	98,883.62	877.57	824.03	53.54	98,830.08
25	98,830.08	877.57	823.58	53.99	98,776.09
26	98,776.09	877.57	823.13	54.44	98,721.65
27	98,721.65	877.57	822.68	54.89	98,666.77
28	98,666.77	877.57	822.22	55.35	98,611.42
29	98,611.42	877.57	821.76	55.81	98,555.61
30	98,555.61	877.57	821.30	56.27	98,499.34
31	98,499.34	877.57	820.83	56.74	98,442.59
32	98,442.59	877.57	820.35	57.22	98,385.38
33	98,385.38	877.57	819.88	57.69	98,327.69
34	98,327.69	877.57	819.40	58.17	98,269.52
35	98,269.52	877.57	818.91	58.66	98,210.86
36	98,210.86	877.57	818.42	59.15	98,151.71

EXHIBIT 14-1 *(concluded)*

112	91,972.53	877.57	766.44	111.13	91,861.40
113	91,861.40	877.57	765.51	112.06	91,749.34
114	91,749.34	877.57	764.58	112.99	91,636.34
115	91,636.34	877.57	763.64	113.93	91,522.41
116	91,522.41	877.57	762.69	114.88	91,407.53
117	91,407.53	877.57	761.73	115.84	91,291.69
118	91,291.69	877.57	760.76	116.81	91,174.88
119	91,174.88	877.57	759.79	117.78	91,057.10
120	91,057.10	877.57	758.81	118.76	90,938.34
121	90,938.34	877.57	757.82	119.75	90,818.59
122	90,818.59	877.57	756.82	120.75	90,697.84
123	90,697.84	877.57	755.82	121.75	90,576.09
124	90,576.09	877.57	754.80	122.77	90,453.32
125	90,453.32	877.57	753.78	123.79	90,329.53
. . . .
212	74,728.65	877.57	622.74	254.83	74,473.82
213	74,473.82	877.57	620.62	256.95	74,216.87
214	74,216.87	877.57	618.47	259.10	73,957.77
215	73,957.77	877.57	616.31	261.26	73,696.52
216	73,696.52	877.57	614.14	263.43	73,433.09
217	73,433.09	877.57	611.94	265.63	73,167.46
218	73,167.46	877.57	609.73	267.84	72,899.62
219	72,899.62	877.57	607.50	270.07	72,629.54
220	72,629.54	877.57	605.25	272.32	72,357.22
221	72,357.22	877.57	602.98	274.59	72,082.63
222	72,082.63	877.57	600.69	276.88	71,805.74
. . . .
352	7,582.14	877.57	63.18	814.39	6,767.76
353	6,767.76	877.57	56.40	821.17	5,946.59
354	5,946.59	877.57	49.55	828.02	5,118.57
355	5,118.57	877.57	42.65	834.92	4,283.66
356	4,283.66	877.57	35.70	841.87	3,441.78
357	3,441.78	877.57	28.68	848.89	2,592.90
358	2,592.90	877.57	21.61	855.96	1,736.93
359	1,736.93	877.57	14.47	863.10	873.84
360	873.84	877.57	7.28	870.29	3.55*

*Does not equal $0 due to rounding.

Nontraditional Mortgages

There are nontraditional mortgages available to homeowners. Unlike traditional mortgages, most nontraditional mortgages do not have the same monthly mortgage payment for the entire term of the mortgage. We will confine our discussion to two types of nontraditional mortgages that have been the underlying mortgages for pass-through securities—graduated payment mortgages and adjustable rate mortgages.

Graduated Payment Mortgages (GPM).   With a GPM, the interest rate and the term of the mortgage are fixed, as with traditional mortgages. However, unlike a traditional mortgage, the monthly payment is smaller in the initial years but larger in the remaining years of the mortgage term. There are several GPM plans available. For example, one GPM plan for a 30-year, $100,000 loan at 10% would require initial monthly mortgage payments of $734.58, graduating up to a monthly mortgage payment of $987.20. Recall that for the traditional mortgage, the monthly mortgage payment is $877.57.

The Federal Housing Administration (FHA) first introduced GPMs in late-1976. GPMs were created to give individuals with rising incomes the opportunity to purchase a home at a monthly mortgage payment that they can afford. As their incomes rise, they can then afford to pay the higher mortgage payments. In 1979, GPMs became eligible for pooling in certain types of pass-through securities that will be discussed later in this chapter.

Adjustable Rate Mortgages (ARM).   The major difference between a traditional mortgage and an ARM is that the interest rate on the latter is adjusted periodically; for the former, it is fixed over the entire mortgage term. The interest rate on an ARM may adjust every month, 6 months, year, 2 years, 3 years, or 5 years. A survey conducted by the Federal Home Loan Mortgage Corporation and the Federal Home Loan Bank of San Francisco found that the most popular term of adjustment is 1 year. The index rate on which the ARM interest rate is based generally coincides with the term of adjustment. For example, the most common index used to adjust a 1-year ARM is the 1-year constant maturity Treasury security. Also, for many ARMs there is a cap on the interest rate adjustment over the life of the mortgage and/or for each adjustment period.

PASS-THROUGH SECURITIES

A pass-through security is created when one or more holders of mortgages form a collection (pool) of mortgages and sell shares or participations in the pool. A pool may consist of several thousand mortgages or only one mortgage. The cash flow of the pass-through depends on the cash flow of the underlying mortgages; as we indicated earlier, that underlying cash flow consists of monthly mortgage payments representing interest, the scheduled repayment of principal, and any prepayments.

The amount and the timing of the two cash flows, however, are not identical. The monthly cash flow for a pass-through security is less than the monthly cash flow of the underlying mortgages by an amount equal to servicing and other fees. The servicing fee, which is a fixed percentage of the outstanding mortgage balance, represents a fee retained by the originator of a mortgage (or someone the originator sold the servicing to) in the pool. Servicing the mortgage includes sending payment notices to mortgagors, reminding mortgagors when payments are overdue, keeping records of mortgage balances, sending out tax information at year-end to mortgagors, administering an escrow account for taxes and insurance, and, if necessary, initiating foreclosure proceedings. There is another fee charged by the issuer of the pass-through security—it guarantees the issue (discussed later).[1] Typically, the coupon rate on a pass-through security is .5% less than the coupon rate on the pool.

The timing of the cash flow is also different. The monthly mortgage payment is due from each mortgagor on the first day of each month. There is a delay in passing through the corresponding monthly cash flow to the security holders. The number of days that the payment is delayed varies by the type of pass-through security.

ISSUERS OF PASS-THROUGH SECURITIES

There are three major issuers of pass-through securities: Government National Mortgage Association, Federal Home Loan Mortgage Corporation, and Federal National Mortgage Association. Exhibit 14–2 summarizes the different securities issued by them. For each security,

---

[1]Actually, the servicer pays the fee to the issuer.

EXHIBIT 14-2   Features of Selected Mortgage Pass-through Securities

| | GNMA | | | | Mobile Homes | FHA Projects | FHLMC PCs | FNMA MBS |
	GNMA I	GNMA II	GNMA Midgets	GNMA GPM				
Type of mortgages	Level payment FHA/VA	Level payment FHA/VA	Level payment FHA/VA	Graduated payment loans (mostly 7.5%)	Level payment FHA/VA	FHA project FHA/VA	95% single family	Level payment single family
	New originations	New originations	New originations	New originations	New originations	New originations	New or seasoned conventional loans	New or seasoned conventional loans
Term	90% must be 20 years +	90% must be 20 years +	15 years	30-year original term	4 types ranging from 12–20 years	Most are 40 years	97½% level payment mostly 30 years (also, a relatively new 15-year term)	30-year original term 20-year original term (also, a relatively new 15-year term)
Minimum pool size	$1 million 12 loans	$7 million	$1 million	$1 million	$.5 million	$.5 million 1 loan	$100 million (except Guarantors Program—$5 million)	$1 million
Geographic features	Highly regional	Regional or national	Highly regional	Highly regional	Highly regional	Highly regional	National	National
Mortgage coupons allowed	.5% over P-T rate	.5%–1.5% over P-T rate	.5% over P-T rate	.5% over P-T rate	3.25% over P-T rate (approx.)	.25% over P-T rate	.5%–2.5% over P-T rate	.5%–2.5% over P-T rate
Range of coupons	5.25%–17.000%	8.00%–14.50%	7.25%–13.50%	9.00%–17.50%	6.00%–16.75%	8.00%–14.25%	4.25% 16.50%	4.00% 17.00%
Stated delay (days)	45	50	45	45	45	45	75	54
Actual penalty (days)	15	20	15	25	15	15	45	24

SOURCE: Adapted from Kenneth H. Sullivan, Bruce M. Collins, and David A. Smilov, "Mortgage Pass-Through Securities," in *The Handbook of Mortgage-Backed Securities*, ed. Frank J. Fabozzi (Chicago, Ill.: Probus Publishing, 1985), Exhibit 1.

Exhibit 14–2 indicates the type of mortgages, the term of the mortgages, the minimum pool size, the geographic characteristics of the mortgages in the pool, the mortgage coupon allowed as a servicing fee, the range of coupons available, and the actual penalty in days due to the payment delay.

For all three types of pass-through securities, the minimum purchase price at original issue is $25,000, with subsequent increments of $5,000 for the securities issued by the Government National Mortgage Association and the Federal National Mortgage Association, and subsequent increments of $25,000 for the securities issued by the Federal Home Loan Mortgage Corporation. In the secondary market, there are discounted securities that may be purchased for less than $25,000. At the time of this writing, Federal Home Loan Mortgage Corporation securities with $1,000 denominations may be offered.

Unlike coupon Treasury, agency, corporate, and municipal bonds, which pay interest semiannually, all pass-through securities make cash flow payments monthly.

Government National Mortgage Association (GNMA)

The Government National Mortgage Association, popularly known as Ginnie Mae, guarantees the mortgage pass-through securities issued by other entities (such as banks and thrifts). Ginnie Mae pass-throughs represent the largest class of mortgage pass-through securities. Ginnie Mae is a wholly-owned U.S. government corporation that exists within the Department of Housing and Urban Development. Only FHA-insured mortgages and VA-guaranteed mortgages are contained in the pool. Six Ginnie Mae programs in which the underlying mortgages are fixed-rate mortgages are summarized in Exhibit 14–2— GNMA Is, GNMA IIs, GNMA Midgets, GNMA GPMs, GNMA Mobile Homes, and GNMA FHA Projects.

The pass-through securities issued by Ginnie Mae are guaranteed by the full faith and credit of the United States government with respect to timely payment of both interest and principal. By timely payment it is meant that the interest and principal will be paid by Ginnie Mae when due[2]. Despite the guarantee, the interest on Ginnie Mae securities is not exempt from state and local taxes, as is the interest on Treasury securities.

---

[2]A pass-through security that is guaranteed with respect to timely payment of both interest and principal is said to be a *fully modified pass-through security*.

Federal Home Loan Mortgage Corporation (FHLMC)

The second largest issuer of pass-through securities is the Federal Home Loan Mortgage Corporation. This issuer, popularly known as Freddie Mac, is a corporate instrumentality of the United States government. Its stock is owned by the 12 Federal Reserve Banks.

The securities issued by Freddie Mac are called participation certificates. Most of the pools of mortgages consist of conventional mortgages, although participation certificates with underlying pools consisting of FHA-insured or VA-guaranteed mortgages have been issued. Freddie Mac guarantees the timely payment of interest. Until recently, the scheduled principal is passed through only as it is collected, Freddie Mac guaranteeing that the scheduled principal will be paid no later than 1 year after it is due.[3] Freddie Mac has a new program where timely principal pass-through also is guaranteed.

A guarantee by Freddie Mac is *not* the guarantee of either the U.S. government or the Federal Reserve Banks. Yet, most market participants view the credit worthiness of the Freddie Mac participation certificates as similar, but not identical, to that of Ginnie Mae pass-throughs that are fully guaranteed by the U.S. government. That is one reason why Freddie Mac pass-throughs offer a higher yield than Ginnie Mae securities with the same coupon and remaining term.[4]

Federal National Mortgage Association (FNMA)

The Federal National Mortgage Association (Fannie Mae) is another issuer of pass-through securities. Fannie Mae is a U.S. government-sponsored corporation whose stock is entirely owned by private stockholders. Fannie Mae pass-through securities are similar in many respects to the Freddie Mac participation certificates. However, Fannie Mae guarantees the timely payment of both interest and principal. Just as in the case of Freddie Mac participation certificates, the Fannie Mae guarantee is not the obligation of the U.S. government. Most market participants, however, believe that the U.S. government will not permit Fannie Mae to default.

---

[3] A pass-through security with this type of guarantee is referred to as a modified pass-through security.

[4] The higher yield for Freddie Mac pass-throughs is also due to the prepayment characteristics of the Freddie Mac loans. Conventional loans tend to prepay more quickly than FHA/VA loans used for Ginnie Mae pass-throughs.

MEASURING YIELDS ON PASS-THROUGH SECURITIES

To compute a yield on an investment that you are considering, you must know the timing and amount of the cash flow from the investment. As we mentioned earlier, except in the case of default or call, the cash flow of the other debt obligations discussed in this book are known if the obligation is held to maturity. The investor must also consider the reinvestment rate that will be available when interim cash flow payments are paid. It is the uncertainty of the reinvestment rate that prevents an investor from determining an exact yield. As we explained in Chapter 7, this is the reason for the popularity of zero-coupon securities—there is no reinvestment risk.

In the absence of prepayments, the only uncertainty about the yield on a pass-through comes from reinvestment risk. However, prepayments do occur. Thus, an investor in pass-through securities does not know what the cash flow will be and cannot determine a precise yield.

Quoted Yield

As the mortgage-backed security market developed, a convention evolved to quote yields based on a "12-year, prepaid life assumption." With this convention, it was assumed that all the mortgages in a pool would prepay exactly after 12 years. That is, the cash flow from the underlying pool was assumed to be the interest payment and scheduled principal payments for the first 12 years and at the end of year 12, all the mortgages in the pool paid off. The quoted yield based on a 12-year, prepaid life assumption was used for new mortgage pools and seasoned pools.[5] Therefore, if a pass-through with an original stated maturity of 30 years was issued 10 years ago, the quoted yield would assume that there would be no prepayments for the mortgages in the pool for 12 years, and then all the mortgages would be prepaid.

Although yields based on the 12-year, prepaid life assumption standardized the way in which yields on pass-through securities are quoted, the yield measure is not useful for making investment decisions.

---

[5] Seasoning refers to the time since origination or age of a mortgage pool.

Cash Flow Yield

Most money managers make some assumption about prepayment rates for an individual pool in order to estimate the cash flow that can be expected from the pass-through. Based on the estimated cash flow, a yield can be computed. A yield computed in this manner is called a *cash flow yield*.

FHA Experience. At one time, the most commonly used benchmark for estimating prepayment rates was the prepayment experience for 30-year mortgages derived from a Federal Housing Administration (FHA) probability table for mortgage survivals. Using FHA experience, cash flows were forecasted for a pool assuming that the prepayment rate was the same as the FHA experience (100% FHA) or some multiple of FHA experience (faster than FHA experience or slower than FHA experience). For example, using one half the FHA experience is referred to as 50% FHA; using double the FHA experience is referred to as 200% FHA.

Despite their popularity, prepayment rate forecasts based on FHA experience are not necessarily indicative of the prepayment rate for a particular pool. The reason is that FHA experience represents an average of prepayments over various interest rate periods. Since prepayment rates are tied to interest rate cycles, what does an average prepayment rate over various cycles mean? To some people, not much. Consequently, since the cash flow forecast based on prepayment rates using FHA experience may be misleading, the resulting cash flow yield may not be meaningful for making investment decisions.

Conditional Prepayment Rate (CPR). Another approach to estimating prepayments and cash flow yield is to simply assume that some fraction of the remaining principal in the pool is prepaid each month. The prepayment rate assumed for a pool is based on the characteristics of the pool and the economic environment. The advantage of this approach is its simplicity; what's more, changes in economic conditions that impact prepayment rates can be analyzed quickly.

There are cash flow yield tables for pass-through securities that assume a range of CPRs—they are published jointly by Salomon Brothers and Financial Publishing Company. A sample page from the three-volume set is shown as Exhibit 14-3. The sample page is for

EXHIBIT 14-3 Sample Page from Yield Book

12½% POOL RATE — YIELD TABLES FOR SINGLE-FAMILY GNMA SECURITIES — YEARS REMAINING **30**

PRICE	QUOTED YIELD (30/12)	CONSTANT PREPAYMENT RATE 0%	2%	4%	6%	8%	10%	PRICE	QUOTED YIELD (30/12)	CONSTANT PREPAYMENT RATE 0%	2%	4%	6%	8%	10%
90	14.18	13.92	14.11	14.31	14.52	14.74	14.96	98	12.75	12.71	12.73	12.76	12.79	12.82	12.85
90⅛	14.16	13.90	14.09	14.29	14.49	14.70	14.92	98¼	12.71	12.67	12.69	12.72	12.74	12.77	12.79
90¼	14.13	13.88	14.07	14.26	14.46	14.67	14.88	98½	12.66	12.64	12.65	12.67	12.69	12.71	12.73
90⅜	14.11	13.86	14.04	14.24	14.43	14.64	14.85	98¾	12.62	12.60	12.62	12.63	12.64	12.66	12.67
90½	14.08	13.84	14.02	14.21	14.41	14.61	14.81	99	12.58	12.57	12.58	12.59	12.59	12.60	12.61
90⅝	14.06	13.82	14.00	14.18	14.38	14.57	14.78	99¼	12.54	12.53	12.54	12.54	12.55	12.55	12.56
90¾	14.04	13.80	13.98	14.16	14.35	14.54	14.74	99½	12.50	12.50	12.50	12.50	12.50	12.50	12.50
90⅞	14.01	13.78	13.95	14.13	14.32	14.51	14.71	99¾	12.46	12.46	12.46	12.45	12.45	12.44	12.44
DURATION	5.9	6.9	6.1	5.4	4.8	4.4	4.0	DURATION	6.2	7.4	6.6	5.8	5.3	4.8	4.3
91	13.99	13.76	13.93	14.11	14.29	14.48	14.67	100	12.42	12.43	12.42	12.41	12.40	12.39	12.38
91⅛	13.97	13.74	13.91	14.08	14.26	14.45	14.64	100¼	12.38	12.40	12.38	12.37	12.35	12.34	12.32
91¼	13.94	13.72	13.88	14.06	14.23	14.42	14.60	100½	12.33	12.36	12.34	12.33	12.31	12.29	12.26
91⅜	13.92	13.70	13.86	14.03	14.20	14.38	14.57	100¾	12.29	12.33	12.31	12.28	12.26	12.23	12.21
91½	13.90	13.68	13.84	14.00	14.18	14.35	14.53	101	12.25	12.30	12.27	12.24	12.21	12.18	12.15
91⅝	13.87	13.66	13.82	13.98	14.15	14.32	14.50	101¼	12.21	12.26	12.23	12.20	12.16	12.13	12.09
91¾	13.85	13.64	13.79	13.95	14.12	14.29	14.47	101½	12.17	12.23	12.19	12.16	12.12	12.08	12.04
91⅞	13.83	13.62	13.77	13.93	14.09	14.26	14.43	101¾	12.13	12.20	12.16	12.11	12.07	12.03	11.98
DURATION	5.9	7.0	6.1	5.4	4.9	4.4	4.0	DURATION	6.2	7.5	6.7	5.9	5.3	4.8	4.4
92	13.80	13.60	13.75	13.90	14.06	14.23	14.40	102	12.09	12.16	12.12	12.07	12.02	11.97	11.92
92⅛	13.78	13.58	13.73	13.88	14.03	14.20	14.36	102¼	12.05	12.13	12.08	12.03	11.98	11.92	11.87
92¼	13.76	13.56	13.70	13.85	14.01	14.17	14.33	102½	12.02	12.10	12.05	11.99	11.93	11.87	11.81
92⅜	13.74	13.54	13.68	13.83	13.98	14.13	14.29	102¾	11.98	12.07	12.01	11.95	11.89	11.82	11.76
92½	13.71	13.52	13.66	13.80	13.95	14.10	14.26	103	11.94	12.03	11.97	11.91	11.84	11.77	11.70
92⅝	13.69	13.50	13.64	13.78	13.92	14.07	14.23	103¼	11.90	12.00	11.94	11.87	11.80	11.72	11.65
92¾	13.67	13.48	13.61	13.75	13.90	14.04	14.19	103½	11.86	11.97	11.90	11.83	11.75	11.67	11.59
92⅞	13.64	13.46	13.59	13.73	13.87	14.01	14.16	103¾	11.82	11.94	11.86	11.79	11.71	11.62	11.54
DURATION	6.0	7.0	6.2	5.5	4.9	4.5	4.1	DURATION	6.3	7.7	6.8	6.0	5.4	4.9	4.5
93	13.62	13.44	13.57	13.70	13.84	13.98	14.13	104	11.78	11.91	11.83	11.75	11.66	11.57	11.48
93⅛	13.60	13.42	13.55	13.68	13.81	13.95	14.09	104¼	11.74	11.87	11.79	11.71	11.62	11.53	11.43
93¼	13.58	13.41	13.53	13.65	13.79	13.92	14.06	104½	11.71	11.84	11.76	11.67	11.57	11.48	11.38
93⅜	13.55	13.39	13.51	13.63	13.76	13.89	14.03	104¾	11.67	11.81	11.72	11.63	11.53	11.43	11.32
93½	13.53	13.37	13.48	13.60	13.73	13.86	13.99	105	11.63	11.78	11.69	11.59	11.49	11.38	11.27
93⅝	13.51	13.35	13.46	13.58	13.70	13.83	13.96	105¼	11.59	11.75	11.65	11.55	11.44	11.33	11.22
93¾	13.49	13.33	13.44	13.56	13.68	13.80	13.93	105½	11.55	11.72	11.62	11.51	11.40	11.28	11.17
93⅞	13.46	13.31	13.42	13.53	13.65	13.77	13.89	105¾	11.52	11.69	11.58	11.47	11.35	11.24	11.11
DURATION	6.0	7.1	6.2	5.5	5.0	4.5	4.1	DURATION	6.3	7.8	6.9	6.1	5.5	5.0	4.6
94	13.44	13.29	13.40	13.51	13.62	13.74	13.86	106	11.48	11.66	11.55	11.43	11.31	11.19	11.06
94⅛	13.42	13.27	13.38	13.48	13.60	13.71	13.83	106¼	11.44	11.63	11.51	11.39	11.27	11.14	11.01
94¼	13.40	13.25	13.35	13.46	13.57	13.68	13.80	106½	11.40	11.60	11.48	11.35	11.23	11.09	10.96
94⅜	13.37	13.23	13.33	13.44	13.54	13.65	13.76	106¾	11.37	11.57	11.44	11.32	11.18	11.05	10.91
94½	13.35	13.22	13.31	13.41	13.51	13.62	13.73	107	11.33	11.54	11.41	11.28	11.14	11.00	10.85
94⅝	13.33	13.20	13.29	13.39	13.49	13.59	13.70	107¼	11.29	11.51	11.38	11.24	11.10	10.95	10.80
94¾	13.31	13.18	13.27	13.36	13.46	13.56	13.67	107½	11.26	11.48	11.34	11.20	11.06	10.91	10.75
94⅞	13.29	13.16	13.25	13.34	13.43	13.53	13.63	107¾	11.22	11.45	11.31	11.16	11.02	10.86	10.70
DURATION	6.0	7.1	6.3	5.6	5.0	4.5	4.1	DURATION	6.4	7.9	7.0	6.2	5.6	5.1	4.6
95	13.26	13.14	13.23	13.32	13.41	13.50	13.60	108	11.18	11.42	11.27	11.13	10.97	10.82	10.65
95⅛	13.24	13.12	13.21	13.29	13.38	13.47	13.57	108¼	11.15	11.39	11.24	11.09	10.93	10.77	10.60
95¼	13.22	13.10	13.18	13.27	13.36	13.45	13.54	108½	11.11	11.36	11.21	11.05	10.89	10.72	10.55
95⅜	13.20	13.08	13.16	13.24	13.33	13.42	13.51	108¾	11.07	11.33	11.17	11.02	10.85	10.68	10.50
95½	13.18	13.07	13.14	13.22	13.30	13.39	13.47	109	11.04	11.30	11.14	10.98	10.81	10.63	10.45
95⅝	13.15	13.05	13.12	13.20	13.28	13.36	13.44	109¼	11.00	11.27	11.11	10.94	10.77	10.59	10.40
95¾	13.13	13.03	13.10	13.17	13.25	13.33	13.41	109½	10.97	11.24	11.08	10.91	10.73	10.54	10.36
95⅞	13.11	13.01	13.08	13.15	13.22	13.30	13.38	109¾	10.93	11.21	11.04	10.87	10.69	10.50	10.31
DURATION	6.1	7.2	6.3	5.7	5.1	4.6	4.2	DURATION	6.5	8.0	7.1	6.3	5.7	5.2	4.7
96	13.09	12.99	13.06	13.13	13.20	13.27	13.35	110	10.89	11.18	11.01	10.83	10.65	10.46	10.26
96⅛	13.07	12.97	13.04	13.10	13.17	13.24	13.32	110¼	10.86	11.15	10.98	10.80	10.61	10.41	10.21
96¼	13.05	12.96	13.02	13.08	13.15	13.22	13.29	110½	10.82	11.13	10.95	10.76	10.57	10.37	10.16
96⅜	13.02	12.94	13.00	13.06	13.12	13.19	13.25	110¾	10.79	11.10	10.92	10.73	10.53	10.32	10.11
96½	13.00	12.92	12.98	13.04	13.10	13.16	13.22	111	10.75	11.07	10.88	10.69	10.49	10.28	10.07
96⅝	12.98	12.90	12.96	13.01	13.07	13.13	13.19	111¼	10.72	11.04	10.85	10.65	10.45	10.24	10.02
96¾	12.96	12.88	12.94	12.99	13.04	13.10	13.16	111½	10.68	11.01	10.82	10.62	10.41	10.19	9.97
96⅞	12.94	12.87	12.92	12.97	13.02	13.07	13.13	111¾	10.65	10.98	10.79	10.58	10.37	10.15	9.92
DURATION	6.1	7.3	6.4	5.7	5.1	4.6	4.2	DURATION	6.5	8.1	7.2	6.4	5.8	5.3	4.8
97	12.92	12.85	12.89	12.94	12.99	13.05	13.10	112	10.61	10.96	10.76	10.55	10.33	10.11	9.88
97¼	12.87	12.81	12.85	12.90	12.94	12.99	13.04	112¼	10.58	10.93	10.73	10.51	10.29	10.07	9.83
97½	12.83	12.78	12.81	12.85	12.89	12.93	12.98	112½	10.55	10.90	10.69	10.48	10.25	10.02	9.78
97¾	12.79	12.74	12.77	12.81	12.84	12.88	12.92	113	10.48	10.85	10.63	10.41	10.18	9.94	9.69
WEIGHTED-AVG. LIFE YEARS		23.0	18.1	14.6	12.0	10.0	8.4	WEIGHTED-AVG. LIFE YEARS		23.0	18.1	14.6	12.0	10.0	8.4

Reprinted by permission of Salomon Brothers, Inc

single-family GNMA securities with a 12½% pool rate and 30 years remaining to maturity. To use this table, first look up the price or the quoted yield. (The "30/12" under quoted yield means that it is based on a 30-year life and a 12-year, prepaid life assumption.) Suppose, for example, the price is 94. Looking down the column for 94 and then across, we see that the quoted yield would be 13.44%. The next six columns show the cash flow yield for annual CPRs of 0%, 2%, 4%, 6%, 8%, and 10%. For example, if a CPR of 8% is assumed, the cash flow yield is 13.74%.

Bond Equivalent Yield

To compare the yield estimated for a pass-through security to that of a Treasury or corporate bond, an adjustment must be made. The reason is that a Treasury bond and a corporate bond pay interest semiannually while a pass-through has a monthly cash flow. This gives the investor of a pass-through the opportunity to generate greater annual interest than a bond investor who receives coupon payments semiannually by reinvesting the cash flow monthly. Therefore, the yield on a pass-through security must be adjusted upward to make it comparable to a bond's yield to maturity. This is done by computing the *bond equivalent yield* for a pass-through security by assuming that the monthly cash flows from the pass-through are reinvested at the cash flow yield until the end of each semiannual period.

RETURN, LIQUIDITY, AND RISK

By now it should be clear that it is not possible to determine an exact yield for a pass-through security; the yield depends on the actual prepayment experience of the mortgages in the pool. Nevertheless, it is often stated that pass-throughs offer a higher yield than Treasury securities. Typically, the comparison is between Ginnie Mae pass-through securities and Treasuries since both are free of default risk.

Exhibit 14–4 shows the historical yield levels and spreads between long Treasuries and current-coupon Ginnie Maes over bond market cycles. The same information is provided in Exhibit 14–5 between 10-year Treasuries and current-coupon Ginnie Maes. The yields shown for the Ginnie Maes are based on the quoted yield expressed on a bond equivalent basis. While the spread has varied, Exhibits 14–4 and 14–5 clearly indicate that Ginnie Maes offer a higher yield than Trea-

EXHIBIT 14–4 Historical Returns and Spreads over Market Cycles: Long Treasuries versus Mortgage Securities

Period Ending First of Month	Market Cycle	Months in Cycle	Total Return			Yield Spread Relationship			
			Long Treasuries	Mortgage Index	Advantage of Mortgage Index	Long Treasuries Yield	Current Coupon GNMAs	Current Coupon GNMAs Yield[a]	Basis-Point Spread off Long Treasuries
September 74						8.70%	9.0%	10.14%	144bp
March 75	rally	6	14.2%	18.8%	4.6%	7.83	8.0	8.34	51
October 75	decline	7	–3.2	–2.6	0.6	8.55	8.5	9.41	86
January 77	rally	15	26.6	25.5	–1.1	7.30	7.5	7.53	23
April 80	decline	39	18.5	–6.5	12.0	12.27	12.5	14.26	199
July 80	rally	3	24.8	22.1	–2.7	9.94	11.0	11.55	161
October 81	decline	15	–22.3	–19.2	3.1	15.20	17.0	18.53	333
December 81	rally	2	18.3	21.6	3.3	13.03	15.0	15.19	216
July 82	decline	7	1.7	2.7	1.0	13.84	15.0	16.38	254
May 83	rally	10	41.9	39.7	–2.2	10.50	11.5	11.85	135
June 84	decline	13	–12.2	–2.1	10.1	13.71	13.5	14.80	109
January 85	rally	7	25.6	21.8	–3.8	11.58	12.0	12.58	100
10.3-Year Period			108.6%	178.9%	70.3%				

[a] Bond equivalent yield to 12-year prepaid life.

source: Michael Waldman and Steven Guterman, "The Historical Performance of Mortgage Securities: 1972–84," in *The Handbook of Mortgage-Backed Securities*, ed. Frank J. Fabozzi (Chicago, Ill.: Probus Publishing, 1985), Table 7.
Reprinted by permission of Salomon Brothers, Inc

EXHIBIT 14-5 Historical Returns and Spreads over Market Cycles: Ten-Year Treasuries versus Mortgage Securities

Period Ending First of Month	Market Cycle	Months in Cycle	Total Return			Yield Spread Relationship			
			Ten-Year Treasuries	Mortgage Index	Advantage of Mortgage Index	Ten-Year Treasuries Yield	Current Coupon GNMAs	Current Coupon GNMAs Yield[a]	Basis-Point Spread off Ten-Year Treasuries
January 77						6.79%	7.5%	7.53%	74bp
April 80	decline	39	-8.9%	-6.5%	2.4%	12.60	12.5	14.26	166
July 80	rally	3	19.0	22.1	3.1	9.98	11.0	11.55	157
October 81	decline	15	-14.8	-19.2	-4.4	15.76	17.0	18.53	277
December 81	rally	2	15.8	21.6	5.8	13.27	15.0	15.19	192
July 82	decline	7	2.2	2.7	0.5	14.32	15.0	16.38	206
May 83	rally	10	37.2	39.7	2.5	10.18	11.5	11.85	167
June 84	decline	13	-7.8	-2.1	5.7	13.78	13.5	14.80	102
January 85	rally	7	21.5	21.8	0.3	11.45	12.0	12.58	113
8.0-Year Period			68.0%	92.1%	24.1%				

[a]Bond equivalent yield to 12-year prepaid life.

SOURCE: Michael Waldman and Steven Guterman, "The Historical Performance of Mortgage Securities: 1972–84," in *The Handbook of Mortgage-Backed Securities*, ed. Frank J. Fabozzi (Chicago, Ill.: Probus Publishing, 1985), Table 10. Reprinted by permission of Salomon Brothers, Inc

suries. This higher yield reflects the greater uncertainty of the cash flow for the pass-through security.

The actual performance (returns) of mortgage pass-through securities, as measured by the Salomon Brothers Mortgage Pass-Through Index, and Treasuries over bond market cycles, is also shown on Exhibits 14–4 and 14–5. Although there were a few years in which the Treasuries outperformed the mortgage pass-through index, for the period overall, pass-throughs outperformed Treasuries.

While historical performance and initial yields suggest that you can increase your return, there is still the risk of uncertainty about the cash flow when you buy an individual pool. For example, suppose you purchased a single-family, 30-year Ginnie Mae with a pool rate of 12½% for 100. If interest rates drop, you would expect the price of your Ginnie Mae would rise, as would the price of a bond if interest rates decline. However, when you buy a Ginnie Mae, you are giving the mortgagors the option to pay off their mortgage at any time. This is analogous to buying a callable bond. The issuer may call the bond when interest rates have declined, preventing the bond's price from rising too far above its call price if interest rates fall low enough and investors feel a call is likely to occur. Moreover, if the bond is called, you are forced to reinvest the proceeds at a lower rate. Similarly, the option you give to the mortgagors is more likely to be exercised if interest rates drop sufficiently and it therefore becomes economical for mortgagors to refinance. As interest rates drop, prepayment rates will increase. This means that you must reinvest the prepaid portion of the cash flow at a lower rate.

If you are smart enough or lucky enough to buy a pass-through security selling at a large discount, say 85, and the mortgages in the pool prepay quickly, you'll enhance your return. You'll be recovering $100 quickly for every $85 you invested. If interest rates have gone up in the meantime, you get to reinvest the prepayments at a higher rate; even if interest rates have gone down, you have the advantage of being able to invest a larger sum, $100 per $85 of initial investment in our example.

Buying a pass-through that sells at a premium is particularly dangerous. A premium exists because the coupon rate is greater than current market rates. Although a pass-through with a high coupon rate may offer a high current yield, there is greater risk that the mortgagors will prepay faster as interest rate decline compared to current-coupon pass-throughs (those selling near par) and low-coupon pass-throughs (those selling below par). You are then faced with reinvesting the proceeds at a lower rate. Moreover, if you invest say

$110 for $100 of par value, you'll be recovering only $100 when mortgagors prepay. Therefore, you may not realize the benefit of the higher coupon for a long enough period of time; instead, over a short time period you'll be repaid less dollars than you invested.

Greater uncertainty about prepayments, and, therefore, cash flow, is present in pass-through securities with a small mortgage pool compared to a large mortgage pool, especially for discount and premium securities. While institutional investors can reduce this uncertainty and produce more stable investment results by buying pass-through securities of many small mortgage pools, an individual investor who purchases pass-throughs of one small pool cannot. Therefore, to reduce the risk of a poor return, individual investors should avoid pass-through securities with small mortgage pools. Alternatively, purchasing shares of mutual funds invested in pass-throughs achieves the same diversification of prepayment risk.

Also keep in mind if you buy a pass-through, the cash flow you receive does not represent just interest; part of it is a recovery of principal. Should you be dependent on current income for consumption, don't make the mistake of spending the entire cash flow believing it is all interest. You'll have to reinvest a portion of the cash flow to keep your invested assets intact.

There is no risk of default for Ginnie Mae pass-throughs. Fannie Maes and Freddie Macs have negligible default risk, which results in higher "offer yields" compared to Ginnie Maes for a given CPR. Although there is an active market for pass-through securities, you are still exposed to price risk when you purchase any pass-through security. As we mentioned throughout this book, the longer the term of a bond, the greater its price risk. However, a 30-year pass-through does not have the same price risk as a 30-year Treasury. Pass-throughs are less volatile because principal is being repaid monthly. A commonly used measure of the life of a pass-through is the weighted average life, which is the weighted average time (in years) over which principal is repaid. The weighted average life depends on the assumption about prepayments. The higher the prepayment rate assumed, the lower the weighted average life. The lower the weighted average life, the less volatility for a pass-through security. The last row in Exhibit 14–3 shows the weighted average life for a 30-year pass-through with a 12½% pool rate. Notice that the weighted average life is always less than the 30-year term of the pass-through and that it decreases for higher CPRs.

Bond Funds

15

A bond fund combines the monies of a number of different investors and reinvests the proceeds in a large number of securities that attempt to meet a certain set of investment objectives. The money market fund that we discussed in Chapter 5 is an example of a bond fund that invests in money market securities in order to provide liquidity. In this chapter we shall discuss bond funds that invest in the securities that we described in earlier chapters (U.S. Treasury and agency notes and bonds, municipal securities, corporate bonds, convertible bonds, and mortgage-backed securities). For many investors, bond funds are an ideal vehicle for investing a portion of their funds earmarked for the bond market.

Bond funds offer shares to investors. There are three kinds of bond funds: open-end funds, closed-end funds, and unit trusts.

OPEN-END BOND FUNDS (MUTUAL FUNDS)

Open-end bond funds, which are commonly known as mutual funds, continuously offer new shares for sale to the public and stand ready to redeem their shares at a price that is computed daily at the close of the market.

The structure of a mutual fund consists of a board of directors (or trustees), an advisor responsible for making the investment decisions, and a distributing and selling organization. Typically, a mutual fund enters into a contract with a management or advisory company that engages in research to meet the fund's investment objectives. Advisory fees are one of the largest costs of administering a mutual fund. Typical advisory fees usually equal .5% to 1.5% of the fund's average assets, but the fee per dollar of asset is determined on a sliding scale that declines as the size of the fund increases. Unfortunately, some advisory organizations charge high—and, in some cases, excessive—fees.

In addition to advisory fees, mutual funds incur other expenses that are included in the cost of services offered to investors. For example, they act as custodians of the assets in their portfolio and provide record keeping services. They ensure that securities are properly transferred and registered. And they pay officer salaries, rent, and other operating and selling costs. Mutual funds also incur transaction costs in buying and selling securities for the portfolio. However, because mutual funds have greater clout, transactions costs are less than what an individual investor would pay if he traded the same number of securities. The total annual cost of administering a fund usually ranges from 1% to 2% of the funds managed. Thus, for example, if an investor has $10,000 in a mutual fund, then the annual amount that he effectively pays in the form of a reduced return for all expenses relating to the administration of that fund, including its advisory fee, will range from $100 to $200.

An investor can get information about the costs of managing and operating a particular mutual fund by reading the prospectus, the publication which describes the mutual fund and offers the sale of its shares.

Buying and Selling Costs

Mutual funds that impose a sales commission are known as *load funds*. These funds add the sales commission to the price of the share. The commission typically ranges from 8.5% on small amounts invested down to 1% on purchases in the amount of $500,000 and over. The load charge works as follows. On an investment of $10,000, for example, the mutual fund may deduct $800 and purchase $9,200 worth of shares for the investor. This increases the sales commission to an effective rate of 8.7% ($800/$9,200).

A mutual fund that does not impose a sales commission is called a *no-load fund*. No-load funds compete head on with load funds and appeal to many investors who object to paying the high initial fee charged by load funds. The relative attraction of no-load funds has forced many mutual funds to convert to no-load status. Generally speaking, there is no difference between the performance of a load compared to a no-load fund. Therefore, if you believe the mutual fund route is the way to invest any portion of your capital, look for a no-load mutual fund.

Even though a fund may not charge a commission for share purchases, it may still charge investors a fee to sell shares. Such funds, referred to as *back-end load funds,* may charge a fee of from 4% to 6% of the net asset value. Some back-end load funds impose a full fee if the shares are redeemed within a designated time period after purchase, such as 1 year, reducing the fee the longer the investor holds the shares. Therefore, be sure to check the prospectus to determine whether a fund you are considering will charge you a fee to sell shares—a back-end load may exist despite advertisements that there is no commission to buy shares. If a fee to sell shares is imposed, check to see how long you must hold the shares to avoid this fee.

There are funds that do not charge an up-front fee or a back-end fee but instead take out up to 1.25% of average daily fund assets each year to cover the costs of selling and marketing shares. Securities and Exchange Commission Rule 12b-1 allows funds to use such an arrangement for covering selling and marketing costs; consequently, such funds are referred to as *12b-1 funds*.

The Price of a Mutual Fund Share

The price of a mutual fund share is quoted on a bid-asked basis. The bid price, which is the price that the mutual fund will redeem the shares for, is the net asset value per share of the fund. A share's net asset value is determined by subtracting the fund's liabilities from the market value of its portfolio of assets and dividing the result by the number of mutual fund shares outstanding. For example, suppose that the market value of the fund's assets is $10 million, its liabilities are $1 million and there are 1 million shares outstanding. The net asset value per share is $9.

The asked or offer price is the price that the mutual fund will sell the shares for. It is equal to the net asset value per share plus the sales commission. For no-load funds, the bid and the asked prices are identical. Market quotations for mutual funds appear in the financial or business sections of most daily newspapers. The bid price is shown under the column "NAV." You can tell from the quotation page whether the mutual fund is a no-load or load fund. When a mutual fund is a no-load fund, "N.L." appears under the column "Offer Price."

Keep in mind that unlike money market funds, the price of a mutual fund is not constant. When interest rates rise, the value of the portfolio of securities will decline and its price will decline. The opposite occurs when interest rates fall.

Services Provided

Mutual funds offer an investor many valuable services in addition to professional portfolio management and diversification.

First, rather than requiring the investor to take physical possession of certificates and face the danger of loss or theft, mutual funds provide an open account record that credits the buyer with dividends and interest, and shows the change in the account's value. A periodic statement is issued to investors for their record keeping. Exhibit 15–1 is an example of a periodic statement. This is an efficient way of dealing with the problems of transferring and registering securities.

Second, investors can choose whether they prefer to receive a steady income from mutual funds or to have their dividends, interest, and other returns automatically reinvested in more shares of a fund. Mutual funds allow automatic reinvestment regardless of how small the reinvestment dollars may be, thus relieving the investor of the necessity of continually deciding how to reinvest any return distributions paid by the mutual fund.

In addition, most mutual funds allow investors to write checks on their account, and some funds allow investors to transfer from one mutual fund within a family of funds to another with just a phone call. *However, the transaction will be treated as a sale for income tax purposes.*

And finally, although most mutual funds require a minimum initial investment varying from $250 to $3,500, they accept additional investments in amounts as little as $100 and allow investors to purchase fractional shares. This is a great convenience for investors, particularly those who make periodic investments too small to purchase

EXHIBIT 15-1

THE**Vanguard**GROUP
A member of
OF INVESTMENT COMPANIES

Vanguard
MUNICIPAL BOND FUND

INSURED LONG-TERM
PORTFOLIO

VANGUARD MARKETING
CORPORATION

FOR ACCOUNT SERVICE
CALL TOLL FREE:
1-800-662-CREW

TAX IDENT. OR SOC. SEC. NO.
ACCOUNT NO   ALPHA

WHEN WRITING TO VANGUARD, PLEASE INCLUDE YOUR FUND NAME AND ACCOUNT NUMBER AND MAIL TO: VANGUARD FINANCIAL CENTER • P.O. BOX 2600 • VALLEY FORGE, PA 19482

CONFIRM DATE	TRADE DATE	TRANSACTION	DOLLAR AMOUNT OF TRANSACTION	SHARE PRICE	SHARES THIS TRANSACTION	TOTAL SHARES OWNED
		BEGINNING BALANCE				.000
1/30	1/30	PHONE EXCH FR VMMT FED	3,000.00	10.45	287.081	287.081
2/01	1/31	INCOME REINVEST	.80	10.43	.077	287.158
3/01	2/28	INCOME REINVEST	21.79	10.13	2.151	289.309
4/01	3/31	INCOME REINVEST	21.96	10.11	2.172	291.481
5/01	4/30	INCOME REINVEST	21.95	10.37	2.117	293.598
6/03	5/31	INCOME REINVEST	21.83	10.64	2.052	295.650
7/01	6/30	INCOME REINVEST	21.94	10.65	2.060	297.710
8/01	7/31	INCOME REINVEST	22.25	10.60	2.099	299.809
9/03	8/31	INCOME REINVEST	22.75	10.50	2.167	301.976
10/01	9/30	INCOME REINVEST	22.84	10.27	2.224	304.200
11/01	10/31	INCOME REINVEST	22.99	10.50	2.190	306.390

BASED ON THE AVERAGE SHARE PRICE FOR THE MONTH OF OCTOBER OF $10.37,
THE AVERAGE ANNUALIZED NET YIELD FOR THE INSURED LONG TERM PORTFOLIO WAS 8.74%.
LOOK INTO A VANGUARD ROLLOVER IRA IF YOU ARE LEAVING A CORPORATE RETIREMENT PLAN.

YOUR DISTRIBUTION OPTION IS		SHARES YOU NOW OWN		
INCOME DIVIDENDS	CAPITAL GAINS	CERTIFICATE SHARES HELD BY YOU	UNISSUED SHARES HELD BY AGENT	TOTAL SHARES OWNED
REINVEST	REINVEST		306.390	306.390

PAID THIS CALENDAR YEAR						
(1) TOTAL DIVIDENDS AND OTHER DISTRIBUTIONS	(2) INCOME DIVIDENDS	(3) ORDINARY TAXABLE INCOME	(4) TAX-EXEMPT INCOME	(5) AMT OF (2) QUALIFYING FOR EXCLUSION	(6) LONG TERM CAPITAL GAINS DISTRIBUTION	
201.10			201.10			

either a bond or 100 shares of a stock. For example, if you want to invest $250 per week, you will not have enough money available each week to acquire a bond. In addition, the transaction costs would be high for such a small investment. Instead of waiting until you accumulate enough to purchase a bond, however, you could invest the entire $250 in a mutual fund. Let's assume for example, that you decided to purchase shares of the XYZ No-Load mutual fund, which requires a minimum initial investment of $1,000 and which sets the minimum investment for purchasing additional shares at $100. After making your initial investment, you can invest $250 weekly. If the net asset value per share when the mutual fund receives your check for $250 is $8.45, you will receive credit for purchasing 29.586 shares. By allowing periodic investments of small amounts, mutual funds encourage people to invest.

One of the more innovative approaches in recent years is the service that allows mutual funds to offer tax-sheltered IRA and Keogh plans. An investor can establish an IRA or Keogh with a mutual fund and the record keeping is done by the fund and the investments can accumulate on a tax deferred basis.

CLOSED-END FUNDS

In contrast to mutual funds, closed-end bond funds sell shares just like any other corporation and usually do not redeem their shares. Shares of closed-end bond funds sell on either an organized exchange, such as the New York Stock Exchange, or in the over-the-counter market. The price of a share is determined by supply and demand; therefore, the price can fall below or rise above the net asset value per share. Investors who wish to purchase closed-end bond fund shares must pay a commission at the time of purchase and again at the time of sale.

The structure of a closed-end bond fund is similar to an open-end bond fund—there is a board of directors (or trustees) and an advisor who receives a fee. The portfolio is actively managed so that the composition of the portfolio changes over time—this results in transaction costs.

UNIT TRUSTS

A unit trust is similar to a closed-end bond fund in that the number of unit certificates issued is fixed. However, it differs from both a mutual fund and a closed-end bond fund in several ways. First, there is no active trading of the bonds in the portfolio of the unit trust. Once the unit trust is assembled by the sponsor (usually, a brokerage firm or bond underwriter) and turned over to a trustee, the trustee holds all the bonds until they are redeemed by the issuer. Usually the only time that the trustee can sell an issue in the portfolio is if there is a dramatic decline in the issuer's credit quality. This means that the cost of operating the trust will be considerably less than that incurred by both an open-end and closed-end bond fund. Second, unit trusts have a fixed termination date while open-end and closed-end bond funds do not. Third, unlike the open-end and closed-end bond fund investor, the unit trust investor knows that the portfolio consists of a specific collection of bonds and has no concern that the trustee will alter the portfolio.

Interest income and proceeds received by the trust when securities mature, are called or are sold due to credit quality deterioration are distributed to investors. Unlike distributions from mutual funds, cash distributions from a unit trust cannot be automatically reinvested in the fund since the number of shares of the trust is fixed.

All unit trusts charge a sales commission. The initial sales charge for a unit trust is 3.5% to 5.5%. There is often a commission of 3% to sell units; however, trusts sponsored by some organizations do not charge a commission when the units are sold. For an investor who intends to hold a unit trust for at least 5 years, the effective annual cost of acquiring a unit trust is reduced.

In addition to these costs, there is the spread that an investor indirectly pays. When the brokerage firm or bond underwriting firm assembles the unit trust, the price of each bond to the trust includes the dealer's spread.

TYPES OF BOND FUNDS

There are a wide variety of bond funds available. United States government bond funds invest only in U.S. government bonds. They offer lower yields than other taxable bond funds because there is no default risk. Corporate bond funds, on the other hand, vary with respect to investment objective. For example, there are funds that invest primarily in high-quality corporate bonds. However, for investors willing to accept greater default risk, there are funds that invest in triple-B corporate bonds. For those investors willing to accept greater default risk, there are high-current-yield corporate bond funds. There is no quality or maturity restriction for these funds. A portion of the portfolio is invested in what is commonly referred to as "junk" bonds, which were discussed in Chapter 7. For those who are willing to let the fund manager take a more aggressive posture, there are general bond funds. The investment policy for general bond funds spans the spectrum of strategies used by professional money managers.

Convertible securities funds invest in convertible bonds and convertible preferred stock. Investors interested in mortgage-pass-through securities can purchase shares in funds that invest in Ginnie Maes. As we mentioned in Chapter 14, an investment of $25,000 is needed to buy a Ginnie Mae directly. In contrast, the minimum investment for a no-load mutual fund specializing in Ginnie Maes, the Fidelity Ginnie Mae Portfolio, for example, is only $1,000.

For those interested in zero-coupon bonds, there are several unit trusts that are comprised of zero-coupon corporate bonds. The Corporate Bond Trust Discount Series A-1 and Discount Series A-2, both sponsored by PaineWebber, and The Corporate Bond Fund, Discount Series A, sponsored by four firms are examples of such unit trusts. In early 1986, a no-load mutual fund with zero-coupon U.S. Treasury securities was first offered. This fund, the Scudder U.S. Government Zero Coupon Target Fund, permits an initial investment of $240 for IRA investments and $1,000 for nonIRA investments. Keep in mind that there are adverse tax consequences of owning a zero-coupon bond.[1] This is also true for the ownership of unit trusts and mutual funds that invest in taxable zero-coupon bonds. These bond funds should only be purchased for retirement plans that are tax-exempt (IRAs and Keogh Plans) or individuals in very low marginal tax brackets who could have the financial ability to handle a negative cash flow.

A wide range of mutual funds that invest exclusively in municipal bonds is available. There are mutual funds that have no restriction on the length of maturity of the bonds that they purchase but limit the investments to municipal issues that are at least investment quality. There are mutual funds that invest only in intermediate-term municipal bonds—usually, maturities run 10 to 15 years. And, there are high-yield municipal bonds whose objective is to achieve maximum yields. Such funds usually invest in lower-quality municipal issues (junk bonds) and issues with long maturities. Some mutual funds specialize in municipal bonds of issuers within a given state so that investors can take advantage of the exemption of interest income from state and local taxes.[2] For example, for residents of New York State and California, there are more than a dozen mutual funds that invest in bonds from issuers within those two states—interest income is therefore exempt from state and local taxes.

There are mutual funds that invest only in commercially insured municipal bonds.[3] Most of these funds are load-funds; an exception is

---

[1]See Chapter 8.
[2]See Chapter 11.
[3]See Chapter 11.

the Vanguard Insured Long-Term Portfolio. Purchasing a share of a mutual fund that acquires only insured municipal bonds for its portfolio does not mean that an investor can not suffer a loss in share value. The value of the shares still depends on the what happens to interest rates. The value of a share will change in the opposite direction of the movement of interest rates.

There are also unit trusts that specialize in municipal bonds. Unit trusts with portfolios consisting of long-term, intermediate-term, or short-term issues are available. There is even a unit trust (sponsored by Merrill Lynch) that invests in variable-rate municipal bonds. The interest rate on the bonds in the trust is tied to the prime rate, with a minimum rate of 6.5% guaranteed regardless of how much the prime rate falls. For investors in states with high income taxes, there are unit trusts that purchase issues that are exempt within the state.

Since the WPPSS default, insured unit trusts have been a very popular vehicle used by investors for participating in the municipal bond market.[4] As we discussed above, there are mutual funds that buy bonds that are all individually insured by a private company. There are unit trusts structured so that the entire portfolio—rather than individual bonds—is insured by a private insurance company with respect to timely payment of interest and principal. A drawback of insured unit trusts has been the lower yield on these portfolios compared to uninsured unit trusts. The yield sacrifice, however, should not be a concern of the investor—greater comfort is obtained. Moreover, the yield sacrifice is generally not that significant. For example, when insured portfolios were yielding 9.5%, uninsured portfolios, with issues of similar investment ratings, were yielding 9.7%. Once again, keep in mind that, despite portfolio insurance, the investor is subject to price fluctuation caused by changes in interest rates. Finally, note that the issues in the portfolio are only insured so long as they remain in the portfolio. If any have to be sold at a loss due to a deterioration of the issuer's credit rating, this loss is not covered by the insurance.

SELECTING A FUND

If you are interested in bond funds, your first step is to do some research on what is available. There are several publications that provide detailed information about the different mutual funds on the

---

[4]See Chapter 11.

market. Although some publications may be too expensive to purchase, libraries often subscribe to the more well-known services. For example, the Weisenberger Investment Company Services, which costs $295 per year but is carried in many libraries, contains a wealth of information about bond funds. It contains details on the operations and historical record of all funds. Specifically, it describes sales charges, if any; investment policy; portfolio composition; portfolio turnover rates; use of leverage; dividend policies; special services offered, such as automatic reinvestment plans; and where the issue is traded. It also gives a historical record of net assets, net asset value per share, yield received by the fund, expense ratios, dividends paid to shareholders, offering price, and a host of other things. The *United Mutual Fund Selector* and the *Directory of No-Load Mutual Funds* are also useful publications. There are monthly financial magazines such as *Financial World* that periodically publish information about all mutual funds (both common stock and bond funds) including performance statistics.

Information about unit trusts can be obtained from their sponsors, usually brokerage firms and bond underwriters. If you are interested in insured municipal bond unit trusts, the largest sponsor of such funds is Van Kempen Merritt located in Naperville, Illinois. Other sponsors of these unit trusts include Merrill Lynch, Salomon Brothers, and Clayton Brown and Associates, to name a few.

RISK, LIQUIDITY, AND RETURN

Market prices and redemption values of bond fund shares naturally tend to fluctuate with bond prices. Thus, when you invest in a bond fund, you expose yourself to the same price risk that an investor in bonds does.

Both mutual funds and closed-end bond funds offer distinct advantages. On the one hand, the investor who buys shares in a mutual fund that is willing to redeem them at the current net asset value per share has less of a liquidity problem than one who buys shares of a closed-end bond fund and must sell those shares in the open market. However, the mutual fund investor pays a price for that advantage. On the other hand, shares in closed-end funds at times trade at a significant discount from net asset value per share, which, from the buyer's point of view, makes them an especially attractive investment.

The relationship between net asset value per share and market price is something that an investor in a closed-end fund should check.

Premiums above and discounts from net asset value per share are not uncommon, and the investor should ask not only what they are, but what (if anything) they reveal about the market's evaluations of the fund's portfolio and performance.

In addition to the price risk (caused by potential interest rate changes), that is associated with bond fund shares, there is also the risk that such shares may lose value as a result of a downgrading of, or default on, securities in the fund's portfolio. In the case of funds that trade actively and use leverage to raise yield, losses may arise from management miscalculations. For example, such a fund might buy bonds on the margin because the manager thinks interest rates are going to fall but he finds instead that they rise.[5] Investing in convertible bond funds naturally exposes the investor to all the risks of investing directly in convertible bonds.[6]

Generally, the returns on bond funds will be roughly in line with those offered on bonds in the market except that, because of management fees and operating expenses, the funds can be expected to return about 1% less than the return on securities in its portfolio. Naturally, for performance-minded funds, the divergence between market performance and fund performance may be much wider, and the fund may actually outperform the market.

Whether the loss in yield resulting from management fees and expenses is worth the services a bond fund provides is something only you can decide. Certainly, holding fund shares relieves you of various headaches and provides diversification. What's more, professional management may be worth something, although of late such management in an aggressive form has certainly implied a good dose of additional risk.

---

[5] This strategy is discussed in the next chapter.
[6] See Chapter 13.

Swapping: Strategies and Techniques

$$\overline{\underline{}} 16$$

Whenever an investor sells one security and buys another, he is said to engage in a *swap*. Most swaps are designed to increase, sometimes at the price of additional risk, either current or expected future yield on the funds invested. A swap, however, may also be appropriate because an investor's circumstances and investment objectives have changed.

For the institutional investor, swapping is often an important part of overall strategy for maximizing yield. For the individual investor, in contrast, swapping is less attractive because transaction costs are proportionately higher on small trades than on large ones, with the result that the potential gain in yield available through a given swap is smaller for the holder of a few bonds than for the manager of a large portfolio. Also, some swaps demand considerable expertise. Nevertheless, swaps may at times be appropriate for the small investor.

Swaps may be undertaken for various purposes and in various ways. In this chapter we describe only the most basic and common maneuvers. As our remarks below suggest, the whole topic of swaps can be treated in a very elaborate and complicated fashion. We have avoided most of the complications here since most swaps are simply not appropriate for the small nonprofessional investor.

RIDING THE YIELD CURVE

As noted, the normal shape of the yield curve is upward sloping. A yield curve of this sort (see Exhibit 3–2) implies that the longer a security's current maturity, the higher its yield to maturity.

Whenever the yield curve slopes upward, the investor can increase yield on his funds by substituting for a hold-until-maturity strategy one that calls for him to buy a security of a given maturity, hold that security part way to maturity, then sell it and reinvest the proceeds in a security with a maturity equal to the one he originally purchased. This technique of increasing yield, known as *riding the yield curve*, is often used by portfolio managers who need to maintain a large pool of short-term investments for liquidity purposes. Some of the money market funds discussed in Chapter 5 invest solely in T bills, which are safer than commercial paper but yield less. To get yields competitive with those achieved by funds that invest in paper, the funds that invest in T bills only ride the yield curve whenever possible.

To illustrate what is involved, suppose that a portfolio manager starts out in April with a large sum that he wants to keep invested in bills with a current maturity of 6 months or less. Assume that initially he purchases 6-month bills yielding 8.15%. Three months later the yield on these bills has fallen to 7.40%, primarily due to their movement along the yield curve. This decrease in yield means that, if our investor were to sell his 6-month bills after holding them for 3 months, he would realize *more than half* of the total gain he would have earned by holding them to maturity. Suppose that at this point he swaps his original bills, which now have a current maturity of 3 months, for new 6-month bills yielding 7.98%. Three months later yield on these new bills has fallen to 6.10%, due partly to the movement of the bills along the yield curve and partly to a general fall in short-term rates. At this point, our investor sells out.

Has he earned on his swap? The answer shown in Exhibit 16–1 is yes. He originally bought bills at a dollar price of 95.93, which would have yielded a $4.07 gain per $100 of face value purchased had the investor held his bills for 6 months to maturity. By swapping at the 3-month mark, he earns $4.70 per $100 of face value purchased—$2.22 on the first transaction and $2.48 on the second. Moreover, the first swap on an equal par basis actually frees $2.15 of principal per $100 of face value purchased, so by reinvesting these funds he could have done even better.

EXHIBIT 16-1 Gains from Holding Treasury Bills for 6 Months

Date			Yield
No swap along the yield curve			
April	*Buy* T bills maturing October at	$ 95.93	(8.15)
October	*Cash in* matured bills at	100.00	
	Gain per $100 of face value	$ 4.07	
With swap along the yield curve			
April	*Buy* T bills maturing October at	$ 95.93	(8.15)
July	*Sell* same bills at	98.15	(7.40)
	Gain per $100 of face value	$ 2.22	
July	*Buy* T bills maturing January at	$ 96.00*	(7.98)
October	*Sell* same bills at	98.48	(6.10)
	Gain per $100 of face value	$ 2.48	
	Total gain per $100 of face value on both transactions	$ 4.70	

---

*This swap permits a $2.15 takeout of principal for equal par amounts.

To keep things simple, we used a single swap in 6 months to illustrate the potential profitability of riding the yield curve. Actually, large institutional investors who ride the yield curve normally swap bills purchased for newly issued bills every 2 weeks. This constant swapping keeps them long in *current bills* (i.e., new issues), which are the most actively traded of all bill issues and consequently the most liquid.

Riding the yield curve is a technique that can be used to increase yield not only on liquid investments but also on long coupons, provided that the yield curve maintains its upward slope over a wide range of maturities. For example, an investor who puts money into 10-year agency bonds might find that—due to the upward slope of the yield curve—after 5 years he could increase his yield by swapping these securities for new 10-year bonds.

Because of transaction costs, swaps along the yield curve that are advantageous for the large investor may offer little or no profit opportunity for the small investor, especially in the case of bills.

SUBSTITUTION SWAPS

Occasionally it is possible to increase yield by swapping one security for another identical or almost identical security that yields slightly more. Suppose, for example, that a new issue of a borrower with a lot of issues outstanding comes to market. Typically the new issue will be priced slightly below the market so that it can be quickly absorbed. If the issuer has an identical or almost identical issue outstanding, by swapping it for the new issue, the holder of that issue might be able to raise his yield by a few basis points. Because of transactions costs, such opportunities generally exist only for the large investor.

INTERMARKET SPREAD SWAPS

As noted in preceding chapters, yields on debt securities vary not only because of differences in maturity but also because of differences in type and quality. Generally pros in the market, who keep their eyes glued to quote sheets, have some idea of and feel for what normal spreads are between different types and qualities of securities. When an abnormal spread develops, a swap becomes potentially attractive.

For example, agencies typically yield more than governments, but on occasion an agency that is close to a Treasury bond in coupon and maturity can be found yielding the same or almost the same yield as the Treasury does. In that case, the investor holding the agency issue could normally profit by swapping it for the government issue and reversing the swap when the yield spread widened again, either through a rise in the price of the government or a fall in the price of the agency.

To illustrate what is involved, let's construct a simple example. Consider an investor who holds 7% 4-year agencies priced to yield 7% to maturity. He finds that 7% governments with a 4-year current maturity are also priced to yield 7% to maturity. Normally, the agencies should be priced to yield more than the governments, so our investor sells his agencies at 100 and buys governments at 100. Suppose now that the yield spread between the two widens over the next 6 months from 0 to 50 basis points. This could occur because the agency issue was initially overpriced, with the result that its price falls over the holding period, driving its yield to maturity to 7.50%. In this case (see Case A in Exhibit 16-2) when he reverses his swap, the investor is able to buy back the agencies he sold for 100 at 98.49—at a gain of $1.51 per $100 of face value. Alternatively, the government issue might have been underpriced so that over the holding period its price rises, forcing down its yield to maturity to 6.50%. As Case B in Exhibit 16-2 shows, in reversing his swap, the investor is able to sell his governments for $101.54—a gain of $1.54 on the total transaction.

Naturally, there is no reason to expect all the price movement to occur in the value of just one of the swapped securities. The swap might have worked out profitably because the agencies fell in price

---

EXHIBIT 16–2 Results of a Swap between Agencies and Governments

---

			Yield to Maturity
Case A.	The agencies were initially overpriced		
Step 1:	*Sell* 7% agencies maturing in		
	4 years at	$100.00	(7.00)
	Buy 7% governments maturing		
	in 4 years at	$100.00	(7.00)
Step 2:	(6 months later):		
	Sell 7% governments purchased		
	in Step 1 at	$100.00	(7.00)
	Buy 7% agencies sold in Step 1 at	98.49	(7.50)
	Gain per $100 of face value	$ 1.51	
Case B.	The governments were initially underpriced		
Step 1:	Same as above		
Step 2:	(6 months later):		
	Sell 7% governments purchased in		
	Step 1 at	$101.54	(6.50)
	Buy 7% agencies sold in Step 1 at	100.00	(7.00)
	Gain per $100 of face value	$ 1.54	

---

while the governments rose. Thus, Exhibit 16–2 shows only two of the many possible ways in which the swap might have worked out profitably.

Note, by the way, that in a swap, reverse-swap transaction of the sort we just described, the swapping per se will be profitable so long as the yield spread widens to normal size. If interest rates fall during the transaction, the price of the security sold will tend to rise but so too will the price of the security purchased, and vice versa if interest rates rise. The swap in no way mitigates the price risk for the bondholder but, on the other hand, the existence of this price risk has little (if any) affect on the profitability of the swap per se.

Naturally many variations on the swap theme described above are possible. An abnormally large spread between agencies and governments would call for the investor to sell governments and buy agencies. Also, an investor might swap a utility of one grade for a utility of another grade if the yield spread between the two seemed out of line, or he might swap a utility for an industrial, etc. Swaps of this sort require that the investor be extremely well informed about historic relationships. In addition, the investor has to pay a lot of attention to current market conditions because what seems like an abnormal yield spread may be due to some new factor and therefore will not be reversed.

If an investor, who thinks that bond B is yielding too little compared to bond A, swaps A for B and the yield spread between the two subsequently fails to return to the historic pattern or, worse still, diverges even farther from that pattern (which might occur, for example, as a result of a major movement in interest rates), the investor will lose money when he reverses the swap. Or, if he doesn't reverse the swap, he will end up holding securities worth less than those he would have held if he had not swapped. Moral: Intermarket spread swaps may increase yield but they expose the investor to a real risk of capital loss.

The investor making an intermarket spread swap is essentially gambling that the relationship between two yields will narrow or widen over time. The period required for this to occur is often referred to as the *workout time*. Frequently, intermarket spread swaps call for swapping bonds with different yields to maturity. If the bond purchased has a lower yield to maturity than the bond sold, the investor is betting that the higher priced bond is still underpriced at current prices. In swaps of this sort the length of the workout period becomes a crucial factor in determining the ultimate profitability or unprofitability of the swap. The longer the swap takes to work out, the more yield losses during the workout period will offset any price gain yielded by the swap.

As our remarks suggest, intermarket spread swaps are best left to professionals both because of the knowledge of and attention to bond market conditions required and because of the nonnegligible transaction costs on small trades.

RATE ANTICIPATION SWAPS

If an investor thinks that he can predict where interest rates are going and is willing to gamble on his predictions, various sorts of *maturity swaps* become attractive.

Suppose, for example, that the investor feels that interest rates are poised for a substantial decline. Then a switch from short- to long-term securities would be appropriate, since a long coupon would appreciate more than a short coupon in the face of falling interest rates. Alternatively, if the investor already holds long coupons, a switch from a current coupon, long bond to a deep-discount bond might be appropriate, since the deep-discount bond would appreciate more in the face of falling interest rates than would the high-coupon security (recall Chapter 7).

To illustrate the possibilities here, let's consider an investor who on September 1 is holding 9% government notes due to mature in 20 months (Bond S). Our investor, who has good intuition, correctly guesses that interest rates are going to tumble. So he swaps out of his short coupons into 6.75% government bonds maturing in 14 years and 8 months (Bond H). Fortunately for him, interest rates fall as he predicted and by January 1 the price of Bond H has risen substantially more than has the price of the bonds he sold, (Bond S), due partly to a general drop in interest rates and partly to a steepening of the yield curve. At this point, our investor reverses his swap and earns a capital gain of $2.78 per $100 of face value, as Exhibit 16–3 shows. The swap, however, costs our investor interest income because he swapped a high-coupon bond for a low-coupon bond. When this interest loss, which amounts to $0.75 per $100 of face value,[1] is taken into account, our investor's net gain is reduced to $2.03 per $100 invested.

There is, of course, a real risk in maneuvers of the sort just described. An investor who gambles that interest rates are going to fall and then finds that they actually rise, will suffer a capital loss. Moreover, this loss may be quite substantial, depending on how long a coupon he buys and how far interest rates rise.

If the investor anticipates that interest rates are going to rise rather than fall and if he wants to invest long-term, the appropriate policy might be to park his funds temporarily in a series of short-term investments while waiting for rates on long bonds to rise to the anticipated higher level. Of course, if the yield curve is upward sloping, this strategy will result in a short-term loss of yield. Thus whether parking funds short-term turns out ultimately to be profitable or not depends not only on whether long rates rise but also on how fast they rise.

Maturity swaps, unlike the others mentioned, may be profitable for the small investor if he anticipates substantial changes in interest rates—say, because he expects a major change in Fed policy. In that case, the resulting movements in bond prices are likely to be quite substantial relative to the transaction costs involved in the swaps.

---

[1]Assuming a 4-month holding period, the loss of interest is calculated as follows:

$$\left(\frac{4 \text{ months}}{12 \text{ months}}\right) \times (9\% - 6.75\%) \times 100 = \$0.75$$

EXHIBIT 16-3   A Rate Anticipation Swap in Treasury Securities

---

		Yield to Maturity
Step 1: September 1		
Sell Bond S: 9% T notes maturing in 20 months at 101–11*		(7.95)
Buy Bond H: 6.75% T bonds maturing in 14 years and 8 months at 98–8		(8.46)
Principal freed per $100 of face value on an equal par basis	$3.09	
Step 2: January 1		
Sell Bond H: at 103– 4		(7.82)
Buy Bond S: at 102–26		(5.94)
Principal needed per $100 of face value on an equal par basis	$0.31	
Gain per $100 of face value	$2.78	
Interest lost per $100 of face value due to swap	0.75	
Net gain per $100 of face value	$2.03	

---

*The number following the hyphen represents 32nds.

PURE YIELD PICKUP SWAP

A second sort of swap appropriate for a small investor is a swap to raise yield to maturity or to raise current yield. A swap to raise current yield might involve, say, trading governments of a given maturity and coupon for similar but higher-yielding agencies. The amount by which swaps from low- to high-coupon bonds can increase current yield depends on the maturity of the securities held, the general level of interest rates, and the relationship between yields to maturity on the swapped securities.

A PURE TAX SWAP

A final sort of swap that the individual investor might find useful is what we might call a *pure tax swap*. When interest rates have increased, bonds provide an ideal vehicle for postponing the payment of taxes to a future tax year by employing this swap strategy. In a pure tax swap, a bond issue that has declined in value is sold and a similar but not identical one is purchased. The loss realized from the sale of one bond issue can be used to reduce ordinary income of up to $3,000 or used to offset a capital gain from the sale of another security during the taxable year.[2]

For example, suppose that an investor owns an issue of bonds which has a maturity of 20 years, a coupon rate of 7% and is rated single-A. Suppose further that these bonds have declined in value from $5,000 when they were purchased to $3,000. If you sell these bonds for $3,000 and purchase a similar issue of bonds which is rated single-A, has 19 years to maturity, and a 7% coupon, then you will realize a loss of $2,000. Yet, your portfolio will be virtually unchanged. If you have capital gains from the sale of other securities during the tax year, the loss can be used to offset them.

Tax swaps are popular because the bond market, unlike the stock market, uniquely allows you to swap securities in a way that both satisfies IRS regulations for claiming a capital loss and at the same time leaves the composition of your portfolio substantially unchanged. The IRS tries to discourage tax swaps by refusing to recognize a tax loss if you purchase "substantially identical securities" within 30 days before or after you sell the securities for a loss. The IRS labels such a transaction a "wash sale." This IRS regulation makes it virtually impossible to use stocks to make a tax swap. If you sold stock to generate a capital loss, you would be prohibited from purchasing the same stock within 30 days before or after the sale and claiming the capital loss. And if you purchased some other stock to replace the sold stock, the composition of your portfolio would change. The replacement stock will not have the same investment characteristics as the stock sold because no two stocks of different issuers are identical. If you sell bonds to realize a capital loss, however, you can easily find replacement bonds having similar maturities, coupons, and credit ratings, even though they may be of different issuers. They will have the same investment characteristics as the bonds you sold to generate the loss, since changes in interest rates will influence the two securities in exactly the same way. And the IRS will not treat a tax swap involving two different issuers as a wash sale.

---

[2]See Chapter 8.

Glossary

Accrued Interest. Coupon interest accumulated on a bond or note since the last interest payment or, for a new issue, from the dated date to the date of delivery.

Active. A market in which there is much trading.

Advanced Refunded Bonds. Municipal bonds for which monies have been already placed in escrow to be used for paying debt service.

After-tax Real Rate of Return. Money after-tax rate of return minus the inflation rate.

Agencies. Federal agency securities.

Arbitrage. Buying something where it is cheap and selling it where it is expensive.

Asked. The price at which securities are offered.

Balloon Maturity. An inordinately large amount of bond principal maturing in any single year.

Bank Discount Basis. Yield basis on which many short-term, non-interest-bearing securities are quoted. Yield on a bank discount basis understates yield calculated on a bond equivalent yield basis.

Bank Discount Rate. Yield basis on which short-term, non-interest-bearing money market securities are quoted. A rate quoted on a discount basis understates bond equivalent yield. That must be calculated when comparing return against coupon securities.

Bankers' Acceptances. A draft or bill of exchange accepted by a bank or trust company. The accepting institution guarantees payment on the bill.

BANs. Bond anticipation notes are issued by states and municipalities to obtain interim financing for projects that will eventually be funded long term through the sale of a bond issue.

Basis Point. One 1/100 of 1 percent.

Basis Price. Price expressed in terms of yield to maturity or annual rate of return.

Bear Market. A declining market or a period of pessimism when declines in the market are anticipated. (A way to remember: "Bear down.")

Bearer Security. A security whose owner is not registered on the books of the issuer. A bearer security is payable to the holder.

Bid. The price offered for securities.

Bond Equivalent Yield. A yield on a money market instrument or pass-through security computed so as to be comparable to a yield computed on a coupon security paying semiannual interest. (Also called corporate bond equivalent.)

Bond Insurance. Insurance purchased by an issuer for either an entire issue or specific maturities that provides for the payment of principal and/or interest. This additional form of backup security will provide a higher credit rating and thus a lower borrowing cost for the issuer.

Bond Premium. The amount at which a bond or note is bought or sold above its par value without including accrued interest.

Book Entry Securities. The Treasury and federal agencies are moving to a book entry system in which securities are not represented by engraved pieces of paper but are maintained in computerized records at the Fed in the names of member banks, which, in turn, keep records of the securities they own as well as those they are holding for customers. In the case of other securities for which there is a book entry system, engraved securities do exist somewhere in quite a few cases. These securities do not move from holder to holder but are usually kept in a central clearinghouse or by another agent.

Brokered CD. A CD issued by a deposit-accepting institution using a broker.

Bull Market. A period of optimism when increases in market prices are anticipated. (A way to remember: "Bull ahead.")

Callable Bond. A bond that the issuer has the right to redeem prior to maturity by paying some specified call price.

Cash Flow Yield.   A yield on a pass-through security based on a projected stream of monthly principal and interest payments. The yield will vary with the prepayment assumption that determines the cash flow pattern.

Carry.   The interest cost of financing securities held.

Certificate of Deposit.   A time deposit with a specific maturity evidenced by a certificate.

Commercial Paper.   An unsecured promissory note with a fixed maturity. Commercial paper may or may not be interest-bearing.

Conditional Prepayment Rate (CPR).   A measure of prepayment which assumes that each month a constant proportion of then outstanding mortgages will prepay.

Convertible Bond.   A bond containing a provision that permits conversion between the issuer's bonds and common stock at some fixed exchange ratio.

Corporate Bond Equivalent.   See **Bond Equivalent Yield.**

Coupon Rate.   The specified annual interest rate payable to the bond or noteholder.

Current Issue.   In Treasury bills and notes, the most recently auctioned issue. Trading is more active in current issues than in off-the-run issues.

Current Maturity.   Current time to maturity on an outstanding security.

Current Yield.   The ratio of the coupon rate on a bond to the dollar purchase price; expressed as a percentage.

Cushion Bonds.   High-coupon bonds that sell at only a moderate premium because they are callable at a price below that at which a comparable noncallable bond would sell. Cushion bonds offer considerable downside protection in a falling market.

Dated Date.   The date carried on the face of a bond or note from which interest normally begins to accrue.

Dealer.   A dealer, as opposed to a broker, acts as a principal in all transactions, buying and selling for his own account.

Debenture.   A bond secured only by the general credit of the issuer.

Debt Leverage.   The amplification that occurs in the return earned on equity funds when an investment is financed partly with borrowed money.

Debt Securities.   IOUs created through loan-type transactions—commercial paper, bank CDs, bills, bonds, and so on.

Deep-discount Bonds.   Bonds selling at a large discount because their coupon is below going market rates.

Default. Failure to pay in a timely manner principal and/or interest when due, or the occurrence of an event as stipulated in the Indenture of Trust resulting in an abrogation of that agreement.

Denomination. The face or par amount that the issuer promises to pay at a specific bond or note maturity.

Direct Paper. Commercial paper sold directly by the issuer to the investing public.

Direct Placement. Selling a new issue not by offering it for sale publicly but by placing it with one or several institutional investors.

Discount Basis. See **Bank Discount Rate.**

Discount Rate. The rate of interest charged by the Fed to member banks that borrow at the discount window. The discount rate is an add-on rate.

Discount Securities. Non-interest-bearing instruments that are issued at a discount and redeemed at maturity for full face value; e.g., U.S. Treasury bills.

Diversification. Dividing investment funds among a variety of securities offering independent returns.

Dollar Bond. Generally a term bond that is quoted and traded in dollars rather than in yield to maturity.

Dollar Price of a Bond. Percentage of face value at which a bond is quoted.

Eurobonds. Bonds issued in Europe outside the confines of any national capital market. A Eurobond may or may not be denominated in the currency of the issuer.

Eurodollars. U.S. dollars deposited in a bank outside the United States.

Federal Deposit Insurance Corporation (FDIC). A federal institution that insures bank deposits, currently up to $100,000 per deposit.

Federal Home Loan Mortgage Corporation. Also known as FHLMC and Freddie Mac. FHLMC is a private corporation authorized by Congress, which sells participation certificates and collateralized mortgage obligations backed by pools of conventional mortgage loans.

Federal Housing Administration. The FHA is a division of the Department of Housing and Urban Development, whose business includes insuring residential mortgage loans under a nationwide system.

Federal National Mortgage Association. Also known as "Fannie Mae" and "FNMA." FNMA was created by Congress to support the secondary mortgage market. A private corporation, it buys and sells residential mortgages insured by FHA or guaranteed by VA. FNMA also issues mortgage-backed securities backed by conventional mortgages.

FHA Experience. A statistical series, revised periodically, which represents the proportion of mortgages that "survive" a given number of years from their origination.

FHLMC Participation Certificates. Securities backed by a pool of mortgages owned by FHLMC. Certifies ownership interests in the specific pool of mortgages.

Federal Savings and Loan Insurance Corporation (FSLIC). A federal institution that insures thrift deposits, currently up to $100,000 per account.

Flat Trades. (1) A bond in default trades flat; that is, the price quoted covers both principal and unpaid, accrued interest. (2) Any security that trades without accrued interest or at a price that includes accrued interest is said to trade flat.

Floating-rate Note. A note that pays an interest rate tied to a benchmark rate. The holder may have the right to demand redemption at par at specified dates.

Flower Bonds. Government bonds that are acceptable at par in payment of federal estate taxes when owned by the decedent at the time of death.

Foreign Bond. A bond issued by a nondomestic borrower in the domestic capital market.

Full-coupon Bond. A bond whose coupon rate equals going market rates and consequently sells at or near par.

Fully-Modified Pass-Through. A pass-through security for which the timely payment of principal and interest is guaranteed by the issuer. A GNMA is an example of a fully-modified pass-through.

General Obligation Bonds. Municipal securities secured by the issuer's pledge of its full faith, credit, and taxing power.

Government National Mortgage Corporation. Also known as "Ginnie Mae" or "GNMA." A wholly owned U.S. government corporation. As part of the Department of Housing and Urban Development, GNMA issues and guarantees mortgage-backed securities which are backed by the full faith and credit of the United States government.

Governments. Negotiable U.S. Treasury securities.

Graduated Payment Mortgages (GPM). Mortgages which differ from conventional mortgages because not all payments are equal. There is a graduation period where payments start at a relatively low level and rise for some number of years.

High-Yield Bonds. High-risk bonds that have low ratings or are actually in default. (Also called junk bonds.)

Indenture of a Bond. A legal statement spelling out the obligations of the bond issuer and the rights of the bondholder.

Insured CD. A term used to describe a CD that is issued by a depository institution, sold by a broker, can be resold in a secondary market, and is insured by either the FDIC or FSLIC.

Investment Banker. A firm that engages in the origination, underwriting, or distribution of new issues.

Junk Bonds. High-risk bonds that have low ratings or are actually in default. (Also called high-yield bonds.)

Liquidity. A liquid asset is one that can be converted easily and rapidly into cash without substantial loss of value.

Liquidity Diversification. Investing in a variety of maturities to reduce the price risk to which holding long bonds exposes the investor.

Long Bonds. Bonds with a long current maturity.

Long Coupons. Bonds with a long current maturity.

Long Position. Owning a debt security, stocks, or any other asset.

Make a Market. A dealer is said to make a market when he quotes bid and offered prices at which he stands ready to buy and sell.

Marginal Tax Rate. The tax rate that would have to be paid on any additional dollars of taxable income earned.

Marketability. A negotiable security is said to have good marketability if there is an active secondary market in which it can easily be resold.

Money Market. The market in which short-term debt instruments (bills, paper, acceptances, and so on) are issued and traded.

Money Market Fund. A mutual fund that invests exclusively in money-market instruments.

Money Rate of Return. Annual money return as a percentage of asset value.

Mortgage Bonds. Bonds secured by a lien on property, equipment, or other real assets.

Municipal Bond. Bonds issued by any of the 50 states, the territories and their subdivisions, counties, cities, towns, villages, and school districts, agencies, such as authorities and special districts created by the states, and certain federally sponsored agencies such as local housing authorities. The interest paid on these bonds is exempt from federal income taxes and is generally exempt from state and local taxes in the state of issuance.

Municipal Notes. Short-term municipal obligations, generally maturing in 3 years or less. The most common types are (1) bond anticipation notes, (2) revenue anticipation notes, (3) tax anticipation notes, (4) grant anticipation notes, (5) project notes, and (6) construction loan notes.

Municipals.   Securities issued by state and local governments.

Negative Carry.   The net loss realized when the cost of carry is greater than the yield on the securities being financed.

Negotiable Certificates of Deposit.   A large denomination (generally $1 million or more) CD that can be sold but cannot be cashed in before maturity.

New-issue Market.   The market in which a new issue of securities is first sold to investors.

Offer.   Price asked by a seller of securities.

Original Maturity.   Maturity at issue. For example, a 5-year note has an original maturity at issue of 5 years; 1 year later, it has a current maturity of 4 years.

Over-the-Counter (OTC) Market.   Market created by dealer trading as opposed to the auction market prevailing on organized exchanges.

Paper.   Money market instruments, commercial paper, and other.

Par Value.   Face value of a debt security.

Pass-through Security.   A security which derives its cash flow from underlying mortgages where the issuer passes through to the investor the principal and interest payments made on the mortgages on a monthly basis.

Positive Carry.   The net gain earned when the cost of carry is less than the yield on the securities being financed.

Presold Issue.   An issue that is sold out before the coupon announcement.

Price Risk.   The risk that a debt security's price may change due to a rise or fall in the going level of interest rates.

Price to Call.   The yield of a bond priced to the first call date rather than maturity.

Primary Market.   The new issue market.

Prospectus.   A detailed statement prepared by an issuer prior to the sale of a new issue, giving detailed information on the issue and on the issuer's condition and prospects

Put Bond.   A bond that can be redeemed on a date or dates prior to the stated maturity date by the bondholder.

Quoted Yield.   The yield on a mortgage pass-through security quoted on the basis of a 30-year term and a 12-year, prepaid life.

RANs (Revenue Anticipation Notes).   Securities issued by states and municipalities to finance current expenditures in anticipation of the future receipt of nontax revenues.

Ratings.   An evaluation given by Moody's, Standard & Poor's, Fitch, or other rating services of a security's credit worthiness.

Red Herring. A preliminary prospectus containing all information required by the Securities and Exchange Commission except the offering price and coupon of the new security.

Redemption. Process of retiring existing bonds prior to maturity from excess earnings or proceeds of refunding bonds.

Registered Bond. A bond whose owner is registered with the issuer and on which interest and principal are payable only to the registered owner.

Reinvestment Rate. Interest rate assumed to be earned on the reinvestment of coupon payments or other interim cash flow payments.

Repo. A financial transaction in which one party "purchases" securities (primarily U.S. government bonds) for cash and simultaneously the other agrees to "buy" them back at some future time according to specified terms.

Revenue Bond. A municipal bond whose debt service is payable solely from the revenues derived from operating the facilities acquired or constructed with the proceeds of the bonds.

Risk. Degree of uncertainty of return on an asset.

Rolling over Securities. Exchanging a maturing security for a new issue.

Savings Deposit. Interest-bearing deposit at a savings institution that has no specific maturity.

Seasoned Issue. An issue that has been outstanding for some time and is traded actively in the secondary market.

Seasoning. The aging of a mortgage. The amount of time that has elapsed since origination.

Secondary Market. The market in which previously issued securities are traded.

Securities and Exchange Commission (SEC). Agency created by Congress to protect investors in securities transactions by administering securities legislation.

Serial Bonds. A bond issue in which maturities are staggered over a number of years.

Servicing Fee. The fee collected by the issuer of pass-throughs, or the originator of whole loans.

Short Bonds. Bonds with a short current maturity.

Short Coupons. Bonds with a short current maturity.

Short Sale. The sale of borrowed securities. A short sale must eventually be covered by a sale of the securities sold short.

Sinking Fund. Indentures on corporate issues often require that the issuer make annual payments to a sinking fund, the proceeds of which are used to retire randomly selected bonds in the issue.

Subordinated Debenture. The claims of holders of this issue rank after those of holders of various other unsecured debts incurred by the issuer.

Swap. Selling one security and buying another.

TANs. Tax anticipation notes issued by states or municipalities to finance current operations in anticipation of future tax receipts.

Taxable Equivalent Yield. The yield an investor would have to obtain on a taxable corporate or U.S. government bond to match the same after-tax yield on a municipal bond.

Technical Default Bond. Failure by the issuer to meet the requirements of a bond covenant.

Tender. The act of offering bonds to a sinking fund.

Term Bonds. A bond issue in which all bonds mature at the same time.

Thin Market. A market in which trading volume is low and the liquidity of the security traded may consequently be low.

Time Deposit. Interest-bearing deposit at a depository institution that has a specific maturity.

Tombstone. An advertisement placed for information purposes, after bonds or notes are sold, that describes certain details of the issue and lists the managing underwriters and the members of the underwriting syndicate.

Trading Position. The holding of bonds for purposes of buying or selling.

Treasury Bills. Negotiable, non-interest-bearing debt securities issued by the U.S. Treasury with an original maturity of one year or less.

Underwriter. A dealer who purchases new issues from the issuer and distributes them to investors. Underwriting is one function of an investment banker.

Variable-rate Bond. A bond whose coupon interest rate is not fixed but is adjusted periodically according to a prescribed formula.

When-issued Trades. Typically there is a lag between the time a new bond is announced and sold and the time it is actually issued. During this interval, the security trades, **wi,** "when, as, and if issued."

Yield Curve. A graph showing, for securities that all expose the investor to the same credit risk, the relationship at a given point in time between yield and current maturity. Yield curves are typically drawn using yields on governments of various maturities.

Yield to Call. Return available to call date taking into consideration the current value of the call premium, if any.

Yield to Maturity. Return available taking into account the interest rate, length of time to maturity, and price paid. It is assumed that the coupon reinvestment rate for the life of the bonds will be the same as the yield to maturity.

Zero-Coupon Security. A security in which no current interest is paid, but instead at maturity the investor receives compounded interest at a specified rate.

Index